# The
# Issue
# Is
# Power

First Edition
10-9-8-7-6-5-4-3-2-1


Aunt Lute Foundation Books
P.O. Box 410687
San Francisco, CA 94141

Cover Art: Melissa Levin
Cover and Text Design: Pamela Wilson Design Studio
Typesetting: Joan Meyers
Production: Jayna Brown
            Patti Casey
            Martha Davis
            Chris Lymbertos
            Cathy Nestor
            Renée Stephens
            Kathleen Wilkinson

Printed in the U.S.A. on acid-free paper



Library of Congress Cataloging-in-Publication Data

Kaye/Kantrowitz, Melanie.
    The issue is power : essays on women, Jews, and violence / by Melanie
Kaye/Kantrowitz. — 1st ed.
        p.    cm.
    Includes bibliographical references.
    ISBN 1-879960-17-6 : $19.95. — ISBN 1-879960-16-8 (pbk.) : $9.95
    1. Women, Jewish—United States. 2. Feminism—United States. 3. Lesbianism—
United States. 4. Antisemitism—United States. 5. Power (Social sciences) 6. Jewish-
Arab relations. I. Title.
HQ1172-K39 1992
305.42'0973—dc20                                        92-19840
                                                            CIP

# The Issue Is Power

**Essays on Women, Jews, Violence and Resistance**

**Melanie Kaye/Kantrowitz**

*aunt lute books*
SAN FRANCISCO

For the movements of the nineties
which must free us

# Acknowledgements

After my first book came out, I swore to say something general the next time around, avoid naming people and suffering from omissions later. Yet, especially with these essays, I feel the weight of what I've received from others. Friends who read essays, speeches, reviews, sometimes in chaotic form, and offered advice, criticism, encouragement. Strangers who wrote notes thanking me for my work; others, who became friends, who used their time to organize events, workshops, tours for me to present my work. Women who housed and fed me, picked me up and dropped me off at airports. All of this supplied me not only, sometimes, with money, but always with information about the various communities of lesbians, women, Jews, and progressives.

Bernice Mennis has been there at critical times with her huge heart and clear vision. Sally Covington offered a critical, sane, and supportive voice. Margaret Blanchard gave the most useful advice when it came to rewriting the masses of material on violence: start in the middle. Tania Kravath provided, in her steady commitment to making art, an image for the joy and necessity of hard work. Helena Lipstadt has always urged, go deeper. Irena Klepfisz was for years my comrade and inspiration in *gerangl*. Lisa Weisbach, Alissa Blackman, Naomi Winiwarter, Erica Moore and Sarah Feldstein brought me to Oberlin for several fruitful exchanges. Laura Wernick has been an apt and energetic comrade. Rochelle Ruthchild told me a million times I was a talented writer and I should keep doing it. Linda Vance was with me for the writing of many of these essays, which have been sharpened by her keen intelligence. My sister Roni Natov has been unswervingly loving and loyal. Sarah Jacobus has been a sister in a struggle and a kindred spirit. Vera Williams, dear friend and long-time pacifist, pushed me to think carefully about violence. Gloria Anzaldúa has consistently modelled commitment to writing as a life-organizing principle; in addition, Gloria, an old friend, and Chrystos, a new one, gave me courage to write honestly about violence. Sharon Jaffe encouraged me through her own commitment to both activism and culture; she has invariably heard my words exactly as intended, and besides sent me an essay by James Baldwin at a critical moment. I thank Mindy Shapiro, of Swarthmore-Bryn Mawr-Haverford Hillel, Clare Kinberg of *Bridges,* and Felice Yeskel, of the Program for Gay and Lesbian Concerns at the University of Massachusetts, Amherst, each for her distinct commitment to progressive Jewish life, and for help in bringing my work to its audience. Naomi Shihab Nye, for her poems, sisterhood, and heart. Naomi Nim for work we shared designing workshops on anti-Semitism and racism. Dalia Sachs and Chaya Shalom, from the Israeli women's peace movement, for their passionate commitment to both Israel and Palestine, and for their friendship. Kathleen Saadat for steady determination to neglect no issue or community. Richard Wiener for political comradeship, and for the meeting in Crown Heights we went to together. Evelyn Beck for her groundbreaking work on Jewish issues in the feminist and lesbian movement, and for *Nice Jewish Girls: A Lesbian Anthology,* where so much began. Toby Miroff for her listening and her intuition. Maureen O'Neill, for her fidelity to writing, for thoughtful criticism on the violence essay, and for her faith in me.

I thank Joan Pinkvoss for her devotion to women's publishing, for her hard work, her editorial care; Joan and Cindy Cleary for hospitality and friendship, and all the women at Aunt Lute whose labors bring books into the world, especially Chris Lymbertos and Jayna Brown, who supervised production for this one. Sarah Bolden for her photographs. Martha Davis for copy-editing, and Patti Casey for speed-demon proofreading.

Finally, I acknowledge the tutelage of the late and much-missed Lil Moed, whose lessons resonate for me and so many of us.

A few institutions also need to be thanked. The Women's Resource and Action Center at the University of Iowa has demonstrated an ongoing commitment to include Jewish issues (and I thank the Jewish women whose struggles bore fruit in the WRAC's commitment). The MacDowell and Millay Colonies, where I worked on earlier versions of the women and violence essay, provided space and solitude, not to mention heat, electricity, and hot water in a time when these things were not normal parts of my life. And the Helene Wurlitzer Foundation in Taos, where I dotted the final i's of this book, has been unfailingly generous and flexible. New Jewish Agenda, with whom I was active in local chapters in Vermont and Manhattan, as well as on the National Steering Committee for two years; and Jews for Racial and Economic Justice, in New York City, where I work as director, have granted me recent opportunities to turn theory into action.

# The Issue Is Power: Essays On Women, Jews, Violence, And Resistance

# *Introduction*

## I. THEMATIC CONNECTIONS

**1.**

First I learned about rape. I mean, I always knew, cannot remember learning.

First I learned about the Holocaust. I mean, I always knew, cannot remember learning.

**2.**

When did I learn the meaning of these things? That rape happened not rarely but all the time. That battering, incest, sexual harassment formed a pattern. That it was built in. That even when the reality did not touch me directly, I was still driven by fear of that reality—all the freedoms I didn't choose: the walks not taken, the bar not stopped in even though I had to pee so bad. The risks I took when I was 17, 19, 20 years old: coming home on the subway at 3:00 in the morning, hitchhiking, accepting a place to crash from this or that man. I would in my twenties, married and dissatisfied, remind myself I was lucky because "he works steady, doesn't drink, run around, or beat you."

When did I learn the meaning of these things? That the Holocaust was an exaggerated but logical extension to a pattern. About pogroms, including the one in Kielce, Poland, in 1946—after the Holocaust. That it was not a long time ago but just before my life began. That my mother was screamed at for causing the war. That America didn't want the Jews, nobody wanted the Jews. That they starved gassed shot millions of people and shovelled their bodies into ovens. That the sun went on shining and ordinary people went about their lives. That some people still say it didn't happen. That some people still say it's too bad Hitler didn't finish the job.

**3.**

Imagine 1969. Imagine women naming rape as a political fact of patriarchal oppression.

Imagine the fear women have of the term and the concept and the feeling, *manhating*. Men get raped too, we say. And they do. But who rapes them? We hesitate to place responsibility squarely where it belongs. Clarence Thomas as Anita Hill's *victim?* William Kennedy Smith as Patricia Bowman's *victim?*

Imagine Jews just now naming the Holocaust. Imagine trying to talk about it without saying the word *Nazi.*

**4.**

In 1982 I was speaking about women and violence, and a woman—another Jew, as it happened—asked if I thought it was a contradiction to be a feminist and a pacifist. I answered quickly, without thought: *First of all, I think it's a contradiction to be a Jew and a pacifist.*

This is where I begin.

**5.**

I bring to this question of violence and victims three lessons. I have mentioned only two: violence against women and the Holocaust.

Here the lessons of what it means to be a victim reinforce each other. Victims resist every way they can. To understand, look inside the experience for resistance, for dignity, for survival. Learn, in the words of Meridel Le Sueur: *sometimes survival is an act of resistance.* But pacifism is a luxury. Victims must fight back. Violence in the hands of victims may prevent violence.

When it comes to liberation from brutal violent murdering oppression, Malcolm X was exactly right. Any means necessary. You use what you can. Everything you can. Do I regret the German lives taken by the Warsaw Ghetto Uprising? It would be an obscenity for me to do so.

Do I regret the life of Francine Hughes' husband, or Jennifer Patri's, or Joan Little's jailer, or Inez Garcia's rapist? It would be an obscenity for me to do so.

**6.**

And the third lesson, the lesson by which I re-evaluate: Israeli soldiers in the Gaza Strip and the West Bank. The haunting question asked by Jerome Segal in *Creating a Palestinian State:* do victims only wait their turn?

What does it mean to be *a victim?* How does one/can one use violence to free oneself? And then how does one stop? When is one strong enough to stop?

And the stunning question that encompasses all other questions: Is history of no use?

I write because I need history to be of some use.

**7.**

To bring the past into the present means understanding the whole steady sickness of the nation-state. The ghost of the Holocaust says *be tough, no one's your friend, no one gives a shit about you but your own.*

Where is the voice to oppose that voice, to assert the present, to make possible the future?

How to remain human—which means not only feeling deeply but acting morally. To escape the paradigm of oppression with its brutal shallow dualism of victim and victimizer. Women, as a group, have not yet had to struggle with the other side of power, though as teachers, employers, owners, and most of all as mothers we have tasted it.

The language that justifies oppression is the language of congressional committees. *They are evil, we are threatened, we need more weapons money men men men.* Men in power.

Someday it will be women in power. And then?

Who would have believed Jews would use power to drive out another people, to squash a people's uprising?

Who would believe even a few Black people in Crown Heights would chant *Heil Hitler?*

## 8.

On the other hand, who would believe the story Naomi Shihab Nye told me, of her father, born in Palestine, emigrated to the U.S. He flew back to attend the funeral of his brother, who had been Mayor of Sinjil, a West Bank village. The Israeli soldier checking his passport at the Tel Aviv airport said *Welcome home.*

Who would believe the story Bernice Mennis told me of a young man in the prison class on autobiography: white, Italian, he wrote his paper on Richard Wright's *Black Boy.* At first he hated the book, and later realized it made him angry, because the pain Wright describes reached him and he felt guilty. Or another story from Bernice, another young man in the class, African American, who read Primo Levi's *Survival at Auschwitz* and said at first he thought, why are we always hearing about the Holocaust, never about the Middle Passage and slavery. Levi made him see the Holocaust as itself.

In these stories, there is room for everyone. No one's suffering mutes or crowds anyone else's. Hearts enlarge instead of shriveling.

Where are the stories we will struggle to believe of men who stand against male bonding, male privilege, male maleness to oppose the violence of their species? I see my nephew's rage at sexism. *I can't believe what happens to women,* he says over and over. Is there a new generation of boys raised to cherish women as equals?

And how do we balance then against now against later? To hang on to our own anger, hatred even, long enough...but no longer?

## II. WRITING

I was the kid who would escape Flatbush because I was smart. And I did. But all the way through graduate school I, who loved literature and who had found reading always the most blissful escape, was plagued by the knowledge that I was not a very good writer. I was told this by my short story teacher at CCNY and by my lit crit professors at UC Berkeley; my writing, they said, was Germanic. Ironic, prophetic. I was trying to write like them.

Not until the women's liberation movement revealed the *I* voice of women and unlocked my vocal cords did a less Germanic, more Jewish voice emerge. The very circumstances that have made it possible for me to write have been political, and always I have wrestled with the relationship between art and politics—the relationship that *is* and the relationship I seek.

The theme that circles these essays, the continuous thread through them is, of course, power. Power between women and men and the need to disrupt the imbalance; power as the partial result of violence-as-tool; power as the mark of the Jew, the too-powerful, scapegoated for all power imbalance. And the result: the woman, the Jew, the abused child taught, on every level imaginable, to fear her own power.

What happens when she begins to contact her power?

What happens when we begin to contact our collective power?

I've dated these essays because they are a journey, one step at a time. These writings come from a fifteen-year span of my life. A certain amount of inconsistency, on the one hand, and repetition, on the other, seem inevitable. From the beginning I have written about the need for utter transformation, new language, new modes, theory and practice together. Some writing which I tried—and failed—to contain in essays came naturally when I turned to fiction. I found in fiction that I didn't have to be right, didn't have to have all the answers. Contempt dropped out and compassion and complexity dropped in. In preparing this collection I have tried, where appropriate, to return the interrogative mood to the essays.

But many of these essays are purposeful, written to cover certain territory: speeches for an occasion, pieces for a particular issue of a particular journal. I have often had a clear idea of audience and purpose. In the last few years, speaking to and doing workshops with students, my sense of purpose has happily extended. There is a new generation of radicals. There is a generation of Jews hungry for a sense of itself as both radical and Jewish (though I have sometimes been shocked by the degree of self-hate among many progressive Jews, young and not so young). There is a generation of women whose strength, competence and confidence awes me. They stand firmly on the ground my generation created for them. I have learned a great deal from them. I thank them especially for the window they offer into the future.

# The
# Issue
# Is
# Power

# *Women, Violence, and Resistance, Naming It War 1979–1992*

# Women, Violence, And Resistance: Naming It War 1979—1992

For:

*Inez Garcia    Joan Little    Yvonne Wanrow    Jennifer Patri    Claudia Thacker
Sharon McNearney    Evelyn Ware    Janice Hornbuckle    Hazel Kontos
Lenore Coons    Carolyn McKendrick    Margaret Pratt    Wanda Carr
Francine Hughes    Diane Davis    Agnes Scott    Marlene Roan Eagle
Miriam Greig    Gloria Maldonado    Julia Parker Price    Bernestine Taylor
Darlene Lis    Virginia Tierce    Elizabeth Mae Fulmer    Gloria Timmons
Evelyn Graham    Jenna Kelsie    Roxanne Gay    Dessie Woods    Shirley Martin
Alta Bryan    Patricia Evans    Cathy Thomas    Barbara Jean Gilbert
Janice Painter    Donna Ferth    Nancy Stilson    Barbara Carpenter    Judy Wagner
Georgia Wondel    Nada Alayoubi    Christina Pratt    Sharon Crigler    Lorilyn Allan
Janet Billey    Barbara Eacret    Idalia Mejia    Sandra Lowe    Janet Hartwell
Eva Mae Heygood    Betty Jean Carter    Lea Murphy    Beverly Ibn-Thomas
Mary Melerine    Maxine Waltman    Eva Diamond*

and all defenders of the self.

# Prologue

*March 17, 1992. I am working on final revisions of the essay on violence. I read in the* New York Times *about Shirley Lowery, stabbed to death by her ex-"lover." Shirley Lowery was 52, African American, divorced for almost 20 years. She'd earned money as a domestic worker to raise her five children, took care of her sick father until he died. Then she got a job as a bus driver, a huge step forward.*

*A man on the bus flirts with her. She has been alone for how long—17, 18 years? They become lovers. He moves in. Two years later her daughter finds out the man was raping, terrorizing, threatening to kill her mother. She helps her mother move out, hide, get a restraining order. And when Shirley Lowery shows up in court to apply for a two-year injunction, the man is waiting. He stabs her 19 times.*

*What haunts me is the bright smiling picture of Shirley Lowery with her round cheeks. It's her words quoted by her daughter, Vanessa Davis: "My mother was embarrassed about what was happening to her. But when we moved her out, she said she felt free for the first time in a year. She said, 'If he kills me tomorrow, at least I know what it's like to be free again.'"*

*What haunts me is the picture of Vanessa with her husband and infant son: Vanessa's face, bleak, staring away from the camera, the husband sweetly focused on the baby. It seems Shirley Lowery raised her daughter with a sense of options that her daughter then fed back to her to help her escape. But options weren't enough. He wouldn't let go.[2]*

*What haunts me also are the statistics. Millions of women beaten every year by male partners. At least 20% of all women seeking emergency hospital assistance are injured by domestic violence.[3] In 1990, of 4,399 women murdered in the U.S., 30% were killed by boyfriends or husbands.*

*Almost four women every single day. Each with her own story.*

## I. Men's War Against Women

Frances Thompson (colored) sworn and examined. By the Chairman:
2919. State what you know or saw of the rioting. [Witness] Between
one and two-o'clock Tuesday night seven men, two of whom were

policemen, came to my house. I know they were policemen by their stars. They were all Irishmen. They said they must have some eggs, and ham, and biscuit. I made them some biscuit and some strong coffee, and they all sat down and ate. A girl lives with me; her name is Lucy Smith; she is about 16 years old. When they had eaten supper, they said they wanted some women to sleep with. I said we were not that sort of women, and they must go. They said, "that didn't make a damned bit of difference." One of them then laid hold of me and hit me on the side of my face, and holding my throat, choked me. Lucy tried to get out of the window, when one of them knocked her down and choked her. They drew their pistols and said they would shoot us and fire the house if we did not let them have their way with us. All seven of the men violated us two. Four of them had to do with me, and the rest with Lucy.

2912. Were you injured? I was sick for two weeks. I lay for three days with a hot, burning fever.
—from "Memphis Riot and Massacres,": Congressional Report, 1865-66[4]

I got his number from a friend as someone who might fix my furnace cheap. He came by early evening. He seemed nice enough. He checked out the furnace. Then he came into the living room where I was reading. I started to ask him about the furnace and he grabbed me. I pushed him away and the next thing I knew he was on top of me, tearing at my clothes, saying things. I know he punched me a couple of times. When it was over, he just got up, zipped his pants, said goodbye, and left. He actually said goodbye. And he sent me a bill for the furnace.
—conversation, Portland, Oregon, 1978.

Even though I hate it, if he needs it, then I feel I ought to do it. After all, I'm his wife.

I tell him I don't want to do it, but it doesn't do any good. If it's what he wants, that's what we do.
—interviews with married women, 1976[5]

## NAMING IT WAR

In 1977 I taught Feminist Theory and Practice at Portland State University, which pointed me in a direction for the next several years of my life. I had asked the class, all women, to look at our lives as the raw material for change, and to seek commonalities as bases for action. The unanimity that emerged from the fairly diverse group was striking.[6] Every one of us saw violence as a central issue in our lives. Every one of us lived in fear of rape; many of us had been raped. Some of us had been beaten by male partners. The more we talked, read, gathered information, from the then-few books and from other women, the more obvious it became: violence against women coiled at the heart of our oppression. We understood that trivializing and eroticizing rape and beatings suited the abusing male's experience of abuse, while our experience included terror, nightmares, injury, and even death, as well as interference with and destruction of our sense of integrity and capacity for sexual pleasure.

When the term ended, about a third of the class formed the core of an action group, and we helped plan the first Take Back the Night march in Portland. I and another group member were hired into CETA-funded positions at the Rape Relief Hotline. As I immersed myself in the issue, talking on a daily basis to women who'd been raped and beaten, learning the statistics, studying the legal remedies, I still was not prepared for what I found. Somewhere in the U.S. a woman was being raped every minute or two. Two or three women were being beaten every minute. Every minute. It was painful to look at a clock.

So much of what I learned then is now such common knowledge that it's hard to recreate the moment of discovery. Sexual harassment from bosses, teachers, landlords, etc., was a yet-unnamed concept, though virtually every one of us had come up against it. We hated it, just as we hated boring jobs, anxiety about money, and harsh weather. But not until then had any of us questioned the inevitability of dealing with male sexual demands in the course of trying to get an education, earn a living, find a place to live, get a cavity filled or an abortion performed.[7]

Information about rape, race and class was especially disturbing. Prior to women's liberation, rape was a political subject only in white racist circles, identified only as a crime committed by Black men against white women—or, really, against white male ownership of white women.[8] The response of liberal and radical men of all colors was to dismiss the subject as a function of sexual uptightness, or as a racist plot. What rape meant to women, including women of color, was barely addressed.

At Rape Relief Hotline, as we heard from woman after woman who'd been raped by doctors, teachers, ministers, bosses, from African American and Native American women who'd been raped by white men, I realized it was anyone's guess how many women are raped by men in positions of authority, how many professional men are sexually abusive, how many women of color are raped by white men.[9] Few of these women reported to the police. I learned that a great many rapes were committed not by strangers, but by dates, co-workers, repairmen, friends of the family.[10] Especially shocking was information about group and gang rape. Many women had been gang-raped at parties— a common initiation to college life or the hideous outcome to a barmaid or waitress job. I learned that rape by men working in pairs and groups was on the rise.

I learned that most rapists were not sex-starved, relationless psychopaths, but by all psychological profiles perfectly normal men with functioning sexual relationships.[11] That it was not a spontaneous crime of passion: three out of four rapes were planned. I grasped that our feminist definition of rape as a crime of violence describes women's experience of rape, but masks a sickening truth: many men consider rape "sex." Many can't tell rape apart from sex. Many can, but still find rape sexy. Later I'd come upon the words of an honest rapist: mocking the psychiatrists who call him troubled, fearful, sick, and hostile, he says the truth is, "I find rape enormously stimulating and very exciting. It's fun."[12]

I learned that just as rape was not "about" race, battering was not "about" class, though women's ability to leave violent relationships is of course connected to money and often to literacy—everything from "do I have cab fare?" to "can I support myself?" But batterers can't be typed by psychological or sociological profile any more than rapists. Most startling, higher education actually seems to increase acceptance and approval of marital violence.[13]

Incest was the biggest shock of all. At that time, the word still conjured up Oedipus, Tobacco Road, Egyptian royalty. To answer the Hotline phone and hear a young girl's voice, a child's voice, say, *um, um, my father keeps bothering me and I don't know what to do*; or, *he says if I tell he'll kill me*; or, *he says if I leave he'll do it to my little sister*; or, most painful, *my mother says I'm lying....*I learned that daughter rape, far from being an aberration, was, in the words of Florence Rush,

> ...an unspoken but prominent factor in socializing and preparing the
> female to accept a subordinate role; to feel guilty, ashamed, and to
> tolerate, through fear, the power exercised over her by men.[14]

And I learned the most insidious aspect of daughter rape: girls discover not only their own powerlessness, but also their mother's. This violation of trust between mother and daughter, woman and girl, undermines feminist unity at its most intimate level.[15]

When I looked at legal remedies, the picture was grim. Legislation about restraining orders was just being enacted, though of course there were problems with enforcement. Incest was barely addressed by the legal system.[16] And rape? I learned what happened to the one out of ten rapes that actually got reported to the police. 15% would be unfounded—that is, disbelieved or otherwise invalidated by police—and a decision made not to proceed. (When women police officers investigate rape charges, rates of unfounding drop to 3%, about the same as for other crimes.) In half the remaining cases, the rapist would be caught, and three-quarters of those arrested would be prosecuted. Between 3% and 53% of those prosecuted would end in conviction, often on a lesser charge.[17]

In other words, when 1000 women are raped (and in 1990, on an average *day* nearly twice that number got raped), at best less than seventeen rapists get convicted, often on a lesser charge; at worst, less than one gets convicted.

## War or Massacre?

The jovial image of "the war between the sexes," suggesting as it does sexual bantering, cloaks an authentic war waged by men against women. The out-of-uniform army functions with implicit orders. Young men rape, making the world dangerous to women, warning women we need protection from other men. On dates, in fraternities, in thousands of "acquaintance" situations, men assert their right to have sex when they want it, and contribute to breaking women's will. The need for male protection, not to mention male access to money, locks many women into the nuclear family, where men can use the threat of violence to control; they can demand sex, from their wives/women, their daughters and sometimes sons. Sexual harassment acts it out in the workplace.

The war. Or, I thought then and think still, it would be more accurate to call it a massacre, because it is hard to find the injury we women are inflicting back on men.

And yet we have no name for this war. In writing I feel keenly this lack. Rape, battering, incest, sexual harassment—each word points toward a particular, often a legal, definition. Abuse, the generalized term, is vague and colorless. There is no word that includes all sexual violation and physical brutalization, the physical component of male domination of women.

You could say, if we had power to shape the language we would probably also have power to stop the acts.

But sexism was once a new word. So was consciousness raising. So was clitoris. We didn't need liberation to name our oppression or our experience, only a willingness to confront our oppression and claim our experience. That we have no word for the violence against us reflects some collective unwillingness or inability to grapple with the issue.

## CHANGES AND LIMITS

In the context of a vigorous movement for women's liberation, women began to change our consciousness about rape and other sexual violence so that we would no longer accept these things as natural events. From this different way of seeing the world, we acted: to create rape centers, hotlines, battered women's shelters, free taxi and escort services, self-defense training; to perform aggressive political action, in defense of these centers and shelters, against institutions, events, and individual men who perpetuated abuse; and to change the laws so that women who were raped or beaten had more options. As women blame ourselves less for the abuse that lands on us, we avail ourselves more of legal remedies. In many states, a woman's sexual history can no longer be dragged into court. A woman being beaten by a man, including her husband, can get a restraining order against him. Marital rape is now a crime in several states. The milk carton in my refrigerator carries an ad for the National Domestic Violence Hotline, with a toll-free number.

Women can sue men who abuse them, and victims of incest, especially, have been availing themselves of this remedy.[18] There has been massive public education about rape, battering, sexual abuse of children, and at least some children grow up being taught they have a right to control their own bodies, to trust and act on their feelings about good touch/bad touch.

In 1977, when I wrote "women & violence" and listed 56 names of women who had defended themselves,[19] hardly anyone knew these names or these stories. By now, feminist legal teams all over the country have defended women whose crime was self-defense, and women have organized support for these defenses, including community education about the "battered woman syndrome" —the psychological impact of continued violence on a woman's ability to make choices.[20] Information is at least available about what should be called the "battering man's syndrome"—his frequent refusal to accept the relationship's end, his pursuit, threats, increased violence. The collusion of police, clergy, and often therapists and family members to preserve the holy family, no matter what cost to the woman, has been exposed to feminist scrutiny, if not to common scrutiny. In this climate, created by feminists, governors in several states have granted clemency to formerly battered self-defenders who swell the ranks of women imprisoned across the country.

Popular culture reflects and re-enforces these changes too. Farrah Fawcett played Francine Hughes in *The Burning Bed* on network television. Greta Rideout's story, the first rape-in-marriage trial, was also a made-for-TV movie. Julia Roberts in *Sleeping With the Enemy* was the final glitz on the subject, and however glitzy, she escapes and kills her crazed, persecuting ex—and I don't believe a person in the movie theater ever objects. The success of *Thelma and Louise*, its leap into the culture, makes it clear that a vacuum had existed: women had been waiting for such a story. The male response, frantic about man-bashing, was likewise instructive.

But we should note the cultural rip-off. Among the first *known* self-defenders against rape or other male violence were Inez Garcia, Joan Little, and Yvonne Wanrow: all women of color, as are many self-defenders. Yet every treatment—docudrama or not—has depicted white women. Such erasure robs all of us of accurate history and role models, obscures the relation between self-defense and a strength perhaps derived from surviving oppression, from learning to fight for yourself because you can't depend on a cushion of privilege.[21] It reinforces a notion of "white feminism," by not acknowledging that some of our century's greatest feminist practitioners are women of color.[22]

The conflation of women's liberation and the contemporary health consciousness has created a generation of young women, especially but not exclusively middle and upper class, who stay in shape, work out, pursue athletics. And though this new feminine norm is exploited, in classic American fashion, as a money-making industry, and though it constitutes yet one more demand on the would-be perfect modern woman, the fact is young women can no longer be counted on to be unathletic or physically passive. What this often means, however, is that men up the ante. Partner and gang rape, rape with weapons, rape with brutal beatings are all on the rise. Men are responding to women's new strength with more violence.

### Service and Ideology

In the late seventies a vital movement to stop violence against women came into existence, strongly tied to women's liberation. By the early eighties, the practice of the movement had split in two directions: service providers and anti-pornography activists.

Service providers took on the backbreaking labor of sustaining shelters, counselling centers, etc., including—once the Jimmy Carter-CETA funding which initially supported many of these projects was cut—the burden of raising funds to sustain the services. And fundraising is an inherently conservatizing task.

I say "inherently conservatizing" as a fact, not a judgment. Few of us get paid, at least not for long, to make social change. So the fiery activists of the pre-funding days became an organizational liability. Women began to define our projects into forms which United Way et al. would sanction. Boards of directors were formed of community notables, often potential donors or those who have achieved their status through actions and views which don't threaten potential donors. Lesbians, who founded many of the shelters and anti-violence groups, were asked "to be cool"—that is, keep closeted. Executive directors were hired with MSWs and impeccable manners to lunch graciously with the moneyed, on whom the projects now depend.

Susan Schechter describes the tensions between service and activism, and speaks eloquently in favor of an activist battered women's movement where politics and service/advocacy are not separate, and where confronting homophobia and racism is an essential part of movement work.[23] Many shelter projects and anti-violence coalitions also offer community education, train police, sometimes work with abusive men to help them change. Many organize demonstrations, lobby for legislation, infiltrate and pressure in the public arena so that some services once provided on a volunteer or scantily funded basis are now part of city and state budgets.

But in many places, the work of service providers focuses, of necessity, on helping abused women get on with their lives, rather than on the political work of stopping the violence.

The anti-pornography activists raised a different set of issues. Kathleen Barry, Susan Brownmiller, Andrea Dworkin, Susan Griffin, and Diana Russell, five major theorists from the seventies about sexual violence against women— along with Catherine MacKinnon, who broke ground on sexual harassment— emerged in the eighties as theorists and activists against pornography.[24] Such concordance seemed to suggest anti-pornography activism as the natural next step for those who wish to stop violence against women. 'Pornography is the theory, rape is the practice,' went the short-form analysis, as the militant wing of the violence against women movement galvanized against pornography. Even the anthology published in 1980, which gathered feminist opinion against pornography, sports the title of the stop-violence-against-women marches, *Take Back the Night*[25]; as if pornography and violence were identical phenomena.

It's a good thing when women rise in outrage against degrading and violence-inspiring media, as it is a good thing when we rise in outrage against anything we find oppressive. And early feminist campaigns against violence-provoking media were feisty empowering protests.[26] They also represented one aspect of a then-diverse movement, which was experimenting with a broad range of strategies and tactics, at least some of which targeted individual abusive men. In the eighties and nineties, pornography as the lone target of this militant energy seems singularly narrow: a swerve towards ideology and away from practice.

True, pornography is also the practice. Women have been abused in production of pornography, some in horrible ways. But, a straightforward feminist approach would assume that sex workers, like any other women, deserve support to improve the conditions of their lives and work.[27] Instead, anti-pornographists sometimes seem motivated not by a concern for the women directly abused in the sex industries, but by a conviction that pornography causes sexual violence against *other* (decent?) women.[28]

The conviction that pornography causes sexual violence ascribes a great deal of power to pornography. Ann Jones, for example, tells the story of a brutal torturer and murderer of a young woman who explained, "Ever since I was a young boy I have wanted to torture a beautiful young girl." She concludes archly, "Now where do you suppose he got an idea like that?"[29] She expects us to answer "from pornography," though I can think of a hundred gothic, horror, and detective films and novels which might give him the same idea, albeit in less graphic sexual detail.

The point is not: where did he get his idea?

The point is: *where did he get the idea that he could act out his idea?*

*Pornography is the theory, rape is the practice*, goes the saying. But isn't the point that men have the power to practice their theory?

Isn't the point that we are not powerful enough to practice ours?

Although a movement against pornography inspired many women with anger and horror at incredibly cruel and disgusting images, this strategic twist also drained the potential of the violence-against-women movement. As an issue, anti-pornography has drawn mostly middle class women, often college students and church women. College is where people learn to identify ideas with reality; to overemphasize theory and undervalue experience. Church is one locus of sexual repression, often equated with morality.[30] Middle class people are less apt than poor and working class people to regard capitalism as a brutal system; and whites are more likely than people of color to seek a quick patch-up to what they think is a basically sound society, as opposed to considering the possibility that the entire enterprise is rotten. These perspectives limit the vision of the anti-pornography movement.

Pornography, as an industry, garners millions and millions of dollars by exploiting and degrading women's sexuality. Anti-pornography activists often neglect to situate pornography as an aspect of capitalism, on a continuum— along with advertising, popular culture, many service and office jobs, etc., all of which also exploit women's bodies for profit. Instead, emphasis has often fallen on explicit depictions of sexuality, as if sex or women's sexuality were the problem, instead of *forced* sex and *exploited* sexuality.

Confusion between explicit sexuality and violence in pornography has obscured, to some extent, the horror perpetuated in art and in popular culture. Wandering through Western culture with a newly acquired feminist consciousness is disorienting, to say the least, from Leda and the Swan to Lolita, the Rape of the Sabine Women to Manet's Picnic on the Grass, with its fully clothed bourgeois men and fully naked women. Popular culture, too, teems with images of violence against women: both white and Black popular music, much of what passes for comic routines, and money-making sleazy soft-porn—from ads for skin-tight jeans to movies in which women are violated and killed in graphic detail, but the killer gets caught so it's not as if the movie is really pro-violence, right?[31] X-rated flicks have no edge on the following random (misogynist and racist) blip from AM radio: the DJ, after airing Shelly West's playful song about getting drunk on tequila, quips, "Thank you, Shelly—and Shelly, the whole Mexico City Soccer Team thanks you too."

The result has been a powerful movement split into false categories of pro-sex and anti-sex, privatizing and psychologizing a real honest-to-god war which rages happily, violently on, totally unconcerned with how any woman *feels* about sex.

Most significantly, as violence against women is an oppression, a terror, and an experience we share across lines of class, race, and culture, a movement might have been created to cross these lines. I do not ignore what *has* been created: the battered women's movement in particular and the anti-violence movement in general. But as the militant activist wing of the movement veered to focus on pornography, the potential for a movement to join us across lines of class, race and culture was undermined. It is this potential that must be actualized if we are to stop the violence.

We help the victims. We attack the theory.
Who is attacking the practice?

What we did was significant, and now I refer to the larger *we*, a huge sweep of feminist activity that has to some extent transformed the conditions of our lives. We ignore important victories if we don't register the impact of the women's liberation movement on this issue.

## But What Has Really Changed?

Are women any safer walking down the street? Are women beaten less by their lovers and kin? Are girls, and boys, abused less by male family members? A recent study found that 683,000 adult women had been raped in 1990, more than one a minute. This doesn't even count those under 18—*and 61% of all women raped endured this rape before age 18; 29% before age 11.*[32] Another recent study found that perfectly ordinary men, when angry, become sexually aroused in response to descriptions of rape: "With the right combination of factors, most men can be aroused by violent sex," concluded the researcher.[33] Campus rape, including acquaintance rape, and sexual harassment in the workplace and in schools, are being exposed as so common that they practically constitute a norm—though exposure is also the first step towards change.[34]

The criminal justice system has improved somewhat, for the classic street rape situation, though, as I've discussed, the chances of a rapist being caught, prosecuted, and convicted remain minuscule. Beneath the iceberg tip of street violence looms the much larger structure of sexual violence that rests on male entitlement to sex from women, the valuing of male needs and priorities over female ones.

And while there is much more awareness, support, and some legal protection concerning incest, most of the discussion has shifted from political to psychological grounds: away from the deep structure of feminist insight into the danger, for girls and women, of the patriarchal family; and towards the psychological damage out of which the individual once-abused abuser continues the cycle of abuse; away from examining male power over women and children, towards exploring our shared genderless condition as victims. [Meanwhile the male power base, though challenged, goes along pretty much unchanged.]

1991 will be remembered as a banner year, in which privileged men who sexually abuse women got exposed...and nothing happened to them. Clarence Thomas, William Kennedy Smith, and the St. Johns' rapists (white male students charged with gang-raping a Black female student) illustrate the immunity with which privileged men still sexually abuse women. These particular men may be more cautious from now on, but women, too, learn caution. We learn—if we didn't already know—that our charges will be met with disbelief. How many of us have pasts or presents that can stand up to scrutiny like Anita Hill's? "A Quickie for Willie" read the *New York Post's* headline, about Smith's acquittal. (The jury took just over an hour).[35] A male friend of the St. Johns' rapists testified to witnessing them rape the woman whose testimony was nevertheless deemed by the jury "too contradictory" for conviction.

Most cases of course get neither publicity nor much legal attention. It's obvious that the legal system is inadequate against men of privilege; it was, after all, designed to protect their rights.[36] We face the virtual uselessness of the criminal justice system, the civil courts, the legislature; the near-impermeability of these institutions to feminist impact.

Yet something *is* happening. Thomas, Smith, the St. Johns' rapists all escaped legal damage. But Anita Hill abruptly and irrevocably raised national consciousness and made visible the chasm between male and female experience.[37] Despite Hill's treatment by the Senate committee, she has enlarged the space in which women who have been sexually harassed can decide how to respond. As the 1992 election nears, women are seeking political office in record numbers; some, like Lynn Hardy Yeakel, specifically in response to the sexism made sickeningly visible in the Hill-Thomas hearings. Patricia Bowman, who charged "Willie" with rape, has become an ardent anti-rape activist. The most famous last words of all may be NOW President Patricia Ireland's: "When we get screwed, we multiply."

## REFOCUSING THE ISSUES

### The Degendering of Male Violence

In the activist anti-pornography wing of the movement, sexism remains a clear focus, though the line between sex and violence often blurs. But more generally we have witnessed a depoliticization of the issue of male violence against women. Husband battering—a relatively rare phenomenon—receives a flurry of publicity. The same is true about the rape of men and boys—not at all a rare phenomenon, but what gets obscured in the attention lavished on male victims is that the agents of sexual violence are almost always men, and the act is usually designed to "womanize" the victim, to assert male power over him. As a man abused by his uncle at age ten remarked astutely: "I felt dirty, disgusting, and nasty. Just like a girl."[38] Homophobia only underscores the role of sexism and male dominance in male sexual violence. Faggots are hated because they don't act like real men; therefore they will be treated like women. Sexism needs to be reintegrated into our analysis of male sexual violence.

### Rape and Race

At the same time, the connection with racism in particular and privilege in general needs to be more deeply understood. In a racist culture, with its history of slavery and lynching, its present of prisons disproportionately full of men of color, violence must be considered through a racial—and class—lens.[39]

What are the issues? First, media and police attention is skewed toward those cases where privileged white women are attacked by men of color (the rape and beating of the "Central Park Jogger," for example, was headlined for days, during a week when some twenty-eight other women in New York City also reported being raped). Second, black-on-black and color-on-color crime is generally treated as trivial, especially when these are instances of men abusing women. Third, what happens when white men or wealthy men commit crimes against women or less privileged men? Take the example of Jeffrey Dahmer, a white man charged with the sexual abuse and murder of seventeen men and boys. One of these, Kontarek Sinthasomphone, a young Cambodian, was reported by at least two women to the police as wandering naked and apparently hurt. The police looked at the hurt naked child, saw "a lover's quarrel," and returned Kontarek to Dahmer, who killed him. Perhaps their racist limited vision kept them from seeing that Kontarek was a child. Should we be pleased that the police "honored" what they saw as a homosexual relationship, as they would a heterosexual one, by condoning abuse?

Fourth, the extra vulnerability of poverty, which often intersects with color. Poor women have less choice about housing, less police patrol and less reason to believe in police protection, less money to drive cars or take taxis instead of using public transportation, less possibility of refusing night jobs, or jobs which include sexual harassment or generally expose us to unsafe conditions. Poverty keeps us from seeking paid counselling, and often prevents us from leaving abusive relationships. Women of color, frequently poor, are often exposed to abuse in dangerous neighborhoods and in demeaning jobs. Women surviving on women's wages—single women, lesbians—are frequently poor. Perceived as unprotected because "man-less," we are particularly vulnerable to abuse by men, especially if we live outside our own cultural or racial community: outsider women are marks, and visible lesbians are doubly outsiders.

A clear response from the left or from communities of color on the issue of violence against women has not been forthcoming. White men feel threatened because they fear either accusation or diminution of privilege. Men of color, in addition, fear the racist use of the rape charge. More recently, African American men have focused on the rape of African American women by white men. But the rape and other violence done to women of color by men from their own community has been addressed almost exclusively by women of color.[40] Many women of color, Jewish women, and other non-dominants have refrained from naming the abuse dealt them by "their" men, fearful of fueling bigotry. And no one can have failed to notice the difference in how even celebrities are treated by the courts when one is William Kennedy Smith and the other is Mike Tyson.

Meanwhile, as long as any woman fears how the issue of male violence against women will be used against her sons, brothers, and husbands—ntozake shange's "the suspect is always black and in his early 20s"[41]—we are all blocked from the very unity we need.[42]

### Rape As Hate Crime

The connection between rape and racism has strategic implications. Legislation to classify bias or hate crimes and to treat them with special gravity has been considered in many cities and states and passed in some. There have been vigorous battles over whether to include or exclude lesbian and gay bashing. But battering and sexual violence against women has rarely been classified as they warrant: as bias/hate crimes against women.[43]

Yet rape is always a crime of woman hate: as performed against women, or as a "womanizing" act against boys and men.

Indeed, there are casual or occasional rapists, who rape almost as an afterthought, along with robbery—*might as well*—or as an evening activity. But this property-theft attitude on the part of rapists, or property-abuse on the part of batterers, implies deep contempt for women. It's risky, however, to focus too much on the feelings of the abuser: his anger, his hatred of women (which usually gets laid at the doorstep of his overbearing mother). There are many ways to express anger and even hatred. In our culture, rape and battering are relatively low-risk ways. This fact suggests profound societal apathy about the condition of women and children.

The point of classifying violence against women as a bias crime is to raise its priority on civic agendas. This classification would promote alliances between feminists and communities of color, Jews, lesbians and gays, and offer opportunities for mutual struggle against sexism, racism, homophobia, and anti-Semitism. It would force feminists to integrate a racial lens into anti-violence work, as it would force activists of color, Jews, and gay men to integrate a gender lens into anti-bias work.

# II. Blocks To Resistance

## IMAGINATION: TO CONSIDER VIOLENCE

A woman raped by a landlord showing her an apartment remarks, "the only degrading thing I can recall about it is simply not being able to hit the guy. I just really wanted to sock him in the teeth."[44]

Another woman, awakened and raped with a knife at her throat:

...You never forget it and you're never the same.... It hits you where you're most vulnerable.... About six months to a year later some of the vulnerability disappeared. It was replaced by rage. Oh, I wish now I had hit him. Or killed him.[45]

Listen to women cheer at karate demonstrations simulating attack when the woman playing "victim" strikes back. Think about women's reaction to *Thelma and Louise*.[46] In response to violence, it's natural to consider violence.

Yet as a movement, we don't.

If a woman is abused and strikes back, we often work for her defense. We respond to her risk. But we do not ourselves shoulder it, even as a movement. Nor do we encourage women to avail ourselves of violence as a serious, perhaps effective option.

Why?

Obvious response #1: *Violence is wrong.*
Obvious response #2: *Violence won't work.*

What do we mean, *wrong?* What do we mean, *work?* When women are prepared to use violence, they are less likely to get raped, abused and murdered.

Listen.

...all of a sudden he got this crazy look in his eye and he said to me, "Now I'm going to kill you." Then I started saying my prayers. I knew there was nothing I could do. He started to hit me—I still wasn't sure if he wanted to rape me at this point—or just to kill me. He was hurting me, but hadn't yet gotten me into a strangle-hold because he was still drunk and off balance. Somehow we pushed into the kitchen where I kept looking at this big knife. But I didn't pick it up. Somehow no matter how much I hated him at that moment, I still couldn't imagine putting the knife in his flesh, and then I was afraid he would grab it and stick it into me.... [47]

*I couldn't imagine.*
*I was afraid.*

*I couldn't imagine* corresponds to *it's wrong.* Sticking the knife into his flesh is unimaginable, too horrible.

This horror, this failure of imagination might have cost her life. Her life against his, and she chooses his.

*I was afraid* corresponds to *it won't work*. Using the knife might make it worse. But how much worse could it get? He's already threatened to kill her.

Is this in women's interest?

If we avoid the question of using violence because it makes us uncomfortable, many men have no such compunctions. They continue to rape, mutilate, beat and kill us. So we are not avoiding violence, only the guilt we associate with using it. Something about innocence is dangerous here. We are innocent because helpless. As long as we insist on maintaining our innocence, we lock ourselves into helplessness. In this way we become complicit with our oppression.

A few feminists have touched on the question. Phyllis Chesler, M.F. Beal, Karen Haglund conclude similarly; in Chesler's words:

> Women, like men, must be capable of violence or self-defense before their refusal to use violence constitutes a free and moral choice rather than "making the best of a bad bargain."[48]

But how do we become capable? What if we are already capable? And what if we don't refuse?

Let us begin to imagine putting the knife in his flesh. If we choose not to, let the reason *not* be that we couldn't imagine doing it. The women who wrote the excellent *Women's Gun Pamphlet* have an answer to the *violence is wrong* voice:

> The only way I've figured out to try and eliminate the all-nurturing masochist in each of us is to remember that the man or men who attack, rape, mutilate, and try to kill you, have done and will do the same to as many women as they can. While you defend yourself, bear in your mind all the women you love that you are fighting for, especially those you know who have been attacked.[49]

## Violence and Power

Yes, I'm talking about violence. But the violence did not originate with us. If we submit, evade, fight back directly or indirectly—no matter what we do we are responding to a violence that already is. Janet Koenig has described how the oppressor's violence

> becomes routinized and ritualized. It becomes so part of the environment, of the school, factory, prison, and family that it is barely perceived consciously. Ideology distorts the perception of violence. The source of violence now appears to be not the system but those who rebel against it.[50]

And Assata Shakur succinctly remarks:

> Women have been raped throughout history, and now when we fight back, now that we have the consciousness to fight back—they call us violent.[51]

To avoid this conceptual error, Ti-Grace Atkinson would call responsive violence, the violence of rebellion, by another name:

When "violence" appears *against* "oppression," it is a *negation of institutionalized* violence. "Violence," these opening blows are a positive humane act—under such circumstances. Such acts are *acts of bravery*...It is a betrayal of humanity, and of hope, to represent such acts as shameful, or regrettable.[52]

Not to deny the horror of violence. Or to invalidate or mock the part in us that does not want to harm. We have an honorable past on this subject. Often life has been preserved solely because of our efforts to feed, wash, clothe, and keep our families in health. We have been active in movements to stop slavery, wars, imperialism, lynching, and abuse of all kinds.

It's hard to transform such concerns into a willingness to cut down another woman's son.

Nor am I saying violence should be leapt to lightly. But the situation is hardly light. I am saying only that using violence should be thinkable. And that the grounds on which we decide whether or not to commit violence against men be *our* grounds: *is it in our interest?*

Violence is an aspect of power. In a conflictual society, where power imbalance exists, so does the possibility of physical force to meet physical threat. "Women," Karen Hagberg points out,

> are called violent (indeed, we actually consider ourselves violent) whenever we assert ourselves in the smallest ways. One woman recently described the verbal challenging of men on the streets as an act of violence.[53]

This is absurd or tragic. Yet the piece of embedded truth is that any woman's challenge to male power—from a calm "I'm not interested" to an assertive "please turn down your stereo"—may be perceived as aggressive and met with violence. Most of us know we risk danger in even a mild confrontation with a man. Every male-female interaction assumes: *in a physical fight he will win*. Every man assumes this about every woman. This is the assumption behind rape. As Ellen Willis remarked in 1968, *Men don't take us seriously because they're not physically afraid of us.*

### An Analog: African American Liberation from Slavery

Recent scholarship about African Americans in the South during and after the Civil War sheds intriguing light on the relationship between violence and freedom. When the war began, the great abolitionist and former slave, Frederick Douglass,

> immediately called for the enlistment of slaves and free blacks into a "liberating army" that would carry the banner of emancipation through the South. Within thirty days, Douglass believed, 10,000 black soldiers could be assembled. "One black regiment alone would be, in such a war, the full equal of two white ones. The very fact of color in this case would be more terrible than powder and balls. The slaves would learn more as to the nature of the conflict from the presence of one such regiment, than from a thousand preachers."[54]

But Northern white men were not so sure. As they debated the question of arming Blacks—slaves or freedmen—three fears were repeated. They feared slave insurrections against slaveholders who, though the enemy, were, after all, white. They feared Black incompetence; no less a personage than President Lincoln speculated that, if Blacks were armed, "in a few weeks the arms would be in the hands of the rebels." But perhaps the deepest and most revealing fear was that Blacks would prove competent. As one Union congressman noted,

> If you make him the instrument by which your battles are fought, the
> means by which your victories are won, you must treat him as a victor
> is entitled to be treated, with all decent and becoming respect.[55]

In the South, the same debate was much more anxiety-laden: would armed slaves turn on their masters? (The transparency of the "happy slave" myth is evident in these musings.) What would happen if distinctions were levelled? "The day you make soldiers of them is the beginning of the end of the revolution," warned General Howell Cobb. "If slaves will make good soldiers, our whole theory of slavery is wrong."[56]

In fact, Black soldiers were crucial to the North, and their performance in the Union army, by all accounts courageous and impressive as Douglass had predicted, revealed that "the whole theory of slavery" was more resilient than General Cobb had imagined, surviving as it did the institution of slavery itself. But whether violence is a tool, a back-up to power, a psychological release or an inevitable response to oppression,[57] *being able* to use violence may be a critical aspect of freedom. Listen to Felix Haywood, a former slave in Texas:

> If everymother's son of a black had thrown 'way his hoe and took up
> a gun to fight for his own freedom along with the Yankees, the war'd
> been over before it began. But we didn't do it. We couldn't help stick
> to our masters. We couldn't no more shoot 'em than we could fly. My
> father and me used to talk 'bout it. We decided we was too soft and
> freedom wasn't goin' to be much to our good even if we had an
> education.[58]

Couldn't shoot them. Soft. The definition of manliness that depends on murder may be the saddest comment on patriarchy anyone can dredge up. As W.E.B. DuBois remarked with some disgust,

> How extraordinary, and what a tribute to ignorance and religious
> hypocrisy, is that fact that in the minds of most people, even those
> of liberals, only murder makes men. The slave pleaded; he was
> humble; he protected the women of the South, and the world ignored
> him. The slave killed white men; and behold, he was a man.[59]

What about the women? Slave women were vulnerable to sexual abuse by white and Black men alike, though solidarity between enslaved women and men appears to have been very strong.[60] Many women resisted, sometimes with violence. Rose Williams tells of taking a poker to the man chosen by her master for her to marry (i.e., breed with), and of capitulating only after her owner threatened her with a whipping.[61] Cherry Loguen used a stick to knock out a man armed with a knife who tried to rape her. Two women attacked by an overseer waited till he undressed and "pounced upon him, wrestled him to the ground, and then ran away."[62] It's likely that women were able to resist assaults and unwanted attention more forcefully from other slaves than from their owners, though Linda Brent's excruciating narrative of resistance to her owner's sexual demands demonstrates the lengths to which some women went to preserve their sexual integrity.[63]

Did women resist enslavement? During the Middle Passage, women, unlike men, were not chained or confined to the hold. While this freedom left them vulnerable to sexual abuse by the ship's crews, it also left them freer to rebel, and there are several reported instances of women inciting or assisting insurrections at sea.[64] On the plantations,

> Some murdered their masters, some were arsonists, and still others refused to be whipped.... Equipped with a whip and two healthy dogs, an Alabama overseer tied a woman named Crecie to a stump with intentions of beating her. To his pain and embarrassment, she jerked the stump out of the ground, grabbed the whip, and sent the overseer running.[65]

A Union official recorded several women entering the Union camp with marks of severe whipping. The whipper was caught and a male slave first lashed him twenty times, and then the women, one after another, gave him twenty lashes, according to the official, "to remind him that they were no longer his";[66] but maybe also because releasing rage where it belongs is one step towards healing.[67] There are also instances of women fighting against their men being taken away.[68]

The ability to defend oneself, one's people, one's dignity, to struggle for one's own liberation, is clearly a survival skill. As Robert Falls, former slave, summed it up: "If I had my life to live over, I would die fighting rather than be a slave again...."[69]

Observations by Black and white, Southerners and Northerners indicate that the Black soldiery affected everyone strongly. Blacks felt pride. Whites felt fear. Both groups recognized that consciousness changed radically when the Black divisions marched through.

And not only consciousness. In New Orleans free Blacks formed two regiments for the Confederacy, in part to improve their status and esteem by learning firearms (though they were never called for combat duty).[70] We could argue the absurdity and tragedy of such a stance, not unlike the arguments that have swirled around Black police or military today. Yet Blacks understood that a Black soldiery might be fair, might protect them, would not automatically assume they were chattel and without rights. A Black soldiery gave Black—and white—people a vision of a differently ordered world: a hint that perhaps the whole theory of slavery was, indeed, wrong.

The analogy is suggestive. Women police officers, fire fighters, soldiers do challenge "the whole theory of slavery,"[71] as do women athletes and construction workers, as well as physicists. But particularly since physical domination so characterizes male-female relations under patriarchy, if women were to defend ourselves and other women, could avail ourselves of violence when needed; and if this potential for self-defense became an expectation, a norm, then patriarchal definitions of male and female would be shaken. Not only minds would change, but reality. Would men begin to wonder if *perhaps the whole theory of patriarchy is wrong*? Would women?

## FEAR OF THE SELF/FEAR OF OUR POWER[72]

If in a patriarchal system violence is an aspect of power, if capacity for violence is a basis for resistance, it's obvious whose interests are served by *it won't work* and *it's wrong*; by the implied fear and horror.

Women often learn to see with the eyes of the dominant culture: male eyes. Especially middle-class heterosexual white women are taught to fear strong women, women with power, women with physical strength, angry women who express that anger forcefully. *It isn't ladylike. It isn't nice.* Even those of us who have long rejected these norms (or accepted our inability to live inside them) still may fear the explosiveness of anger—though this fear obscures the reason for our deep anger, which is our powerlessness. Instead of learning to cherish this rage and to direct it effectively, we often try to suppress it, in ourselves and in others. It's exactly as if we have an army we're afraid to mobilize, train, and use.

Yet we are not always victims. We can be violent. How have we managed to avoid noticing? The idea that men are inherently violent, women inherently non-violent, is dangerous, not only because it is a doctrine of biological superiority, and such doctrines have supported genocide.[73]

The idea that women are inherently non-violent is also dangerous because it's not true. Any doctrine that idealizes us as the non-violent sex idealizes our victimization and institutionalizes who men say we are: intrinsically nurturing, inherently gentle, intuitive, emotional. They think; we feel. They have power; we won't touch it with a ten-foot pole. Guns are for them; let's suffer in a special kind of womanly way.

Such an analysis dooms us to inappropriate kindness and passivity; overlooks both our capacity for and experience with violence; ignores in fact everything about us that we aren't sure we like, including how we sometimes abuse each other. Whatever we disapprove of, we call *theirs*, and then say, when women do these things—talk loud, use reason, fuck hard, act insensitive or competitive, ride motorcycles, carry weapons, explode with rage, fight—they are acting like men.[74]

But who defines "like men," "like women"? On what basis? Remember Sojourner Truth's challenge to restrictive definition: *ain't I a woman?* All women defined as deviant might well echo her words. We may be numerous enough to redefine the "norm." When we find many of us doing what only men are supposed to do, and nearly all of us expressing in some form what is supposed to be a male behavior, then maybe we need to enlarge our notion of who *we* are. The woman who is violent is not acting like a man. She may be announcing a host of contradictions: that her condition is intolerable; that she is or isn't afraid; that she feels entitled; that she has nothing to lose or something to protect; that she needs physical release; that she's a bully; that she has lost or given over or seeks control. But always, in addition, she announces that women are not who men say we are.

TO SEE WOMEN'S VIOLENCE AS A FIELD INCLUDING: SLASHING YOUR WRISTS STANDING UP TO A THREATENING LANDLORD KILLING A RAPIST ATTACKING A WOMAN AT THE BAR FIGHTING AN ABUSIVE HUSBAND PUNCHING YOUR LOVER PUNCHING A MAN WHO MOUTHS OFF AT YOU LEARNING KARATE KICKING A DOG SHOOTING UP WRESTLING FOR MONEY DRINKING TOO MUCH ALCOHOL WRESTLING FOR FUN BEATING YOUR CHILD KILLING ANOTHER WOMAN'S RAPIST

To see women's violence as a wide range of behavior which can serve, protect, endanger, or violate women and children—or be neutral.[75] To expose the taboo which clothes even our questions about violence. To admit that when we don't fight back against men's violence, it's not because we're passive, not even because we're good: but because we're afraid of what they'll do back.

And for good reason. Consider these words from two married women:

*Sometimes I get so mad I wish I could hit him. I did once, but he hit me back, and he can hurt me more than I can hurt him.*

*When he's so much bigger and stronger, and you got four kids to take care of, what's a woman supposed to do?*[76]

Consider the implications of the fact that in the late seventies a full 40% of the women imprisoned for homicide in Chicago's Cook County jail had killed men in response to physical abuse by these men.[77] Even though judges in some states have ruled to release women serving time on such convictions, many women still remain in prison.

The fact is, fighting back, even supporting women who fight back, can be dangerous. The wife who feigns sleep when her husband comes home drunk; the child who lies to avoid getting beaten; these are tactics based on experience. Sometimes evasion works better than confrontation. At least it has sometimes kept us alive.

We worry about making things worse. "If you do what I say, I won't hurt you," says the rapist, but the woman who trusts him forgets, in her desperation and terror, that he is, after all, a rapist: hardly a basis for trust. With the husband or mate, while appeasement may be plausible, it's hardly desirable as a way of life.

What happens to women who actively resist violence? The facts, especially about street violence, flatly contradict the usual police/male advice of "don't fight it." When a woman resists a rape *in any way*—saying NO like she means it, screaming, kicking, running, fighting—her chance of escaping ranges from 60-80%.[78]

Whereas *if she doesn't resist her chance of getting raped is 100%.*

**Women and Guns**.

From my journal, 1978:

*For three or four years I've dreamed about rape regularly. The can't run dreams. The can't scream ones. Dreams where I'm being attacked and I have a knife in my pocket but I can't get it, or I'm afraid to use it. The dream that keeps extending into more complication, more danger, until there he is again, "my" rapist. I even had a dream where I'm sitting by a lake and a man swims up, sticks his head out of the water, and says: "I'm your rapist."*

*In many of these dreams, I don't recognize the danger early enough to respond.*

*Since I bought a gun and have learned to use it, my dreams have changed. Whatever the situation, whatever the form of attack, I simply whip out my gun. Sometimes I shoot. Sometimes I don't even need to shoot, I just aim and he is suddenly harmless. The man who called himself "my rapist" laughs at me when I draw my gun; he says, "The hospital can suck those bullets out in no time." But I know, and he doesn't, that it's a .38 I'm holding, and I shoot, confident that the bullets will do the job.*

If resistance alleviates abuse and increases dramatically our chances of escape, how can we increase our ability to resist? The most certain way to refuse violation would be to keep a gun handy.

Many women immediately reject this option. Some call guns "masculine." Many are simply terrified of guns' murderous power. But aside from fears of legal repercussions or male retaliation, fears which are realistic and need to be addressed—is a gun really more dangerous than, for example, a car? Is owning a gun more dangerous than not owning one? Past the realistic fears is, I believe, a fear of our own selves.

I've talked with many women about getting a gun and learning to shoot.

R. tells me, "I'm afraid I'd kill my husband."
Not to dismiss killings that happen in rage because a gun is handy (though how many of these killings are committed by women?) But to recognize that in her mind she's protected against killing her husband only because she lacks the means.

K. says she's afraid she'd shoot the first man she saw acting like an asshole. I ask what she means by "an asshole." She says, "Like some man beating up on some woman." Again, she is protected (from her best impulses) only by her inability to act.

N. says she's afraid she'd shoot her nose off.
As if a woman who has learned to cook, play the recorder, ride the subway, drive a car, and change a diaper couldn't learn to shoot.

H., B., C., E., many many women say, "I'm afraid if I have a gun it'll get used against me."

Of course this is exactly what men tell us. For example, in Boston in 1979, after the sixth Black woman in as many weeks had been killed, police still advised Black women against carrying weapons because they could be used against them. Yet what alternatives did the police offer?

In fact I've rarely heard of a real-life woman's weapon being used against her, though I've seen it happen over and over again on TV and in the movies. I've heard of a 14-year-old woman who shot her assailant with his gun; a 17-year-old who sliced her attacker's jugular vein with his knife; a mother who shot with his gun the policeman who threatened her child—she killed him and wounded his partner.[79] Maybe it's men who shouldn't carry weapons. But no one tells them that.

I also discover among my friends women who aren't afraid of guns. L., who teaches me to shoot, grew up around guns in rural Oregon. P. learned to shoot in the army. F.'s father hunted. M's grandfather was a gangster. Against the dominant experience of women—which is to have little acquaintance with deadly weapons—an alternative perspective emerges: that of women who were taught to shoot as girls; country women who'd as soon live without a knife in the kitchen as a gun in the bedroom; women who recognize a gun as a tool: useful, dangerous but controllable, like a book of matches.

The first time L. took me shooting with a handgun, I tried a .22 pistol for a while, practiced aiming again and again till it came easy. Then I tried the .38. Fire leaped from the barrel, my hand jumped. TV and movies lie about the sound of guns: it is unbelievably loud. The noise, even with earplugs, shook me. After the first round I sat down, took a deep breath, and said, "I feel like I can't control it."

"It feels like that," L. said, "you just have to get used to how it feels."

After a few minutes, I got up to try again. I started to hit the target.

A learning experience, like a million others in a woman's life. Yet so many of us consider ourselves tiny children when it comes to guns. We're afraid a gun—a source of possible protection—will be turned against us. This fear deprives us of strength, lest our strength benefit them, not us. We're afraid what we'd do *if we could*—which, again, keeps us powerless, lest we use our power badly.

To fear ourselves is to use them as model:
*they abuse their power, therefore we would too*
is to imagine only helplessness keeps us in line:
*the more choices we have, the worse we'll be*
is to insist in some hidden corner of the body:
*we need oppression*

Like, *you can't take the law into your own hands.*

But what better hands to take the law into?

Our fear of ourselves then is fear of ourselves empowered. As we worry about what we'd do if we could, we are undermined in our attempts to end our oppression. We are partly afraid we can't be trusted with freedom.

## Mother Cultures

The one doctrine of my mother's teaching which was branded upon my senses was that I should never let anyone abuse me. "I'll kill you, gal, if you don't stand up for yourself," she would say. "Fight, and if you can't fight, kick; if you can't kick, then bite." Ma was generally willing to work, but if she didn't feel like doing something, none could make her do it.
—from "Unwritten History of Slavery: Autobiographical Accounts of Negro Ex-Slaves"[80]

Women who commit violence, aggressive or defensive, are not as rare as we've been led to think. In literature by and about women who are invisible in mainstream generalizations about women—poor women, street women, women of color, lesbians—experiences with destruction, violence, and power emerge as a steady theme. It might seem paradoxical that women with the least worldly power often have the least fear of our own power. Often we have the clearest sense of our capacity for violence. Often we perform physical work, know our bodies' strength. Often we know how to fight. We're apt to be less mystified about physical abilities, perhaps because no mystification is required to keep us in line: reality suffices. We are not fed the virtues of helplessness. Constantly exposed to violence, had we not known how to fight, we would not have survived.

In these cultures, too, women often have a strong effect on the next generation of young women. Mirra Komarovsky's classic prefeminist work *Blue-Collar Marriage* notes that white working-class wives tend to rely primarily on their mothers for advice and support; while more highly educated, upwardly mobile white working-class women tend to view the husband as the appropriate confidant and supporter, and to believe that remaining too close to one's mother is a betrayal of the marriage. In other words, white middle class culture, at least prior to second-wave feminism, directly undermined mother-daughter bonds.[81]

Gloria Joseph, investigating Black mother-daughter bonds in a 1981 study,[82] found "a decisive 94.5% [of daughters] expressed respect for their mothers in terms of strength, honesty, ability to overcome difficulties, and ability to survive." She also found that what daughters feared in their mothers was often an aspect of what they respected; that is, strength and guts could manifest as temper, discipline, assertion of will, and sometimes physical punishment. Comparing family patterns among African Americans and immigrants, Joseph discovered that immigrant children were more likely to try to assimilate, learn English, separate from their mother's culture and knowledge.

Nevertheless, the relationship between respect and fear towards the mother was similar among African American women, regardless of class, and white working-class women. African American mothers and white working-class mothers were likely to teach their daughters that men are no good; that they should marry but, as one Black women put it, "keep your own stash." White middle-class women, on the other hand, were more likely to fear *becoming* their mother, and to desire independence from her. Messages about men and marriage from white middle class mothers tended toward the romantic—"marry for love"—and did not urge self-protectiveness or independence.

Those of us who come from cultures where women have been powerful in relation to the family men may have been labelled "old fashioned," at best; castrating bitches, at worst. My search for literature about women's experience with violence led directly to literature by and about working class women and women of color. Daughters from these cultures often tend to rest easier with powerful women, trust them, be willing to become them.

Vicki, for example, whose story is documented in *Heresies 6.*[83] Vicki is young, has grown up in the South Bronx, belongs to the Roman Queens, a girl gang. She is heterosexual and she is tough. She knows how to shoot and she carries a gun. She teaches her daughter to take care of herself: "You hit back because they only going to fuck over you if you don't hit back.... But I don't tell her go, go around hitting everybody in the head.... I just tell her, when somebody hits you, you hit back." Men don't push Vicki around. "I know you know I'm not as strong as a man and really they kick my ass, you might as well say. But I've proved to them that when you raise a hand on me, I'm going to raise one back." She says men have left her for this.

This is survival training. Street kids get it; poor kids; woman-raised kids. In *Yesterday's Lessons*, working class lesbian Sharon Isabell's father tells her,

> If you ever come home and tell me you lost a fight, I'm gonna beat
> the shit out of you.... Sharon, if anyone says anything to you knock
> 'em down, and be god dam glad you ain't no runt.

And her mother says it clearly for poor women:

> I'm telling you, Sharon, you got to get some guts or you're never going
> to make it.[84]

Pilate, in Toni Morrison's *Song of Solomon*, is a lesson in toughness. When Pilate's daughter Reba is beaten by her boyfriend,

> Pilate looked up from a fourth-grade geography book she was reading
> and closed it. Slowly...she walked over to a shelf that hung over the
> dry sink, put the geography book on it, and removed a knife. Slowly
> still, she walked out the front door—there was no back door—and
> as soon as she did, [you] could hear Reba's screams and the man's
> curses.... approaching the man from the back, she whipped her right
> arm around his neck and positioned the knife at the edge of his heart.
> She waited until the man felt the knife point before she jabbed it
> skillfully about a quarter of an inch through his shirt into the skin.

Still holding his neck, so he couldn't see but could feel the blood making his shirt sticky, she talked to him.

"Now, I'm not going to kill you, honey. Don't you worry none. Just be still a minute, the heart's right here, but I'm not going to stick it in any deeper. Cause if I stick it in any deeper, it'll go straight through your heart. So you have to be real still, you hear? You can't move a inch cause I might lose control. It's just a little hole now, honey, no more'n a pin scratch. You might lose about two tablespoons of blood, but no more. And if you're real still, honey, I can get it back out without no mistake. But before I do that, I thought we'd have a little talk."

The man closed his eyes. Sweat ran from his temples down the sides of his face.... [85]

Pilate doesn't have to kill. She knows exactly how to use minimal violence for maximum results. No wonder her granddaughter a couple of pages later is telling a boy she can probably beat him up.

Sometimes instead we turn violence on ourselves. Pauline, in Joyce Maupin's "A Trip to Chicago," is ready to kill herself out of sheer terror that her ex-husband will find her and force her to return to him, when suddenly

...[she] gasped as she saw the way out. He had physical feelings like anyone else. A knife cutting into his flesh would hurt and the wound would bleed. This time he must react, raising his voice in a cry of pain.

Instead of killing herself, kill him! A murderous joy possessed her.[86]

Pauline's fantasy suggests one function violence can serve: equalize vulnerability. She makes the startling, if obvious, realization that the most appropriate direction for her violence is not against herself but against her persecuting husband.

Or we turn it on each other. In *Song of Solomon* again, a roomful of African American men learn of Emmett Till's murder, two begin to bicker, call each other cowards, and are about to fight, when a third interrupts:

"There is no cause for all this. The boy's dead. His mama's screaming. Won't let them bury him. That ought to be enough colored blood on the streets. You want to spill blood, spill the crackers' blood that bashed his face in."[87]

But in the crunch of pressure and fear, we are not always clear about where the violence belongs, and a lot of it comes out on whoever's accessible: ourselves, our people and our children. In Linnaea A. Due's "The Light," in the closed world of dykes at "a school full of boozers," Maggie insults Beka and Beka jumps her.[88] In Sharon Isabell's "20 Days," women in the county jail are poised to jump each other at the slightest affront.[89] Or listen to these statements by two working-class lesbians, one African American, one Jewish:[90]

*Yeah, I used to beat up my lovers, I was butch, that's what a butch was supposed to do. I didn't know I was in a rage. I didn't know there were other ways to be butch.*

*Boiling anger rises rises ready to explode and I grab her hair and shake her head knock her down on the bed and bang her head on the mattress. This time she doesn't resist, doesn't hit me back. Power swells in me along with a sickness in my heart.*
No wonder we're afraid of our power.

## Fear of the Mother

If we have seen women with worldly power it has probably been a false power; for example, low-level bureaucrats, bank officers, the only woman professor in the department. These women have usually achieved power by identifying most clearly with male interests. Feminist struggles have often opened the gates for a few tokens, even opportunists, who may feel little responsibility towards other women.

But especially when we were children, the women we knew with power had power over us. We did not understand their powerlessness in the world, "powerless responsibility," in Adrienne Rich's phrase.[91] We just knew that many of our mothers did not deal well with this power. Many of us felt controlled, throttled, badly schooled in our womanhood. Many of our mothers beat us. Seventeen percent of the women in Judith Arcana's study were beaten by their mothers (only seven percent by their fathers).[92]

Feminists are familiar, by now, with stories like that of Joanne Michulski, mother of eight, who murdered and chopped up her two youngest;[93] or Bernadetta King, 21 years old, eight months pregnant, three young children, who beat to death her 23-month-old daughter.[94] The total responsibility women bear for their children, coupled with powerlessness: who cannot imagine going over the edge? Yet in our imaginative grasp of these extreme situations, we identify with the desperate mother. What do we feel towards that mother if we identify with the child?

According to Dorothy Dinnerstein, since children are raised primarily by women, they experience mothers as powerful and fathers as absent. Mothers are blamed for all frustration. Thus, she claims, as adults continuing this pattern of blame, both women and men will have trouble with powerful women.[95] Dinnerstein's analysis is provocative, but misses the critical point, which is women's relative lack of power in the world outside the family. There is no transition, no bridge between the mother's absolute power over the child and her powerlessness in the larger world. The chasm between this absolute power, on the one hand, and powerlessness, on the other, prohibits the mother from directing her power to somewhere besides her children, and prevents the growing child from modulating her/his understanding of empowered women.

Having learned as girls that women who have power will dominate and control us, how can we trust one another, except in victimization? It's a cliche by now that the feminist movement has helped women more in achieving strength than it has dealt well with women once they develop this strength.

Arcana's research indicates that women tend to forgive their fathers everything, their mothers nothing: women still see their mothers from a child's perspective, as all-powerful. But even an intellectual grasp of our mother's actual powerlessness still leaves many of us feeling queasy around the conjunction of women and power—as we are meant to feel. Were we not so afraid of what we'd do if we could, did we not fear taking the law or any other form of power into our own hands, we might struggle wholeheartedly for power over our lives instead of turning on one another. We still don't trust. If we trusted, we might win. If we were not afraid of our empowered selves, we might not tolerate powerlessness.

## WOMEN, MEN AND PATRIARCHY

If women can't defend ourselves adequately against abusive men unless we're prepared to take our lives more seriously than we take theirs—what if the abuser is a woman? Must we apply the same remorseless logic?

Men's violence against women carries with it a great deal beyond the personal interaction. For one thing, a man who raises his arm, who even raises his voice, is, in a sense, already hitting.[96] He is probably larger than the woman, heavier, better trained in fighting and in defensive physical response.[97] He may have been in the armed forces, gone through boot camp; he may have killed, maybe several times; he may have raped, mutilated, tortured. All of that experience—or potential experience—is invoked by a man when he raises his arm. Even a weak or timid man draws on the fear bank created by the cruelest and most violent of the species. How's a woman to know the particulars she's faced with, especially if she's never learned to confront male violence?

I am saying, a man's arm falls with the weight of patriarchy.

A woman's, at most, has the force of the victim's mother.

Often she *is* the victim's mother. But when you consider the pressure of motherhood, and that the percentage of women whose mothers beat them— 17%—is about half of common estimates of how many women are beaten by men they live with (about 33 1/3%), you begin to get an idea of mothers' restraint.

Still, it is as mothers that women most carry authority; and the extreme violence women do in this role is testimony to the destructiveness of authority under patriarchy. People are as reluctant to intervene on behalf of an abused child as on behalf of a woman being beaten. The expected response—*it's none of your business*—is buttressed by the privatized nuclear family. Besides, decent alternatives to the family are scarce. Most children don't want to be taken from their mothers, painful and debilitating as her beatings may be[98]—especially not to be placed with a foster family, where the chance of further abuse is very high.

But whereas battering men most often justify their behavior—it is never their fault—the violent mother usually feels intense shame. Corporal punishment by parents is still considered a norm by many, but the violent mother is not supported by an entire culture ringed with jokes. Usually she knows that even when the children "deserve" some kind of punishment, they don't deserve what she's dishing out.

Women's guilt over childbeating is wildly painful. Yet maternal violence—child beating—is so common that only the secrecy surrounding it explains why the woman who wrote the following is so ashamed.

Does motherhood release rage and cruelty in anyone except me and "sick" child batterers?...My children, when they were about a year old, released in me terrifying fantasies of torture and cruelty. They did it by being children, with normal childish traits of persistence, nagging, crying, curiosity.

Fantasy films unwind in my brain...I...seize a child by the heels, swing it round, and smash its head into the wall, watching the blood and brains flow down.... Sometimes...I leave them in the house alone and just run way.... After the fantasy films run out I look at my babies and realize I could never do those things.... I love my children too much. Then I am able to be tender and gentle with them once again. But I really have, in anger...kicked at their legs, spanked, pulled hair, and pushed them to the floor.... I understand how the battered children become that way...

I am ashamed to admit I...really have hit and kicked my little children....

I spend so much time in self-hate.... [99]

The mushrooming of Parents Anonymous groups, organized and developed mostly by women, suggests that women would rather not be beating their kids. I don't see Batterers Anonymous or Rapists Anonymous springing up.

Whose authority is reinforced by male and female violence? We know that men's violence supports patriarchal constraints on women, terrorizes women as a group, and reinforces male power. Whose interest does women's violence serve?

Parental violence against children, whether exercised by fathers or mothers, strengthens patriarchal authority. Children are often beaten for breaking social rules; the discipline mothers enforce is in the service of male-centered society, not of feminist rebellion. Judith Arcana remarks:

Hitting their daughters is one of the ways mothers, albeit against their will or understanding, enforce society's oppression of woman....

How better to impress submissiveness on us than to force us to submit?[100]

Women who are violent against other women have a mixed relationship to patriarchal authority. The fact of women dealing violence to anyone other than children violates patriarchal definitions. Yet lesbian violence hardly threatens patriarchal power. As does any in-group violence, lesbian violence protects the status quo, by deflecting rebellious energy away from the seats of power, and by doing the oppressor's work for him: demeaning and demoralizing the oppressed. If we look at women's violence from the perspective of its relationship to patriarchy we find that maternal violence supports patriarchy; women's violence against men challenges it; and lesbian violence straddles it, challenging its definitions but ultimately bolstering its force.

## LESBIAN VIOLENCE

### What is Battering?

That I have not needed to define battering before now suggests one basic difference between lesbian violence and heterosexual male violence. With lesbians it's not always obvious what is battering and what is something else. Sandy Butler, a lesbian counselor, tells me, "if a heterosexual woman walked in and said she was in a battering relationship, I'd assume I knew what she meant, and 98% of the time, I'd be right. If a lesbian said the same thing, I'd have to ask a bunch of questions before I knew what she was talking about."

I define battering as the systematic use of violence in an intimate relationship to control and dominate. Some lesbian relationships include physical fighting; ugly and debilitating, it may have nothing to do with domination, everything to do with inadequate controls. Sometimes women are learning anger management and it doesn't happen smoothly. Sometimes two women in love have radically different tolerances for shouting, for physical gesture; what seems normal to one is terrifying to another. Many lesbians describe temper tantrums, rage, sexual confusion. Sometimes it's a matter of women (usually, of course, victims of abuse themselves at some point) being "able" to express violence against an intimate for the first time, because of relative equality of size and power. Sometimes abuse of alcohol and drugs is involved.

Then, too, the coming out process—uneven and different for each woman, and sometimes lasting years—demands so much rule breaking about female behavioral norms that sometimes lesbians retrace growing up, in order to develop new, more appropriate behaviors. Expressions of sexuality and anger have often been so shaped by male dominance that lesbians, freed in intimate relationships from this overarching construct, sometimes need to relearn how to fuck and how to fight. Violence sometimes surfaces as part of a more generalized confusion.

And sometimes lesbians do exactly batter other lesbians, use violence on a regular basis to control and dominate.

I don't minimize how any of this feels. Whatever the source or intent, violence in an intimate relationship is frightening, degrading and exhausting. Violence has a way of escalating: what seems not dangerous can suddenly explode—when someone angry is driving a car, for example, or stands within arm's reach of a boiling kettle. In addition, even a pattern of relatively "mild" violence tends to catapult a relationship into fear, isolation and shame. A woman brutalized verbally or physically will often do *anything* to avoid the onset of abuse; in this way the abuse controls her life, whether actualized or not. Anyone who has lived through abuse in an intimate relationship knows the way violence seems to blanket everything, as metaphor and as fact: one experiences an utter lack of control, over oneself, over one's life.

**Victims Are at Least Innocent.**

In 1979, when I began this work, I knew almost no one but Michaele Uccella who even mentioned the existence of lesbian violence. Since then, the topic has surfaced in virtually every lesbian community. Many have issued statements about it, through groups identified with the battered women's movement (in which of course lesbians work in large numbers) and through specifically lesbian groups. In 1986 the Seal Press published an anthology, *Naming the Violence: Speaking Out About Lesbian Battering.*[101]

Most of this discussion follows a formula. To establish the importance of the subject, equalize its importance with some other subject deemed worthy of attention. Thus some have described lesbian violence as "equal in severity" to the problem of male violence. Ann Russo, in a mostly excellent essay in *Sojourner,*[102] claims that one-third of all lesbian relationships involve battering, a horrendous figure, equal to the statistics about male heterosexual battering. Russo's subject is denial, which makes it hard for me to question the figure—what am I, in denial?—but I do question it.

For one thing, as I asked above, how is battering defined? Some women I've talked to use this term to describe one episode of violence, whereas, to me, battering implies a pattern, not an isolated incident. One woman, self-described as a "battered woman," revealed, in response to specific questions, that her ex had slapped her twice. Yes, something; even a devastating something; but not the whole experience. And why was she so anxious to claim it?

I know, too, that many of us don't speak of the violence in our relationships. Even so, my impressionistic sense of lesbian violence reaches nowhere near one-third, and I have lived in many different lesbian communities, geographically and culturally. I've wondered if the term "battering" has sometimes been seized to ensure visibility; as if otherwise, our experience won't count.

On the other hand, a friend whose ex-lover, a public figure, has died, can't bring herself to talk openly about the violence in their relationship, feeling protective of the dead woman's reputation. Another turns over and over in her mind the one punch her ex-lover landed on her, as a terrible truth she can't speak, for similar reasons. Why can we talk about all sorts of pain and shame, and cradle these with compassion, *except when women are the agents?*

Again, the love affair with innocence.

It's true that when one human being does violence to another, an observer does well to be cautious about comparing the pain, severity and significance. But if we recall that every minute three of four women are being beaten by men—does anyone really claim this about lesbians?

Most discussion of lesbian violence focuses entirely on the victim, at least in part because the discussion has been largely shaped by the shelter movement. *From the victim's point of view, the abuser's gender may not be significant. Abuse is abuse.*

But from the point of view of strengthening community and political organizing, the abuser's gender is critical.

Here we smack into a cultural wall. We are so accustomed to think in terms of the individual that it is hard for us to also think politically. A psychological analysis focuses on the individual, while a political analysis broadens to include the group.

As feminists attempting to resist men's war on women, women are our community and our constituency; this is even truer for lesbians, living with neither heterosexual privilege nor the dubious protection of men. A lesbian who abuses her lover may be just as nasty and dangerous as any given man. What is different is the possibility of turning her around. She is engaging in horizontal hostility, taking out her frustration and rage on someone she can reach, someone vulnerable to her. She must be stopped, but proper guidance and challenge (and often sobriety) may well lead her to direct her anger against the systems that oppress both her and the woman she is victimizing. We can fairly assume that this abuse is against her best interest, an assumption we cannot make in the case of men.

What about working-class men who beat their wives, or other marginalized men who beat women of their own race, culture, or class? Certainly any revolutionary movement worth its name will demand that men stop beating women and direct their anger where it belongs. But male violence is such a norm that it takes considerable political sophistication, self-discipline, and feminist education to challenge the idea that men are entitled to beat and rape "their" women. Let me take a moment to encourage men of all oppressed races, classes and cultures, to recognize the comradeship of their sisters, and to confront their brothers about sexist violence.

That is their work. And confronting lesbian batterers is work for lesbian activists.

From the perspective of how to stop the abuse, or what the abuse means in a lesbian community, lesbian violence is vastly different from male, or heterosexual, violence. A battered lesbian may try extra hard to keep a relationship together, to absorb her lover's abuse, to be the perfect "wife," in order to compensate for deviating from female norms by being a lesbian. If she has not examined and resisted internalized homophobia, she may think she deserves abuse. An incomplete feminist analysis may actually block an abused lesbian from sticking up for herself, concluding that since her lover is not a man, this must not be battering.

Men—even those oppressed by the larger world—when they abuse, are often backed up by male power, and by an entire culture, including police-doctors-ministers-family. When a lesbian relationship explodes in violence, though the violence may be as severe, the pain and humiliation as great—these things feel terrible no matter who dishes them out—the abusing woman is not supported by anyone or anything.

Further, discussions of lesbian violence have ignored what seems to me a significant difference. Male violence and male sexuality are practically synonymous under patriarchy. This is not true of women. Less than 1% reported sexual abuse is committed by women, against males or females; even assuming a high degree of underreporting, the definition of sexual violence as a mostly male activity is clear. Lesbians do not go out on the street and attack women, nor do they climb in windows or assault them on dates. How often do you hear of a lesbian serial rapist or killer? Some of us—lesbian and heterosexual—remember as children making smaller children take their clothes off, playing sexual games, exercising the small power we had over smaller ones who had less. But even as sexual abuse of children explodes in the media, and women figure as abusers in several of these cases, *most* people of whatever age and gender victimized by sexual abuse are victimized by men.[103]

When lesbian sex and violence tangle, the context is usually very specific. I know of women who have been raped by women, their lovers or ex-lovers; I say this not to excuse the rape, but to point out the specificity. Lesbian rape remains rare. Even the stories of women raped in prison seem to vanish when you track them down and may even be projections based on male sexual behavior in prisons.[104]

Instead of approaching abusive lesbian relationships as if identical to heterosexual ones, a better approach might model on maternal violence. The immediate goal, of course, is to interrupt the violence; but the goal does not focus entirely on the children. The mother is also defined as a sister in trouble and feminists will agree she needs help.

Yet when a woman beats a woman, the tendency is to disown her, call her male, boot her out of the community. I think this is partly a result of internalized homophobia, a fear that violent lesbians will give all of us a bad name. The other cause I've already named: the pernicious feminist love affair with the victim. Do we only merit community support when we're victimized? A friend who had been severely violent in a relationship some years back reads a statement on lesbian battering, and says, "I had an image of women coming into my house, putting their arms around D. Then they turn their back on me, or kick me out. *I'm still a woman*," she cries. It's politically reactionary, even dangerous, to turn your back on your own people instead of helping them past destructive behavior.

We pride ourselves, in our communities, on facing issues. But our way of facing this one, paradoxically, is to make it only half ours: to exclude wrongdoers from the lesbian community. It's understandable that we don't, and don't want to, rely on the criminal justice system for protection against other lesbians. Therefore, we need to create alternatives.

But the impulse to exclude smacks of denial. In Ann Russo's survey of the movement to stop violence against women, I read that male batterers receive counselling and help from shelter projects, only to discover, a few sentences away, that lesbian batterers should be excluded from the community. Why is this? So our communities remain pure? Do we think we can shove wrongdoers "out there," like garbage, for someone else to clean up? Where are they supposed to go? Who will deal with our abusers, our shadow, our difficult and dangerous ones, if we don't?

Finally, I want to suggest that in many "outlaws" is a strength our movement needs. Not to romanticize hard-core batterers, or to forget that some people, including some women, may be beyond the realm of change. But women who can tap their rage and channel it fast into physical power can be good fighters. With all our wisdom about abused children and the critical role of self-esteem, empathy groups for rapists, anger management techniques for violent adolescents, can't we imagine training/therapy for violent lesbians, combined with political organizing to channel the rage where it belongs?

## Personal Narrative

I have tried to write this book without saying directly, I was involved in a violent relationship. For a lot of reasons I've wanted not to say this. Because I struggle with shame; because I can imagine being named "a batterer": I was not only the one who got hit. Sometimes I hit her.

I'm not proud of this. It took months for me to learn control and stop, though I did stop, and would never again stay in a relationship that contained violence. But the language—*battering lesbian*—pins me, and her, as though this is our essence, *who we are.*

I know some would analyze the origin and pattern of abuse in our relationship and say she battered, I resisted. But this represents, I think, a false stab at control-by-categorizing. It omits the explosive violence I felt in myself and expressed, and which I think may be more characteristic of lesbian violence than the control-and-dominate model of heterosexual battering. Besides, whoever started what, no one should be hitting anyone.

Growing up, my mother beat me and my sister on a weekly basis, that's just what Saturday was like. This pattern began when my sister reached adolescence—I was ten—and she also got beaten by both parents for suspected misbehavior with boys, while I became extremely secretive, a habit that pursues me into the present.

When I was 20 I went with a man who hit me when he got drunk, which was often, and I learned to walk out at the first sign of drinking. He never hurt me much because I didn't stick around. Years later, when battering got named, I recognized it as what he'd done, because he'd tried to control me. But I wasn't vulnerable to his control. Men beating women was not in my lexicon. It was completely unacceptable.

Whereas women beating women they're supposed to love? This was definitely in my lexicon.

In my first long-term lesbian relationship, a difficult relationship with a woman who had her own story of childhood abuse, this early training in violence translated two ways. I had a lot of pent-up violence and rage in me. And I found anger very frightening: any sign meant I'd get hit. Now I wonder, was anyone asserting control? Not me. The violence, for me, was about abandoning control, falling into a hideous pit—but it had been waiting for me all those years.

The first time she hit me I thought I would pass out from shock. She punched me in the mouth, my lip blew up, and she said she couldn't look at me, it made her sick with shame. We went into a little bar in Santa Fe on the Plaza, where I had never gone before nor have I since, where it was dark and no one could see my lip, and I drank a bourbon to warm away the terror.

It happened again. At some point, maybe six months later, I hit her. Then sometimes I hit and sometimes she did, and sometimes we fought. For me, the more blighting influence on the relationship was that I would do almost anything to avoid her anger, verbal or physical. This evasion controlled the five years we were together: the first two years, when violence was a steadily recurring nightmare, and the last three, when we "only" screamed.

What I needed (and, I think, she needed also) was intervention. Reality check. Friends to cut in on us and say, *This is terrible what you're doing to each other, you have to stop.* I did *not* need someone to decide which of us was the batterer and exclude that person from the community.

Having said that, this is what it looks like from the inside.
From my journal:
*She said, could I hit her on the body, not the face, the face really hurt. Ashamed. My shame is self-indulgent. Can I stop myself? Can I see myself in a context of batterers, I a violent woman? My actions make me sick; as long as I wallow in guilt—what? I resolved once never to hit her again—when did I start, can't remember now. This time I grabbed her, lost it, hit, kicked, knocked her down, part of me is gleeful still to have done it. Can I do nothing else? What do I get from it?*

*WHAT DO I GET FROM IT? Do I get any control through it? Does she? I will go to extremes of lying and placating to avoid the fight itself. And she—she also avoids my anger. Our anger—our mothers' anger—perhaps our fear of our mothers' anger is so extreme that we neither of us is willing to be honest—*

*Today I gave up in to the impulses that seem not like me, like another person, a crazy woman. I'm not like this, I say. But I have been this person, will be again. So maybe I am, maybe I need to claim this woman who punches and slaps and kicks her lover. Today was the worst ever and it was over in a minute.*

*She says, you think you're violent?—sort of mocking, trying to comfort at the same time. I do think this. It scares me. She assures me that she can protect herself, that I haven't done damage. Perhaps I need not to think of myself as a victim of violent impulses—my own—and ask again what I get from being violent. Imagine violence as choice—*

*and the answer flashes upon my brain: release, a familiar kind, plugging into my mother's release, once a week, letting go, what I saw in her; what I would have liked deep deep inside me to do to her as she beat me. This I bring to my lover, like a trunkful of ghosts, myself a clumsy marionette tied to their ghostly strings.*

And again from my journal, months later:

*I can identify suddenly with my mother's crazy rage and frustration exploding as violence, so powerless, so enraged at her snotty infuriating selfish kids she gave up everything for—So who asked you to? we'd say, and she'd go right up the wall....*

*Sometimes I am out of control. A few times I hit her and I'd feel some ecstatic release, the freedom of losing control. Once I acknowledged that, I came to realize I did not really want to physically hurt her, though I was enraged. That is, I became an adult with my violence and, if I feel it coming, I say, I have to go out.*

And some months later:

*Stopped for lunch at the country barbecue/suburban bar. I look up from the check I'm writing to find the bartender's hand near my breast.* Get your hand away, *I snap. He mumbles something about helping me get my ID.* I get my own ID out of my own pocket, *I say. He becomes abusive, sputtering,* Don't take this bitch's check. *I'm livid.* Listen you. *I bellow, shaking my finger at him,* you better watch it! *He shuts up.*

*Let me not omit that he was small, just a couple of inches taller than I am; and drunk. That no one around him was going to help him out. That X was with me. But this is realistic assessment of a situation. Something has changed in my relationship to violence. I learned something about strength. I can take care of myself. I can choose to rely on violence as back-up. I know this comes from the violence I have seen in myself. I'm talking about a power that comes with release, rage, letting go: maybe as simple as knowing you can count on adrenalin, can trust your body. This wild creature who can tap her anger, translate it into physical energy violence fast, she is not frozen by concern for an attacker. She will never say,* Somehow I couldn't imagine putting the knife into his flesh. *If she can tap the violence, she can protect herself*

## REMOTHERING

As women began to talk among ourselves about violence against us, a feminist analysis developed that said sex and violence had nothing to do with each other, that power equalled domination, that rape was a crime not of sex but of violence. At the same time, in a separate and seemingly unrelated sphere of activity, women theorized that since patriarchy blamed mothers for everything, we would exonerate mothers entirely: either by honoring their strength, courage, and devotion; or by recognizing their victimization, their helplessness to do better.

In 1977 when I first began to write about women and violence, I was startled to discover in women's poems, letters, and journal writings, in conversations—everywhere except in feminist theory—that when women spoke of violence, three other themes kept surfacing: sex, power, and mother.[105] The observations and information seemed chaotic, contradictory and threatening.

For example, rape is a crime of violence, not sex. This statement, a crucial truth about women's experience of rape, attempted to move rape from the realm of dirty jokes into the arena of criminal, terrifying violence, where it belongs. But, as I've mentioned, this line omits a crucial truth about men's experience. Men who rape get off on it. Male sexuality is often tangled with domination, anger, and violence. Women's sexuality has often been shaped and deformed by sexual abuse.

Similarly, the truth about heroic or victimized mothers omitted the times they sided with our fathers or brothers against us. Often they could not or did not defend us. Often they had power over us. Sometimes they beat or abused us.

What had sex to do with violence? Most obviously, women's numerous experiences of abusive sex and sexualized violence. But beyond these, the link seemed to be power, and women's fear of being powerful, physically or sexually. Because we are constricted in our power, unaccustomed to exercising it, any powerful action may seem violent. Sex and violence are two visceral areas where women have been heavily constricted, pinned to a skinny little norm of permissible activity (coming in the missionary position; slapping a man's face, not hard). Women who act against these norms are erased, punished, or presented as totally aberrant, so much so that in the dominant culture, acts of sexual or physical aggression are considered "male" acts. In *Female Sexual Slavery*, for example, Kathleen Barry consistently uses the term "sexual power" to mean male sexual domination: sexual power is what enforces female sexual slavery.

But what is sexual power for us?[106] Sex and violence are two capacities women need to explore, a need which I believe explains much of the preoccupation in lesbian communities in the late seventies and early eighties with sado-masochism. S/m, as sexual practice and as discussion topic, offered a place—often the only place—where lesbians could explore issues of violence, sexuality, power, strength and helplessness. And as some feminists labelled strong sexuality, sexual power, even penetration as inherently male, others, who saw and felt things differently and chose not to lie about this difference, became alienated from "feminist" practice and were declared or declared themselves sexual outlaws. Yet at least half of what I heard women talk about as hard-core sadomasochism during this period, I would call experimentation and explora-tion. The sense of taboo was extraordinary in a movement dedicated to women's freedom, a movement that initially built its theory out of the contradictory, complex threads of women's experience. From feminist mouths came some of the ugliest name calling—on both sides—that I have ever heard, about an area where we are almost all tender and vulnerable; none of us needed to have her sexuality mocked.

Sex and violence are two areas where many of us learn to fear ourselves, the more we fear ourselves, the less we try for freedom.[107] This lack of self-trust is particularly evident and poignant around issues of sexuality, because sexuality is so individual. Just as our dreams are uniquely our own, our sexuality might also be uniquely expressive, we might be truly ourselves in it were we not made especially afraid. And since sexuality is such a powerful aspect of ourselves, to the extent that we are shamed in it, we are that much controlled.

One way men have dealt with sexual shame is by projecting sexuality onto "bad" women. Often the projection is race or class defined as well, to distance the sexual ambiance, and to buttress master-race-and-class dominance. Excessive sexuality has been attributed to the poor under capitalism,[108] the "natives" under colonialism and imperialism, African Americans after Emancipation,[109] and Jews in all anti-Semitic portraits, including Nazi propaganda.[110] The point is to dehumanize the underclass by animalizing them. Animalizing the "other" in one fell swoop frees the overclass from fear of their own sexual impulses, secures for privileged men sexual access to women, and justifies control of the underclass through rape and other forms of violence, often sex-linked (e.g., lynching, often connected with charges of rape and accompanied by castration).

Being defined by the dominant class as inherently or excessively sexual hardly frees the various non-dominants to express sexuality.[111] But white middle-class christian heterosexual women—defined as the virgin/mother, as opposed to the whore—were forbidden any sexuality until the last few decades.[112] Contemporary emphasis on sexual availability and simultaneous orgasm changes this norm only superficially. Women are still not permitted an autonomously defined sexual practice.[113]

What about sex and mother? Under patriarchy, the split between the two is absolute: *sex* means *whore* and *mother* means *sexless*. But the common thread that binds both *sex* and *mother* to *violence* is *power*. Because the first powerful woman was the mother. Because many of us learned violence or passivity from her. Because for lesbians, especially, when we face each other as lovers, opening our bodies to each other, the woman with power over and with our bodies is always in some sense the mother.

To the extent that women have avoided or resisted male dominance, we are positioned to love and protect other women, to act towards women as true daughters (to honor) and true mothers (to nourish and protect). I don't think this means only lesbians, though I am sure it means choiceful sexuality and love for women. When the woman in Alice Walker's story "Coming Apart" realizes that she finds her mother sexy, she is prepared to stick up for her own sexuality in struggle with her husband.[114]

But lesbian or heterosexual, we knew power first from a woman, and mother-daughter relationships have often been fraught with grief. We can see this as an inevitable fact under patriarchy. Even those women whose family men were not especially powerful in the world that is, most women, who are not white, not middle and upper class—for whom a salient growing-up initiation is witnessing the humiliation of her father, of her people's men; even these women have seen that inside the family and subculture, a male often receives special attention, honor, heeding, sexual privileges at the expense of the women and girls. He's also likely to earn more money, which carries both literal and symbolic power.

(The less trammeled strength of African American women, relative to white middle-class women, as noted in Joseph's study,[115] is reflected in the daughters' respect for their mothers. But the odd skew to many male discussions of African American male unemployment and disempowerment reflects dominant cultural assumptions: that the problem is not the poverty and oppression of *all* African Americans, but the demasculinization of the men relative to the women. After all, men are supposed to dominate women, and it's unfair that African American men don't get to. Such discussion also ignores the persistent facts of female impoverishment: employed white women still earn less than those Black men who are able to find paid employment, and Black women still earn least of all.)

Those of us whose mothers beat us may be especially afraid of powerful women, or apt to confuse love, sex and violence. But each of us had a mother who was powerful compared to the child. We don't straight away know much about woman-love that doesn't include some level of control. What many of us need in order to work through confusions, through this inaccurate training, is profound re-education, and at such a basic level we have to call it remothering.

If girls were taught openly about violence—what it is, who uses it, what it's for—we would be better able to choose or reject it on our own terms. Remember Vicki instructing her daughter: *I just tell her, when somebody hits you, you hit back.*

What might remothering mean on this issue of violence? I think separating out the issues of shame, self-control, power-tripping, physical fighting, "male behavior," cultural difference, would help us to look at our actual behavior, positive and unacceptable. To stand outside the learned circle of responses available to the powerless. To understand ways in which our mothers were not helpless; what they might have done instead of what they did; their choices and our own.

The first step in the process is speaking: what our relationship to violence has been. This is not to condone women's abuse of children or of other women. Violence in process must be interrupted. But women who have been violent need to talk about it, release the shame, begin to understand and forgive themselves. We need to confront and to comfort the child-self, to see the behavior as patterned.

The same is true for women who have never fought, who feel reluctant to take on what we perceive as "maleness," violence. We need to do the work outlined here, taking apart violence-power-maleness-femaleness-mother-helplessness, to radically reconstruct these concepts from a woman's perspective. We also need to beware self-hatred, the male's contempt for the female, the femme who doesn't know how to fight, isn't athletic, the lowest of the low in a patriarchal context: "like a girl." We need to look hard at our perceived choices, in the past, as we grew up and assumed womanhood, and now. This way we may learn to know our violence and tap it as needed, instead of taking it out on our kids, loved ones, or ourselves.

## Consciousness Raising as Remothering

We need to speak, and we also need to listen. To understand the range of our experience. We need to move beyond the private into the political, via the same route as early women's liberation: the small group of women in a circle, sharing experience so that we can create both theory and change.[116]

From our original CR groups came both theory and practice. You could say anything. *Anything.* And if it didn't belittle or deny someone else's experience (if we lived up to our theory, which we didn't always), no one would say you were wrong. Your experience had to be accounted for. A group of women worked together to understand our lives from what we knew.

And this is no longer true.[117]

It's inevitable that those who develop a movement in its early stages are blissfully free—because everything remains to be said. Those who come later are building on something. Ideas codify. It makes sense to pass on what we discover. And women wrote books and read books by other women, took classes taught by women in programs which women had fought for—but now these books and classes and programs have become givens, with obligatory citations of French feminists and midterms and papers of 10 typed pages with 3/4" margins.

Yet in some key areas, more experience needs to be shared. I think we don't need to be told anything right now, we need to remember and to pool the memories; to retreat from models of hierarchy, accusation, and correctness, and talk to each other; try to recapture what we know. We need to do this in an atmosphere where nonconformity is cherished.

To ensure honesty and trust we may need to divide into women who perceive ourselves as having been victimized and women who have used violence (though I believe, when we are honest, most of us will belong in both camps). We need all of us to talk about victimization, face our vulnerability, and examine all the ways we have stayed alive. We need to look at where we have harmed each other and ourselves, and at the connections between harming ourselves and harming others.

# III. Forms of Resistance

## FROM DEFENSE TO RESISTANCE

### Survival as an Act of Resistance[118]

My goal in the preceding sections has been to clear away some space on the subject of violence so that we can begin to look at how to resist without preconceived notions. It seems obvious. If you talk about violence, you talk about resistance: those of us who live have lived through something. Women resist not only with simple defense against simple aggression, though there's plenty of that:

> He tried to grab me and I punched him in the nose—and broke it.
> He climbed into my sleeping bag and I flipped him off me and got him pinned.

But most of the violence we face is not "simple" street violence. As women and girls are attacked and abused inside the structures of ordinary life, marriage, and family, we resist. Children hide under the table; have tantrums; feign illness; run away; make fun of the abusive adult; cherish fantasies of rescue or of power; focus hatred, which is often a measure of reluctance to internalize punishment or to accept abuse. Women who are beaten/raped by men who are intimates may leave, disrupt the pretense of the happy family, withdraw love, or tolerate vastly ambivalent feelings. We learn to keep a secret money stash, to take a cab and get away; to hide an extra set of car keys; to signal a friend or neighbor, so a "surprise" visit or phone call can offer protection. If not free to leave—or not choosing to do so—we work out ways to survive with some dignity. Women keep their living space off limits to men. Women try to provide models of toughness and assertion for little girls. Some women develop big mouths, cultivate words as weapons. Women gain weight, take on size, refuse the dainty delicate image of femininity. Women take comfort from sisters, friends, allow ourselves to fall apart under the protection of other women. Finally, women resist by participating in the struggle to end the violence.

All this in addition to women who know how to use keys as weapons, learn karate or street fighting, strenghten our bodies, carry knives, buy guns and learn to shoot, and teach other women to do these things.

I've been talking about self-defense in its most limited form: a man attacks and then a woman chooses to fight or not, according to her options, preparation, ingenuity, rage, adrenalin, whether or not she owns a weapon, has it on hand, etc. But if we consider that any time a woman is raped or beaten, a climate of abuse is strengthened—the woman fearful and damaged, the man knowing he got away with it, each of them in contact with others: her fear, his conquest, rippling out into society....

Then we begin to recognize that violence against any woman is violence against every one of us. Further, that any act which resists this violence, viewed now as a mass assault against a vast people, constitutes self-defense.

**Who is the Self?**

Some of the cases typically included as women's self-defense actually include defense of another. Dessie Woods, for example, an African American who killed the white insurance salesman who tried to rape her and her friend. Yvonne Wanrow, a Colville Indian, and one of the early self-defense cases, was actually protecting her child and a friend's child from a known child-molester, a white man.[119] Many women who defend themselves against abusive husbands are also protecting their children.[120]

But the notion of self-defense is even larger. It is another name for solidarity. For example, the inspiring action performed by Joan Lester and reported by her:

LIKE TWO SHIPS THAT PASSED IN THE NIGHT

On Thursday, November 10, I was walking by the subway station at Grand Army Plaza in Brooklyn at 10 p.m. I saw a man and a woman coming out of the subway; the woman looked as if she was struggling against the man, who had his arm around her. I asked, "Is everything all right?" He answered, "This is my woman." I was uneasy. They were going in the direction opposite from me, so I reversed direction and began to follow them. The man kept looking back at me. After a third of a block, I said to the woman, "Are you OK?" She grimaced and shook her head no. The man was holding her tightly. He looked at me and said, "If you say anything, I'll kill you." I saw three men approaching about half a block away and I yelled, quite loudly, "This woman needs help. Help this woman." They began to run toward us, the attacker released the woman who ran over in my direction, and suddenly one of the running men pulled out a gun, aimed it at the attacker and said, "I'm a policeman." A second man pulled out a walkie-talkie, they had the attacker against a wall, and in a minute or two one or more police cars were on the scene, and the attacker was hustled into the police car.

Meanwhile the woman had run to me, shaking and sobbing, saying, "Thank you, thank you." I held her and I said (which I find one of the most amazing parts of the whole drama, in retrospect), "You are my sister." In a few minutes the plainclothesmen came over and took her name, of which I have no memory, her age (27), and her address (somewhere in the Village.) Before they took her with them I asked them to show us their ID to prove they were cops, and asked for a woman counselor to assist and support the woman who had just been attacked. She said that she had come off the subway and the man had grabbed her from behind. He had a knife and had cut her ear and was forcing her to go with him. The first thing the police said when they came over to us was, "We are pretty sure this is the guy who did 100 rapes in Brooklyn."

Among the many amazing things that occurred during that twenty or twenty-five minute episode was the fact that the cops spoke not one word directly to me. They didn't thank me for intervening, they didn't take my name as a witness, they did not acknowledge me, and although I had my arms around the woman as they were asking her to tell what had happened, the whole thing was suddenly over when they took her away to their car, and I was left alone on the street, my heart pounding violently.

I want to make this event public for several reasons: first, people should know about a case where intervention DID WORK. The woman was probably saved from rape, physical injury, or murder; I was not hurt; and the attacker was captured. Although it was pure luck that two plainclothesmen were walking by at the exact instant I yelled, I think the attacker was preparing to run anyway, as soon as I yelled. I am pretty sure he released the woman as soon as I yelled, and he did *not* move toward me....

Second, the woman involved played a great part in saving herself by struggling continuously against her attacker. If she had not been so evidently struggling I would not have had the clue as to what was going on. Resistance was effective.

Third, women should know that this happened, since it occurred at a place and a time that most of us would have considered relatively "safe": a busy well-lit subway station and intersection at 10 p.m.

I hope that I can trace the woman. We shared a profound moment. Her face, with her mouth stretched wide, exposing her teeth, her eyes enormous with fright, and her courage in continuing to struggle and to act on her own behalf by shaking her head when I asked if she was all right, although he must've had the knife against her—all these images of her keep going through my mind, and it would be good if we could connect again, and perhaps put a close to the event.

There are other reasons too, for wishing to reconnect. Perhaps she needs emotional or legal support to prosecute, and together we could search out women's groups which could give that support. Perhaps we could share our experience with other women and give them a feeling of strength, for after all, we, two women, did act in concert in a violent confrontation with a street attacker...and we were victorious....[121]

You don't need to be Wonder Woman to stick up for another woman in this way. You do need to look at the male world with the eyes of ntozake shange:

before i ride the subway
buy a paper or drink
coffee from yr hands i must know
have you hurt a woman today
did you beat a woman today
throw a child cross a room
are the lil girl's pants
in yr pocket[122]

You hear screaming outside your window. You see a woman attacked on the street. The car in front of you is driving funny, weaving (could be a drunk, or, as I once discovered when I followed the car, could be a woman grabbing the steering wheel to escape an abusive husband). The neighborhood child, the little girl at the day care, the niece who acts out sexually, or draws explicit sexual pictures. The upstairs neighbor screaming as, you think, her husband is beating her. We must begin to take responsibility for one another, and this means smashing through the barriers around our private lives, including our families.

Women have developed some inventive strategies to transcend the limitations of police/court options. In Portland, we formed a group called the Godmothers, who would protect battered women in their own homes. Women in a number of places across the country have developed public exposure formats. On March 8, 1977—International Women's Day—the Kitty Genovese Project in Dallas published and distributed to 25,000 women the names of 2,100 men indicted for sex-related offenses in Dallas County. Women post leaflets identifying a particular rapist—an especially strong tactic for closed communities, like campuses. Santa Cruz Women Against Rape confronted men at work, though since they, unlike the Kitty Genovese Project, were not dealing with public record, they were subject to libel suits.[123] Imagine if Anita Hill had confronted Clarence Thomas back in 1980. This kind of exposure is especially shattering to those men best protected, by class status, from the criminal justice system. Women have filed civil suits against rapists, and this has occasionally been successful, but as with criminal cases, class and race biases are powerful. Generally the same woman whose chances look good in criminal proceedings also fare well in civil court.

One woman created with some friends a life-size dummy dressed in the distinctive style of the man who'd raped her. The dummy, labelled with his name and the word "rapist," its crotch painted gorily red, was delivered to the man's place of work. Another woman, a new, single mother suffering post-partum depression, went to her doctor for help. He paid her the unusual courtesy of a home visit, seduced her, got her pregnant, and then refused to support her in her choice to have the baby. He did offer her an abortion (in his hospital). A flyer telling the story and naming the doctor was distributed around his hospital. In both these cases, the women who had been abused and humiliated felt gleeful and dignified.

In one city, several women had been raped in a park by a pair of rapists; when the police refused to patrol the area, women set up weekend patrols, thus discouraging the two rapists from their chosen hunting ground. Pam McAllister, in "Feminist Law Challenging Actions," reports on a number of creative feminist responses to abusive men: painting *rapist* on the front door of doctors and other professionals who abuse clients; catching rapists, shaving and dying their heads bright colors; "haunting" a harassing man—that is, following him, pointing to him in public places, saying "Do you know what this man has done?" (a technique developed in the Indian resistance movement against the British).[124]

Some of these tactics run the risk of exploding into violence, and women need to be prepared. But most of the actions I'm describing have a strong element of theater. The problem is not danger so much as time and energy, tight commodities in a tightening world. In order to create these actions, we need to feel effective enough to commit the time and energy. We need to see our dramatic but small strategies as part of a larger whole.

There are reports of an underground rape squad in Sacramento, California, that castrated one rapist a month during 1974, based on court records,[125] and rumors of Los Angeles lesbians running decoys against the Hillside Strangler. The story goes that ten men who attacked women during that time were killed. The Hillside Stranglers were finally apprehended, but the word on the women's circuit is they were driven out of L.A. by the women.

At this point we wander into the shadow ground between herstory and mythology, precisely around the difficult question of using violence by choice. Whether or not these acts took place, it's worth considering: what do we think of such acts? How do they make us feel? Do we think they are effective? Can we imagine doing them?

Personally, the thought that L.A. dykes went after the Hillside Strangler(s) and killed ten rapists makes me feel stronger. I'm inspired by the women's courage, and—let me say it openly—pleased by the thought of ten less woman-violators on the planet. I'm also terrified by the risks the women ran.

The Sacramento castration squad, on the other hand, arouses mixed feelings: relying on police records.... Who are the women—what is their class and race makeup? Who did they go after? Besides, castration as a tactic carries hideous historical baggage, as well as supporting the analysis that blames the penis.[126]

In considering action, we need to ask: would women feel strengthened by this act? Would abusive men feel intimidated? What is the risk to women? How much can we trust one another's courage and calm, not to mention loyalty? Activist Marcia Womongold was set up by a police informer when she shot into a pornography theater.[127] She had good legal workers and publicity, and was sentenced to a year's probation, but I don't like to think about what would have happened to her had she shot one of the men in the theater. Women who have been involved in discussions of getting rapists and batterers—and many many women have had these discussions—report these periods in their lives as fraught with paranoia.

A case of three women in Lowell, Massachusetts, charged with killing the man who raped one of them, provides a chilling scenario. Debra Midgley, the woman who'd been raped, was acquitted, after testifying that she had not been at the scene of the murder. She also testified to watching Marcia McWhinney, charged with the actual murder, strap on her gun. McWhinney was convicted and sentenced to life. Magui Yero, charged as an accessory, was also convicted. McWhinney and Yero are lesbians. The District Attorney told the jury, "There is a philosophy among gay people that is different from those of others."[128] Stories about Marcia McWhinney and Magui Yero ran in the *Boston Globe*, sometimes in the column next to reports on the "Holbrook Five"—teenage males who viciously gang-raped and beat a woman, claimed she'd asked for it, pled Guilty and received suspended sentences, whereupon public (i.e., feminist) uproar forced the judge to impose prison time. He sentenced them to three to five years, so they changed their plea to Not Guilty and were acquitted of all charges but one: they were convicted of damaging the woman's car.

I think about these two stories and I know which one strengthens me. Yet Marcia McWhinney and Magui Yero paid heavily for their contribution. We need to ask: how can we confront, challenge and intimidate abusive men without landing ourselves in prison?

## CREATING A NEW CONSCIOUSNESS

How do we push towards a world where we are no longer victims? How, when we are taught the immutability of the social order, do we begin to imagine such a world? We don't learn history in a way that helps us see that change does happen, has happened, *is* happening, and *will* happen *no matter what we do*. The question we need to ask is not, "can things change?" but "how can we push in the direction of the changes we want?"

Art is a source and a repository of vision. Most art—and I am deliberately not distinguishing between "high" art and popular culture—gives us vision which backs only one set of possibilities in the vast flux which is the present social order as it transforms into the future social order. I do not for a moment imagine that feminists can create through our work and ingenuity and minuscule resources a culture which in and of itself can challenge the mainstream culture. Nor do I believe that culture operates in a vacuum. What we show in our art must somehow reverberate in the society or no one pays any attention.

But feminists can create art which bridges gaps between the society around us and the one we hope to bring into existence; art which articulates those strains in the society which, if emphasized and strengthened, will tilt things in a positive direction; art which starts with *what is*, palpable, and stretches it, so that our consciousness is extended to a point where we can envision new action. This new action shifts consciousness as the mind opens to receive the new action, new possibility. Art can then reflect the new shift and extend it yet again, so that we can yet again imagine new action.

### Feminist Art and Resistance

In 1977 a group of women artists and writers in Portland gathered to talk about how to make art about violence against women. Someone brought a recent cover of *Ms.*, sporting a picture of a model with a huge black eye; a poster announcing a benefit for a rape crisis center, with a graphic of a woman spreadeagled on the sidewalk; and another poster showing a woman looking miserable and ashamed. We agreed that images like these made us feel hurt, humiliated and helpless—all the feelings of the women shown in the pictures.

These images also made us angry: at the men who caused this pain, *and* at the artists who chose to show these images, evoke the terrible feelings of victimization and shame *again*. As if we didn't know. As if we were in danger of forgetting.

*Why*, we thought, *show us what we already know and makes us feel worse?* Granted, we were not an ordinary group of women. Far from living in denial of the issue of violence, we were obsessed with it. But our reactions offered a clue to women's denial. No one wants to feel hurt, humiliated and helpless. Asking women to focus on the violence done us without offering possibilities for resistance was asking a lot.

But we also came to a startling realization. Images of victimization turned us off not only because they're painful but because they're lies. The woman with the black eye puts on makeup, sunglasses, goes about her life. She will devise all kinds of clever strategies to keep the abusive man off her case. She may get help from friends. She may plot and scheme to leave him; she may actually leave. But even when he beats her, she will be bruised and frightened and will probably still go on with her life, like any other woman. Isolating her in the moment of victimization makes her a social service case, not a woman who has lived through an experience which most of us have in one way or another touched. Similarly, the woman who has been raped on the street usually gets up from the sidewalk and survives. To freeze her in an essential post-rape pose belies the truth about rape: that it has happened to so many of us; that we survive and go on. Art that insists on portraying us as victims—or, at its worst, portraying *them*, women not ourselves, as victims—contradicts what we are trying to do, which is resist victimization.

The question was, how to talk about it without making us feel worse?

We also observed that art which was supposed to inspire us with women's strength—images of women in uniform, militias, guerrillas—actually felt unsatisfying and depressing. Not that we were repelled by the idea of women's organized physical might, or by images of women in other countries who carry rifles and perform feats of physical daring.

It was the empty assertion. We have no women's army. Most of us don't yet know how to shoot rifles, much less own them. We liked these images better than the others, because at least they announce our intention to fight, and the possibility that women can fight. But they leave us dangling in the opposite gap, between our contemporary reality and a fantasy.[129]

The thread connecting these critiques is a desire for realism; for images which present us as neither weaker nor stronger than we really are.

In our group, we agreed that images of resistance strengthened us, but only if we could believe them.

Then a woman told about a waitress she'd worked with, a small woman married to a large, brutal man who beat her every time he drank. One night he did the usual and passed out. She stitched his clothes to the mattress, hours of careful, methodical sewing. Then she took a hammer, beat him black and blue, packed her things, and walked out.

As the story concluded, we all laughed and clapped our hands. We applauded the transformation, from oppression to resistance. The young waitress who sewed her husband to the mattress was smart, sassy, and she knew her tools.

Imagine a magazine cover story about this courageous and ordinary woman. Imagine a cover story that showed several women protecting an abused woman, as has happened in many communities and probably throughout history. Or a scene from a woman-run shelter of women giving comfort to one another. Or a photo of Francine Hughes or Patricia Evans or Roxanne Gay or any of the hundreds of women who have killed the men who beat them. Imagine a cover filled with these photographs.

Such stories have two things in common. They show women responding with courage to the fact of violence. And they are true.

Susan Griffin, in *Pornography and Silence*, tells the following anecdote, learned from Frances Jaffer:

> A little girl who was kidnapped and put in the trunk of a car managed to pick the lock from the inside of the trunk and free herself after her assailant drove into a gas station. When she was asked how she managed this brave and mechanically very difficult escape, she responded that she asked herself what Nancy Drew might have done in the same situation.[130]

But Nancy Drew is not the only inspiration at hand. The little girl who escaped is an inspiration. Frances Jaffer by telling the story, Susan Griffin by citing it, I by repeating it, offer women the gift of knowing how some amazingly brave, clever girl outsmarted a grown man who meant her harm.

Or a letter I received from artist Gail Waechter: the right-hand column is a xeroxed newspaper article about two women who escaped a rapist/killer at Point Reyes, California. He, with a rifle, ordered them to lie down and began to tie up one of the women. But she started to struggle, and the second woman grabbed a wine bottle and broke it over his head. The first woman then grabbed his gun (yet another man who shouldn't carry a weapon), cracked him over the head with it, shattering the wooden stock. Then she fired at him. The article said the man might be dead.

In the left-hand column is Gail's comment. "love these women," she writes, with an arrow.

> i went out for a hike alone at the ocean and it was in a secluded place....miles of sand dunes with brush on them...great hiding place...a helicopter was scouting for someone...i watched it and knew because of the eerie feeling that someone was out there...i put on my fierce heart and decided to hike to the ocean anyway.... had my kill self ready. i was going to the ocean and not going to get detained by fear...hard to run in the sand...good for the legs to push against and feel the muscle...
>
> i got to the ocean and a feeling of peace came to me...watching the waves...every once in a while a spray of water would shoot out

horizontal along the crest...saw couple of deer and some rabbits...a good day to kill i thought...let whoever it is who hides here come out and i will give them all my rage...i am just alive...

when i got back to where some friends were in russian river i got the news that a man had been out there and had met with some women who defended their dignity...and he is probably dead out there...

when i was walking back in the dunes i had a vision of a skeleton. this article was buried in back pages...i would have plastered it all over the front page...[131]

If we want to encourage resistance, we should plaster it all over the front page. And since we usually don't have access to the mass media, we need to step outside it. For example, these three leaflets, printed and distributed around Portland in 1977-78, spread news of women's resistance.

STOP RAPISTS! xeroxed a news article: 400 high school girls in Milan beat up a student who had raped his girl friend. The girls also beat up some teachers who tried to stop them from coming after the rapist.

WOMEN BITE BACK told the story of a 76 year old woman in Battleground, Washington, who was attacked by a man dressed in a delivery uniform; she said, "I'm too old for that sort of thing," but when he persisted, and took a knife to her (her knife, which she told him was too dull to cut anything), she bit him. He hit her several times but finally left.

WHO SAYS, DON'T HIT BELOW THE BELT? related how a 15-year-old Portland girl was attacked by two men who tried to pull her into a car where two other men waited; she scratched one and kicked the other in the groin; she ran away and hid until the men returned to their car and left.[132]

Each of these stories strengthens women. Each is true. No analysis or explanation is required, just simple presentation of information. Being on the lookout for these stories, finding ways of sharing them, is one way of nourishing in every woman the part which is strong, brave, and angry.

Some acts of resistance call for total celebration. The two bold women who used sign language to escape from rapists gave me this poem:

SIGN

"Two deaf-mute women used sign language to escape a pair of kidnappers and would-be rapists Saturday morning near Kenton Park, according to police reports....

While one woman led the two kidnappers into the woods, the other locked the car's doors. The woman who had gone with the two men ran back to the automobile and both victims escaped unharmed."

—*Oregonian* 1/77

My fingers move
sly against your palm
Like women everywhere, we speak
in code  Hear me  If            NOW I run
you run, if                     you lock the car
they follow, if                 I run
twigs crack under their shoes   you wait  the car
our bones will hear them        ready  you wait
stumble, unnerved               the car ready  I
by our sudden wisdom: fear      run  I see
is not useful;                  you  the car  the door
doing nothing                   opens
is also dangerous               my breath, your
Show me your hands              hands[133]

Joan Little gave Sweet Honey in the Rock the question pounding through the song "Joan Little": *Tell me who is this girl, and what is she to you, Joan, Joan Little.* Inez Garcia gave Bev Grant the refrain for her song "Inez": *We have the right, we have the right, women have the right to fight.* Yvonne Wanrow's eloquent face appears on t-shirts asserting *We will defend ourselves.* As we speak it, as we hear it, find it resonating around us, we come to believe it is possible. Because it is happening.

We can stretch into what might and must happen. A statue in downtown Portland incited such a stretch. Purchased (for $6000!) by the city of Portland, the statue is a naked dwarfed woman with a surrealistic cape of seductive hair, skinny, powerless legs, and huge, naturalistic breasts which men passing by would sometimes reach out and stroke. Several of us chose the statue as the site of a self-defense ritual, which I'll describe in a moment. The statue later became famous in art circles through a poster captioned *Expose Yourself to Art* of a man's back in the proverbial dirty raincoat held open in front—his bare legs making obvious his nakedness beneath the coat. And what is he facing? The statue at 5th and Washington.

We saw her quite differently, and to this end I wrote the following poem, and distributed copies to women who passed by the statue on International Women's Day, 1978.

THE STATUE AT 5th & WASHINGTON SPEAKS

She stood naked for hours.
The pay stunk. In the end
she tore up his sketchbook
buttoned her coat &
stormed out. Then

he made me
from memory
of an airbrushed photo clipped from a magazine
to hang over his bunk bed in the army—
a mammary gnome with thin
untutored legs, hair long, hips
wide, offering
space for babies to grow
to bind me—that's
how he wants me. She
stands on line at unemployment.
She's not eligible—
he didn't report her wages & now
she wishes she'd torn up him
instead of his visions. I

wait, thinking how
she'll come to meet my hurricane eyes
the better to make the world turn over
so he no longer has power
& she is not poor
afraid
& insulted.

I tell her, *take my hair*
*crackling with rage from every woman*
*waiting tables*
*counting pampers*
*grabbed on the street*
*or stuck with a drunk man—*

I tell her, *squeeze my tongue*
*into a rock to throw at his window*
*breaking silence*
*into a thousand sharp edges*
*for woman-haters to walk on*
*naked, single-file*
*past sidewalks jammed with women jeering*
*& clapping*
*to the corner*
*where I crouch*
*behind a sculpted smile.*[134]

The statue becomes the site of female judgment and power as she joins
with the exploited model to confront woman-haters.

Lisa Siegal's poster advertising free self-defense classes for women depicts a
line of chorus girls, except these women's faces are strong, unsmiling, and their

pose is not a dance routine but a karate kick. Chorus lines do not, as a rule, keep their faces blunt and aware, and I've never seen a chorus line of women in dresses doing karate. But these truths dim before some other facts. In a chorus line women kick in precision their strong dancers' legs. The graphic transforms chorus girls into fighters by drawing on their actual strength. The arm-and-rolling-pin greeting card, also by Lisa Siegal, transforms the housewife into a fighter.

Or the fabulous sticker, by Paula King, of an arrogant little red Queen of Hearts saying *off with their rocks*, with "Disarm Rapists/Stop Violence Against Women" printed across the bottom. Never mind for the moment that castration is not an appropriate tactic. The Queen of Hearts sticker made a lot of women laugh. We recognize her anger, but she's also outrageous: the Queen of Hearts hails from childhood, and "rocks" is a very vulgar word. The form too—a sticker that costs a nickel—invites women to join in outrageousness, and, indeed the Queen turned up all over Portland, in johns, phone booths, mail boxes, Greyhound bus stations, even on police car license plates.[135]

## Humor

We need women to identify with women, to surmount the self-hatred of oppressed people, move past the fear of being trapped as we see women are often trapped. Thus we bond around pain, a first level and a crucial one. But should we stop there, we nurse each other through lingering illness, yet never heal. So we move to rage. Here we encounter more difficulty. It's scary to get angry with the oppressor. For many many women—taught to fear our anger, taught love for men, indeed often taught love as a form of oppression—this anger is truly terrifying (*I'm afraid if I had a gun I'd kill my husband*). To identify with a group of furious oppressed people is a courageous act. We are afraid of the power of our anger, afraid what we'll do with it. We need inoculation against this fear. How to meet this fear, how to anticipate it?

One way, known to artists, servants, women, and court jesters, is to sneak by it, while people are laughing.

Look at these lines from "Admonitions" by Lucille Clifton.

girls
first time a white man
opens his fly
like a good thing
we'll just laugh
laugh real loud my
black women[136]

Behind the fact of a white man opening his fly in the presence of Black women is a history of overwhelming violence: the forced sexual slavery of African women before Emancipation, the vulnerability to rape and sexual abuse since. Add to these the form of alienated labor available to poor women: prostitution.

These are the ordinary contexts in which a white man opens his fly in the presence of Black women. And Lucille Clifton says *girls*—conspiratorial—first time the fool opens his zipper proudly to show off—*we'll just laugh*–the girls of the injunction transformed by this laughter into women, Black women, the poet's people.

The metamorphosis of girls into "my black women" is not simply a poetic trick. Ridiculing an enemy where he is vulnerable is delicious and strengthening. Laughing at someone who has power over you serves several functions. Releasing hostility can allow people to survive with some spirit and joy. Fear of reprisal can be diffused through humor. We can tolerate jokes that are frightening. Look at the humor in *Nine to Five, Thelma and Louise*, the Queen of Hearts. The hostility can be tapped, acknowledged, and released in a relatively safe form.

But there are two other important, change-making functions of mocking the enemy. He is cut down to size. You can always feel superior to someone you mock. The targets of rage are depowered and made resistible. Perhaps most important, the laughers, those who are in on the joke, bond and strengthen through the collective *us* against *them* laughter. When the laughter is public and communal, at a film, play, or poetry reading, for example, those who laugh together experience the possibility of a resistance community.

## Bonding and Separatism

I have written elsewhere critically of the warning to treat people as people, face the enemy with love, etc., and about how, as a Jew, I grew up with knowledge of situations in which "my people" and "our enemies" were clearly defined.[137] I carry this way of seeing into other areas. People who oppress and benefit from oppression of my people are *not* my people. This doesn't mean that they are all bad, any more than it means that "my people," defined situationally—women, Jews, lesbians, workers, teachers, artists—are all good. It means my freedom and safety are linked inextricably to theirs.

Early women's liberation theorists, groping for images to clarify the enormity of our oppression and how it had been obscured, tried to explain the behavior of women who identified strongly with male interests by likening them to those Blacks who, during slavery, worked in the house, close to whites. But the true anomaly of women's situation is revealed by a little research. House workers were not, for the most part, confused in their identification. The "distinctions between house and field slaves seem more pronounced in the literature than in the day-to-day operations of slavery," and, in fact, during the Civil War many house servants "fled at the first opportunity, sometimes entire households, and if they remained, many of them refused to wait upon their masters and mistresses...."[138]

But women's loyalties *are* confused, often claimed by the family in which society reproduces human life, including male life. Loyalties which are essential to women's survival and identity—racial, cultural, and class loyalty—I'm not questioning; I share them. But the institution of enforced heterosexuality presses women into a family structure which often undermines autonomy, threatens physical integrity, makes her responsible for protecting her children while rendering her unable to do so, and demands that she subordinate female to male interests.[139] Add to this the extremely complicated fact that boys, vulnerable as children and entrusted to women's protection, become men—potential violators of the very people socialized to protect them.

Contemporary African American women report clear messages passed through the women: messages about men, love, female power, and money.[140] Feminist historians have uncovered rich evidence of a female culture among white middle-class women in the nineteenth century, running alongside dominant male culture.[141] This is the consciousness possessed by many of our "bitch grandmothers," a psychic separation permissible because women lacked political power or economic means to achieve actual separation.

Now that it is possible for some women to live somewhat independent of men, "separatism" emerges as a dread and maligned phenomenon. But consciousness of women as a people exists quite apart from physical separation. In "A Jury of Her Peers,"[142] a story by first-wave feminist Susan Keating Glaspell, two women—one, a sheriff's wife—are called to the home of a woman arrested for strangling her husband. The men comb the house for clues, seeking a motive, while the women untangle the mystery by decoding the woman's behavior, entering imaginatively into her life. The men overhear bits and pieces of their conversation; they mock the women for focusing on "trifles." One of the women remembers that the arrested woman used to sing, was a joyous person before her marriage. They talk about the dead man's grimness, his lack of kindness or fun. They find the farm house bleak, as she must have. When they discover among her things a canary with its neck broken, wrapped in a little box, they understand everything. Without a word of discussion, they, a jury of her peers, hide the dead bird, the only evidence. Meanwhile the men continue to scratch their heads about the lack of motive.

Women love this story. At the conclusion to a dramatic reading of "Trifles," the play version, women cheer, identify completely with the women's psychological astuteness, their concern with the accused woman's feelings, their solidarity with her. In such bonding there is enormous potential. We need to encourage our loyalty to one another, heighten our awareness of ourselves as a people. This does not mean we identify against the other groups to which we belong, ignore our other issues. It means we have a possibility to bridge the gaps between us.

## Manhating

But what happens when you start talking like this? The banner is raised instantly in the most dangerous kneejerk that feminism has had to contend with: *manhater*. Manhating is the worst possible sin a woman can commit.

Women worry too much about manhating. Straight women because they're sexually dependent on men. Lesbians because they're dependent on men in other ways, and because they're afraid of alienating straight women. Most of us, because of family men, especially sons. Anger towards men is scary. Since men have more power, women fear retaliation. And if you're joined to men in love, sex, kinship, or political solidarity, manhating can seem a dead-end, politically incorrect, immature, or just plain isolating.

But think: the existence of this or that nice—even antisexist—man doesn't shift the reality of sexism. Since men as a group oppress and violate women as a group, perhaps an edge of manhating is a sign of health.

Early women's liberation expressed clearly and boldly a great deal of rage. Somewhere between the late sixties and the present, feminist anger got muted. Robin Morgan sticks up for the nuclear family. Betty Friedan advocates liking men. Bev Grant sings her intensely moving song about Inez Garcia's heroic self-defense, and then says, "I'm not saying this is the *answer* to stopping rape" (yet felt no need to explain that another song—about bazookas being used for liberation of Black South Africa—did not offer the *answer* to stopping oppression). The fiery Take Back the Night marches in some cities slosh liberally into marches for law and order, linking rape and violence against women with urban disorder and rising crime rates, instead of placing these crimes squarely in a context of womanhating, sexual harassment, discrimination and subordination of women to men.

In part, the shift away from focusing on men-as-enemy is a positive result of a deepening analysis by radical women, a grasp or re-grasp of the complexities of race, class, and international domination. The failure of mainstream feminism to tackle these issues has produced a watery agenda of equal shares of poison pie, and has projected an image of feminism curiously unable to link economic concerns with feminist analysis. The tightening economic crunch has increased class antagonism, as well as women's dependence on men and semi-voluntary bonding in the nuclear family, the single existing structure in the entire society defined, at least in part, to meet human needs. As feminists reel from the shock of challenges to reproductive choice and the hypocrisy of the U.S. Senate vilifying or trivializing Anita Hill, the potential for a radical feminist agenda deeply steeped in class awareness re-emerges.

For many women, rage at men will represent only a partial response. Yet one of the functions and values of art is to enable us to try on partial responses. It's useful to encourage women to know, experience, and be able to tap their hatred against men who abuse and against men who do nothing to stop this abuse. Why not try on manhating, see how it fits?

### The Charge of Glorifying Violence

Names of self-defenders collected in "women & violence," formed the basis for a ritual performed on International Women's Day, 1978, around the statue at 5th and Washington described above. Eight women, wearing white masks molded from our own faces, took on the voices of women who had killed abusive men. "My name is Wanda Carr," begins the first woman. "I am 40 years old. My husband beat and abused me for years. I shot him. I was acquitted. California." And the group chants, *I am a woman. I fought back.*[143] Through this ritual the exposed, optionless statue takes strength from women fighters, as we who spoke their stories were strengthened by becoming momentarily fused with them.

This ritual has been performed by women on various occasions, including at Take Back the Night marches. I learned about the one in Washington D.C. from Tricia Lootens' review of Ann Jones *Women Who Kill* and Faith McNulty's *The Burning Bed* (Francine Hughes' story). The review begins:

As part of a recent Take Back the Night march, members of the Washington D.C. Area Women's Chorus enacted a ritual from *Fight Back! Feminist Resistance to Male Violence*.... The ritual is simple: woman after woman takes on a woman's name and her story of violence abuse, her recourse to killing, and her treatment at the hands of the courts. And the refrain is simple: "I am a woman. I fought back." But the emotions it awakened in me were anything but simple—and it has become clear to me since then, both from male reporters' stories and from the reaction of other women that some of the audience was disturbed, even angered, by the ritual's inclusion. I found these women's stories a devastating reminder of the devastating results of oppression and resistance; others found it one more glorification of violence...[144]

Those of us who created this ritual intended it neither as a devastating reminder of what women know only too well, nor as "one more glorification of violence" (though I am curious to see all the other glorifications; they seem to have passed me right by). Since the ritual describes male brutality from the perspective and in the voice of the woman brutalized, it could hardly glorify violence. The ritual was intended to celebrate women's resistance. Each of these women met force which was perhaps deadly and *did not die*. Instead the perpetrator of violence against them died.

It's odd, disturbing, that feminists mourn Kitty Genovese and name an ingenious anti-violence project for her (Dallas); mark all over a city sites where women were raped (L.A.); yet to honor those women who fought back and stayed alive is considered a glorification of violence. If all women could find a way to resist male violence—however we could—we would be freed from a pervasive oppression and fear. This is bad?

What's bad is that women who resist are punished, and that the burden of resistance rests on the individual woman who is attacked. The ritual was also intended to underscore the next-to-final words: *When women resist together, we risk less.*

I wrote the words to the ritual, but the ritual was a collective creation in which seven other women participated. I don't know if the other women still feel moved by it. I do. I have read this ritual, and asked women to read it with me: in discussions designed to explore feelings about violence; in a workshop for volunteers at battered women's shelters; as part of a gun workshop for women. I've recited the names of these women all over the country and asked women to say their names back. I update the list. I explain that these names are part of our history of resistance, that each woman has helped enlarge the possibility of resistance for other women. For me. For each of us.

Women who have been battered have told me how they felt hearing on the radio or TV the story of one or another of these women: Gloria Timmons, Agnes Scott…Feelings like relief; pride; exultation; possibility. I also know two of the women named in the ritual. Both were proud to be included. They knew they had done something heroic and important, and that the ritual recognized their courage, as well as their desperation.

I wish that women who see violence glorified in this ritual would ask themselves: why is this my response? What is frightening to me? What do I think is an acceptable response to attack or violation? What is an acceptable response to women who refuse victimization? To women who use violence successfully against an attacker?

These are important questions. The ritual was in no way designed as a strategic directive. But response to it rests on basic attitudes and assumptions about violence, power, and resistance, assumptions which keep us longing for innocence, resisting action because in action we are possibly culpable.

I know we who performed the ritual felt in that moment many things (aside from self-conscious), some of which I can name. Daring: it's not proper, certainly not feminine, to celebrate women who've killed men. Inspired and inspiring: because if every woman who was attacked responded this way, can you imagine how fast abuse would stop? Bonded with women: because each of us knew in some form the terror of male violence. Threatening: because if these women are honored, abusive men should feel afraid. High: because strengthened. And powerful. Powerful. *Powerful.*

And I know women need to feel these things.

But I do not mean to imply that we should sit back and wait for those women who cannot do otherwise to resist, so we can tell their terrific stories, feeling high or earning a national reputation as we go—and they can, perhaps, rot in prison, or endure years of courtroom battle. The stories must be told. They must also happen. Just as it is men's ability to act out violent pornographic scenarios that makes pornography so threatening, we must assert our ability to pull off some of what we suggest.

## IMPATIENCE

### Whose Hands Are Dripping Blood?

From my journal, 1990:
*And here I am back in New York City. Violence again an issue. Women against men.*

*I walk alone. At night, I prowl, alert as any jungle beast, ears, antenna, nose twitching. At the slightest sign I am out in the street ready to run into traffic. No one escapes my view. Tonight, New Year's Eve, but early, I go out for a walk, a man close by. I spin to observe he is short, Black, older than I am, with a beard and a beret. Arty looking, older: good signs. He's not going to hurt me. (Not that he, like other older, arty men, might not commit other acts of violence against women, but street rape or mugging is simply improbable).*

*K. asks,* Aren't you scared living in New York?
I'm alert, *I tell her,* but what's important is not to let myself be controlled by fear. *Still I usually have a string of* what if *fantasies chanting alongside my confident strides,* what if *I'm attacked and if only I hadn't gone out or hadn't stayed out so long or had chosen another route.... I walk shoving aside* what ifs, *and it is at least as courageous as stepping out into space on some mountain.*

*But here is what I know. When I walk I know that any woman I see is safe. I don't want to hear the one exception, the gang of teenage girls, the true lunatic. When I see a woman coming, whatever size shape or color I know I'm safe and she knows she's safe. Gender is the great reassurer.*

*After that, age. Older men. Men with packages (purpose). Men with children or dogs (ditto). Men with women (chaperoned). Well-dressed men of any age (class)—my threat comes from men who need money and crazy angry men—I am after all a middle-aged woman you'd pass in the street, and I don't look like a mark. No one has tangled with me yet, and each time I say, even think this, my stomach turns over. It could change.*

I am caught in the gap between what I know and what I can bear to do. I know that if every day the papers carried a story about some woman-abuser getting his head blown off, this would begin to change the climate in which we live. Abusive men would no longer feel invulnerable, as they have every reason to feel now. Women would get new ideas, instead of the ideas we are constantly fed, how we are vulnerable and they are not.

I am not writing to encourage women to kill men, though I know (and so do you) that every abuser taken out is one less man around to rape or batter again. I am writing to encourage women to think about our responses to issues of violence; to explore our feelings about ourselves and other women as agents; to distinguish between the violence done to women and children, which must be stopped, whoever the agent, and the resistance women mount against it, whatever the mode (violent or non-violent).

There is a difference between elaborating violence as strategy—a nonsense strategy in a movement that can't even turn out a furious demonstration at the acquittal of William Kennedy Smith—and welcoming the important contribution and extraordinary valor of women who adopt this strategy. A difficult stance. Every time I say it I think, *Well, why don't I do it?* And here are the reasons. Who are my targets? How am I sure? How would I go about it?

And, of course, I'm scared. Scared I'd get caught. Scared I'd kill the wrong person. Scared it would be almost meaningless without a politically strategic context.

On the other hand, I think of Rosa Parks, who of course was not an isolated individual who simply got tired of standing on the bus, but an activist who seized the time. And I think, maybe I too should seize the time. I worry that I am being a hypocrite, and I think I am right to wonder. This ambivalence, uncertainty, self-examination, and pushing relentlessly for honesty about what we will and won't do—and why—seems critical to me.

For example, do I really think women should walk around armed?

Not necessarily. I think women who live in houses or apartments that are not sufficiently secured, who are afraid of invasion, should own a gun and train to use it. They will know they can take care of themselves, and this will help them sleep at night. For women camping, driving long distances alone, for the situations in which we find ourselves suddenly vulnerable, a gun you know how to use is a good thing. Of course any woman who owns a gun should train and be prepared to use it.

The last couple of years I lived in Portland, my mind filled as it was with the facts of street attack, I bought a gun, learned how to shoot, and never went out for a walk at night by myself without it. I was very glad to have it in the apartment when a neighbor harassed and threatened me. I complained to the police, and they came; I complained to the landlord who, miraculously, evicted him. So it never came to the gun, and most of the time it won't and shouldn't. It was never something to wave around, but I knew it was under my pillow, and I could sleep nights.

When I lived in rural New Mexico—as an outsider and a woman not under male protection—I continued this practice of carrying a gun when I went out for walks alone, long solitary joyful walks. But what was obvious became even more obvious when I moved to rural Maine and then Vermont: outside of urban environments, the violence that threatens most women comes from their own homes, the men they relate to or are related to: fathers, grandfathers, uncles, brothers, husbands, lovers, sons. In rural communities, there is no anonymity. You are not threatened by strange men; there are so few strangers that they stick right out. Street violence is minimal; there are no streets. Those of us who did not have male intimates were rarely threatened by male violence. My gun was stolen while I lived in Vermont, and while I regretted its loss, I had stopped depending on it.

I don't know if I'd carry a gun again in a city like Portland; I suspect not. Part of the burden of rape is living with fear and I'm not sure that carrying a gun doesn't exercise its own fear. Back in New York now, I can't imagine packing a gun for my near-nightly walk home from the subway. I am no Bernard Goetz, have no desire to blow away some kid who's after my money, and this is the most likely danger scenario I walk home with.

As for solitude in the country, this is when I miss my gun most, and think to buy another, for I am always nervous and I do restrict my movements. Only in rugged back country do I relax, just from probability. Rapists are lazy cowards who pick what's easy, and are probably not prowling in unpopulated areas seeking a victim. Though it sometimes happens that a violent unhinged man is also a hiker. It is unnerving to have to rely on the probability of men's sanity. I do carry a knife—I don't count on it, but it could come in handy.

We all live with these balancing acts. And it's obvious that, in the big cities, the struggle to stop violence against women cannot be extricated from the struggle against racism and poverty, or against urban violence generally. Rape often accompanies robbery. Street rape is mostly committed by men with little to lose. And none of this touches acquaintance rape, fraternity gang rape, marital rape, daughter rape, or sexual harassment.

Yet this complexity is no reason for women not to sort out the particulars of our lives and decide how we can best protect ourselves. If a woman chooses not to own or carry a gun, let the reason *not* be that she thinks she'd blow her own foot off, or she can't imagine using it. We need to trust in our competency and imagine responding to the danger against us. We need to think about protecting the vulnerable among us, especially the children.

I am concerned about our fear of glorifying violence, of manhating. I believe this is fear of women taking power. Even Andrea Dworkin, usually so fiery, stresses not that we must resist however we can, but that we must never betray the heroic commitment to the worth of human life which is the source of our courage as women. If we do betray that commitment, we will find ourselves, hands dripping with blood, equal heroes to men at last.[145]

When we are more scared of women's hands dripping with blood than of women continuing to be abused and undermined we are in trouble. Compare DuBois' sad comment on the white male definition of manhood: *The slave killed white men; and behold, he was a man.* It is a tragedy that we should need to consider such options, *but the tragedy did not originate with us.* Our choices are not clean hands or bloody ones. The blood is already being spilled.

## The Importance of Being Extremist

In a volatile, active time, organizers, leaders need to exercise caution. The task is to gather people's energies, see that energy is directed to the point of greatest impact, and to protect people as much as possible. But this has been a dulled-out decade, just starting to stir again. The time calls for daring, risk, experimentation, and an unwillingness to settle for things as they are. This is a time for impatience.

I am reserving a legitimate place in the struggle for those who are impatient and willing to take risks. My hope is that women who see more moderate channels as primary or comfortable, who choose the way of greater patience, can also recognize that the wild ones not only have a point, but are essential. Radical demands and tactics push people's expectations about what is moderate. Some of us had best be on the edge. How else will we know where it is?

Lorraine Hansberry, African American radical, playwright, protofeminist, dead of cancer in her thirties, tells of Robert Kennedy's unsuccessful attempt— he was then Attorney General—to get Hansberry and other leading African Americans to dissociate from the militant Civil Rights Movement.[146] Later, as slogans like Black Power and possibilities like race war emerged, the Civil Rights Movement became suddenly more palatable to white America. Martin Luther King's birthday is now a national holiday in 48 states.[147]

A movement that disowns its left inevitably moves right. It will fail to inspire those who are angriest, who have the most rebellion in them. It will take pressure off the dominant culture, which can then point to moderate demands and call them "asking for too much." Good political sense demands a multi-faceted approach to any issue.

So too on the issue of violence. Why not support shelters and lobby for full employment and free self defense classes and firearms training for women and free safety locks and classification of rape as a bias crime and rap groups for women to talk about experience with violence and public speaking by women about child abuse—and where women are brave enough to confront abusive men directly—*why not?*

Even mistrust-the-masses Hannah Arendt acknowledges—quoting from the 1969 *Report on Violence in America*—"Force and violence are likely to be successful techniques of social control and persuasion when they have wide popular support."[148] It's obvious that violence against women has wide popular support from men. But physical resistance could also have wide popular support from women, if we made up our minds to encourage and build this support. The support may already exist: think again about the response to *Thelma and Louise*.

*Doing nothing is also dangerous,* I imagine one of the escaping women in the poem "Sign" saying to the other. I say this to myself all the time. The danger persists, haunts us. Our first desire ought to be to minimize the danger. We need to admit that if, as a movement, we do not confront this danger in every way imaginable, then we leave the burden on individual women, especially those most vulnerable to attack and least likely to be supported by the legal system.

I am not urging that we land ourselves in prison. Yet we've barely even discussed the possibilities of extra-legal approaches. Walking the edge may be less perilous than we think. One of the costs of an apolitical atmosphere is that we come to see the tiniest disobedience as highly risky. Nadine Gordimer's words about anti-apartheid struggle in South Africa, are useful here: "...there are positions between the bulldozed ivory tower and the maximum security prison."[149] We must not get frozen by images of men as omnipotent, whether as abusers or as law-enforcers. Think how men get away with rape and murder. Surely it's obvious that not all outlaws get caught.

In fact, some outlaws spark movements toward revolution. The unwillingness to endure abuse any longer springs from what is holiest in us, our desire for freedom and dignity. Listen to Lorraine Hansberry:

> I think, then, that Negroes must concern themselves with every single means of struggle: legal, illegal, passive, active, violent and non-violent. That they must harass, debate, petition, give money to court struggles, sit-in, lie-down, strike, boycott, sing hymns, pray on steps—and shoot from their windows when the racists come cruising through their communities.
>
> And in the process, they must have no regard whatsoever for labels and pursed lips in the light of their efforts.

The acceptance of our present condition is the only form of extremism which discredits us before our children.[150]

As feminists, shouldn't we be saying this to each other?

*The acceptance of our present condition is the only form of extremism which discredits us before our children.*

1979-1992

## NOTES

1. I want to acknowledge general indebtedness to the work that preceded or has accompanied the writing of this essay. The first feminist speak-out on rape, in New York City in 1971, was documented in Noreen Connell and Cassandra Wilson, *Rape: The First Sourcebook for Women* (1974). Susan Griffin, *Rape: The Power of Consciousness* (1979) includes her earlier essay, which is still one of the best discussions of the issue. Andrea Medea and Kathleen Thompson, *Against Rape* (1974) remains useful, as does Susan Brownmiller, *Against Our Will: Men, Women and Rape* (1975)—the classic, limited but essential. Early work on battering includes Erin Pizzey, *Scream Quietly or the Neighbours Will Hear You* (1974), Betsy Warrior, *Battered Lives* (1974) and Del Martin, *Battered Wives* (1976). Susan Schechter, *Women and Male Violence: The Visions and Struggles of the Battered Women's Movement* (1982) remains the best single text on battering to combine service-provider and activist consciousness. On incest, Florence Rush's early work is included in the *Sourcebook* noted above, and her book *The Best Kept Secret: Sexual Abuse of Children* (1980) contains the earliest discussion of how Freud suppressed information and revised his theory, based on his women patients' experience of incestuous abuse by male relatives, in favor of his oedipal theory that women fantasized this abuse. Sandra Butler, *Conspiracy of Silence: The Trauma of Incest* (1978) remains one of the clearest treatments built from women's experience, compassionate and politically savvy. Also, Judith Lewis Herman, with Lisa Hirschman, *Father-Daughter Incest* (1981). General books on violence against women: Andrea Dworkin's *Woman Hating* (1974) and *Our Blood* (1976); Kathleen Barry's *Female Sexual Slavery* (1979); and Frederique Delacorte and Felice Newman, eds., *Fight Back! Feminist Resistance to Male Violence* (1981). Pauline B. Bart and Patricia H. O'Brien, *Stopping Rape: Successful Survival Strategies* (1985), and Evelyn C. White, *Chain Chain Change: For Black Women Dealing with Physical and Emotional Abuse* (1985) are extremely useful.

I want also to acknowledge general indebtedness to numerous conversations in the late seventies with Paula King and Michaele Uccella, and to the many thinkers and activists with whom I worked in the Portland, Oregon movement to stop violence against women. Many women have read pieces of this essay over the years and shared their responses with me: Gloria Anzaldúa, Margaret Blanchard, Sandy Butler, Chrystos, Irena Klepfisz, Helena Lipstadt, Fabienne McPhail-Grant, Bernice Mennis, Maureen O'Neill, Linda Vance, and Judy Waterman, in addition, of course, to Joan Pinkvoss, my editor and publisher at Aunt Lute. I alone am responsible for its weaknesses.

2. According to psychiatrist Carole Warshaw, "The greatest risk of getting killed is when the woman attempts to leave.... The husband or the partner can't tolerate the idea of her leaving." Information drawn from the *New York Times* (3/15/92).

3. The term "domestic violence" may conceal some instances of women abused by women. Lesbians in the emergency room might well fabricate a male abuser or allow assumptions of heterosexuality to protect them from further exposure to scrutiny and humiliation. On the whole, though, one suspects that lesbians often pursue the same course as heterosexual women, blaming phantom doorknobs, stairs, etc., rather than acknowledge battering. With murder, it's another story; probably the gender of the killer is accurately ascertained. It does not appear that lesbians regularly kill their lovers or ex-lovers.

4. US Document 1274, 39th Congress, 1st Session, 1865-66. House Reports, Vol.3, No. 101, in Gerda Lerner, ed., *Black Woman in White America* (1973), 174.

5. Lillian Rubin, *Worlds of Pain: Life in the Working Class Family* (1976) 139-40. These fairly ordinary quotes ought not to be construed to support the mistaken idea that working class men rape their wives more than men of other classes, though of course the married woman's ability to assert her rights, leave the marriage, etc., is closely connected to independent resources.

6. Diverse in terms of age, class, sexual preference, ethnicity/religion, partnered and single, mothers and non-mothers; racially not diverse, 15-20 white and one Japanese American. While more immediate survival concerns may preoccupy poor women, including many women of color, I am still convinced that violence against women is a key issue for all but the most powerful, protected and independent of women. As such, it still has the potential to unite women across differences, when we approach the issue informed by our differences.

7. Before abortions were legalized, seeking an abortion was like putting your body on the meat rack.

8. The myth of the Black rapist dates from Reconstruction, and was used to justify white terror against emerging Black freedom. See Frederick Douglass, "The Lesson of the Hour" (pamphlet, 1894), quoted in Angela Davis, *Women, Race and Class* (1981), 184. In the lexicon of patriarchy, rape by Black men of white women constitutes theft of white male property. (The myth, by sexualizing Blacks, disguises and justifies sexual abuse of Black women, and repression of Black men).

Most of this myth-dashing material, except about race and class, comes from Menachem Amir's classic study, *Patterns in Forcible Rape* (1971). Amir's work is extremely useful for information on the police-blotter rapist, but his reliance on statistics from the criminal justice system excludes consideration of all those rapists who are protected by privilege from this system. Thus his conclusion, that rapists fit squarely within the subculture of violence, describes only those rapists who get caught and punished. A more accurate conclusion is that rapists fit squarely within the dominant culture of patriarchy.

9. Latinas rarely used the Hotline at that point; later two Chicanas were hired to translate Hotline literature, to do community outreach in Spanish, and to staff the phone line with Spanish speakers.

10. Statistics indicate that men tend to rape women of their own race and class. But statistics reflect only the small percentage, 10% by FBI estimates, that filters through the criminal justice system. Acquaintance rape, which tends to go unreported, usually reinforces the same-race, same-class category. But contradicting this category is the also seldom-reported category of privileged men who rape women of lower class or race status.

11. One study of thousands of men revealed "only one third [who] said there was no possibility that they could be sexually violent toward women"; Mary Kay Blakely, in "The New Bedford Gang Rape: Who Were the Men?," *Ms.* (July, 1983), 50 ff., citing the research of Neil Malmuth and Edward Donnerstein. This and other research on the subject is surveyed and critiqued in several articles in

*Take Back the Night: Women on Pornography,* Laura Lederer, ed.,(1980). Cf. Medea and Thompson, note 1, "from all data available it appears that normal men rape normal women," 134.

12. In *Heresies 6: Women and Violence* (1979), 52, from Nadia Telsey and Linda Maslanko, with the help of the Women's Martial Arts Union, Self-Defense for Women (1974). See also Catherine MacKinnon's discussion in *Sexual Harassment of Working Women* (1979), 218-221; Lilia Melani and Linda Fodaski, "The Psychology of the Rapist and His Victim," in *Sourcebook,* note 1, 84, and Irene Diamond, "Pornography and Repression: A Reconsideration," in Catherine Stimpson and Ethel Spector Person, eds., *Women, Sex and Sexuality* (1980), 129-44.

13. Martin, *Battered Wives,* note 1, 20.

14. Florence Rush, "The Sexual Abuse of Children: A Feminist Point of View," in *Sourcebook,* note 1, 73-74. It was startling during the Thomas hearings to see the incest pattern mirrored; the defense—that Thomas wasn't the sort who would do such a thing—is often heard about "upstanding members of the community" when girl children charge them with sexual abuse.

15. Butler, note 1, 97, 100; Herman, note 1, cites restoration of the mother- daughter bond as the major task of therapy for incest survivors, 144 ff.

16. In the most typical scenario, a girl victimized by incest can report to the police, or talk to a doctor, psychologist, teacher, social worker, etc., each of whom is legally obligated to report to the police. Then, if the mother refuses to exclude the abusive man (very often the case and quite the challenge to visions of universal sisterhood), the girl is yanked out of her home and placed in foster care where the chance of further abuse runs very high. That is one option. The second: she can put up with it and wait to turn 18. Third: she can run away, often to support herself by prostitution. Margot St. James, organizer of COYOTE (the prostitute's union, Call Off Your Tired Old Ethics) estimates that 80% of girls under 18 who become prostitutes are incest victims (Diana Russell and Nicole Van de Ven, eds., *The Proceedings of the International Tribunal on Crimes Against Women,* 1976, 180) though I wonder if this huge figure simply means that incest is far more widespread than anyone imagines. (Similarly, Schecter, note 1, points out that the many battered women who were incestuously abused as girls may only indicate "that incest is much more widespread than anyone has previously recognized," 213.)

17. Statistics from Brownmiller, note 1, 175.
     Calculations: With a base of 1000 actual rapes, 100 women will go to the police, and 85 of them will be believed. In half the cases (42.5 rapes), a perpetrator will be arrested. Three quarters of them will be prosecuted (31.9 rapes). Of these anywhere between 53% (31.9 x 53% = 16.9 rapes) and 3% (31.9 x 3% = .95 rapes) will end in a conviction. (1000 rapes x 10%= 100 x 85% = 85 x 50% = 42.5 x 75% = 31.9 prosecuted; 31.9 x 53%= 16.9 convictions; 31.9 x 3% =.95 convictions, often on a lesser charge). What may have changed in the past 15 years is the rate of reporting; some estimate as many as half the women raped will report to the police.

18. Legal battles to exempt such cases from statutes of limitations have been critical, since it may take many years for a woman to remember the sexual abuse she endured as a girl, or to learn that she has some legal recourse.

19. The idea of collecting these names was Paula King's.

20. Lenore E. Walker, *The Battered Woman* (1979).

21. Anita Bracy Brooks, discussing cultural differences about violence remarks,
     [the black woman] has been socialized to live with violence on an everyday basis. She may observe daily in the community one-to-one physical violence inflicted in states of anger, sexual exploitation, and accommodation for goods and services, as well as family violence, and be powerless to intervene. Or, she may find she must defend herself against aggression because she does not have any expectation of anyone coming to her rescue or protecting her from physical or emotional harm, even the police. Thusly she learns to not only protect herself or avoid encounters, but to fight back if necessary....
     The advocate must be aware of and examine her/his own threshold and attitude toward the tolerance of anger/violence because Black people experience anger and violence differently.

Anita Bracy Brooks, "The Black Woman Within the Program and Service Delivery Systems for Battered Women: A Cultural Response," *Battered Women: An Effective Response,* Chapter 2, Minnesota Department of Corrections, June, 1980, 7, quoted in Schecter, note 1, 272.

22. A disproportionate number of sexual harassment charges have been filed by Black women (MacKinnon, note 12, 53), which may mean that Black women are disproportionately harassed on the job—given the way racism and racist myths about Black sexuality function, this should come as no shock (See Lerner, note 4, 150 ff. and *passim*)—and may also mean that Black women are choosing to fight sexual harassment more.

23. Schechter, note 1, alone among those who have written the major texts on the subject, comes from the service end of the spectrum, and her work remains the best combined practical/theoretical work on the subject.

24. See notes 1, 12

25. note 11.

26. Especially against Warner Brothers' record albums which depicted bruised and beaten women; Nikki Craft's work against pornography magazines; Marcia Womongold shooting into a porn theater, documented in Marcia Womongold, "Setting a 'Bad' Example," in *Fight Back,* note 1, 222-25.

27. The woman whose sexual—and domestic—slavery takes place in the family apartment is only more invisible, not freer, than the prostitute—like the file clerk, who may or may not be subject to sexual harassment and she performs the world's dreariest work.

The servitude of any woman reinforces women's oppression, but feminists do not talk about forcing housewives and file clerks to stop what they're doing. We talk about creating options.

Historian Judith Walkowitz points to the experience of nineteenth century middle-class women who tried to help prostitutes reform, only to discover that, while there were those who accepted the opportunity to earn "an honest day's pay," there were also quite a number who looked at the reformers like they were demented, offering backbreaking work for hardly any money. "The Politics of Prostitution," in *WSS*, eds., Stimpson & Person, note 11, 145- 56. In another essay Walkowitz discusses the casual and occasional nature of prostitution for English working class women prior to the mid-nineteenth century (when the Contagious Disease Acts were introduced, 1864-1869). One result of the Acts was to isolate prostitutes, make of them a distinct class of women, and destroy their mobility. "The Making of an Outcast Group," in *A Widening Sphere, Changing Roles of Victorian Women*, ed., Martha Vicinus (1977), 82.

28. Brownmiller is one of the worst offenders, joining with repressive church groups to protest at Times Square. Kathleen Barry, on the other hand, is an exception to this; she alone of the theorists has devised some innovative practical suggestions for reducing female sexual slavery, including monitoring bus stations for young runaways (who are often escaping abusive homes and are marks for pimps), providing childcare to women who work as prostitutes and attempting to reach them through their concern for their children. She also suggests a source for funding: that portion of city budgets spent policing and prosecuting prostitution. Dworkin's rage and compassion on behalf of women victimized by sex work is unmistakeable.

29. Ann Jones, "A Little Knowledge," in *TBtN*, note 10, 184.

30. Lesbians, whose sexuality is illegal in several states, may find this equation especially contradictory to our vision of feminism. See Lisa Orlando, "Bad Girls and 'Good' Politics," *Literary Supplement, Village Voice* (#13, December 1982), and Ellis Willis's classic "Feminism, Moralism and Pornography," in *Beginning to See the Light* (1981), 219-227.

31. Some activists criticize popular and high culture as well, like those who picketed the Broadway production of *Lolita* or *Miss Saigon* (the latter, picketed by The Heat Is On Miss Saigon, a multiracial coalition of mostly lesbians and gays outraged by the play's racism as well as sexism). But most anti-pornography work has been directed at places like Times Square and hardcore low-class porn.

32. *New York Times* (4/24/92).

33. *New York Times* (12/10/91).

34. See Ann Russo on campus rape in the *Women's Review of Books* (Feb., 1992). At one small private New England college in 1990, for example, three charges of sexual harassment were reported in a single department. Now, sexual harassment charges are popping up all over in the wake of Anita Hill's consciousness-raising charges against Clarence Thomas.

35. About Smith, sympathetic newscasters commiserated that he had to spend his entire fortune, two million dollars, on his defense (poor thing, soon to become a doctor, he possessed a personal fortune of two million dollars, and he'll inherit millions more). Did anyone remark that the law, created by (and often for) lawyers, leaves unrestricted the amount of money that individuals may spend on defense?

36. Some of these rights (the right to bear arms, to free speech, etc.) are spelled out in the Constitution and Bill of Rights, because they're being asserted against kings, governments, and the like, while other rights (the right to beat wives and children; to obtain sex from wives by force; to own Black men, women and children) are not even articulated; they are simply assumed.

37. What if Hill had been white? Would she have waited ten years to speak? Would the Senate have dared to disbelieve publicly a privileged professional white woman charging a Black man, even a privileged Black man, with a sex crime? Might they have voted not to confirm—not because women have the right to a work environment free of sexual harassment but because white men have exclusive rights over the bodies of white women? This is the public stance I would predict, though privately some of these enlightened spirits might well have responded as white officials at Notre Dame reacted to a white woman who charged with rape several Black members of the football team. "We believed the boys," they said—these boys being, presumably, the kind of Blacks up-to-date college officials would adopt as "best friends." In that same incident, the more old-fashioned, also white police ranked race over gender and believed the woman. From Dworkin, "The Rape Atrocity and the Boy Next Door," *Blood*, note 1, 38-42.

38. Butler, note 1, 32. On incestuous abuse of children, Butler notes 87% girls, 13% boys, 3.

39. This means recognizing, honoring, but not depending on the resistance skills of those women most burdened by sexism. Working class women and butches often have developed their ability to physically fight. Single women and lesbians often do not depend on male money.

A poll following the Hill-Thomas hearings showed that working class women (not identified by race) tended not to believe Anita Hill because they'd all had to cope with sexual harassment and they didn't see why she hadn't told the fucker off. At the same time, see note 22, on the disproportionate number of sexual harassment charges filed by Black women. Women who are less tied into the system also may have the clearest vision.

40. Alice Walker's depiction of Black male violence against Black women in *The Color Purple* was roundly condemned by some Black men as "white feminist."

41. ntozake shange, *nappy edges* (1978).

42. See, for example, Anne Braden, "A Second Open Letter to Southern White Women," *Southern Exposure* IV.4 (1977), 50-53. Braden, a white Southern anti- racist activist, recalls attending a lecture by Susan Brownmiller where a Black woman asked, "What you are saying may help me protect myself, but how can I protect my son?" Feminists need to throw our collective weight behind the abuse of those women least empowered by the system. This also means respecting the concerns of women of color about the random and unequal persecution of their men.

43. In Brooklyn, in January, 1992, a fifteen-year-old white girl was raped by two Black men. This was labelled a bias crime, because of two mentions of race, one of which was reported as: she asked, "Why are you doing this to me?" and one rapist answered, "Because you're white and perfect." Does the "white and perfect" remark make this a bias crime? Is retaliatory rage the same as racist hate? I don't excuse rape of any sort. But I'd hate to see hate crime labelling used most frequently for crimes against whites, christians, men and heterosexuals.

44. *Sourcebook*, note 1, 49.

45. Brownmiller, note 1, 363.

46. Interesting that in patriarchal western culture, revenge is considered practically a sacred duty for men, Hamlet and Orestes being only two of the more obvious examples (both sons avenging their fathers in part against their mothers). But women are not even supposed to entertain vengeful feelings.

47. Griffin, *Consciousness*, note 1, 21.

48. Phyllis Chesler, *Women and Madness* (1973), 292; see also M.F. Beal, *S.A.F.E. House* (1976) and Karen Hagberg, "Why the Women's Movement Cannot Be Non-Violent," *Heresies* 6, note 12, 44.

49. *The Women's Gun Pamphlet by and for Women* (1975), 3.

50. Janet Koenig, "The Social Meaning of Violence," *Heresies* 6, note 12, 91.

51. Assata Shakur, from an interview in *Plexus* by Women Against Prison, quoted in Beal, note 49, 111.

52. Ti-Grace Atkinson, *Amazon Odyssey* (1974), ccxlix. The term *violence* she reserves to represent "a class function," available as a *tactic* only to the oppressor class (200).

53. Hagberg, note 49, 44.

54. Leon Litwack, *Been in the Storm So Long: The Aftermath of Slavery* (1980), 65-66.

55. Litwack, note 55, 66.

56. Litwack, note 55, 43. What is being said here? First, the "whole theory of slavery" boiled down to an assumption of African inferiority, less-than-humanness. Second, military prowess dominated patriarchal notions of humanness: only competent soldiers, i.e., men who could act like "real men," were equal human beings. Consider that slaves were not an unknown people but the very people who not only performed necessary physical labor, but also raised white Southern children and tended the white Southern sick; obviously, tenderness, intelligence, caring, etc. did not challenge "the whole theory of slavery." See Deborah Gray White, *Ar'n't I a Woman: Female Slaves in the Plantation South* (1985).

57. Frantz Fanon, *The Wretched of the Earth* (1963), discusses the political implications of the oppressed's psychological need to release rage.

58. Litwack, note 55, 46.

59. W.E.B. DuBois, *Black Reconstruction* (1935), quoted in Litwack, note 55, 64.

60. See Angela Davis, "The Legacy of Slavery: Standards for a New Womanhood," in *WRC*, note 8, 3-29, and Linda Brent, *Incidents in the Life of a Slave Girl* (1973; 1st pub. 1861), which depicts extreme sexual harassment and abuse suffered by enslaved Black women from white men, and solidarity among Black women and men, both enslaved and free. Of course Brent was writing an abolitionist document.

It appears that women employed all the forms of resistance used by men, direct and indirect. But unlike the men, the women had no access to the military, no institutional focus through which to transform capacity for violence into organized strength. And if "manliness," as DuBois caustically remarked, meant murder, "womanliness" translated into what Black women were deprived of, the right to be protected by their men, and to raise their own babies.

61. White, *Ar'n't I a Woman*, note 57, 102-03, citing B.A. Botkin, ed., *Lay My Burden Down: A Folk History of Slavery* (1945), 160-62.

62. White, note 57, 78.

63. Brent, note 61.

64. White, note 57, 63-64.

65. White, note 57, 77-78.

66. Litwack, note 55, 65.

67. Toni Morrison's *Beloved* (1987) and Sherley Anne Williams' *Dessa Rose* (1986) both imagine permutations of violence from enslaved women.

68. Litwack, note 55, 76, 114.

69. Litwack, note 55, 46.

70. Litwack, note 55, 42.

71. Susan Brownmiller argued in *Against Our Will* for the critical importance of integrating by gender the military and the police. Though we have seen some signal changes as some gender integration occurs, and though women police and soldiers may improve their individual status, challenge stereotypes, and offer better service or protection to women, it's no more an adequate solution to

rape than Black soldiers were an adequate solution to racist violence. The missing link in Brownmiller's argument is the role of the army and police in the U.S., which is to safeguard the interests of the powerful at home and abroad. This means men. Until or unless male institutions truly serve our interest, we can't adequately fight for women through them. During the Civil War and Reconstruction the interests of northern capitalists uniquely coincided with the interests of the slaves.

72. An earlier version of part of this chapter appeared in *Fight Back*, note 1, co-authored by me and Michaele Uccella. The ideas emerged in our discussions; the actual writing was done by me.

73. Andrea Dworkin argued this in "Biological Superiority: The World's Most Dangerous and Deadly Idea," *Heresies 6*, note 12, 46.

74. "The belief that violence is somehow gender-linked is amazingly prevalent throughout all literature, even feminist literature.... Obviously it would be stupid and cruel to say that women are not brutally victimized, systematically, institutionally, across all age, class, and race barriers. Quite the contrary. But the assumption that women are inherently incapable of violence is something else. My own inquiry into the matter has shown me that this assumption is simply not true." Michaele Uccella, *Lesbian Violence*, presented at Goddard College and at the Montpelier (Vermont) Women's Center, September, 1978.

75. The theory that a woman's capacity for doing violence (however covert or unacceptable the expression) is also a capacity for resistance was developed by Michaele Uccella in *Lesbian Violence*.

76. Two women quoted in Rubin, note 5, 117, 42.

77. C. McCormick, "Battered Women" (1977), cited by Schneider, Jordan, and Arguedas, "Representation of Women Who Defend Themselves," in *Heresies 6*, note 12, 100 ff.

78. Police statistics from Portland, Oregon, 1976, indicated a 60% rate of escape for women who use some form of resistance. Considering that many women who get away don't bother to report to the police, the higher rate of 80% indicated by other studies seems plausible. (Of course many many women who don't escape also refuse to report to the police, perhaps as many as 90% of all women who get raped.) Bart, note 1, has compiled resistance strategies from women who escaped.

79. The first escape was recorded in the *Portland Oregonian* sometime in 1979; the second came from the *New York Post*, 1/31/79. Neither of these women was charged. Also note the following divine judgment: "An axweidling Portland youth was killed early Friday when he accidentally struck himself in the side of the neck while allegedly threatening two girls in the parking lot of a convenience market." *Oregon Journal*, 7/19/78.

80. Social Science Documents No. 1 (Fisk University Social Science Institute, 1945), 284-91, in Lerner, note 4, 35.

81. Mirra Komarovsky, *Blue-Collar Marriage* (1967).

82. Gloria I. Joseph, "Black Mothers and Daughters: Their Roles and Functions in American Society," in Gloria Joseph and Jill Lewis, *Common Differences* (1981), 75-126. Joseph notes that her sample of white women was small, but sufficient to reveal trends.

83. Excerpted from a videotape by Martine Barratt, *Heresies 6*, note 12.

84. Sharon Isabell, *Yesterday's Lessons* (1974), 20-22.

85. Toni Morrison, *Song of Solomon* (1978), 93-94.

86. Joyce Maupin, "A Trip to Chicago," in Judy Grahn, ed., *True to Life Adventure Stories*, vol. I (1983).

87. Morrison, *Song of Solomon*, 82.

88. Linnaea A. Due, "The Light," in Grahn, note 87.

89. Sharon Isabell, "20 Days," in Grahn, note 87.

90. The first quote is from a conversation with an African American lesbian; the second from a journal by a Jewish lesbian.

91. "Motherhood without autonomy is one of the quickest roads to a sense of having lost control." Adrienne Rich, *Of Woman Born* (1976), 26.

92. Judith Arcana, *Our Mothers' Daughters* (1979), 90-91.

93. Story cited by Rich, *OWB*, note 92, 256-58, 263-65.

94. This was reported in 1977.

95. Dorothy Dinnerstein, *The Mermaid and the Minotaur* (1976).

96. I'm indebted to Becky Birtha's unpublished discussion of the power invoked by simple male gestures, "The Threat of Violence—to Keep Her in Line."

97. On an average, 3 inches taller and 24 pounds heavier, according to Brownmiller, note 1, not as much as you'd think.

98. Tania Kravath described to me a film for teachers on child abuse in which a child, black and blue and swollen from the mother's beatings, is being taken from the mother by a social worker; the child is shrieking *mama, mama*. When abuse and love are tangled, we cling.

99. From the autobiography of a student in a class in Women's Biography, California State College at Sonoma, in Deborah S. Rosenfelt, ed., "Learning to Speak: Student Work," *Female Studies X* (Feminist Press, 1975), 54, quoted in Rich, *OWB*, note 92, 277-78.

100. Arcana, note 93, 90.

101. Edited by Kerry Lobel. The anti-violence newsletter *Athena* announced in (1991) two forthcoming issues: "Lesbian Battering," and "Ex-batterers Speak Out." The proximity of the two titles suggested to me, at first, that the latter title was for lesbian ex-batterers, and was glad that someone was recognizing that there are exes. A second reading of the notice informed me that "ex-batterers" was not gender defined, and while I assume that the issue will also include lesbian testimony, I was disappointed by the invisibility of lesbians who are violent but stop and change.

102. (November, 1991.)

103. But see Kate Millett's *The Basement* (1979) about the sexual abuse and torture of a young woman by a somewhat older, heterosexual, woman. The story is as atypical of woman's violence as serial killers are atypical of male violence, but Millett's concern with sexual power clearly drew her to explore this agonizing material: a brave, early, and flawed attempt to confront complexity.

104. See Carlene Faith and Robin Ruth Linden, "Sex Is Always the Headliner," *Sinister Wisdom 16*, 2-10.

105. In response to a questionnaire modelled on the one Michaele Uccella had designed and administered for her study on lesbian violence. This questionnaire was published in *Sinister Wisdom 10* and distributed around Portland, Oregon, at various women's gathering places by Diane Nowicki. An article based on selected aspects of these responses was written by me, in consultation with Michaele, and published as "Survival is an Act of Resistance" in *Fight Back*, note 1. See pp. 118.

106. Or, as the *Diary* (1982) from the Barnard Conference on Sexuality notes, the question "what do women want?" can be a real question now that *we* are asking it. See "Sexual Power." Also see *Heresies 12*, "Sex Issue" (1981).

107. According to Susan Griffin's persuasive explanation of the pornographic mind, in *Pornography and Silence* (1981), drawing on Wilhelm Reich's *The Mass Psychology of Fascism*, virtually all of us learn not to trust ourselves with freedom.

108. One of many examples: Eunice Lipton, "The Violence of Ideological Distortion: the Imagery of Laundresses in the 19th Century French Culture," *Heresies 6*, note 12, 77-85.

109. Frederick Douglass, "The Lesson of the Hour" (pamphlet, 1894), reprinted as "Why is the Negro Lynched," in Foner, *The Life and Writings of Frederick Douglass*, Vol.4, 498-499; quoted in Davis, *WRC*, note 8, 184.

110. Anti-Semitism has flourished in many different historical periods and under a range of social and economic systems. Today Jews in the western world are less likely to be considered animalistic and more likely to be seen as perverse (similar in this way to stereotypes about Asians). Jewish men are often considered effeminate, "faggy," not real men; Jewish women are depicted alternately as insatiable and promiscuous or as frigid and sexually withholding.

111. Sylvia Witts Vitale, "A Herstorical Look at Some Aspects of Black Sexuality," in *Heresies 12*, note 106, 64-65, notes that Black people and especially Black women have had their sexuality defined by non-Blacks.

112. See the illuminating discussion of Black and white women's sexuality in *Differences*, note 83.

113. The medical "discovery" of a vaginal ejaculatory gland only suggests the abyss of ignorance contained in official definitions of female sexuality. Now the knowledge of this biological structure brings the experience of millions of women who knew they came wet into line with scientific norms. Some of us spent years trying not to. Noteworthy that it was a woman and a nurse practitioner who identified the gland. It's worth observing that this "discovery"—sort of like the "discovery" of America—made nowhere near the impact of the "g-spot" which promises female orgasm through intercourse, thus reinforcing heterosexual practice based on male practice (god forbid he should have to do something extra!).

114. Alice Walker, "Coming Apart," in *You Can't Keep a Good Woman Down* (1982).

115. In *Differences*, note 83.

116. Consciousness raising has been suggested as a strategy for confronting racism (for example, Tia Cross, Freada Klein, Barbara Smith and Berley Smith, "Face-to-Face, Day-to-Day—Racism CR," in *Top Ranking: A Collection of Articles on Racism and Classism in the Lesbian Community*, Joan Gibbs and Sara Bennett, eds., [1980], 65-69) and on exploring sexuality (Cherrie Moraga and Amber Hollibaugh, "What We're Rollin Around in Bed With," *Heresies 12*, note 106, 58-62).

117. A number of feminists have pointed to an out-of-hand dismissal of "outsider" feminist perspectives. Cherrie Moraga and Amber Hollibaugh, for example, in the piece cited above; Joan Nestle in *Restricted Country* (1988?); the editors of *Lesbian Contradiction*; Karen Lindsey, in several pieces in *Sojourner*.

118. The quote is from Meridel Le Seuer. I regret editing and changing this section from its earlier appearance in *Fight Back! Feminist Resistance to Male Violence*, in which Michaele Uccella and I compiled the stories of eleven women. One of the contributors chose to withdraw her section, because of changes in her world view, and since her piece was crucial to the whole, rather than disrupt and patch together, I have written in summary, incorporating much of the data. I refer readers to that original version.

119. Wanrow's case, after eight years in the courts, won for women the Wanrow Instructions, which demand that a jury take into consideration the difference in experience and perception between an average-size woman (in this case, whose leg was broken, in a cast) and a much larger man who is attacking her. Another Native American, Marlene Roan Eagle, an Oglala Sioux, 20 years old, was beaten many times by her husband (she was hospitalized twice from these beatings, once for a month). When she was seven months pregnant, he beat her with a broom handle. She grabbed a knife and stabbed him, and was found not guilty, on grounds of self-defense and defense of her unborn child (*Newsweek* [1/30/78], 54). Clearly her self-defense was perceived as more acceptable because of her pregnancy, and the legal precedent is both significant—many men beat their pregnant wives—and dangerous, fuel for anti-choicers. A third Native American women, Rita Silk-Nauni, fleeing a man who had abused her, was harassed by police who manhandled her child. She somehow got one of the cop's guns, killed him and wounded his partner. Were it not for support and visibility given Silk-Nauni by feminist and Native communities, she would have been convicted of murder one instead of manslaughter.

See "Rita Silk-Nauni" in *Fight Back*, note 1, 164-67; also Rita's letters from prison, in Beth Brant, ed., *A Gathering of Spirit: Writing and Art by North American Indian Women* (1984).

120. Esther Lee Clay shot—as he sat in the police station—the man who had raped her eight-year-old daughter (he survived, partially paralyzed). She spent six months in mental hospitals, but was cleared on grounds of temporary insanity, and is now free (*Oregonian*, Portland, Oregon, early 1978). The rapist had been indicted, but the case against him was dismissed after a psychiatrist testified that Esther Lee Clay and her daughter were "too emotionally overwrought to undergo cross-examination." Mary McCarthy and Alta Bryan, two Oregon women, each killed an abusive husband to protect herself and her children. Marianne Bachmeier entered a courtroom in West Germany in 1981, and shot and killed the man accused of murdering her seven-year-old daughter Anna. The man had twice been convicted of sexually abusing young children, and had been voluntarily castrated; a doctor was giving him hormone shots to restore his sex drive. I have not been able to find out what happened to Marianne Bachmeier. A class of schoolchildren was visiting the courtroom when she shot her daughter's killer (*Albuquerque Journal* [3/7/81]).

121. Joan Lester, "Like Two Ships that Passed in the Night," *off our backs* (January, 1978).

122. ntozake shange, "with no immediate cause," in *Heresies 6* (1979), 12.

123. Janet Bode, *Fighting Back* (1978), 217. In the final section, Bode describes some alternative actions against rape.

124. Pam McAllister, in *Fight Back*, note 1, 212-221.

125. McAllister, note 124, 212, quoting from "Short Currents," *Lesbian Tide* (July/August 1977).

126. Besides, check out the story of Anna Bachmeier, note 120 above. The man who murdered her had been castrated.

127. Womongold, "Setting a 'Bad' Example," in *Fight Back*, note 1, 222-25.

128. *Boston Globe* (6/9/83).

129. Since early women's liberation, images of women engaged in liberation struggles against colonial domination or repressive regimes have inspired us. It's important for North American women to know about women's lives, courage and risks in other parts of the world, especially for those of us in the U.S. whose government so often bears some responsibility for the risks under which other women labor.

Yet too often we idealize revolutionary movements. Long-time left activists know this revolutionary hit parade, beginning with the former Soviet Union, then China Cuba Vietnam Cambodia Nicaragua South Africa... The danger of such idealization is multifaceted. Idealization blocks an accurate grasp of the nature of revolutionary change, so that we in our country come to see societal transformation as something happening always elsewhere, magically (because the underclass of other cultures is inherently braver and more virtuous than oppressed peoples here). It allows us to continue to envision people in the Third World as the vanguard, thus avoiding our own responsibility for making change here and leaving them always out in front, taking the brunt of danger. And finally, as problems, contradictions, difficulties with these foreign struggles emerge, and especially now as socialism falls apart nearly worldwide, activists who have not learned how to support and be critical at the same time risk disillusionment: *It's not perfect so what's the point?*

130. Griffin, *Silence*, note 107, 213.

131. Gail Waechter, letter (Winter, 1982).

132. Stories from, in order, *Parade Magazine* (Portland, Oregon; 6/26/77); *Oregonian* (6/24/78); *Oregonian* (8/27/78).

133. from Melanie Kaye/Kantrowitz, *We Speak in Code: poems & other writings* (1980).

134. Note 133.

135. "Off With Their Rocks" was also used imaginatively to transform a billboard in Portland in 1977. A blonde woman lounging seductively in a black gown with the caption "Black Velvet feels smooth on the rocks" was graced with a voice balloon announcing "Off With Their Rocks"; "Disarm Rapists" was painted across the billboard. No one could get offended by the voice balloon's vulgarity without acknowledging the gross sexual content of the original slogan.

136. Lucille Clifton, "Admonitions," in *Good Times* (1969).

137. See "Some Notes on Jewish Lesbian Identity," pp.

138. Litwack, note 55, 156-57. Luisah Teish exposes the myth "that the Black concubine was a privileged 'house nigger'" in *TBtN*, note 11, 115-116.

139. See Adrienne Rich's classic essay, "Compulsory Heterosexuality and Lesbian Existence," in *Blood, Bread and Poetry* (1986).

140. *Differences*, note 83, esp. 75-126.

141. See, for example, the work of historian Carroll Smith-Rosenberg, *Disorderly Conduct: Visions of Gender in Victorian America* (1985).

142. "A Jury of Her Peers" and *Trifles* were reissued in 1991 by The Feminist Press. As a playwright, Glaspell worked with the Provincetown Players, as did Eugene O'Neill; they were considered peers. The play version, *Trifles*, has been taught in some high schools, probably because it's a one-acter with few characters, and in accordance with Virginia Woolf's notion that if a work is threatening to a culture, it will often be categorized "for children," as a way of absorbing it without dealing with its content; Woolf notes *Gulliver's Travels*, *Moby Dick*, and the poems of Emily Dickinson as examples.

143. Published in *Code*, note 133, and in *Fight Back*, note 1.

144. *off our backs* (December, 1981).

145. Dworkin, "The Sexual Politics of Fear and Courage," *Blood*, note 1, 65.

146. Lorraine Hansberry, *To Be Young, Gifted, and Black* (1989).

147. In early May, 1992, I predict that the L.A. riots will strengthen the political clout of African American moderates and progressives. Even to Bushites, progressives like Ron Dellums and Marian Wright Edelman look like saints compared to the specter of L.A. burning.

148. Hannah Arendt, *On Violence* (1970), 19.

149. Nadine Gordimer, "The Essential Gesture," in *The Essential Gesture*, Stephen Clingman, ed., (1988), 294-95.

150. Hansberry, note 146, 222.

# To Be a Radical Jew
# in the Late 20th
# Century

# Some Notes on Jewish Lesbian Identity

Published in *Nice Jewish Girls,* ed. Evelyn Torton Beck. 1st ed. Watertown, MA: Persephone, 1982. 2nd expanded ed. Boston: Beacon Press, 1989.

That I am lesbian is my usual awareness. My close people are almost all lesbians, mostly not Jewish. I live in Santa Fe, among gentiles; and though I am lonely for Jews, I don't go to *shul,* and never did; and don't pray, or even know the prayers. I think Israel a boiling contradiction; and besides, they don't give queers citizenship.[1]

But the rise of Klan activity, Reagan and his white-on-white cabinet, synagogues bombed in France, have me in a sweat. Dreams of the camps. I need to know the tradition, what binds us besides danger.

## JEWISH TRADITION

This year I made a menorah from a stick of wood, hammered in nine nails, eight and one for the special candle (angry I'd forgotten its name). Lighting the candles each night, I remember Hanukah with my parents and sister, the presents (a little one each night, and a big one on the last night). We never said prayers, though my father, raised orthodox, must have known them. I remember their menorah, a music box in its base played the *Hatikvah.* I thought all menorahs played the *Hatikvah;* and this Hanukah, each night as I light the candles I hum, can't keep from humming the *Hatikvah.* My body feels warm: for thousands of years people have lit candles to celebrate freedom, millions of Jews are doing it right now.

On the seventh night I rushed out early and forgot to light the candles; later discovered it was the eighth and last night, and I'd missed it. I had started Hanukah a day late. I felt ridiculous; and deprived. So Friday at sundown I lit a candle for the sabbath and stood in front of it, wanting to do something special—but what? wondering, what is it we do, we Jews on Friday night when we light candles—what is precious in this, is it just centuries and endurance? All I could imagine doing was crossing myself, which made me very nervous, evoking my imprinting; to do anything christian is to sin, not against god but against Jewishness; to betray my people.

Liberals and pacifists often challenge the notion of "one's own people." Liberals "don't like labels"; pacifists say, "face your enemy with love."[2] Both say, "people are people." I think Jews are haunted—intelligently so—by spectres of cattle cars packed to the top with our people. Some of who I am roots in the knowledge, as early as I can remember: there are people who did not want us to exist—millions of them. For these people, there is no love. It's easy for me to think in terms of "my people" and "our enemies."[3]

I learned this way of thinking from my parents; both are anti-religious, fierce in their hatred of everything German, suspicious of the gentiles (though they are polite and try not to say *goyim*), and passionate in their communication of certain truths: never cross a picket line; all men are brothers *(sic)*; nothing is more important than school (corollary: the best job you can get is teaching; security, and the same hours as your children).[4]

Of course, there would be children. I think I am a disgrace to my family, as a lesbian, as a childless woman. Also, I am to them a nice girl: though instead of providing for my parents, I occasionally need to borrow from them, at least I have an education and write books. The content of these books is not so important to them; one uncle bought two copies of my poetry book, which celebrates women who kill abusive men.

My family are good people: they would take care of me, any of them. They welcome my (gentile) lover as if she were a husband (to her discomfort!). They do not disown—family is family. I sometimes feel ready to dissolve in a great wash of tears because I have no child to contribute to this brave pool of survivors. As if I owe these parents aunts, uncles, cousins a birth—for those who died?

The grandparents are all dead now, and none of us born in this country knew their families, only great-uncle Abram who barely spoke English—all the rest died in the camps, except one cousin was saved and shipped off to Israel (Palestine, then), the only survivor from the Old World (and I know he would take care of me too).

Maybe because I can't imagine very far back, having no language to remember with, no name for my grandmother's *shtetl,* or even for her mother or father, no photographs, maybe for these reasons those of my family who still live loom for me with such solidity. A child would bind me to them, would give both me and the child this solidity: there would always be Thanksgiving and people to have birthdays with, celebratory and irritable, people who overeat and go on diets, who play mah jong and poker, or who avoid these things, but all of us would *know* these things. I feel a visceral tug of family, especially at a distance. I choose to live far from them, among lesbians, women who are all somewhat outside the cultures which raised us. Jewishness is a leitmotif in and out of my brain; not the main theme.

But sometimes—a TV program called "Kitty: Return to Auschwitz"; the sound of a Yiddish melody I don't know by name but have heard in the air, in my sleep, my whole life; a crossword puzzle, twenty-four down, "German Chancellor," the answer is "Hitler"—something forces my awareness not that I am Jewish—I am always Jewish—but that others are not.

For example, excerpts from journal, May 1980
*writing—i stop to pee—in the bathroom through the door i can hear
m's radio, news, jewish school in hebron attacked, five dead, how many*

*wounded? in 1929 the jews fled hebron, escaping an arab massacre.*
*now the israelis settle there. i am crying, in part because the non-jewish*
*world—the goyim—will explain and justify the killings with and through*
*hatred of jews, will not care much because it's only jews. on the left,*
*pro-arabs; on the right, nazis. i feel alone.*[5]

or a month later:

*i meet r., a dyke visiting from arkansas—i hadn't thought to ask myself,*
*is she jewish? but her car sports a huge star in the rear window. i ask*
*if she's not afraid to be so identifiable, especially in the south. she says,*
*"i decided it was time to come out." the thought scares me. invisibility*
*is sometimes a comfort. at the same time i see how the star made our*
*conversation possible—that we welcomed each other as jews because*
*i knew she was jewish and would welcome me.*

I begin to identify myself as Jewish, often—not in visual ways but with words; I discover Jewish women everywhere—yes, like coming out.

## JEWISH IDENTITY

Historically, Jewish people have vacillated between forced identification and forced assimilation. A brief chronology:

1215 The church's Fourth Lateran Council decrees that Jews must wear distinctive dress (a large hat, a yellow or crimson circle over the heart to mark them as targets).

1290 Jews expelled from England.

1306 Jews expelled from France.

14th-15th c. Jews expelled from German countries.

1492 Jews expelled from Spain.

1800's In France, under the revolutionary government, and in Germany: passports and identification cards marked to identify the Jews.

1804 Jewish Statute passed in Russia, obliging the Jews to—among other things—take last names (patronyms), against their own custom and in keeping with the gentile way.[6]

1850 Russian Jews ordered to stop wearing their traditional dress: men had to cut their *peyes* (long sideburns); women to stop shaving their heads on the eve of marriage.[7]

1938 Jews in Germany who had changed their names (before 1933) were forcibly restored to their "original" names; all Jews had to take the middle name Sarah (for females) or Israel (for males); new babies had to be named from a government list.[8]

Jews in Germany had to get their passports stamped with a big red J.

1940 Jews in Germany had to get their ration cards stamped with a big red J.

1940s Jews in Germany and throughout Reich-occupied territories had to wear a Jewish star as mandatory public identification.

1940s (and earlier) Jews deported to the camps.

Exposed or isolated, deprived of our culture or locked into it, our power-lessness to define ourselves culminates in the camps: take Primo Levi, a chemist, deported from Italy to Auschwitz in 1943, one of millions: "Levi's number—174517—was tattooed on his left arm in a swift and slightly painful operation....Only by showing the number could 174517 get bread and soup."[9] Levi speaks:

> *Nothing belongs to us anymore; they have taken away our clothes, our shoes, even our hair; if we speak, they will not listen to us, and if they listen, they will not understand. They will even take away our name: and if we want to keep it, we will have to find in ourselves the strength to do so, to manage somehow so that behind the name something of us, of us as we were, still remains.*[10]

## JEWISH NAMES

Jews have always had to exist "behind the name." In the new world too, many of us, like other immigrants, lost our names or heard them mutilated, out of gentile ignorance, laziness, or hostility. Some of us shed our names like a ragged coat.

My father's name is Kantrowitz, my mother's Wolfgang (I slip over the ordinary erasure of female to male name). He changed his name to Kaye just before the first child—my sister—was born in 1942. My mother tells how she threatened to name the baby Forsythia if he didn't change it, Forsythia Kantrowitz. I have heard her tell this story a dozen times at least; always there is an assumed comicality about the name. My father says everyone called him Mr. K. anyway, at the vacuum cleaner store where he did sales and repair. For business, because Kantrowitz was too long, too hard to say.

(think about Gloucester; McLoughlin)

(think about 174517)

At the dyke bar in Portland I tell Amy Kesselman, my best Jewish friend, that I'm thinking about taking back my mother's maiden name—as far back as I can go through the women—or my father's name—or both. "Kaye is a made-up name," I say, "It has no history." Amy, historian, tells me, "Just because a history isn't pretty doesn't mean it isn't history."

Kaye is both history and closet. History of a kind of closet. Kaye is Kantrowitz Kaminsky Keminetsky Kowalsky Klutz Korelowich Ka....

(think about asking every Jew you know: what *was* your name?)

I recently met a woman who knew me through my written work. "Oh," she said, "I expected you to be tall and blond." I joked, "I must be doing something wrong"—but it made me feel funny.

Also recently, a woman asks my name and I find myself about to say Melanie Kantrowitz, just to hear it. To toot her face. If I called myself Melanie Kantrowitz, no one would ever expect me to be tall and blond.

I grew up laughing at names that were typically ours—not Deborah or Naomi, bible names, but old-fashioned names like Yentl, Sadie, Rivka. My whole generation of girl children born Jewish mid-forties New York City was named

Susan, Ellen, Judy and sometimes Jane. Any given school class would have its Ellen C., Ellen R., Susan A., Susan L., Susan W., Jane S., Jane L....

But whatever the name, if you looked like a Jew, you couldn't hide.

## LOOKING LIKE A JEW

In the Jewish resistance, women did much of the courier, weapon-gathering, smuggling, communication, and guide work—in part because they could pass more surely than the men, who might be asked at any moment to drop their pants. The many Jews—women and men—who did pass testify to how many Jews look "Aryan."

Yet at least one woman resistance fighter was stopped leaving the Warsaw Ghetto because she had a Jewish nose.

This historical flash may put into perspective the painful, expensive operation which men (often Jewish ones) make jokes about—the nose job. In the heyday of Barbra Streisand, it's hard to remember that every Jewish teenage girl of my generation whose nose "looked Jewish" longed for another chance. Parents who could pay, paid. When my cousin Susan turned fifteen, she got a nose job. When I saw her a week later, she still looked like someone had beat the shit out of her—her face bruised, puffy—and a swollen nose which, a few months later, "reverted." More money, more nose-breaking, more pain. Again, it reverted. She had her nose re-done three times. I can't remember what it looks like now, whether or not the nose job was "successful."

We all knew Jewish noses were ugly. Never asking, "*why* ugly?" or answering, "because Jewish."[11]

When I was a tiny girl, my aunt Edna said of me, "look at that, a nose like a *shiksa.*" I snuck into the bathroom to stare in the mirror, sobbing, "I don't look like a *shiksa,* I don't"—this, before I knew what a *shiksa* was. But later I took a strange sickish pleasure in "my nose" and would tell people what my aunt had said, partly to make them notice my nose.

Through my teens and halfway through my twenties I was setting and sometimes bleaching, sometimes straightening my hair. What I did to my eyebrows will be understood only by those women who also have black bushy eyebrows. I was not trying to look like a *shiksa*—I was trying to look pretty.

(why ugly? because Jewish.)

I was also trying to sound pretty (cultured).

## SOUNDING LIKE A (LOW-CLASS) JEW

Sometime around ninth grade, words like *yenta shmate bubbe* began to embarrass me. I—as I thought of it then—aimed higher. What I meant by this was vague but included museums, foreign films, and an escape from Brooklyn—dates, engagement parties, weddings at temples with booze and cocktail franks and longline bras and girdles and dyed-to-match shoes and a band playing Anniversary Waltz while uncles made cracks about wedding nights. It also meant escape from a six-days-plus-two-nights-work-week selling longline bras and girdles in "the store"—my father's and his sister's business, where all of us worked, full-time, part-time, summers, christmas, at various times in our lives.

And words like *shmate* trapped me—no matter who said them—marked, stripped and revealed me. I came from people who talked *like that.* I came from them and would be stuck with their lives. In case I needed proof of the connection between their lives and that accent, I had only to attend C.C.N.Y. and discover that in order to graduate, I had to learn NOT to talk *like that.* [12]

But last night I sang Yiddish songs with a dozen Jewish women. L., a woman in her twenties was teaching us the words, I was moved by her pleasure in the words, the sound and lilt—pretty. She seemed like a daughter I might raise, braver and less scarred—the sounds she speaks, her inflections are the very sounds I grew up trying not to make:

*zuntig, bulbes*
*muntig, bulbes*
*dinstik un mitvokh, bulbes* [13]

In these songs the ways words sound good is to sound *like that,* not "uneducated English," but Yiddish, a language.

I borrow from L. a book, *Der Yidisher Lerer (The Yiddish Teacher).* My eyes have always wobbled at the sight of Hebrew or Arabic letters, but the first word in this book is *bubbe;* the second is *mame.* These words leap from my blood, my mouth knows how to say them. At two letters a day I'll have the alphabet in a couple of weeks. *shvester. zogt. vaser. vos vil di bubbe? di bubbe est a zeml.* My tongue.

In the Jewish Women's Group I have felt ashamed of my ignorance—of Hebrew, of religion. I've muffled words to songs rather than ask anyone to slow down. Passover with these women, each of us reads something from the service, adding something of her own. I talked about my grandmother Helen Wolfgang who had just died that week—how she had left Poland as a teenager and was rebellious against religion because Jewish orthodoxy had been stifling to her freedom—how we always had a seder at her house, but with bread on the table as well as matzoh. One woman—bless her—said, "let's drink to her—what was her name?" But from many others there, I felt disapproval so clear it was visceral. I thought, many of these women were raised by professional parents, sent to Hebrew school, taught cultural pride. A poor Jew trying to climb out of her class learns to associate her lower-classness with her Jewishness (also her femaleness).

I notice in the group that P. who knows Hebrew commands much respect. She's been researching Jewish ceremony, looking to create a matriarchal religion, and she performs an evening prayer for us, closing the shabbes, something to do with the new moon. All the while she holds and rocks and tips the glass of wine (which is really grape juice, none of these women drinks) she has poured very full; and L. whose house it is and whose rug it is not keeps bending over P. to steady the glass, her face showing anxiety about the juice and the rug but P. will not sip off the top, she keeps waving her arms and the juice slops dangerously to the edge and some drops spill on the blanket, yes, on the rug, but there's no stopping P. as she performs the ritual—

(and I think, this is why I don't like religion, she is wonderful in the rabbi role, absorbed and holy, but *she* won't have to clean up the spilled juice)

I also notice that P., in her knowledge of Hebrew and religion, those arenas of Jewish male activity, is more heeded than L. who is younger, softer, and knows Yiddish and hundreds of songs, and worries about her friend's rug. The hierarchy of Hebrew over Yiddish, male over female, rich over poor replicates here.[14] If you're going to be Jewish, at least be refined; not female, especially not Jewish female.

## ACTING LIKE A JEWISH WOMAN

As Jewish women, we are often blamed for our strength. When I became a lesbian and no longer had to care what men, Jewish or otherwise, thought of me, I came into my power. As a lesbian, I learned fast and ecstatically that women liked me to be strong. I began to enjoy, build, and relax into my full self.

On the other hand, a few months ago, I was applying for jobs and was interviewed by an all-women's collective for one job, and by english department faculty (women and men) for another. I found myself comfortable with the "english" people—the school was a city college, and most of them were either Jewish or very accustomed to women "like me." With the women's collective members—several of whom were lesbians—I had an eerie sense of unbalance. None of them were Jewish; I was a surprise to them.

This unbalance can explode into bitter repercussions. In one group, several of the women were having a hard time with "my style." It had never occurred to me to count noses. But I counted noses. They didn't look Jewish. Most of the women troubled by me had been sent to expensive colleges by their fathers; they spoke with well-modulated voices, and they quaked when I raised mine. They didn't understand that to me anger is common, expressible, and not murderous. They found me "loud" (of course) and "emotional." Interestingly, I got along fine with all the women of color in the group, one therapy buff, and one middle class WASP woman who was also a dyke and a radical and my best friend at the time—and who hipped me to the covert anti-Semitism (she explained since *she'd* been afraid of me, she could recognize it in others.)

But I'm talking not just about differences and fear of difference. I'm talking also about power to suppress difference. Why ugly?

So when women say things like
   she has a "difficult" style
     as well as
       aren't all Jews rich? (or, the more
         sophisticated version, aren't all
         Jews middle class?)
       or, there are *so* many Jewish teachers
       writers filmmakers Jewish women
         in the women's movement [15]
   or, when they don't say these things but assume them, we are not being paranoid if we hear familiar themes: pushy, loud, moneygrubbing, exploitative,

and—especially—there we are taking over again, in the schools, the art world, even the movement.[16]

Nor are we being paranoid if we point to anti-Semitism, in the United States, or in the women's movement; and they say it isn't really. Or, as happened last year in San Francisco, tell Jewish women wanting to meet as Jews, that this is divisive, that Jews are "really" white; or "really" European.[17] Or, if they hint that "all that" is over now, why are we making a fuss.

Or, if their ignorance compels us to explain that gentiles persecuted the Jews for thousands of years before the Nazis got efficient at it;[18] and that a year after the Nazi defeat, in Kielce, Poland, a mob stormed a Jewish community center and killed, out of the tiny number of surviving Polish Jews who remained in Poland, forty-one Jews. And that pogroms then erupted all over Poland. That even now, with a Jewish population of five to eight thousand (from 3.5 million pre-Hitler), anti-Semitism rises again, accelerates, in Poland.[19]

I am pulled back to the theme of danger as the shared Jewish identity. As Jewish women, we need also to define ourselves by ourselves, on our own terms.

## JEWISH WOMEN

As women and as lesbians we have learned to reclaim names like
dyke
bitch
manhater
golddigger
shrew
harpy
whore
cunt
amazon
(even) lesbian
even *woman* had first to be reclaimed from a place of squeamishness.

As Jewish women and Jewish lesbians, we need to reclaim words like
pushy
loud
politico
power trippy
cheap
dominating
garish
sexy
emotional
always screaming
bossy
scary temper

difficult style

(and, of course) Jewish mother

(and) Jewish princess

Take Jewish mother. Who accuses her of the heinous crime—of let's face it—pushiness? Often, Jewish men; especially those who have climbed out of her class because of her help. Ironic, too, that success often comes to Jewish boys through an education which teaches them to be ashamed of their Jewishness, and of their mothers. Perhaps the familiar put-downs of Jewish women by Jewish men stem from male resentment of the strong mother; indignity that a successful Jewish man, unlike his idealized WASP counterpart, has to contend with uppity women.[20]

As Jewish women, we need to look at our people with our own eyes. To see Judith, who saved the Jewish people; she flirted with the attacking general, drank him under the table; then she and her maid (whose name is not in the story) whacked off his head, stuck it in a picnic basket and escaped back to the Jewish camp. They staked his head high over the gate, so that when his soldiers charged the camp, they were met by their general's bloody head, looming; and they ran away as fast as their goyishe little feet could run. Then Judith set her maid free, and all the women danced in her honor.[21]

That's a Jewish princess.

Or Anzia Yezierska, who told, in Yiddish-like-English, stories of Jewish immigrants, especially women's struggles for love, freedom, and education. Of her work, she wrote: "It's not me—it's their cries—my own people—crying in me! Hannah Breineh, Shmendrek, they will not be stilled in me, till all America stops to listen."[22]

That's a nice Jewish girl.

Or Violette Kaye, who recently when I asked, ashamed, to borrow money for an airline ticket back East, and she said, of course; and then told me they're retiring, and I said, this isn't a good time for any of us, and she said, listen, if I have it, and I do, it's yours.

That's a Jewish mother. (Mine).

## JEWISH FOREMOTHERS

I began with the Holocaust. I want to know how it happened—not how the Jews let it happen (the question sprouts so easily on gentile tongues) but *how* did it happen? I come from people who were killed like that, for that. An odd identity, but a compelling one.

Especially I need the stories of resistance laced through the horror, as an amulet, inspiration, and warning. To know that our efforts at resistance came too late, too frail for six million. To swear "never again," uncertain of what this oath might entail; but in some corner of my brain on guard.

Most stories of the Holocaust, like most other stories, have been told by and about men. I don't reject them for this, they are Jewish and mine. But as a woman, I need to know about the women, and that many Jews fought back, as they could, Jewish women among them.

To fortify myself, I collect names and as much information as I can find. About women who fought inside the camps. Say their names.

Rosa Robota; Esther, Ella, and Regina, all hanged for crucial parts in the Auschwitz resistance.

or, Sala Lerner who fought at Sachsenhausen.

or, Mala Zimetbaum, the "Runner," who had worked in the Belgian underground, was caught and sent to Auschwitz, and escaped, and inspired the women to wait, to survive, to believe that liberation would come; though she was caught again and killed.

or, Olga Benario and Charlotte Eisenbletter, who gathered the women's resistance at Ravensbrück.

—that there was a *Women's Resistance* at Ravensbrück—

or, Fania Fenelon, a member of the Auschwitz women's orchestra, privileged to survive—and anyone who survived the camps was privileged (and lucky); she played Beethoven's Fifth at Birkenau, for the prisoners to delight in the signature tune of the Free French Broadcasts; and arranged a Jewish (therefore, forbidden) song as a march, so the prisoners marched to a Jewish song, while the SS tapped their feet, ignorant.

or, Kitty's mother, who survived as a hospital worker at Auschwitz, and hid her sick daughter under a mattress with a dead body on it; who hissed at her, *run, run,* because those who could run, when the commandant said *run,* survived.

and Kitty herself, who worked the gas chambers, and doesn't lie about it; who stole from the dead (only from the dead) and hoarded the gold to buy explosives to blow up the Auschwitz ovens. They blew up one of the Auschwitz ovens.

and the hundreds—thousands?—of women who fought in the Warsaw Ghetto Uprising—like Niuta Teitelboim, known in the resistance as Wanda "of the braids," who organized a women's detachment, guided Jews out and smuggled weapons into the ghetto, often posed as a whore or shy girlfriend to gain access to Nazi officials and kill them; blew up Nazi trains and clubs, robbed a bank; was tortured and killed by Nazis, but not before she smuggled out a note, assuring her comrades that she wouldn't betray them.

or Mira Fuchrer, a factory woman's daughter, polished speaker, practiced in surviving where she wasn't meant to. Her comrades describe her as a sprite, everywhere at once. She said, we'll stay alive only by resisting every rule we possibly can.

or Dvorah Baron, a rich man's daughter, blond, with a nose like a *shiksa*— an expert messenger because she could pass; emerged first from a bunker on the fourteenth day of the uprising, using her looks to shock the Germans into pausing while she threw a grenade in their faces.

or Regina Fudin, the champion guide of the Warsaw sewers.

or Zivia Lubetkin, a commander of the ZOB; when she escaped from the ghetto; she almost killed a fellow commander because his orders left behind some of her people.

or Pola Elster, captured fighting in the Brushmaker's District of the Ghetto; crammed into a cattle car with hundreds of people for days, mothers with thirsty babies two three four days in the car giving the babies piss to drink, the only fluid, and watching the babies die in convulsions; Pola Elster suggested they file down the window bars and try to escape. The others were afraid it would make things worse—but how, she wondered, could they get worse?[23]

In the book where I learn about the Warsaw Ghetto Resistance, there are pictures of these women. I read their stories; study their faces, turn to the introduction to see who was actually interviewed, who survived. Almost forty years later I feel pain at each discovered death. I stare especially at the picture of Pola Elster. Her hair is short, slicked back, she's wearing a tie. She looks like a dyke. I ponder the contradiction that some of my Jewish people will think I'm being insulting and disrespectful to suggest this.

I read about Krysia Frimer, whose brother was a resistance fighter but he forbade her to join because it was too dangerous—yet she was killed first. I mourn all the women deprived of the right to fight back, who were not thereby saved; and all the women whose names have not survived, who took messages food weapons in and out of the ghetto, who whored to the soldiers leaders cops for somebody's life freedom food information, who kept themselves and their children alive.

Those were Jewish women. I come from women who fought like that.

I want a button that says *Pushy Jew. Loud Pushy Jew. Loud Pushy Jew Dyke.*

*—Santa Fe, New Mexico*
*Summer 1980-Winter 1981*

---

NOTES

I would like to thank Michaele Uccella for her grueling editing and intellectual, political and emotional inspiration and sustenance (not to mention physical assistance in meeting publication deadline).

Israel is hardly unique in its discrimination against gays, though predictably more than a fair share of criticism is directed against Israeli policy. As a Jewish lesbian, I find homophobia in Israel especially heartbreaking when I consider that the Nazis would have killed me for being gay as well as Jewish (estimates on how many homosexuals were imprisoned in the Nazi death centers range from the conservative figure of 220,000 to 900,000).

1. "Jews who are homosexual are not allowed to obtain Israeli citizenship under the Israeli law of return" Miriam Socoloff, Leo Schlosberg, and Jeffry [Shaye] Mallow, "Why We Write About Gay Liberation," in *Chutzpah: A Jewish Liberation Anthology* (San Francisco: New Glide Publications, 1977) p.28.

2. See Barbara Deming, *Prison Notes* (Boston: Beacon Press, 1966) for a sensible and moving account of non-violent struggle in the South. But the perspective is that of a white, who can choose to enter the struggle.

3. See Andrea Dworkin's useful concept of "primary emergency" in *Woman Hating* (NY: E.P. Dutton, 1974) p.23; also my column in *Sinister Wisdom* 8 ("Scrambled Eggs: Politics as an Act of Love").

4. In fact, I am a teacher (though I teach mostly college-level, above my parents' aspirations; and though being a public lesbian creates a considerable fly in the ointment of security).

5. It's odd, considering how active Jews have been on the left, that positions and attitudes taken by radicals toward the Jews have rarely reflected Jewish interest. We find among radicals all the anti-Semitism prevalent in other quarters; for example, in late nineteenth century Russia, some radicals "adopted the tactic of fusing class with national antagonism": one "revolutionary" group issued a leaflet praising pogroms and urging the "honest Ukrainian people" to rise up against "the kikes." See Milton Meltzer, *World of Our Fathers* (NY: Dell, 1974), pp.200 ff. See also Susan Schechter, "To My Real and Imagined Enemies, and Why I Sometimes Can't Tell You Apart," and Steven Lubet and Jeffry Mallow, "That's Funny, You Don't Look Anti-Semitic: Perspective on the American Left," both in *Chutzpah*.

6. Meltzer, *World of Our Fathers*, pp.38 ff., notes that until this point, the Jews of Eastern Europe had used Hebrew names; and that distinctions between two Jews of the same given name were made through common sense—nicknames, street where you lived, your wife's or husband's name—not through patronyms. Russian Jews got to choose their surnames. In Austria, Jews had to select from a list which included some deliberately offensive names.

7. This kind of regulation, where women are forbidden a practice of "their" culture which is oppressive to them, evokes ambivalent feelings. The issue, as usual, is choice.

8. The list of acceptable names specifically excluded Hebrew names (e.g., Esther, Ruth, Adam, Daniel); and included names like Scharne, Scheindel, Schneine, Schewa (for girls); and Faleg, Feibisch, Feisel, Feitel (for boys). See Raul Hilberg's flawed but infinitely useful *The Destruction of the European Jews* (NY: Harper & Row, 1979; c. 1961), pp.119-120. All information in this brief chronology not otherwise cited is from Hilberg. Hilberg's "flaw" is rigid adherence to his thesis of Jewish passivity, in the face of clear evidence of courageous and sometimes effective Jewish resistance. See Milton Meltzer, *Never to Forget* (NY: Dell, 1976) pp.135-189; and Yuri Suhl's inspiring collection, *They Fought Back: The Story of Jewish Resistance in Nazi Europe* (NY: Schocken Books, 1975; c. 1967).

9. Meltzer, *Never to Forget*, p.121.

10. Quoted, *ibid.*

11. "What's a weed? A weed is a plant you don't want." Michaele Uccella, conversation, Summer 1979.

12. When I went to City College of New York (the sixties) students—who were mostly working and lower-middle class immigrant once-removed children—were required to pass four units (two to four classes) of speech, where the emphasis was on learning not to dentalize (sound consonants harshly, against your teeth); dentalization is characteristic of Yiddish, Italian, Polish, Russian, etc.

13. "Sunday, potatoes/Monday, potatoes/Tuesday and Wednesday, potatoes," Yiddish folk song.

14. Hebrew, the language in which educated male Jews spoke to god; Yiddish, the tongue to which (Ashkenazi) women and poor men are restricted. So Yiddish was the people's tongue; also, to some Jews, a brand of exile. The split among activist Jews tended to occur along political lines: Bundists (intent on building worker consciousness) opted for Yiddish; Zionists chose Hebrew. Survivors of the Warsaw Ghetto Uprising report that in the hidden bunker at Mila 18 on the nineteenth day of battle, an argument broke out about the merits of Yiddish vs. Hebrew! In Dan Kurzman, *The Bravest Battle: The 28 Days of the Warsaw Ghetto Uprising* (NY: Pinnacle Books, 1980). The book is irritatingly slick but invaluable for details of conversations, events, photographs of resistance fighters.

15. Some women who teach women's studies report being questioned about why there are "so many lesbians on the reading list," when, in fact, there may be three or four articles out of twenty-five or so. Sometimes "so many" equals "too many" equals "any." On the other hand, the Jews' honorable commitment to intellectual and, especially, political work is either idealized (all Jews do these things) and/or considered a sign of our tendency to take over. "It was never dealt with in a way that might have helped us to understand it or that might have helped us to feel good," Ruth Balser, "Liberation of a Jewish Radical," in *Chutzpah*.

16. Evidence indicates that quotas often and still function to exclude Jews. See Alfred Kazin's remark that Lionel Trilling was hired as THE Jew at Columbia University, in *New York Jew* (NY: Alfred Knopf, 1978). In my own time, Columbia one year abandoned quotas for students, with the result that they were flooded by New York Jews (all males, of course).

17. It's depressing that these women, many of whom had burned out trying to explain to male lefties their need to meet as women, couldn't generalize.

18. See Hilberg, *The Destruction of the European Jews*, pp.1-30.

19. See, for example, an article in a recent *New York Times*, "Anti-Semitism Without Jews? A Polish Riddle," by John Darnton, March 15, 1981, IV:4.

20. That women lose personal power in heterosexual relationships as their men gain class power in the society seems obvious. Upwardly mobile in earning power and/or self-image, men want their due. See discussion the *The Jewish Woman in America* by Charlotte Baum, Paula Hyman, and Sonya Michel (NY: Plume Books, 1976), pp.235-261, an excellent source.

21. I am indebted to J.J. Wilson for this story, from her presentation on women artists (published as *Women Artists*, co-authored with Karen Petersen [NY: Harper & Row, 1976]).

22. Quoted in the introduction to *The Open Cage: An Anzia Yezierska Collection* edited by Alice K. Harris (NY: Persea Books, 1979) p. vi.

23. These women's stories are available in Suhl and in Kurzman; in Fania Fenelon's *Playing For Time* (written with Marcelle Routier, translated by Judith Landry [NY: Berkeley Books, 1979]); Kitty's story is from a recent PBS television broadcast of the film Kitty made of her return to Auschwitz, to teach one of her sons about Auschwitz. Zivia Lubetkin survived and went to Israel after the war, and with others, founded Kibbutz Lochamai Hagetaot (Ghetto Fighters' Kibbutz) in Western Galilee.

# Ani Mamin, *5749*

**Published in the Barre-Montpelier *Times Argus* September 22, 1988**

A few days before Rosh Hashanah opened the Days of Awe and the Jewish year 5749, I was backpacking in the Adirondacks. I am not a veteran hiker, and our task—to complete a 36-mile trail in just over 48 hours—took more strength than I had. Yet there was no choice. After a low point a few miles along, where I seriously considered walking back out, there was no turning back and I trudged along alternately frightened and comforted by this knowledge. There was only one way to go: forward.

So I walked pushing hard, contemplating the metaphor, the sense of peace it occasionally conferred: if I fulfilled this task, I was doing everything required. At the same time, my 43-year-old not-particularly-trained body lagged behind the others, and I needed to keep my spirits up. As at so many other needy, exhausted or terrifying points in my life, I sang to keep moving, and among the songs I found myself singing was an ancient Hebrew melody, *ani mamin:* the first words of the 13 articles of faith of Maimondides—what each Jew is supposed to subscribe to.

*Ani mamin* means simply "I believe." But its history, and how it comes into my possession, are not simple. I know this song from a book called *Songs of the Holocaust,* because—we are told—religious Jews from the Warsaw Ghetto, realizing they were about to be murdered by the Nazis, went to their deaths singing this song, affirming their faith—in Judaism in general and in the coming of *hameshiakh* (the messiah) in particular.

The piercing cadence of the song, the stillness and solitude of the woods, turned this fact over and over in my mind. What it means to go to one's premature, vicious, utterly monstrous death believing. What it means to be a Jew blessed with knowing this song and its history, privileged with time and health to undertake this difficult, exhilarating—and in the context of Jewish history, astonishingly safe—hike. What it means to be both deeply Jewish—in culture, history, identification—and secular, not religious, an atheist. Finally, what it means to be a Jew in the middle of her life about to embark on the 5749th year of her people's history.

And so I came naturally enough to a question. When I say *ani mamin,* "I believe," in my own voice, what follows? What are my articles of faith? And what have these to do with being Jewish?

Here is what I found, in myself, in the woods: no surprises, but some thoughts to contemplate for the new year, to move in the one direction possible: forward.

The community, not the individual, is the unit of solution. Judaism specifically incorporates time for each individual to make private prayer, allows for a huge range of debate and disagreement. But one is not truly Jewish alone: one is Jewish in community with others. Problems are conceived of in collective terms, and solutions likewise. What this means in the late twentieth century, when problems are global, is that solutions must also be global.

Poverty is not, as in traditional Catholicism, a blessed state; nor, as in Calvinism (the root of Protestantism), is it an indication of sin. Instead, poverty is an instance of someone denied her/his rights, and the entire community is responsible to right this wrong. The Hebrew word for charity—*tzadekah*—also means "righteousness." Unique (as far as I know) to the Jewish conception of charity is the assumption that neither the giving nor the receiving is acknowledged. The poor are not shamed, their need is taken on by the community as a whole. The wealthy are not honored, they just spread around the excess.

*Am israel chai:* The Jewish people lives. To mark our holidays—our year against the calendar of the dominant culture—reminds us how far back we reach, that we persist because of labor, desperation, and bold hopeful leaps of those who preceded us. The survival of this peoplehood against great odds is a cause for celebration, and the distinct identity and culture of the Jews should be preserved and treasured. Culture has a supremely important role in defining and sustaining a people.

Non-Jews are to be treated as equals. Non-exclusive: no one has to be Jewish to be saved. One law: treat the stranger as yourself, for you were strangers in Egypt. The experience of alienation and slavery—political, social, geographical, cultural, religious—stays with us, remembered each *pesakh* (Passover) along with our deliverance. This history, this memory should teach us compassion: to extend ourselves to strangers, to bring the outsider into the community, and to oppose slavery and oppression of all kinds.

I have said I am an atheist, but there is one aspect of the Jewish god in which I believe. Rabbi Milton Steinberg defined god as

> the power working within individuals and peoples that will not permit them to acquiesce in servitude, their own or that of others. He [sic] is the spark that kindles them into rebellion and the iron that makes them stubborn for freedom's sake.*

This capacity for resistance, this longing for freedom is the holiest thing I know, in myself and in others.

For Jews, debate about the origin and meaning of evil is less important than the commitment to oppose it. Once you are of an age to know what is going on in the world, you are responsible for every injustice committed. But Judaism is a non-perfectionist faith. You do what you can. If you've done wrong, you try to make things right.

Life is good. The body is good, the mind is good; human connection, pleasure in solitude, in nature, sexuality, food, the arts—all these are the goods of life, to be enjoyed. This is not an ascetic faith or a faith that postpones pleasure, justice, beauty. Not surprising that "Bread and Roses," that terse summary of working people's demands, comes from a speech by Rose Schneiderman, a worker, a woman, and a Jew.

Finally, everything good is possible and already prefigured in the beauty and goodness that now exist. Our job is to pursue, enhance, and make available these goods, not to deny their importance or to pretend we don't want them or point towards pie in the sky for the disenfranchised.

These are a few tenets about which I say readily, *ani mamin*. I would like to imagine that all Jews believe as I do, that the particular threads of Jewish tradition which I wind together are the dominant, the only threads. But I know better. The tradition holds many contradictions. At the same time, I feel buoyed in my beliefs by a community of Jews who share them, here in Vermont, across the U.S., and internationally. Perhaps it is this cluster of beliefs that explains why many Israeli Jews cry shame against their own government for its repression of the Palestinians; why Jews continue to be strongly represented all over the world in movements for social justice—from Argentina to South Africa—though not always visible as Jews. In the U.S., where "Christian" is too often considered synonymous with "decent" or "human," Jews need to claim our heritage, to say publicly, "we do this work because we are Jews," to embody our values in our lives. However difficult, weary, or frightening, there is only one way to go: forward. But singing.

NOTES

*Milton Steinberg, *Basic Judaism* (Northvale NJ: J. Aronson Inc., 1987).

# To Be a Radical Jew in the Late 20th Century

*For Irena Klepfisz who pushed me*

To be a Jew in the twentieth century
Is to be offered a gift....
—Muriel Rukeyser, "Letter to the Front, VII," 1944

**Published in The Tribe of Dina: A Jewish Women's Anthology, eds.
Melanie Kaye/Kantrowitz and Irena Klepfisz. 1st ed. Montpelier: Sinister
Wisdom Books, 1986; 2nd expanded ed. Boston: Beacon Press, 1989.**

*Portions of this essay were first developed as talks given in Mankato and Minneapolis, MN, on
"Anti-Semitism, Racism, and Coalitions" (1984); a workshop given at the 1985 Women & the
Law Conference on "Dealing with Racism as Jewish Women" and as a review of Yours In Struggle
which appeared in* off our backs *(10/85). I thank the women who attended these events and
talked with me about these issues. Much of the essay was also developed in conversation with
Irena Klepfisz. I thank Linda Vance for her critical acumen, generous editorial attention, humor,
and patience. Responsibility for the opinions and analysis is mine alone.*

*So, Melanie, what's with all the Jewish?* This was my father speaking,
sometime in 1982, the year he died. I answered him clearly, carefully, the way I
did that year because he often got confused, but the answer was not hard to
find. I had been away from New York since I was twenty—I was then thirty-
seven— and I had noticed two things: my own hunger for Jewish culture, music,
food, language, humor, perspective, Jewish *people;* and the anti-Semitism,
palpable—and growing—around me.

Twenty years earlier I had marched on my first demonstration, against
nuclear testing. My parents had not pushed me into activism, yet clearly they
raised me to these things. Their parents had come to this country from Eastern
Europe, Poland and Russia. None had been political. Yet, as a teenager in the
Depression, my father had belonged to the Young Communist League; and, even
as an adult, his major hero remained his dead friend Aaron, a Communist who
had spoken on street corners and fought in Spain. My mother had circulated
petitions against the Korean War, walking up to people on the streets of Flatbush
during the peak McCarthy period, and she had been spat on. Later she became
president of the PTA at Walt Whitman Jr. High, and fought to bring blacklisted
performers to sing at the annual PTA meeting.

My mother often says, "When Melanie was three years old, I knew it would
be Melanie against the world, and I was betting on Melanie." One of her favorite
stories of me dates from 1950, when my class and my older sister's had been
given dog tags—issued to New York schoolchildren, as to soldiers—so that in
the event of a bomb, our bodies could be identified. My sister, seven years old,
asked what the dog tag was for, and my mother told her. I listened. And had
bombs ever been dropped? Roni asked. Imagine the discussion, my mother
explaining to a seven-year-old about war, about Hiroshima and Nagasaki....And

the next time the five-bell signal rang for a shelter drill and my kindergarten teacher said, "Now, children, it's only a game, remember, under your desk, head down," I, five years old, stood up and said it was not a game, it was about dropping bombs on children and they, our own government had dropped bombs on children and their eyes had melted and people were burned and killed. The other five-year-olds began crying and screaming, and the principal summoned my mother to school. "What are you, crazy, telling a kid things like that," the principal is reputed to have said, and my mother to have answered: "I will not lie to my children."

My mother's version of this story emphasizes my role: as class conscience and rebel. But what delights me in the story is *her* courage: though a good student, she had dropped out of high school at fifteen and was always convinced that educated people were smarter. Yet she had the political and intellectual backbone to defend me and defy authority.

This was my Jewish upbringing, as much as the candles we lit for Hanukah, or the seders where bread and matzoh shared the table. My father had been raised observant, my mother, not. But to us breaking religious observance was progressive, the opposite of superstitious; when we ate on Yom Kippur, it never occurred to me that this was un-Jewish. I knew I was a Jew. I knew Hitler had been evil. I knew Negroes—we said then—had been slaves and that was evil too. I knew prejudice was wrong, stupid. I knew Jews believed in freedom and justice. When Eisenhower-Nixon ran in 1952, I noticed Nixon's dark wavy hair, like my father's, and said: "He looks like Daddy." My mother was furious: "Nothing like him!" and went on and on explaining how Nixon had gotten elected to Congress only by smearing Helen Gahagan Douglas (the liberal Congresswoman). I was seven years old.

Soon we would get our first TV, so my mother (and I) could watch the McCarthy hearings. I knew the whole fate of humanity hinged on these hearings, as surely as I knew the Rosenbergs had been good people, like my parents, with children the same age as my sister and me. I knew government people, like McCarthy, had killed the Rosenbergs, and I was terrified, but it literally did not occur to me that real people, people I might meet, people who had children and went to work, hated the Rosenbergs, thought they should die. Nor did it occur to me that there were people who thought unions were bad, people who did not know you never cross a picket line, did not know prejudice was wrong and stupid.

This is not to say I never heard alternate views, but my parents—though not formally educated or trained in political analysis—had very definite opinions about right and wrong which they passed on to me like the Ten Commandments, ideas I have yet to find wanting.

That this set of principles was Jewish never occurred to me. Around me was Flatbush, a swirling Jewish ghetto/community of first and second generation immigrants, including Holocaust survivors (though they were noted in my mind simply as the parents who brought umbrellas to school when it rained, spoke with my grandparents' accents); there were clerks, trade unionists, salespeople, plumbers, small business people, radio and TV repairmen, people like my parents and their friends; there were teachers and there were even doctors who lived in what we called "private houses" in the outreaches of the neighborhood at the point where not everyone was Jewish.

But where I lived, everyone was, or almost. Jewish was the air I breathed, nothing I articulated, everything I took for granted.

1963. I was seventeen, working in the Harlem Education Project.[1] HEP had organized a tutoring project, several rent strikes, an anti-rat campaign;[2] had pressured schools for decent facilities and a Black history curriculum, and helped to create freedom schools for children to attend in protest. A block organization was gradually turning a lot filled with garbage (and once or twice dead bodies) into a park. It was my first experience with a mobilizing proud community and with the possibilities of collective action. I was hooked, though it took me years to recognize how my upbringing had brought me to 133rd St. and Lenox, and primed me for this commitment.

It was also my first experience in a non-Jewish environment. Harlem was the center of Northern Black culture; there were community people, students— some from other cities and communities—some from middle-class homes, some travelling back and forth from the South with stories of Fannie Lou Hamer, James Farmer or of the past: a grandfather lynched in Florida, a great-great-aunt who learned to read in slavery in Mississippi (and Mississippi is still the most frightening word I know). And there were white people, these almost all young, almost all students, some who were my first contact with WASPs; some Jews, though I barely registered that fact since they were not like the Jews I knew. All these students went to colleges like Columbia and Sarah Lawrence, while I went to no-tuition City College, riding the subway three hours a day to classes and to Harlem, and would the next year—at eighteen—move into my own apartment and become financially self-supporting.

At the end of my first summer in Harlem, on the bus returning from the historic March on Washington, a Black man my age flirted with me and I flirted back, and he sang me this song:

*Jew girls from Brooklyn they go wild over me*
*and they hold my hand where everyone can see*
*O they paint their face like whores*
*have me leave them at their doors*
*They go wild, simply wild over me*

Intensely focused on white racism, utterly unaware of racism against Jews, or of the possibility of Jewish danger (the Holocaust was eons ago, irrelevant), I felt only shame at the label—Jew girl from Brooklyn—and at the stereotype— hypocrite, liberal in public but won't bring him home to meet the family. I determined not to be like the others; not to be like myself....

1966. I was twenty, preparing to leave New York for graduate school at Berkeley. I wanted to get away from New York, from my family, my people, to be part of the radical politics developing on the West Coast. At a summer demonstration against the war in Vietnam, I marched with a slim, pale woman from

California. She had long straight blond hair, wore some easy cotton shift and sandals; she seemed not to sweat and her voice lilted when she spoke. I had the same body I still have: sturdy, strong legs, heavy black eyebrows, dark hair which in New York's August frizzed and bushed; my skin glistened with oil. I could not imagine how I would fit into the West Coast.

I discovered in Berkeley that the Brooklyn Jewish accent which in New York had always marked me as lower-class now marked me as one of those smart Jews from New York. Apart from this observation, passed on by an admiring gentile friend, I have few memories of being a Jew in Berkeley, little consciousness that people's reactions to or assumptions about me had something to do with my particular style of Jewish culture. Jewish political issues moved me not at all, including the 1967 war in the Middle East—I did not identify with Israel—and, when in 1968 I had a minor operation, like Tillie Olsen's Anna I wrote "none" next to *religion* on the hospital registration form because "I didn't want anyone mumbling religion at me if I died."

1972. I had just moved to Portland, Oregon and was attending a feminist conference, talking with a woman while we waited for the elevator. I have forgotten the context for what she said: that she did not like Jews. They were loud and pushy and aggressive. This was the first time I had heard someone say this outright. I was stunned, didn't know what to say—"no they're not"?—and I couldn't believe she didn't know I was Jewish. I said, loud, flat, "I'm Jewish." I can't remember what happened next or even her face, only the moment by the elevator.

1975. Yellow Springs, Ohio, at the Feminist Socialist Conference, on the lunch line, the woman in back of me was talking about a Jewish caucus. I didn't ask her anything, didn't even seriously eavesdrop. I couldn't relate to it. I went to a workshop on economics instead. Years later I wonder what they talked about.

1978. I was working at Rape Relief Hotline in downtown Portland doing counselling, advocacy, community education and organizing. I was talking with my best friend and sister organizer—a middle-class WASP woman—about my sense of awkwardness and ineffectiveness with "straight" women—meaning some combination of middle-aged heterosexual non-movement women; that I seemed to have no social skills, everything I said had the wrong beat. A couple of days later a woman called the hotline to talk about her experience some years back of being battered. She wanted to get involved in hotline activities, and I invited her to stop by. She did. The woman was some thirty years older than I, had raised two kids, worked in an office, had never considered herself political. I might have been the first lesbian she'd ever knowingly met. She was everything I was supposed to, by my own analysis, feel awkward around. We went out for coffee, talked for hours, easy. She was a Jew, an East Coast Jew. I realized in some ways I was in the wrong city, the wrong part of the world; I was an alien.

By the time I left Oregon in 1979, I had developed an interest in Jewish immigrant history and an obsession with the Holocaust. I read avidly, vaguely aware that I needed Jews but feeling as out of place as ever with those who'd received religious education, as with those women in Portland who had started getting together on Friday nights to eat and *shmooz*, to "socialize." I was political. My rejection of these Jewish women's gatherings parallelled closely my pre-feminist contempt for women's consciousness-raising groups. My failure to register this similarity is a tribute to the mind's ability to resist information which threatens.

And then a time of moving, from one *goyish* environment to another. A summer in Maine, Down East, the easternmost point in the U.S., and if I thought I had seen a Jewish vacuum before, I hadn't. The house we moved into had a swastika smeared on the bedroom door in what looked like blood. A car parked down the road had swastikas and crosses painted on the doors (we spray-painted over them one night). I was becoming very very conscious. Driving out West, passing signs for Greensboro, Atlanta, Birmingham, Montgomery, Jackson, names I knew as sites of struggle and danger, listening to the radio's furious anti-Arab anti-Iranian aggressively fundamentalist christian tirades, unleashed by the taking of hostages in the Tehran embassy complex; hearing christian hymn after christian hymn, seeing more crosses, more churches than I had ever imagined: I was afraid.

By the time I got to northern New Mexico—where I lived for the next two years—I knew I needed Jews, nothing vague about it. I sought out a Jewish women's group which met on and off. I was reading and writing about Jewishness. My political work was still not Jewish-related—I helped to organize a women's coffeehouse, and a demonstration against militarism at Los Alamos Science Museum, and at these and other women's events I read work with strong Jewish content. Some women hugged and thanked me, especially Jews and others strongly grounded in their own culture; responses which warmed, emboldened and confirmed me. And some looked blank, perhaps wondering why I was bothering, or why I was being divisive, identifying with a patriarchal religion, or...responses which alienated me, pushed me deeper into my Jewishness, sharpened my awareness of difference so that I began to notice and respond to cultural stimuli or casual remarks or jokes or, even, political analysis differently.

1980. I recognized in Reagan's election that the liberalism I had for years seen as the real danger was being superseded, that the right was gaining power, with all its Jewhating, racist, sexist, homophobic capitalist thrust. At the same time the anti-Semitism I was encountering in the women's movement and on the left hurt me more, not because it was more threatening but because the feminist left was where I needed to be: this added to my sense of isolation as a Jew.

I was also reading analyses of racism and discussions of identity, mostly by Black women, and my proximity to Chicana and Native American cultures allowed me tangible lessons in diversity and in non-mainstream survival.

Cultures, people were being defined as Third World or white; where I lived it was Chicana, Indian or Anglo. But none of these categories, none of the descriptive analyses fit me or my culture. I was an English-speaker, my people came from Europe, but we were not Anglo and neither was our culture.

There are many more details, scenes, some I remember and some which still elude me. What is clear to me is this: the more outside of a Jewish ambiance I was, the more conscious I became of Jewishness. For me, it was like Marshall McLuhan's perhaps apocryphal remark: I don't know who discovered water, but I'm sure it wasn't a fish. Inside a Jewish environment, where I could take for granted a somewhat shared culture, an expectation about Jewish survival, where my body type and appearance were familiar, my voice ordinary, my laughter not too loud but hearty and normal, above all, normal...in this environment, I did not know what it meant to be a Jew, only what it meant to be a *mentsh*. I did not know that *mentsh* was a Jewish word in a Jewish language.

As I lived longer outside Jewish culture, as I became more fully aware of anti-Semitism, internal as well as external, as I understood my own hunger for home, kin, for *my people*, I was walking further and further along a mostly unconscious, gradual, zig-zag, and retrospectively inevitable path.

## I. IF I AM NOT FOR MYSELF...

There were many of us on distinct but similarly inevitable paths. What happened as Jewish women began raising Jewish issues inside the women's movement?

Even at the beginning, some of the issues we were raising seemed almost mundane, obvious: issues of direct insult, stereotypes, omission, exclusion, indifference, discrimination, assumptions of sameness, passing, invisibility, cultural difference, concern for cultural survival...I—and I think many of us—expected that the groundwork on these issues had been laid, that the heroic and tedious labor undertaken by women of color, with some white and Jewish support, to raise everyone's consciousness about racism would carry over somewhat to inform response to Jewish women.

Not that I thought white—or Jewish—women had always been adequate in their commitment to fight racism. Not that I assumed experience and issues for Jewish women and for gentile women of color were the same; nor did I expect identical experience and issues for all women of color, including Jewish women of color. But I did expect some analogy to be apprehended. I expected that the movement would continue building on general principles, as well as differentiate what was unique.

And this did not happen. I saw resistance, overt rejection, ridicule, a willful ignorance. Not from everyone. From some I saw respect, support, and desire to extend themselves. From many I saw hypocritical silence masquerading as respect. From some, hostility. And—most often—I saw a bewilderment, an inability to grasp what was being said about anti-Semitism or Jewish identity, an incapacity to recognize why it mattered. And, of course, the too-polite silence, the bewilderment, the hostility intensified my self-consciousness as a Jew.

Examples are not hard to find. The policy statement that doesn't mention opposition to anti-Semitism.[3] The many courses that include readings by women from a variety of cultures but, somehow, no Jews. The decision that to have a Jew as keynote speaker is too particular, too specialized.[4] The 1984 Women & the Law conference, with its theme *Bread and Roses,* which offered, out of nearly 200 workshops, none on Jews or Jewish issues. (Let me honor those Jewish women who ensured that the 1985 conference would have several Jewish workshops and events.[5]) The flyer for an anti-militarist protest which voiced opposition to misogyny, racism, homophobia, ableism, a number of other -isms, but not anti-Semitism; named a string of identities including "Black, Latina, Asian, Palestinian..." but not Jewish.[6] A flyer soliciting material for a feminist journal on issues such as:

Imperialist Intervention

Racism, Sexism, Heterosexism, Ageism...

Hunger Education Reproductive Rights

Disarmament Health Self-Determination Housing[7]

I guess the "..." after "Ageism" is supposed to leave room for the inclusion of anti-Semitism, but the general effect is to make Jews feel invisible, unwelcome, or worse.

Why? Why have the basic points been so hard to get? Why have so many radicals been impermeable to a pro-Jewish analysis and activity? Why are we getting the message that many of our erstwhile political comrades and sisters— including some Jews—think it contradictory to be a radical Jew?

The explanation, as I have tried to track it down, is as tangled as the nature of anti-Semitism; as unconscious, as willfully ignorant as an ordinary American's relationship to the rest of the world; as inadequately grasped and developed as the women's movement's understanding of race and class and why the movement should oppose racism and class hierarchy.

## Anti-Semitism, Race And Class

I am not one who believes anti-Semitism is inevitable, yet I confess my heart sinks when I consider how resilient this hatred is: Jew as anti-Christ, embodying materialism, money, Shylock's pound of flesh; Marx's analysis of the Jew as irrelevant parasite; shameful victims, who went like sheep to the slaughter; the U.N. General Assembly's proclamations on Zionism; killer Israelis.

Nor does Jewish oppression fit into previously established analyses. If capitalism is your primary contradiction, the Jewish people is not a class category. If racism, many Jews have light skin, pass as gentile if they wish. If sexism, why should Jewish women identify with Jewish men? If Jewish is an ethnicity, a peoplehood, why don't you live in Israel, or call yourself Israeli? If it's a religion, how are you Jewish if you don't observe?

But not only does Jewish oppression elude conventional categories, Jewish stereotypes prove that anti-Semitism does not exist. Jews are rich, powerful, privileged, control the media, the schools, the business world, international banking: the Zionist conspiracy rides again. How could such powerhouses ever be in trouble? These stereotypes, I've realized, prevent recognition of how we are threatened or demeaned as Jews.

For example: in 1982 when WBAI, New York City's progressive radio station, broadcasted the disarmament march and interviewed—as the lone voice against the demonstration—an Orthodox Jew, I was one of several who phoned to complain. "Why pick on an Orthodox Jew as the single representative of conservative politics?" I asked. "Why not?" a man answered. "I've always wanted to pick on an Orthodox Jew." When I expressed shock/tried to explain (obviously I was in shock if I tried to explain), he immediately said, "I'm so sick of hearing about the fucking Holocaust" (which I hadn't mentioned). So I called the station manager, who apologized and proceeded to explain how when someone was making $7,000 a year and someone next door was making $15,000 a year (clearly this man knew a lot about neighborhoods) I could understand the resentment.

Sure I could understand. But I had been talking about Jewhatred, not class antagonism. The station manager of New York City's progressive station had leaped from one to the other instantly, automatically. As if all Jews were wealthy. As if all wealth were Jewish. As if anti-Semitism were indulged in only by the poor.

By speaking about anti-Semitism, Jewish women unsettle an unspoken equation in the radical women's movement: in a society like ours, deeply racist and absurdly pretending to classlessness, class comes to be seen as identical to race. People of color are considered the same as working and poor people. Other aspects of racism—cultural erasure, assimilation, self-hate, just to name a few—are simply not heeded, nor are—god forbid—strengths of ethnic or racial minorities acknowledged unless—in a wash of white self-hate—people of color are romanticized as stronger, more authentic, somehow better than whites; but better because they are seen as such victims that mere survival is a miracle.

Meanwhile, these same analyses which ignore class as an independent category, related to but separate from race, ignore the variety of class experience and location of Jews: Jews you remember, are all rich or at least middle-class. Why, then, are we complaining?

Such a non-analysis not only belies the experience of middle-class people of color—the upper middle-class Black families, for example, whose L.A. neighborhood was firebombed in June, 1985; the middle-class Japanese home-land-and-business-owners on the West Coast who had everything confiscated and were imprisoned in camps during the Second World War—but this perspective also erases the existence of Jews of color and working-class Jews, and the entire white poor and working-class; a very substantial group of women.

Related to this unspoken equation: analyses of racism—both on the left and in the feminist movement—have been spearheaded by Black people, and to some extent the experience of Black people in the U.S. provides the model by which we understand racism. And despite the existence and even growth of a Black middle class, the continued grinding poverty of most Black people in this country also suggests an equation of race and class.

And it's true: most immigrant groups have moved up the class ladder, at least to lower middle class or trade union status (which—for men—means pretty good pay), usually pushed up in what has been called "the queuing effect" by a newer group of immigrants against whom prejudice is fresher and stronger.[8] But American Blacks, in their forced passage to this country, in the destruction of many elements of African culture by slavery, in their confrontation with classic American racism against the darkest skin, and in the exploitation of this racism by capitalists to "explain" inequality, have been painfully excluded from the process of queuing. This is evident from the progress of Puerto Ricans and Koreans in New York City, for example, or Cubans in Miami; though more recently arrived than Blacks, these groups have, in effect, cut in ahead of Blacks economically.

But there's another kind of distortion. I have lived outside of New York City for half of my forty years now, and have come to think that the usual explanations of racism and anti-Semitism focus unduly on New York, a focus which has everything to do with location of media and ambitious intellectuals, not to mention a huge Jewish and a huge Black community, each deeply rooted in the city, each a cultural center for their people. And these two communities have often, in the past twenty years, been at odds, not utterly, but noticeably: on community control of schools, in the struggle for the city's limited resources, on affirmative action and quotas. And the contrast—between a visible, relatively secure Jewish community, mostly (except for the old) employed, and a continuing impoverished Black community with an unequal share of the city's resources, unequally protected and unequally harassed by the police, with an astronomical rate of unemployment among Black teenage males and not much prospect of improvement—the contrast has got to seem stark.

It is this sense of contrast that is drawn upon again and again in people's discussion of anti-Semitism as opposed to racism. But when I look more closely at places other than New York—at Boston, where working-class Italians and Blacks have been at odds over school busing; at Detroit, where Iraqi small merchants and Blacks have had racial tension reminiscent of the "Jewish shopkeeper in Harlem"; at northern New Mexico, where Chicana/o and Native American communities may have differences, and where Anglos moving to the area are wresting political control from the Chicanas/os; at Miami, where non-Spanish speakers may resent the bilingualism requirement for civil service jobs dealing with the public—my grasp of complexities of race, Jewishness, ethnicity, class, and culture is greatly enhanced. Instead of being characterized by polarization, in which anti-Semitism is treated as a phenomenon different *in nature* from racism, anti-Semitism can be clearly seen as *a form of racism*.

## The World According To America

There are other factors blocking recognition of the weight of anti-Semitism on Jews. Jewish experience in the U.S., isolated from the experience of Jews around the world, seems fairly rosy. But Jews are an international people, and the nature of Jewish identity, oppression, fear, and danger derive from and connect to experiences outside this country.

Wars between the U.S. and other countries have always been fought *in* other countries; most people in the U.S. live in an extraordinarily protected context. Not only is our country vast and populous and proud of an isolationist spirit (often masking an imperialist reality); but, in addition, the strictly limited immigration during the middle portion of this century has restricted most Americans' knowledge about war, persecution, torture, the experience of refugees. Most Americans seem to believe ourselves peculiarly unaffected by what goes on in the rest of the world. If it didn't happen here, if it isn't happening now, why worry? Nor does a nation busy constructing a California or Texas future over Native American and Chicana/o culture care much about history.

From this vantage point, Jews seem ridiculous when we talk about Jewish danger. We are up against a failure of Americans to take seriously the pitch Jewhating attained so quickly in Europe in the thirties, for example, because Americans think Europe and the thirties so far away. They know about evil Germans, sheeplike Jews, and heroic Americans, but are not taught to see the war against the Jews as a culmination of centuries of Jewhating. Americans are told lies about the base of Nazism, so that we imagine Jewhating goes with a lack of education: working-class people are—as with white racism in this country— blamed. We are not told of the doctors and doctorates trained in Europe's finest universities. For most Americans the Holocaust blurs safely, almost pleasantly, with other terrible events of the past, like Bubonic Plague in the Middle Ages.

Nor have most Americans paid much attention to the persecution of Jews in the Soviet Union, or Argentina, or Ethiopia, unless an ideological point is to be scored against these nations. As for the fact that Jews are *not* in danger in some communities around the world because Jews have been exiled or violently excised from those communities: this is not recognized as a legitimate source of grief and suspicion for Jews to reckon with, a loss—of our people, our culture. Women in the feminist movement, not necessarily educated on these issues, respond pretty much like other Americans.

### The Scarcity Assumption

Then, too, an assumption deeply integral to capitalism has been absorbed by all of us, since it is reflected in so much of what we see. I have called this the Scarcity Theory,[9] not enough to go around: not enough love, not enough time, not enough appointments at the food stamps office, not enough food stamps, not enough money, not enough seats on the subway. It's pervasive. We learn mistrust of each other, bone deep: everything is skin off somebody's nose.

And in the short run, certain things *are* scarce. To what causes do I apply my limited "free" time? Where do I donate "extra" money? What books do I read, what issues do I follow and become knowledgeable about? Where will my passion be deep and informed, able to make connections and inspire others, and where will it be superficial, giving lip service only? The women's movement has only in the last few years and under considerable pressure begun to face its own racism; class is still addressed in the most minimal ways. Meanwhile, international crises—apartheid in South Africa, intervention in Nicaragua, torture and repression in Salvador and Guatemala—compel attention.

Few of us have learned to trust our own rhetoric, that people will fight harder as they also fight for themselves. So when Jews begin talking about anti-Semitism, it's only "natural" that even the left, which should *welcome* a people's coming to consciousness, responds as if we're asking for handouts— and whose pocket will they come out of? Ignoring how much political energy can be generated as groups develop a cohesive identity and analysis, the left accuses Jews of draining the movement, of competing for status as victims, of ignoring advantages and options open to us.

Identity politics of all kinds do contain an inherent potential not only for victim-competition but for splintering movements into 1,000 groups whose members at last feel sufficiently the same: comfy but not a powerful resource.[10] But while the focus of some Jewish women on identity as a source of personal discovery and support is hardly unique, criticism of identity politics has been aimed disproportionately at Jews, sometimes *by* Jews. I'll put this another way: anti-Semitism has sometimes masqueraded as a disdain for identity politics.[11]

## Hurry Hurry

Some—including some Jews who identify, as I do, with the left—if not disdainful of our attention to Jewish identity, seem to be rushing us, implying that we are lingering over what Rosa Luxemburg, a Jewish leftist, called "petty Jewish concerns," that we are evading important struggles, being selfish or self-indulgent. Aren't we done already?

A Jewish lesbian/feminist who has written about racism publishes, as part of a long essay on anti-Semitism and racism, five pages of consciousness-raising questions directed at Jewish women, prefaced by:

Since many women have engaged in consciousness-raising about Jewish identity and anti-Semitism...I have skipped over a basic avenue of inquiry...[12]

New Jewish Agenda, a progressive Jewish organization founded six years ago—and to which I belong—holds its second national convention, Summer '85, inspired by Hillel's second question: *If we are only for ourselves, what are we?* The question has two possible takes: an ethical one (the answer is, "less than human"); and a practical one (the answer is, "a failure," because we are a tiny minority who needs allies). This is the question which prompts joining with others, the question of coalition.[13]

But before Hillel asked, "If I am only for myself," he asked, "If I am not for myself, who will be?" This is the question of separatism, the question that prompts a gathering of one's people. Literally, who will stick up for me if I don't respect myself enough to stand up for myself, if I can't articulate my own concerns so that others understand and care about them? Here is our beginning. Have we been for ourselves sufficiently already? Do we even know who our selves are?

## II. JEWISH DIVERSITY, ASSIMILATION, AND IDENTITY

Who, what is the Jewish people? This question dazed me when I first voiced it. I had always known the Jewish people: we lived in Brooklyn, and those whose fathers made money moved to Long Island. It was simple.

And suddenly it was not simple at all. I began to discover the different experiences, cultures, languages of Jews. I was thirty-four when I learned about Ladino, a couple of years older when I learned of Arab Jews, Kurds, the Beta Israel of Ethiopia, the Colchins of India. The diversity of the Jewish people shocked me.

Even in this country, I realized, there are vast differences: place of origin, part of the country, class background, religious or secular upbringing and practice, knowledge of and attachment to Jewish culture (which one?!), degree of assimilation.

For some Jews, "passing" seems a choice; for others, passing means total denial and pain; for still others, passing is something they do without even thinking, and for still others, passing—as white/American/normal—is impossible. Some Jews have never felt a moment of Jewish fear; others smell it daily. Some were raised in comfortable suburbs, sheltered from knowledge of anti-Semitism; others came from Europe or the Middle East and relive their own nightmares or those of their families; others grew up in mixed neighborhoods where they were beat up every day after school for being the Jew, and especially on Easter.

To observant Jews, a persistent reluctance by others to take Jewish holidays, *shabes,* or dietary customs into account means that they—observant Jews—are not welcome;[14] to others, ignoring these traditions embodies anti-patriarchal struggle. Some Jews are passionately attached to Yiddish culture and want to preserve this; others feel alienated by a Yiddish emphasis: they grew up with Ladino or Arabic, and resent the assumption that Jewish means Ashkenazi roots; some share the rejection of much of the New Left for European anything, and, seeing the future in the Third World and only a moribund or embarrassing past in the remnants of European Jewry, feel no desire to preserve Ashkenazi culture. (Though one might question this last position as self-hating, the people who feel this way do not perceive what they hate as their *selves.*)

Some Jews identify deeply with other Jews; others identify only with white middle-class privilege; some consider themselves people of color. Some invalidate, trivialize or otherwise deny Jewish experience, oppression, and values, say "I'm a Jew" only as a label or a credential, not a perspective. With the diversity of our experience unarticulated in a way that supports all of it, even Jews tend to perceive the needs, complaints, experience of other Jews as extreme, atypical, threatening, not really or not necessarily *Jewish.*[15] Given this lack of agreement about even such basics as the nature of Jewish experience and identity, the parameters of anti-Semitism, how are Jews supposed to work politically as *Jews?*

America is famous for gobbling up cultures, immigrant and native. But in addition, the nature of the Jewish people on the face of this earth has been totally transformed in the past forty-five years by three facts:

—The Holocaust: the partial extermination of European Jewry and the virtual destruction of Ashkenazi culture.

—The expulsion of Jews from the Arab countries and destruction of these centers of Judeo-Arab culture.

—The founding of the state of Israel and the ingathering of many Jews.

We have not yet absorbed these transformations. We don't yet know what it means to be a Jew in the late 20th century.

For many North American Jews (in the U.S. and Canada, half the world's Jews) a key issue is assimilation, a seepage of Jewishness out of diaspora Jewry, except for those who retain or return to religious practice. Assimilation is often treated, by those who would belittle Jewish issues, as privilege, the *ability* to pass, a ticket out of Jewish oppression.

Anyone who has heard—as I have—Jew hating remarks said to her face because to the speaker she didn't look Jewish knows both the survival value and the knife twist of passing. (And consider how some Jews came to look non-Jewish: Jewish women raped by gentile men during pogroms; Jewish women with lighter skin, hair, more gentile features, considered prettier, more desirable than their darker, more Semitic-looking sisters.)

But assimilation is a much larger issue than who you do or don't look like. Assimilation is the blurring or erasure of identity and culture. As I have come to recognize Jewish identity and culture not as givens, there for the taking, but as profoundly valuable and *vulnerable,* assimilation has become a source of pain: loss, some of which I can retrieve, some not: gone.

The point is that Jewish identity is not just about oppression, about anti-Semitism and survival, though clearly this is part of our history and we need our history. We also need our culture, need to know *where we grew.* We need *not* to disappear into the vague flesh of America, even if this disappearance were possible.

Those who call resistance to assimilation a luxury might do well to think about calling "sexual preference" a luxury, or reproductive rights, or access to education or creative expression. None of these is *bread,* but "Bread *and* Roses" was a demand voiced by Rose Schneiderman, a union organizer and a Jew.

What are the roses? As Jews we need our peoplehood, our culture, history, languages, music, calendar, tradition, literature. We need these things because they are beautiful and ours, and because the point of struggle is not bare survival but lives full of possibility.

But Rose Schneiderman's metaphor flounders. Our culture is not a rose, it is our backbone. To say it matters we're Jews; to bond with our people—for a tiny minority, these acts trigger intense fear: fear of being boxed into a perspective that is assumed to be narrow and selfish, fear of being isolated, as we have often historically been isolated.

And the only thing that counters this fear is love for our people, pride in our culture.

*If I am not for myself, who will be?* Hillel could not have predicted the need American Jews in the late 20th century would bring to his first question: the need to know the self, the people, the culture. For several years I have given workshops across the country on anti-Semitism, racism, and more recently, Jewish identity. I have heard Jews talk about gathering as a group, loving the comfort, the opportunity to discuss anti-Semitism, offer support, eat wonderful food, laugh...but then? uncertain what to do next, as Jews. I have watched Jews sob as they grappled for the first time with the meaning of Jewish resistance, of violence and non-violence in the context of the Holocaust. Jewish radicals are just beginning to tangle with Jewish identity and its relationship to Jewish culture, tradition and politics.

So it's not surprising that we are still, many of us, uncertain in our responses. What *is* a good radical Jewish response? How do we take positions that won't be used against us or where we won't be invisible as Jews? How, for example, do we support the struggle against apartheid, confront the anti-Semitic emphasis on Israel as well as the assumption that as Jews we support the Israeli government's position, do all of this without getting crazed or isolated? What is our position on arms sales to Israel? What's our position on Israel generally? Why do we, as Jews, need a position on Israel—on another country's foreign and domestic policy? What is our relationship to the mainstream Jewish community? How do we look clearly at the strength we have, as a people, without worrying that they'll see us as running the world again?

These questions need to be answered by Jews talking with one another, developing political and emotional clarity and cohesion. And this requires Jewish space in which to piece together a deeply felt Jewish identity and perspective inch by inch from the various threads of tradition, literature, ritual, religion, culture, values, politics, language. Some of us will spend our lives building Jewish identity; others will draw on this work as a strong foundation from which to live our politics. Particularly for those of us who are not religiously observant, much confusion attends our grasping—through anti-Semitism and often prodded by anti-Semitism—for something beyond common danger. We need to figure out how to undo assimilation without being nostalgic or xenophobic; how to reach in and out at the same time.

### III. GUILT VERSUS SOLIDARITY

Most feminist theory on identity was developed by women of color and focused on fighting racism.[16] I have come to think that had white women fully grasped the nature of this fight and *their own reasons for joining it,* they would now be grasping what Jewish women are trying to do. For the suspicion which greets a developing Jewish identity—from some Jews as well as gentiles—is only partly explained by anti-Semitism (the sense that Jewish identity *in particular* has no value) and by scarcity (the fear that focus on Jews will detract from other pressing issues). The way Jews have been met with "not you too," the way anti-Semitism becomes the one issue too many, suggest that many white women are angry and resistant to dealing with racism but are too frightened to express that anger openly;[17] suggest further how little our movement has taught us to see struggles against racism as life-giving, nourishing; as our own.

Most white women have learned, instead, guilt: to oppose racism because it's their—I am tempted to say christian—duty, for they seem to offer two models: the missionary and the crusader.

## Guilt: How Not To Build a Movement

If you join a struggle because you know your life depends on it—even if remotely: because you identify with the people, because people you love are involved—you have one attitude toward the people and their struggle.

But if you join because lucky you, you should help out those less fortunate —you have a different attitude: you consider those you deign to help pathetic victims. (It's no wonder Jews remain outside the paradigm, because Jews are pegged as overprivileged powerhouses: gentiles don't feel guilty about Jews.) The missionary in some way sees herself stooping to pick up the white woman's burden, a dangerous attitude, reeking of condescension, of failure to believe in the value or capacity of other people. Besides, "the white man's burden" was a polite name for imperialism. I don't imagine that white women in the women's movement are the British Empire, but people who take this attitude are—at best—focused on themselves. They want that rosy do-gooder glow.

They can be harmless. And sometimes they *do* good. Guilt has prompted some white women to act against racism: white teachers who make sure to include books by Third World writers; white women with access to funds, grants, etc., who make sure that women of color get heard, solicited, funded. These acts are not negligible, whatever their motives. And though people acting from guilt may not be reliable allies, they will do in the short run. Sometimes they're all the allies there are.

The crusader, another sort of frail ally, plays on white guilt. She attacks white women whose racism has showed, isolating and shaming them. I have seen her in women's communities all over the U.S.: in crisis centers, in print, in women's studies programs....Sometimes, I confess, I have been her. And just as crusaders were supposed to gather souls but really killed, so the white knight, I have come to call her, destroys more than she saves.[18]

By doing so, she gains power in her own community—white women are afraid of her—and, besides, she is on to something. The white knight often does useful work: were this not true she would have no credibility—people aren't fools. But instead of enlarging the circle of women doing anti-racist work, fostering an atmosphere in which people believe they can change—by struggling compassionately with other white women, by communicating a vision of why one struggles—the white knight banishes most potential allies, leaving herself and a few others as the only decent white women in town.

Her power thus depends on racism, making her, in the end, no more reliable as an ally than the guilt-responsive missionary, since she has, objectively speaking, a stake in maintaining racism. She can, of course, function overtly as a christian knight and attack other christians who exhibit anti-Semitic behavior, etc.; but since the guilt quotient on Jewish issues is low, she's less likely to get response.

Sometimes acts inspired by guilt or by fear of acting wrong have a positive impact. And, for the most cockamamie reasons, people land in situations from which they change and wisen. I did not take the D-train to Harlem when I was seventeen with my present consciousness, yet I would not have developed my present consciousness without those formative experiences.

But guilt itself, as a motivating factor, is rooted in a way of thinking which does not promote change. Guilt asks: am I bad or am I good? guilty or innocent? racist or not? Very different from asking "is this a racist *act?*" which allows me not to commit it, or to do the work that ensures I never commit it again. For in order to change you have to be willing to expose yourself—at least to yourself— and observe and examine and understand. This takes time, patience, and a respect for process. Guilt prompts a longing to purge all impure impulses quickly, get it over and done with once and for all. Impulses which seem impure are not examined or transformed; they are stifled while you keep busy trying to act as though you have the right impulses.

We've all seen white women act like corpses around women of color, so afraid of doing the wrong thing: meaning, anything natural, treating a person like a person. For guilt is a freeze emotion: you can't think, you can't feel, you can only knee-jerk. This is the infantilizing function of guilt: you lose faith in your own responses because the risk of their being wrong is more than you can handle.

In addition to militating against real change, guilt exercises an uneasy influence over the real difference in resources and options which women may enjoy, leading to downward mobility, pretending to have less, gleefully selecting the most oppressed possible identity: *office worker,* not *daughter of a lawyer and dropout from a prestigious college most office workers never get near (as students).*

And why does someone embrace an identity of oppression? Because it's groovy? The insult of this must be apparent. Because she feels guilty about what she's got? Are money, power, privilege worthless resources to ignore, bury, pretend away? The insult of this ought to be apparent too.

And besides: behind the guilt, the desire to belong, be one with the people, etc., the resources remain, quietly drawn on or untouched by anyone, but ready to be picked up and used at some future date. So guilt helps people hoard what they've got, because they never come to terms with how to use resources productively.

The thing is: anyone who really wants to hoard her money, power, and privilege sooner or later will. She can be targeted for guilt trips—to let go of some of what she wishes no one knew she had—but beneath the guilt had better be fear: fear of exposure, fear of conflict, so she'll stay in line and act right. And how does any sane person react after a while to fear, guilt? Is this a way to build a movement?

Nor can guilt mobilize those who don't feel guilty. Try telling a white working-class woman, for example, to fight racism because of how privileged she is. She may think racism is wrong and may be committed to fight it; she may also think that movement analyses of racism are ridiculous because she is not living the easy life her white skin is supposed to guarantee her. Whatever privilege she may have, she clings to—things are tough—but she hardly feels guilty. Only recognition of a common goal, the possibilities and—I want to say—the joys of solidarity will inspire women who don't feel guilty to join another struggle as their own.

## Solidarity: How To Build a Movement

Solidarity requires the bonding together of a people engaged in common struggle. But solidarity also means standing alongside another struggle, not because you feel guilty but because you recognize it as your own; it means using what you have on behalf of the struggle.

Angela Davis notes, for example, Prudence Crandall, a white woman who risked her life in defense of education for Black girls.[19] Or the strategy suggested by Maria Chapman Weston, a white leader of the Boston Female Anti-Slavery Society: when a white pro-slavery mob burst into a meeting chaired by Weston, she realized that the mob sought to isolate and perhaps violently attack the Black women in attendance, and thus insisted that each white woman leave the building with a Black woman at her side.[20] Or, at the world anti-slavery convention in London, at which the notorious decision was made to bar women from the floor, there were a few men who refused to join the floor but stood with the women in the gallery, silent. Among them was the Black abolitionist Charles Remond, and the white abolitionists William Lloyd Garrison and Nathaniel Rogers.[21] Black leader Frederick A. Douglass, too, at least initially supported the then-radical demand of women's suffrage and used his male privilege on behalf of the emerging women's rights movement.[22] Or, the women workers in the stockyards (mostly Irish and Poles) and in the garment industry (mostly Jews and Italians) who deliberately—and contrary to the practice of the AFL and most of their peers—sought to include and organize with Black women.[23] Or the Women's Trade Union League, upper middle-class college-educated white suffragists who worked in support of immigrant women's unions.[24] Or the Black and white college students—including many Jews—who went south to challenge segregation.

All these actions are examples of informed coalition work. None is a passive giving something up; they are all an aggressive wrapping of two peoples in a cloak only one has. These are acts which build trust between peoples.

But those who performed these acts which build and justify trust—I can't believe that they did not understand that these acts were *also* in defense of *their own freedom,* a freedom without which they, the actors, could not breathe.

*If I am only for myself, what am I?* Lonely. Hungry for sisters, comrades. Listen to the words of the fiery Grimke sisters, white abolitionists who recognized "the special bond, linking them with Black women who suffered the pain of slavery: 'They are our countrywomen—they are our sisters.'"[25] Or the slogan displayed at the April '85 march in Paris to protest increasing violence against Jews and Arabs (many of whom are also Jews) and to protest increasing racist propaganda about purifying France for the French: *Ne touche pas à mon pote*: Keep your hands off my buddy.

None of this is the passionless rhetoric which has come to dominate our movement's discussions of race, class. Obviously if your friends, if your sisters are suffering you put everything you have into the struggle to free them *because you need their freedom as your own.*

Your privilege, insofar as it divides you from others, is *in your way*, unless you resolve how to use it for others, as well as for yourself. This is a non-guilt approach: drawing on what is best in people, not suppressing what is worst.

And let me say something which in this (christian) culture may come as a surprise: what is best in people is not self-abnegation. What is best in people is a sturdy connection between respect for the self and respect for the other: reaching in and out at the same time:

*If I am not for myself, who will be?*
*If I am only for myself, what am I?*

## IV. SOME STRATEGIES FOR ACTION

As we come into our Jewish identity, we feel somehow that to be justified in asserting it, in opposing anti-Semitism, we must be innocent victims, trying to make our oppression palpable to those who don't understand it. My beginning search for Jewish identity focused on the Holocaust and on the immigrant experience only partly because such a search must. So did a number of poems we received for this anthology—not because of direct knowledge, but for some other reason. The only other subjects which appeared in such profusion were "grandmothers" and the "Triangle Shirtwaist Factory Fire."

We need our history/herstory, and these are our handles, what we know. These are also all images of greater persecution than most American Jews are subject to today. As Jews, afraid of the myth of Jewish power; as (white?) feminists, guilty about our skin privilege, we are so hungry for innocence that images of oppression come almost as a relief. Innocence, even suffering, seems the only alternative to guilt.

But innocence has its price: while it relieves us of responsibility, it also denies us our strength. The assumption is: since we have been victims, we cannot ever be anything else. Witness Begin, invoking the Holocaust to justify the invasion of Lebanon. *How could Jews be oppressive after all we've suffered?* From this perspective, class hostility, for example, has no basis in class distinctions but is only a front for Jewhating. We have to recognize that Jews are relatively well-off economically compared with most people of color in this country, as with the rural white poor; and that Jews endure about the same level of poverty as other ethnic groups who immigrated around the same time. Our job is to untangle class hostility from anti-Semitism, not to pretend the Jewish people still work in the sweatshop.

Non-Jews rely on this innocence too, including people of color. Witness how some excused Farrakhan's description of Hitler as a great German. Was it because support for Jesse Jackson's presidential candidacy transcended Jewish danger (which, given Jewish wealth and power, could not possibly be *real* danger)? Or was it because Farrakhan is Black, and a cry of hatred against Jews carries no threat when the speaker is, by definition, powerless? (Need it be said that this is racist as well as anti-Semitic?) From this perspective, the fears of elderly Jews in racially mixed neighborhoods that they will be mugged and robbed are merely a front for racism, instead of reflecting the reality of urban violence: old people are marks, especially when living in communities no longer theirs. Our job here is to untangle concern for safety from racism, not to come up with justifications for mugging.

How this need for innocence translates politically is a disaster. The attitude that claims we—of any group—are essentially victims and so can't be charged with our behavior is destructive to all of us. If we can't do anything wrong, the fact is we can't do *anything* at all—and how in that state of powerlessness are we to build a vast movement sufficient to transform the exceedingly powerful state we live in? Defensive, protective of that dubious privilege of having our suffering acknowledged, we are at something of a standstill. Can't we look at each other and begin to see what we might build? Can't we extend towards each other so that we can draw on each other's strengths, learn to trust that we can use our power in positive ways?

## Working Alone/Working Together

True coalition is not a smattering of tokens. True coalition forms between groups; the premise is that each group has a strong base in a larger community. Thus Jews who want to work in coalition need, not only to know who we are, but to be bonded with other Jews.

For feminists, for lesbians, this presents its own complications. Some of us won't work with men. This is not a flawed choice. Some of us will have to be separatist—as Jews, as women, as lesbians, as whoever we are. Separatism gives strength, a base from which coalition is possible. Some of us—because of desire or need—will choose to be with our own. There are different forms of struggle, and separatists often are in the vanguard, creating a strong identity and consciousness for the whole community, including those who are not themselves separatist.

Those of us who choose to work in coalitions can assert that identity and consciousness to others. I know many Jewish women, myself among them, have participated in anti-racist, anti-apartheid, anti-intervention work, but not visibly as Jews. It is time we became visible as Jews, as some are doing.

Yet we need at the same time strategies for combatting anti-Semitism, for Jewish visibility fans the coals of indifference and passive contempt. An individual visible as a Jew simply attracts, like a magnet, all available anti-Jewish prejudice, or gets written off as an exception. And sometimes we even need strategies to ensure visibility. A Jew who travelled to Nicaragua recently tells of her attempts to be visible as a Jew to the Nicaraguan Press, attempts frustrated by her travel group's leader, whose job it was to inform the press about the group members and who kept "forgetting" to mention the Jewish member. Just as women, as lesbians, need our own groups—for support and as bases for coalitions, a Jewish group travelling to Nicaragua might have had the desired impact, built Jewish pride *and* Jewish-Nicaraguan solidarity. To reach in and out at the same time.

The particular example of Nicaragua offers another possibility for solidarity and coalition. Progressive Jews have something in common with progressive Native Americans who oppose U.S. intervention in Nicaragua, yet are concerned about the status of the Miskito Indians. We might learn from each other ways to express concern about our people without having this concern either used by the right or discredited by the left.

Again, focusing on Nicaragua, there is work to do in the Jewish community, to make sure the justified fear of anti-Semitism is not exploited by the U.S. government—that Jews have access to the facts. There's a need for community education by strongly-identified Jews; there is also a need for honest discussion of liberation theology, of its potential for anti-Semitism (if the revolutionary impulse is christian, where does that leave us?) and of ways we can support the revolution without supporting an unexamined christianity.

But there are fears. Mine are that non-Jews won't care about working with us. Who are *we* that they should bother? Our numbers so small, we are so disposable, a liability almost; dislike of us a point of unity among everyone else. And as women, as lesbians, as underemployed professionals or workers at traditional women's jobs, most of us don't even have money to contribute. Sometimes I am simply afraid that radical Jews are on the wrong side of history, trapped between self-respect, love for our people and culture and what we, politically, ideologically would support were it not tangled with Jewhating. I know I am not the only radical Jew whose stomach ties in knots reading the radical press or attending a rally.

Non-Jews, especially people of color, may fear that Jews will deny differences in experience, will aim for the great white American marshmallow of you're oppressed/I'm oppressed.

No doubt on every side there is prejudice, ignorance, and mistrust. I think of the Jew who uses the names Palestinian and Lebanese interchangeably, has not bothered to distinguish between the two peoples; the Arab who blames Leon Klinghoffer's death on "the fact that the whole country of Palestine has been hijacked by the…Zionist Jews of Europe, America and elsewhere," not only condoning the brutal death of an old man in a wheelchair, but also hiding—with the words "and elsewhere"—the thousands of Jews forced to leave *their* homes in Arab countries.[26] The Jew who says "We made it, why can't they?" or "Who cares, they're all *goyim!*" The Black who says "*They* made it on my back." The Chicana/o who says *"They're* all landlords." There is work to do on all sides.

James Baldwin, in 1967, wrote: "A genuinely candid confrontation between Negroes and American Jews would certainly prove of inestimable value. But the aspirations of the country are wretchedly middle-class and the middle class can never afford candor."[27] A genuinely candid confrontation amongst all of us—a genuinely *specific* and candid confrontation—is much needed; and Baldwin is precise, as ever, in indicating that we must be prepared to go further than liberal acceptance, further than maneuvering for our own (larger) slice of the pie. The theme re-emerges: we must *want* equality, and we must grasp that equality does not coexist with class structure.

As a feminist and a Jew, I am asking women of color not to abandon us as we assert our Jewishness, not to hear this assertion as a lowered vigilance against racism.

And I am asking Jews not to withdraw into self-righteousness, not to insist that gentiles understand everything immediately, yesterday. We are not without dignity if we explain our issues. I am also asking Jews not to be so afraid of being trapped with other Jews—including, perhaps, some whose politics or attitudes offend us—that we forget that people can change, including our own people, including ourselves.

**Commonality**

I am saying there have got to be many points of unity among us. Even in my fear that non-Jews won't care because we are a small and therefore useless minority, I find a connection: with Native Americans who express the same fear, of irrelevance, and another similar fear, genocide—historical and cultural. And I see difference: the grinding poverty in which most Native American people live.

And in my recognition that Jews are better off economically than most people of color, I find connection with some Asian Americans, not the recent immigrants from Southeast Asia who tend to be very poor, but with many Japanese Americans. Looking specifically at the situation of Japanese Americans I see a people also traumatized by events of the past forty years: internment in camps; the atomic bombs dropped on civilian cities of Hiroshima and Nagasaki; a fear of cultural loss and assimilation; and continued economic discrimination, despite their apparent integration into professional and business life. And I see differences: Japanese—and other Asian-Americans—pressed into the sciences, engineering, computers, pushed away from the humanities, the arts, where much Jewish talent has been channelled.[28]

I could go on. And if I am doing my work, I *will* go on, understanding the ways in which Jewish history and experience are like and unlike the experience of other groups, the ways in which the light skin of some Jews has and has not protected them, the issues as *defined by Jews* and the issues as *defined by other groups.*

We might then, as Jews, offer support to Japanese Americans seeking restitution from the U.S. government for their internment and confiscation of property during World War II, and to those still fighting their convictions for refusing to report for "relocation."

We might express—in unison with Japanese American women—our disgust at the stereotype and acronym JAP—a racist name for Japanese people as well as a sexist scapegoating of Jewish middle-class women for the crimes of capitalism.

We might, as Jews, press our religious and community institutions to offer sanctuary to refugees, from El Salvador and other countries, as some are doing, recognizing our own history as refugees. We might, as Jews, support attempts of women garment workers—jobs once held by Jewish and Italian women—to organize for better conditions and pay. We might support bilingual efforts of Chicana, Latina, and Francophone communities, grasping through our own linguistic losses the importance of retaining one's language.

We might decide that even in the midst of vitriolic disagreement about peace in the Middle East, we must never accept or leave unchallenged instances of racism against Arabs, remembering our own history of prejudice and stereotypes.

We might even, as Jews, offer support to people whose struggles and issues are different from ours now and in the past simply because we care about justice; because we know that while nothing guarantees allies, callousness guarantees callousness.

Of late, there are positive instances of coalition. An event in New York City of Jews and Latinas/os (including some who are both) reading and performing their work, much of which is bilingual (Spring, 1984). Prior to several of Farrakhan's most recent appearances, coalitions of Black and Jewish leaders joined to denounce him. (In Baltimore, the same group joined to condemn Kahane prior to his appearance there).[29] In the feminist movement, a Jewish-Palestinian dialogue.[30] A workshop for Black-Jewish dialogue is being offered at the 1986 Women and the Law conference for the second year. It seems that many of us may have learned something from drawing close to the precipice of total withdrawal and isolation.

If we could start working together *before* we trust, understand, or like each other, we might learn to. Black activist and performer Bernice Reagon says we are stumbling because we have to take the next step.[31] We have gotten entirely too theoretical about these issues, expecting that with words, with ideas, we can work it all out in advance. Perhaps we need to engage, even in uncertainty, and work out issues as they arise. Maulana Karenga, a theorist for the Black movement, has pointed out that a coalition on a specific issue does not create reliable allies: he is critical of what he calls the reliance of middle-class Black movement leaders on alliances with Jews.[32]

But the positive side to Karenga's depressing analysis is that you don't need to be reliable allies to form a coalition. Having formed one, it may be possible to overcome mistrust and establish a larger common ground. It is impossible to do this without some concrete basis of unity, and focusing on the task at hand can help reveal commonality.

The problem is not a lack of common issues, not a lack of desperate need. The problem for us, as Jews, is that we are often afraid, afraid to gather with other Jews, afraid to be visibly Jewish, afraid—too often with reason—to know the extent of anti-Semitism in our comrades, neighbors, co-workers, friends. We are afraid of being or of seeming racist; afraid of our own ignorance of Jewish culture and tradition.

And because, as radicals, we have been taught to see dignity in resistance, in the struggle against oppression, we sometimes idealize oppression. We must remember to respect the struggles Jews have waged on behalf of their children, who are, sometimes, us. We must remember: what is beautiful is the resistance, and that people can—and must—resist from their own authentic place in the world.

This means we must reach out to Israelis fighting for peace, civil rights, and feminism without secretly feeling the Palestinians are more beautiful, because more besieged. One of the hardest acts of self-love for American radical Jews is to identify in this way with Israelis, and I have come to believe it is a crucial stretch, for the alternative is denial of the Jewish connection. It is from this solid, self-knowing place that we can work towards peace and justice in the Middle East.

It is also from this place of valuing resistance that we are able to reach out to those in the Jewish community who have themselves been fighters for justice, or supporters of this fight, to ask them to continue this tradition; to ask them for what is best in themselves too.

Last Rosh Hashanah I stood with my friend Mitzi Lichtman at the edge of the Atlantic performing (in our own way) the ancient ritual of *tashlekh*—casting our sins into the water, in the form of stones. And among all the sins we hurled into the ocean, the sin of self-hate and the sin of failing to feel compassion for others mingled, as indeed they should, for they are the same sin.

And Hillel had a third question: *If not now, when?*

## NOTES

1. The Harlem Education Project (HEP) was a branch of the Northern Student Movement (NSM), founded in New Haven as the northern arm of the Student Non-Violent Coordinating Committee (SNCC), the most militant of the southern civil rights activist organizations.

2. The anti-rat campaign consisted of a number of young Black people armed with rifles very visibly hunting rats in Harlem apartment buildings. The sluggish city health department responded immediately to combat the rats.

3. The National Women's Studies Association, pressed by angry Jewish women, agreed to mention opposition "to anti-Semitism against Arabs and Jews." Since hatred and discrimination against Arabs are regularly included by the term "racism"—and since, oddly enough, these same phenomena directed against Jews are often excluded—I wonder why Jews are not allowed to use "anti-Semitism" to mean anti-Jewish racism, its historic meaning.

4. I have heard this a number of times from women who attended conference planning sessions.

5. Cynthia Kern deserves particular credit for her work. Let me mention that these Jewish events were mostly open to gentiles but were attended almost exclusively by Jews.

6. Flyer for Not In Our Name/Women's Resistance Action, Boston Office. See exchange of letters—a critical letter by Mitzi Lichtman and me, and a self-critical response by several Not In Our Name women—in *Gay Community News* (11/17/84).

7. *Heresies.*

8. For a discussion of the queuing effect, see Stanley Lieberson, *A Piece of the Pie: Blacks and White Immigrants Since 1880* (Berkeley, Univ. of CA Press, 1980), pp.296-326; 377-81.

9. See my earlier discussion, "Anti-Semitism, Homophobia, and the Good White Knight," *Off Our Backs* (5/82).

10. Cf. Black activist Bernice Johnson Reagon, on the discomfort of working in coalitions: "[Coalition is] a monster. It never gets enough. It always wants more. So you better be sure you got your home someplace for you to go to so that you will not become a

martyr to the coalition." See Reagon's fine discussion, "Coalition Politics: Turning the Century," *Home Girls*, ed. Barbara Smith (NY: Kitchen Table/Women of Color Press, 1983), p.361.

11. The felicitous wording is Linda Vance's.

12. Elly Bulkin, Appendix to "Hard Ground: Jewish Identity, Racism, and Anti-Semitism," *Yours In Struggle* (Brooklyn: Long Haul Press, 1984), pp.194-98. See my review in *Off Our Backs* (10/85).

13. Adrienne Rich, speaking at the NJA Convention, added another question—"If not with others, how?"—seeming to place the burden on Jews, as if we have refused to work in alliance with Gentiles, whereas in fact the opposite has often been true. The history of Jews engaged in political activity hardly suggests a people unwilling to work with others; what this history reveals, rather is erasure of Jewish participation, Jews drummed out of movements by anti-Semitism, as well as substantial Jewish contributions to revolutionary activity. See, for example, Elinor Lerner, "Jewish Involvement in the New York City Woman Suffrage Movement," *American Jewish History*, LXX (1981), pp.442-461.

14. See Susie Gaynes' moving statement about recognizing how some Jewish women were made to feel unwelcome by just such a reluctance, "Rosh Hashonah 5743," *The Tribe of Dina*, p.321.

15. In this discussion I am drawing heavily on Irena Klepfisz, "When Jewish Women Disagree," unpublished (1983).

16. For an early clear statement of identity politics, see the Combahee River Collective, "A Black Feminist Statement," reprinted in *Capitalist Patriarchy and the Case for Socialist Feminism*, ed. Zillah R. Eisenstein (NY: Monthly Review Press, 1979).

17. See Susanna Sturgis' analysis of feminist resistance to dealing with fat oppression, "Is this the new thing I'm going to have to be p c about?" *Sinister Wisdom 28* (1985).

18. See Kaye/Kantrowitz,"...the Good White Knight."

19. Angela Davis, *Women, Race & Class* (NY: Random House, 1981), pp. 34 ff.

20. Davis, p.38.

21. Davis, p.48.

22. Davis, pp.50 ff.

23. See Eleanor Flexner, *Century of Struggle: A History of the Women's Rights Movement in the U.S.* (Cambridge, MA: Belknap/Harvard Univ., 1978). But also see Rosalyn Terborg-Penn, "Survival strategies among African-American women workers: A continuing process," *Women, Work & Protest: A Century of U.S. Women's Labor History*, ed. Ruth Milkman (Boston: Routledge & Kegan Paul, 1985). Terbourg-Penn cites the occasional interest of mostly white CIO unions in organizing with Black women, but the more common lack of interest.

24. Nancy Schrom Dye, *As Equals As Sisters: Feminism, The Labor Movement and The Women's Trade Union League of New York* (Columbia: Univ. of Missouri Press, 1980), p.93.

25. Quoted in Davis, p.44.

26. M.T. Mehdi, letter, *New York Times* (10/17/85).

27. James Baldwin, "Negroes Are Anti-Semitic Because They're Anti-White," 1st pub. *New York Times Magazine* (1967); reprinted in *Black Anti-Semitism and Jewish Racism* (NY:Schocken, 1972) p.11.

28. See Prof. Ronald Takaki's remarks, quoted in the *New York Times* (9/4/85).

29. See Earl Raab, "Poisoned Good: Understanding the Farrakhan Factor," *Moment*, vol 11, no. 2 (Jan.-Feb. 1986), pp.13-17.

30. The dialogue was organized by New Jewish Agenda.

31. Reagon, p. 368.

32. Maulana Karenga, "The Crisis of Black Middle-Class Leadership: A Critical Analysis," *The Black Scholar* (Fall 1982), pp.16-32.

# *Class, Feminism, and "The Black-Jewish Question"*

(Parts of this essay were presented as a talk at the Tikkun Conference [Reconstituting the Progressive Tradition of American Jewish Intellectuals, December, 1988, New York City], and published in *Tikkun* magazine [July/August, 1989].

This issue of *Tikkun* (July/August 1989) also includes the extremely valuable talks of the other panelists: Cherie Brown, director of the National Coalition Building Institute in Arlington, MA; Congressman Barney Frank; Rabbi Chaim Seidler-Feller of UCLA; and Cornel West, director of Afro-American studies at Princeton University.)

## The Meaning of "The Black-Jewish Question"

Are Jews especially racist against African Americans? Are African Americans particularly anti-Semitic? Why, in a culture that parades a white christian norm—also a male, heterosexual, nuclear family, middle class norm; in other words, a norm that excludes the vast majority of Americans—can't two targeted groups get along? Or, why, in a complex multi-racial society that sets most marginalized groups at odds with one another, do we even talk about *Jewish-Black conflict* as something unique?

There have of course been incidents, often exaggerated by media coverage. But considering the intensity of Italian-Black conflict in Boston or Bensonhurst, for example, or Korean-Black conflict in L.A. or Flatbush, the emphasis on Jewish-Black tension bears examination.

Race relations in the U.S. are usually presented as a Black-white paradigm which disguises both the complexity of color and the brutality of class. For example, the 1992 L.A. riots/rebellions in response to the acquittal of the policemen who savagely beat Rodney King were described again and again as Black anti-white riots, even though a majority of those arrested were Latinos, not Blacks, and businesses owned by Koreans, Chicanos, Iranian Jews and Blacks were attacked, as well as those owned by whites.[1] The paradigm controls how reality is perceived and named.

I believe that the notion of Black-Jewish conflict is related to this conventional Black-white paradigm, for in the new paradigm, Jewish simply displaces white. Whites discreetly vanish, certainly not the source of any difficulty. The new paradigm highlights Black anti-Semitism (and cloaks the barbaric tradition that has for centuries embedded itself in Eurocentric christian culture); it emphasizes Jewish racism (and eclipses the savage legacy that entered the "New" world with the Europeans, and which inflicted such destruction on the indigenous people and on those brought in chains from Africa).

And so? The characterization of anti-Semitism as a Black phenomenon encourages Jews to distrust African Americans, despite a common threat from white supremacists and a frequently similar political and social agenda. Jews, influenced by fear of anti-Semitism, as well as by dominant culture racism from which we are hardly immune, may ignore differences in experience between our peoples—most pivotal, access to resources and ability to pass—to conclude it's not racism but Black genetic code that's the problem (Michael Levin, professor of psychology at City College of New York, has dedicated his career to trying to prove this).

Similarly, as Jews are portrayed as "the iciest of the ice people,"[2] the most culpable of whites, class inequities are again obscured (it's not Jewish alliance with middle class priorities but Jewish genetic code that's the problem), and African Americans are encouraged to distrust Jews as whites, again despite the common threat from white supremacists, and despite the evidence that— Jewish neo-conservatism notwithstanding—Jews remain the most dependably progressive whites in the U.S. (that is, those Jews who are white).[3]

African American scholar Henry Louis Gates, Jr. has argued that African American nationalist leaders who emphasize Jewish culpability in the slave trade are deliberately undermining the possibility of any Black-white alliance, attacking Jews as the flying wedge of white progressives: if the Jews are untrustworthy, all whites are untrustworthy, and a nationalist/isolationist stance is validated. Whereas if possibilities for alliance exist....[4]

Finally all of this Black-white and Black-Jewish ideation masks the complexity of tension—and affinity—among people of color and among all marginalized people, as well as the force fields of entitlement and disentitlement, empowerment and disempowerment in this nation—a series of chasms that must be bridged if we are to create alliances forceful and robust enough to challenge that relatively small, terrifyingly powerful group of, need it be said, mostly white, heterosexual, christian men, growing ever more rich, powerful, and vicious at the expense of all the rest of us, not only in this nation but on this planet.

## A Glance at Jewish History

I am writing this as a Jew, a feminist and a lesbian, and as an activist with a long history of struggling for racial justice. All these factors matter: my gut connection to the Jewish people, my loyalty to women and to lesbians and gays, and my commitment to the aspirations of African Americans. Here I want to clarify what makes it hard for non-Jews (and even for some Jews) to grasp and situate Jewish issues in a context of race-hate and white supremacy.

In the U.S. people tend to be both ahistorical and insulated from the impact of international events. From this tunnel perspective, Jews have it good. What are we worried about? Yet to understand Jewish experience demands looking not only at daily acts of hate and belittlement, exclusions, humiliations, and violence; not only within the limited frontiers of New York City or suburban Chicago; not only at contemporary events or even the Holocaust.

Jews have a history of nearly 6000 recorded years, a history which includes repeated subjection to vicious bias based on our birth, culture/religion, nationality, peoplehood, appearance, identity; repeated cycles of calm then chaos; repeated periods of relative safety and prosperity disrupted by persecution, brutal oppression, murder, and expulsion or exile for the surviving remnant to a strange land where the cycle begins again. Thus Grace Paley tells of her mother in the 1930s commenting on Hitler's rise to power: "It's coming again."[5] *Again* says it all.

In the U.S. much of the bias against Jews has been mitigated by the development of some institutionalized Jewish power, most notably in the areas of education, science, media, and some sectors of business. This should be a cause for celebration. Yet this undeniable success is often used against us, as evidence of our excessive control, power, and greed. We recognize this "evidence" as the toppling domino, shoving us—we fear—from the calm and sometimes prosperous phase of the cycle into danger and chaos.

There are other brakes on celebration. Jewish success—like any other U.S. success—has been achieved inside a severe class structure. Add to this the painful fact that Jews, like many other ethnic and racial minorities in the U.S., have benefitted in concrete ways from racism against Black people.[6]

In Europe the Jews who survived (a weighty reminder, most did not) are still Jews, while in the U.S. we are often, even to the Christian mainstream, white.

This benefit is something like that "enjoyed" by the conventionally feminine-looking lesbian vis-à-vis the stone butch; or by the unaccented-English-speaking Chicana with lighter skin. That is, Jews benefit from not looking Jewish.[7] Think about common response to the ultra-orthodox Hasidic Jews, who dress and look the way all Jews in Europe would have looked throughout the Middle Ages until the 18th and 19th centuries. Physically identifiable, the unassimilated Hasidim are magnets for anti-Semitism. Similarly, anti-Semitic graffiti, vandalism, and even bombing of synagogues demonstrates that identifiable Jewish places are also vulnerable.

That many—by no means all—Jews walk safely down the streets of North America because our Jewishness is not visible is a fact, but not necessarily a comforting one. Many of us would prefer to be both visible and safe. What must be understood is the cost of this passage, the danger of Jewish visibility, the double edge of whatever power Jews manifest, and the peculiar Jewish condition of never knowing exactly what point of the calm-chaos cycle we've reached at any given moment.[8] *Is it coming again?*

Often christians—the national majority, whether people are churchgoing or not—see Judaism only as a religion, and thus consider anti-Semitism as simple religious bias. This ignores both Jewish history and the meaning of Jewish identity. Christianity defines itself as a religion anyone can embrace through belief, an individualistic religion separate from peoplehood and culture.

But Jewishness is a fiercely collective endeavor, a culture/peoplehood/religion: one need not believe in god, but one is hard put to be a Jew without Jewish community. Until the 19th century a separation between Jewish identity, culture, and religion was not even imagined. As Jews in Europe confronted the modern world, they developed separate strands of Jewishness, including not only a diverse religious practice with various degrees of observance, but also an adamantly secular cultural Jewishness which, over time, evolved into two distinct aspects: one, socialist *yidishkayt*[9] (Yiddish culture), by now terribly diminished by the European Holocaust on one hand and the pressure of American assimilation on the other; and socialist Zionism, which animated most of the founders of Israel. (Some would argue that communism represented a third aspect, its Jewishness hidden even from itself.)

Progressives who believe in self-definition need to hear that Jews define ourselves as a people. We have been persecuted for this, we have resisted our persecution, clinging to our Jewishness in a variety of ways. Even this diversity of resistance and self-definition is characteristically Jewish.

At this point a question seems inevitable. I have seen progressives absorb eagerly the information that Native Americans, for example, do not separate the strands of culture, religion, history, spirituality. Such a holistic approach is embraced—indeed, cannibalized—by many feminists. Why is it so hard to grasp that Jews are a people? Why, among progressives committed to fighting other forms of oppression, is there often a reluctance to take anti-Semitism seriously?

Let me suggest three reasons, based in suspicion, fear, resentment, and sometimes anti-Semitism:

—that Jews, in a burst of victim-competition, will deny both responsibility for racism and privileges derived from it;

—that Jews will take up too much of the still-inadequate space/ resources only recently available to people of color;[10]

—that recognizing Jewishness as a peoplehood will mean somehow legitimating Jewish national aspiration.[11]

A fourth reason—and I believe it is the primary reason—brings me to the subject of class. Anti-Semitism—Jewhating—is not taken seriously because it hasn't kept Jews poor.

## Class and the Black-Jewish Question

Class and race are not identical constructs. Yet the connection between them is intricate and sturdy in a country founded on twin poles of Native American genocide and African enslavement, in which profit and exploitation, wealth and poverty have all been justified by racist ideology. Today, Black children

are far more likely to be born into devastating conditions of poverty than they were five years ago. They are twice as likely as white children to die in the first year of their lives, and they are three times as likely as whites to be misplaced in classes for the educable mentally retarded. Afro-American children are twice as likely as white children to have no parent employed, to be unemployed as teenagers, and to live in substandard housing. They are three times as likely as whites to have their mothers die in childbirth. Moreover, those between the ages of fifteen and nineteen are four times as likely as white children to be incarcerated in jails and prisons.[12]

To describe the conditions of growth for a people's children is to describe the people's future. As the proportion of homeless women with children increases—and in New York City, for example, 90% of the homeless are people of color—this will only get worse. The African American future projected only from the present, without change, is bleak; and it is dramatically different from the Jewish American future, projected also without change. This difference must be confronted because it—class—is at the heart of "the Black-Jewish Question."

Yet often race is assumed to determine class automatically. Other aspects of racism—cultural erasure, assimilation, linguistic loss, self-hate, just to name a few—are ignored. Nor, except for patronizing romanticization, are strengths of ethnic or racial minorities acknowledged. Most people in the U.S. are groomed to ignorance about class structure and class oppression: "middle class" means "normal," "not a failure."

But look, for example, at the rural white poor in New England or Appalachia; at class structure among Chicana/os in New Mexico; at the relative financial success of Japanese and Koreans in the U.S. versus the extreme poverty of recent immigrants from Southeast Asia; or at class differences between Barbadian immigrants and African Americans. Look at the complex yet common mix of class inside a heterosexual relationship/marriage where more than twenty years after the explosion of second-wave feminism, the woman still earns 60 cents to the man's dollar, and economic survival depends on what a working couple can earn—even though more and more women of all races and ethnicities are raising children without male support.[13] With all this in mind, we probably recognize that class and race are related but separate, intersecting categories.

But in general people don't look this carefully. And when the related but distinct issues of race and class are fuzzed and confused, this in turn confuses the meaning and danger of anti-Semitism. The dominant culture represents rich WASPS as normal, while rendering poor WASPS and other poor whites as invisible. People of color are depicted as unemployed and on welfare, or inherently suited for the most menial, worst paying jobs, with the exception of some Asians, who are characterized as evil, sneaky, clever, clannish, and good with money (similar to the Jews in this, and in their children's diabolically excellent performance in school).

And Jews: everyone knows about the upward mobility of most Jews into the middle echelons, positioned visibly in cities as teachers, social workers, and managers, thus able to exert some control over the lives of many poor people, including many Blacks. Commonly overlooked is the fact that most economically secure, privileged Jews are men or are affiliated with men; that many old Jews and Jewish women, especially single mothers, are poor; that Jews endure about the same rate of poverty as other immigrant groups who came to the U.S. at the same time, most of whom are white.

But myth looms larger than reality, and according to the myth, not only is anti-Semitism an entirely different animal from racism, anti-Semitism is trivial, and those who complain about it are overprivileged whiners. Indeed, once Jews are defined as "the rich," then healthy and essential class antagonism distorts into anti-Semitism—a phenomenon August Bebel observed in Europe many years ago: *anti-Semitism is the socialism of fools,* he said, but the foolishness pops up at regular intervals, and is even sometimes defended by supposed progressives. Witness populist anti-Semitism, from the Russian Revolution, where some Bolsheviks encouraged anti-Semitism as a form of class rebellion, to those farmers in the Midwest who blame foreclosure on the Jews, to some followers of the Nation of Islam, who hold Jews responsible for all evil.

This is not to say that anti-Semitism is caused by capitalism (anti-Semitism's vigor in the socialist world is evidence enough of deeper roots). It is, however, convenient: hate Jews and don't examine the structure of property. In a word, anti-Semitism protects christian wealth. As economic straits tighten for many, history teaches us to expect a rise in anti-Semitism, as well as racism.

Why does it matter that anti-Semitism be understood in a context of white supremacy? Angela Davis has pointed out that, when she was growing up in Birmingham, around the same time as the Black church was bombed and four young girls murdered, a synagogue was also bombed.[14] White supremacists believe that Blacks and Jews—as well as many other peoples—are inferior, and threaten racial purity. They hate us both. Failure to grasp this commonality separates us in the face of shared and serious danger, from violent skinheads active in 31 states, Aryan Nation, neo-Nazis, the Klan, and other white supremacists. In addition, as the center of U.S. politics continues to move right, African Americans and most Jews—progressives, women, the poor, gays, and the old—face continued, mutual, grave setbacks from a reactionary activist Supreme Court.

Failure to understand the deep connection between anti-Semitism and white racism can lead Jews to overlook the relationship between Jewish survival and the survival of other marginalized peoples. I have heard Jews say, "She's one of those Jews who always stands up for the Blacks but never for the Jews." They may be describing a real phenomenon, the self-hating barely-identified Jew who cares about everyone's struggle but her own. Or, looking at someone who cares deeply about racism, they may assume that she can't care about both. Such is the polarization that African Americans, too, may be accused of kowtowing to Jews, or to whites; of being Uncle Toms, if they object to anti-Semitism. As though we can't care about each other. As though we need not care about each other.

The failure to connect and analyze these oppressions diminishes our ability to challenge and transform society. It means that class, as usual in American politics, is obscured, blocking the possibilities of alliances among people of color who are poor and those who are not but whose lives are threatened by racism; among Jews who are poor and those who are not but whose lives are endangered or constrained by anti-Semitism; and among whites who are poor, even though their lives are not menaced by race-hate. Add lesbians and gays, threatened by homophobia, and women, sick of sexism (with its economic, social and legal manifestations) and we have the possibility of a majority coalition.

As we move towards the 21st century with the hope of a vibrant multi-racial left in which African Americans figure prominently, as leaders and as the nation's most predictably progressive constituency, a failure to grasp the relationship between anti-Semitism, racism, class, sexism and homophobia will constitute an extraordinary, missed opportunity at a critical historical moment.

## The Black-Jewish Split?

To summarize: when it comes to Jewish-Black relations, some of what stands between us is class. But this is not what gets talked about. What gets talked about is Black anti-Semitism and Jewish racism.

I do not minimize these realities. Two almost random examples:

—Steven Cokely, a Black aide of appointed Mayor Sawyer in Chicago who claimed that Jewish doctors are giving AIDS to Black people;

—ZBT, a mostly Jewish fraternity at the University of Wisconsin, Madison, which held a slave auction in which pledges wore blackface and Afro wigs.

But Black anti-Semitism is a subdivision of *American* anti-Semitism, or christian anti-Semitism, or sometimes Islamic anti-Semitism. Jewish racism is a brand of *American* racism, or white racism, or sometimes European racism. The Cokely incident is symbolic of the struggle for power in Chicago city politics following the death of that compelling unifier, Harold Washington. The fraternity incident epitomizes campus backlash, validated by people like Allan Bloom with their great white male books. Neither Black anti-Semitism nor Jewish racism is so special in itself, although both are specially destructive in their implications.

Look at Cokely's bizarre accusation. I am not one who believes in group paranoia; I believe in the fundamental soundness of suspicion and fear. I know that the U.S. tests products on people of color in third world countries. I know food and drugs deemed unsafe here are marketed abroad. I read in the paper recently about a doctor in Dayton, Ohio, who for years performed unnecessary experimental surgery on the sexual organs of hundreds of women without their prior knowledge or consent, and dozens of other doctors knew and did nothing.

So when Steven Cokely claims that Jewish doctors are deliberately inoculating Black people with AIDS, what stands out is, first, a real fear (whether Cokely's or the Black community's, where that fear resonated) that Blacks will be killed or experimented on in deadly ways; and, second, Jews are being scapegoated for this fear.

Similarly, when a Black priest, Rev. Lawrence Lucas, at a recent New York City rally, attacked Jews as "those who are killing us in the classroom...look at the Board of Education...it looks like the Knesset in Israel,"[15] he underscored two points: first, the New York City school system, in which many Jews are employed, is desperately not meeting the needs of Black children; and, second, Jews are being scapegoated for this failure.

There is a third point: media exacerbation of tension. Lots of discussion of the Black-Jewish conflict, but it boils down to the same old rehash of incidents—like the mall bookstores with 10,000 books, only it's 10 different titles, 1000 copies of each.[16] Mainstream media lead the way, but both Jewish and

Black newspapers and radio stations have learned to headline and exaggerate points of tension as a way to sell papers and increase their audience.

How familiar, for example, is the name Albert Raby? He died in 1988, 55 years old. He was the organizer who brought Dr. King to Chicago; he ran Harold Washington's successful campaign in which Jews and Blacks worked together to elect Chicago's first Black mayor; he was co-chair of a group of Blacks and Jews formed to deal with the wake of Cokely's remark. Albert Raby was an important man in the history of Black struggle, of Chicago, of Black-Jewish relations, and how many people have heard of him, compared to another Chicagoan, Louis Farrakhan? For that matter, you'd think from what mainstream and Jewish media reported about Farrakhan that his popularity among African Americans is completely due to the anti-Semitic remarks which those media used to make him nationally famous. Few commentators were analytical or even interested enough to notice the aspirations of African Americans which Louis Farrakhan expressed—of Black autonomy and self-respect, for example—or to examine the relationship between nationalism, isolationism, and anti-Semitism.

Or, think of the difference in attention, the way the media lovingly dwelled on details of conflict between Jesse Jackson and the Jews, downplayed all Jackson's attempts at reconciliation, and only briefly reacted to the news about Bush's 1988 campaign being packed with Nazis. This smacks of a double standard.

## Stereotypes

I want to talk about basic stereotypes, the ones that make me intensely nervous even to name because of how they have been used by gentiles against Jews and by whites against African Americans: the Jewish Landlord and the Black Rapist. In these stereotypes, Jews are rich and Blacks are violent.

Historically these stereotypes have emerged in very different ways. The Jewish Landlord originated in a grain of truth, in neighborhoods where some Jews retained stores and houses after they'd moved away—houses where Blacks lived, stores where Blacks bought. The Black Rapist, on the other hand, originated in the white South's fantasy and propaganda machine. I can't imagine a southern Black man with his mind intact would have raped a white woman, given the danger of such an act, but the myth of the Black rapist served to terrorize and lynch Black men; to constrain white women; and to oppress Black women by making their particular vulnerability to white male sexual abuse invisible and unspeakable.[17]

Any economic analyst can tell you most owners aren't Jewish. Any woman can tell you: *any* man walking behind her on an otherwise empty street might be a rapist. But stereotypes have a powerful life of their own. The landlord, symbol of privilege and exploitation, stands in for all who make money, hoard money, live at the expense of others. And Jews in an anti-Semitic society are peculiarly associated with money. Perfect.

The rapist, symbol of urban violence, stands in for all who disrupt and terrorize innocent people. And Blacks in a racist culture are peculiarly associated with both sex and violence. Perfect.

It's revealing that the Black rapist is always thought of as raping white women, since this assumption ignores statistics, which show that Black rapists mostly rape Black women, and white rapists mostly rape white women. Rapists choose women to rape based on accessibility, and on whether they—the rapists—think they can get away with it.

So why is the rape victim in this myth white? Because she symbolizes white men's property, sexualized to avoid the awkward facts of economic inequity. (Her whiteness, his blackness also cleverly conceal the essentially patriarchal nature of violence against women.) The concern is not with any woman's safety but with Black men's theft of white men's property.

So as landlords stand in for all exploitative owners, those who make money, rapists stand in for all thieves, muggers, those who steal money: the have-nots, the clamorous underclass which perpetually threatens the haves.

You see where these stereotypes connect fundamentally with class. If the problem is Jewish greed and power, if the problem is Black immorality, then capitalism itself is not the problem. So let me say clearly: capitalism *is* a problem, and "The Black-Jewish Question" will be posed as long as there are economically privileged and economically oppressed peoples.

I could spend a lot of energy on why it's unfair that the abuses of capitalism be blamed on Jews. It is unfair. But for Jews to combat the anger's manifestation without also combatting the anger's cause—economic injustice and cruelty—is likewise unfair. I also believe it's stupid and destructive.

The landlord and the rapist, the Jew and the Black, are men. Where are the women? Anyone who pays attention to the disturbing upsurge of hate incidents on college campuses will have noticed an increased number of attacks on Jewish women under the rubric of JAP, that favorite laugh for Jewish male comics. The Jewish American Princess is the contemporary version of the Jewish mother, who at least was nurturing, while the Jewish American Princess does nothing but nag and consume—this at a time when Jewish women, like other women, are working outside the home in unprecedented numbers.

Inside the Jewish community, the JAP epithet is clearly backlash material used by men who seem not to understand or care that the term is not only sexist (and racist against Japanese people), but also anti-Semitic. Outside the Jewish community, the "Jewish American Princess" attracts anti-Semitism, and takes the rap for capitalist consumption. She is the scapegoat on college campuses, signs proclaim *No JAPS Allowed Here*; crowds of students at football games point and chant *JAP JAP JAP* when a woman perceived as fitting the (over-privileged, thus Jewish) stereotype walks by; *SLAP A JAP* is a popular slogan, revived from World War II propaganda. Beyond the campus, in one instance in Arizona, a woman's husband murdered her and was acquitted on a "JAP defense" presented by the same psychiatrist whose expert "Twinkies defense" got off Dan White, murderer of Harvey Milk and George Moscone.

Looking at the African American community from my perspective as a Jewish feminist, I see similarities and striking differences. I see the respected image of the matriarch challenged by whites like Pat Moynihan, who irrationally blamed Black women's strength for undermining Black manhood and the Black family, instead of honoring this strength for its contributions to Black survival. Some Black men, too, have accepted white definitions of maleness that include male domination of women.[18] I see some backlash against assertive women (though not on the scale of the Jewish male backlash). Take Alice Walker, who has got to be the most generous person on the face of the earth, in her persistent belief that practically everybody has the capacity to change. She has been attacked as castrating and hateful toward Black men because she writes about father-daughter incest, battering, and—god forbid—lesbian love. In both communities feminism is often depicted as an outsider plot, splitting the Jewish or Black community in an unnatural way. Black women and men both have expressed criticism of a limited feminism that has too often belittled race and class issues and the need for solidarity between Black women and men. But in both communities male privilege and homophobia have interfered with women acting in their own interest.

In the dominant culture, when white male politicians stop chiding "The Black Matriarch" they and their backlash constituency blame "The Black Welfare Mother" for sucking the country dry. Though "most single Black mothers are the working poor," though over half of all families headed by Black women are over the poverty line,[19] the Black woman continues to be stereotyped as helplessly poverty stricken; she is then not only blamed for her poverty, she is also scapegoated for many of the nation's, and especially the cities', problems. It's her fault taxes are high, (forget the defense budget). She's sexually irresponsible (i.e., only white middle class women should reproduce). She brings up her kids wrong (rotten schools/health care/housing, lack of employment opportunities and the sea of drugs have no relation to problem adolescents; and never mind that it's she and her children who are most ravaged by urban crime). She doesn't understand protein (a charge which ignores both the difficulties of feeding a family adequately on food stamps or a poverty income, and the amazing resourcefulness of many poor women who manage on so little). Mainstream political analysts—white men—blame her for her strength—it makes her man feel unmanly (it never occurs to them that some men might welcome strength and partnership in women)—and for her vulnerability—they claim she's unable to control her children or teach them to escape her poverty. They file her away as the archetypal Black, who spoils Western civilization, and the archetypal female, who spoils her children. They portray her as the passive version of the rapist/mugger (he takes money, she spends money not her own), and as the impoverished version of the Jewish American Princess (she's a parasite who does nothing but consume, the main difference being she can't consume very much).

But we—Jewish and Black women—are not parasites. We do not exist within the parameters of mainstream male definitions, or even within the limits prescribed by men of our own communities. As Jewish and Black women meet, talk honestly about our differences, and entertain possibilities of cooperation; I believe that we—and many other marginalized women—can clarify significant differences, as well as similarities that can help us learn from and support one another: issues such as dual allegiance, to women and to the home culture; women controlling our own bodies versus pressure, grounded in historical reality, to repopulate our decimated peoples; accusations of manhating when we challenge our community's sexism; women raising children alone; the role of the family as an instrument of survival and exploitation; lesbians and our home families; transmitting and transforming the culture, and on and on.

## Women as Solution

Which brings me to women as potential sources of solutions. Flareups on many college campuses—often when a Black student group invites a speaker known for anti-Semitism, such as Farrakhan or Kwame Toure (the former Stokely Carmichael)—have usually resulted in Jews and Blacks denouncing one another as unspeakably disgusting. These unproductive inflammatory posturings are to nobody's surprise, mostly male. Jewish and Black women students, spoken to privately and directly, allow the conflicting authentic issues—Jewish fear, Black autonomy—to emerge with clarity. They say things like, *I was scared* and *They can't tell us who to listen to.* They ask, *Why don't they understand our pain?* and *Why do they assume we're stupid?* They show a refreshing and optimistic grasp of process: *This anger is part of how we learn.*

Instead of being shocked by these bursts of anger, we should expect conflicts to erupt, and create opportunities for dialogue, hearing grievances, and developing working relationships which will allow us to use these conflicts positively: to recognize, assess, and begin to bridge our distance. Here are some useful principles: avoid confrontational tactics, when possible. Respect group solidarity; never try to pit Black against Black, Jew against Jew. Talk among your own people. Find those you know and trust among the others, and talk in intimate conversations and small groups. Don't try to make nice. Tolerate ambiguity.[20]

The women's movement is ahead of the mixed left in communication between Jews and Blacks, for a couple of reasons. First, because our socialization has trained many of us to heed the human cost of abstractions, to see one another also as people. Second, the women's movement is a mass movement. Amorphous and not always full-bodied in its analysis, it has changed the lives of millions of women—and men—and brought women from many different communities into contact with one another. There is barely a city in this nation that does not have explicit women's activities taking place. Any of us who speak on feminist issues or teach returning women students or women's studies classes know that women are discovering feminism every day, and the impact is as fresh as the day it was born. (What's different is that there aren't easy political channels for new feminist insight.) And wherever there is feminism, there is at least a theoretical commitment to combat racism. Attention to Jewishness has been slower coming, but it is coming.

There's another aspect to this scenario. Lesbians have always formed a disproportionately high number of cross-class, cross-race, cross-culture relationships. Often these relationships retain familial status even after breaking up.

Many of us also maintain very close ties with our home communities, so that our cross-cultural relationships spin out into networks, family connections, in-laws, children, and inside these relationships much pain is felt raw. For many lesbians, dealing positively with Black-Jewish tension is not abstractly desirable but concretely necessary. (This is also true for Jewish women who are raising children of color, either adopted or mixed-race birth children.)

It's not surprising that some of the most hopeful developments in Black-Jewish relations have been among feminists and lesbian feminists. The impetus has come more strongly from the Jews, not because we're better but because we're more scared of being excluded, a classic Jewish fear and a realistic one. Progressive Jews know we need Blacks; many Blacks are wary of political alliances with any whites, including Jews, and instead focus on developing self-sufficiency or alliances with other people of color. Nevertheless, out of conflicts in the women's movement have come dozens of dialogue groups, coalitions, and various attempts to work through some of these issues.

But much remains to be done. The usual approach has been to put together a panel of male leaders to swear good faith. Feminists working in the Jewish community need to approach the problem from the source of the division, and insist on leadership from those Jews who share concerns with members of the Black community—namely, women, seniors, and gays. This means Jewish men have to step back and listen to the concerns of the whole Jewish community, not just the part that's comfortable for or visible to them. Healing the Black-Jewish split will also challenge the hierarchy and sexism of the Jewish community, including the progressive Jewish community.

What will a common agenda look like? It will be a long list including: medical care, day care, decent employment, guaranteed annual income, housing, affirmative action (all this talk of Jews opposing affirmative action, when Jewish women have always supported it), reproductive rights, protection for sexual preference, AIDS research and treatment, prevention of violence against women, urban safety, sensible foreign policy (no intervention on the side of repressive governments, foreign aid a right of developing nations), anti-hate legislation, separation of church and state, and a strong education platform—from public schools through college, including multi-cultural, multilingual education.[21]

Though priorities and emphases may differ, let us recognize, in the toxic wasteland of the nineties, how much common ground we share; certainly enough to begin the necessary struggles.

## Solidarity

The Jewish-Black split will not be healed as long as class divisions remain so stark in American society. Many African Americans will regard Jews mistrustfully, through a lens of class bitterness, and many Jews will regard African Americans mistrustfully, through a lens of class protectionism. That understood, what is needed?

Jews need to articulate strongly a pro-Jewish, anti-racist position addressing not just our common ground of discrimination and race hate but our not-so-common ground of economic inequities. Many Jews who are working against racism and on various progressive issues are invisible as Jews, and we need to identify ourselves clearly. We need to develop working relationships, respect and trust inside the Jewish community. A very connected part of this work is building Jewish pride and solidarity.[22]

Jewish visibility is critical when it comes to the issue of South Africa. The battle against apartheid is, of course, close to the heart of the Black community, and Israel's relationship with South Africa is a sore point in Black-Jewish relations. We need to correct inaccuracies in the common view—Israel is hardly alone in trading with South Africa—but without defensiveness. We need to publicize that the Israeli left, like the left here, is working on sanctions against South Africa. We need to name as Jews those Jewish South Africans who have fought and continue to fight apartheid: people like Ruth First, Nadine Gordimer, Abie Nathan, Albie Sachs, Helen Suzman, Janet Levine, and a South African organization called *Jews for Justice*. We need to voice our opposition to apartheid as Jews.[23]

Jewish visibility is also critical when it comes to the Israeli-Palestinian conflict. Many Blacks identify with the Palestinians, because the Palestinians are oppressed economically, culturally, violently by a Euro-dominant government which does not represent them; I imagine that this feels familiar. (Though most Israeli Jews are people of color, the elite and empowered are disproportionately Ashkenazi, and Palestinians are, of course, systematically disempowered.) We need to remind all our comrades that people are not the same as their government and point to the half of Israel that would trade land for peace. It is the left's crime to have forgotten this wisdom, to have ignored the Israeli peace movement and the growing force of progressive Jews in this country. Most people—Jews, Blacks, and everyone else—simply do not know what is going on in Israel. They do not know about the near-identical agendas of the Palestinian people and the Israeli peace camp, or about cooperation between Israelis and Palestinians, especially the women.[24] This information is crucial to prevent polarization.

Finally, Jews should welcome opportunities to work with African Americans in support of many of these issues. Often this will mean welcoming leadership from African Americans, which is itself an opportunity to relearn some of what Jews have learned badly: to develop new relationships, as peers.

I have spoken of what Jews need to do. That I do not presume to advise African Americans does not mean I think the work is all on the Jewish side. I would like to ask African Americans to meet Jews on our common agendas. To recognize that people—including Blacks and Jews—have always been drawn to progressive politics not only out of direst need but also out of longing for community and justice. To hold Jews accountable for our actions, but not to scapegoat us for the crimes of capitalism and racism. I would like to ask African Americans to grasp the history of Jewish persecution, including the Holocaust, as Jews must grasp the history of African persecution, including enslavement. I would like both peoples to realize that the other's history/culture/identity is not only about victimization and suffering, but is also a source of enormous pride, joy, and strength.

When African Americans point to the impoverishment and exploitation of their people, the throwaway attitude of those in power towards their people's lives, Jews must vow not only to fight white supremacy, which threatens Jews as well as Blacks, and the racism which specifically targets Black Americans; we must also vow to dismantle the class structure which insists that someone suffer. When Jews point to the brutal swings of history, African Americans must vow to take anti-Semitism seriously. I want to acknowledge the many Blacks in every community in this nation who do take anti-Semitism seriously, and who oppose it. I believe that as strong representative coalitions against hate groups and for economic and social justice develop, Jews must and will be included, and all our grasp of the complexities of oppression and resistance will strengthen.

A character in a story of mine, revisiting the New York subway, muses, "Today I'm here in Hymietown as Jesse Jackson was stupid enough to call it and never be forgiven for by people every one of whom had heard *schwartze* once in her or his life without protest."25 The time for self-righteousness is over.

But what will pull us together is not an easy, instant trust. Nor is it nostalgia for the falsely golden Thirties or Sixties, when African Americans and Jews worked together with serious, often unacknowledged racism and tension.[26] We need honesty. We need a relationship of equals. We need to feel our frail/sturdy human hearts outraged by injustice and committed to generosity. The time for solidarity is, I hope, beginning.

## NOTES

I want to thank Lisa Weissbach, Ehrai Adams, and others at Oberlin College, for discussion of some of these issues and for their openness and thoughtful responses. More recently, I'm indebted to Jayna Brown, Lisa Hall, and Chris Lymbertos for challenging editorial suggestions. Responsibility for the opinions and analysis is mine alone.

1. Tim Rutten in *The New York Review,* June 11, 1992.

2. Henry Louis Gates Jr., summarizing a popular Afrocentric text which stigmatizes Jews as particularly racist, Michael Bradley's *The Iceman Inheritance: Prehistoric Sources of Western Man's Racism, Sexism, and Aggression;* in "Black Demagogues, and Pseudo-Scholars," NY Times, Op-Ed page, July 20, 1992.

3. It bears repeating that most Jews from the Middle East, India, Latin America, Turkey, Ethiopia and elsewhere are, by definition, people of color. Of course many Ashkenazi Jews are also dark-skinned.

In the 1988 election, among the less than half of those eligible to vote, who bothered to do so, Blacks led in voting progressive; Hispanics second and Jews third. About two-thirds of Jews chose the Democrats, voting in many cases against their economic self-interest. While Blacks have replaced Jews as predictably progressive leaders (see, for example, the voting record of the Congressional Black Caucus), Jews have not turned conservative at the same rate as their immigrant cohorts.

4. Gates (note 2) mentions the Nation of Islam's publication *The Secret Relationship between Blacks and Jews,* which distorts historical fact to charge the Jews with primary responsibility for the crime of slavery. Gerald Sorin, Director of Jewish Studies and Professor of American History at SUNY New Paltz, made a similar point in his presentation on the minor role of Jews in the slave trade at a forum organized by Jews for Racial and Economic Justice in New York City, *Jews and Slavery: Participation and Resistance,* April 8, 1992.

5. Grace Paley, "Now and Then," *Tikkun* (May/June 1989), p.76. In particular, European medieval and Renaissance history from a Jewish perspective reads like a disaster chronicle: expelled from here, massacred there, forced conversions someplace else. Occasionally there is a bright spot: "Jews return to Worms" (from which they had been expelled the year before). "Jews allowed to settle in England" (from which they had been expelled some centuries earlier). The late nineteenth early twentieth century, especially in Eastern Europe, presents a similar wave of persecution, dwarfed only by the magnitude of what followed. Grievous official and unofficial oppression of Jews was a common feature of modern pre-Holocaust Europe.

6. For a fuller discussion of these issues, see "To Be a Radical Jew...."

7. Jews who could pass as gentile, because they looked less Jewish and could speak the dominant language fluently, were more likely to survive the various swings of anti-Semitism. Thus to tell some survivors of the European Holocaust who may have survived by passing "you don't look Jewish" is to twist a painful truth; had the person looked more Jewish, s/he would probably be dead.

8. I do not mean to claim a new and special status of victimization of uncertainty, which may even look appealing to those who face the relative certainty of extreme poverty, high infant mortality, etc.

9. See Irena Klepfisz, "Secular Jewish Identity: Yidishkayt in America," in *The Tribe of Dina: A Jewish Women's Anthology* , pp.32-50.

10. This fear is fed by the anti-Semitic notion that Jews already have way too much, and the familiar scapegoating stance that the scarcity of resources is the Jews' fault. Even recognizing those areas where Jews have flourished, the point is that we need to expand the space for all of us who don't conform to the dominant culture's norms. For example: a white gentile woman at the opening plenary session of a conference remarks on the creation of a Holocaust museum and on the lack of similar memorials for the genocide against the indigenous people of the Americas, and the Africans who died in the Middle Passage. A legitimate observation. But she then asks the Jews at the conference to explain why they created one and not the others. As though Jews by commemorating the Holocaust were acting illegitimately, or *against* the sufferings of others. As though Jews were more responsible for gathering resources to create memorials for other genocides than white gentiles who had no extermination of their own to commemorate.

11. Surely the century of Armenian genocide and *Deutschland Über Alles*—not to mention contemporary Eastern Europe and Germany—has witnessed other dangers of nationalism besides Zionism.

12. From the "Children's Defense Fund, Black and White Children: The Key Facts" (1985), pp.1-2, quoted in Angela Davis, "Slaying The Dream," in *Women, Culture & Politics* (NY: Random House, 1989), p.74. The major report, "A Common Destiny: Blacks and American Society," has found, according to Gerald Jaynes, the study's director, that "the status of blacks relative to whites has stagnated or regressed since the early 1970s" (Julie Johnson, "Blacks Found Lagging Despite Gains," *New York Times* [July 28, 1989], p.A6). The report is available for an ironically steep $35 from National Academy Press, 2101 Constitution Avenue NW, Washington, DC 20418.

13. See Barbara Omolade, "It's a Family Affair: The Real Lives of Black Single Mothers," *Freedom Organizing Series #4 Pamphlet* (Latham, NY: Kitchen Table/Women of Color Press, 1986). Omolade's lucid discussion highlights not only the difficulties but the strengths and survival strategies of Black women raising children without male support; strategies which challenge the norm of the patriarchal family.

14. Angela Davis, plenary speech, *Parallels & Intersections: Conference on Racism and Other Forms of Oppression*, Iowa City (April 9, 1989).

15. At a rally held outside the Board of Education, December 28, 1987; see *Jewish Currents* (February, 1988), p.30.

16. See Cherie Brown's appalling anecdote about a CBS news segment on Blacks and Jews; producers insistently focused only on negative findings and ignored efforts at cooperation, *Tikkun* (July/August, 1989), pp.88-9.

17. See Angela Davis, "Violence Against Women and the Ongoing Challenge to Racism," *Freedom Organizing Series #5 Pamphlet* (Latham, NY: Kitchen Table/Women of Color Press, 1985); revised and reprinted as "We Do Not Consent: Violence Against Women in a Racist Society," in *WCP* (note 9), pp.35-52.

18. Many Jewish sons of the immigrant generation—in which the power and strength of Jewish women were critical to Jewish survival—sought assimilation into American patriarchal culture including their right to dominate their women. This is also a class issue. Poor people need every member of the community to be strong. Middle-class men, and those who aspire to middle-class status, often see male dominance as part and parcel of male/middle-class privilege.

19. As Barbara Omolade (note 10) points out, though a majority of Black single mothers receive some public assistance, a much smaller number are supported by welfare alone: "Most Black single mothers are the working poor." Further, she notes, "If nearly half of all families headed by Black women have incomes below the poverty line...then over half do not," p.4.

20. If these sound like rules for intimate relationships, this is no accident. What we build will depend on how much trust we can create. See Cherie Brown (note 14) for a description of powerful coalition building workshops between Jews and Blacks.

21. Like many Jews, I was educated through the free City College system. It is a disgrace that this option no longer exists, and that the percentage of African American college students, after an upward surge, is decreasing; that after some economic and social gains, the conditions of African Americans' lives are getting worse. See Johnson (note 8).

22. I recommend for all Jewish feminists engaged in this work "*In gerangl/*In struggle: A Handbook for Recognizing and Resisting Anti-Semitism and for Building Jewish Identity and Pride," by Melanie Kaye/Kantrowitz, Irena Klepfisz, with Bernice Mennis, in *The Tribe of Dina* (note 5), pp.334-346. See also Cornel West's Black left perspective on identity, "Beyond Rootless Universalism and Ethnic Chauvinism," *Tikkun* (July/August, 1989), pp.95-97.

23. Jews for Racial and Economic Justice in New York was founded in 1990 initially to offer Nelson Mandela (just released from prison) a visibly Jewish welcome to New York.

24. See "I've Been to Israel & to Palestine."

25. *schwartze*, Yiddish for Black (often pejorative); from "Some Pieces of Jewish Left," in *My Jewish Face & Other Stories* (San Francisco: Aunt Lute Books, 1990), p. 208.

26. See Jonathan Kaufman, *Broken Alliance: The Turbulent Times Between Blacks and Jews in America* (1988) for an intelligent discussion of the Black-Jewish alliance from the fifties to the present.

# We Are the Only Adults

(An earlier version of this essay was originally presented as the keynote address at the New Jewish Agenda Regional West Coast Conference in Portland, Oregon, June, 1990.)

## MAKING CHANGE, KEEPING BALANCE AND
## PROGRESSIVE JEWISH POLITICS FOR THE LONG HAUL

### Making Change

All through the 1980s I'd hear echoes of T.S. Eliot's poem "The Hollow Men":

*This is the way the world ends*
*this is the way the world ends*
*this is the way the world ends*
*not with a bang but a whimper.*

Whimper of environmental disaster. Erosion of hard-won gains. Fragmentation of mass movements. But the eighties are over. We don't yet know what the nineties will bring, but clearly something is happening which demands something new from us.

We're all thinking about this. The *intifada,* and the cooperation between the peace camp Israelis and Palestinians, especially the women; Tienanmen Square. The bizarre events of Eastern Europe, and the Soviet Union, remind us of a basic, forgotten principle: vast unity across broad lines can challenge the very core of power. (The rise in ethnic chauvinism also reminds us—as do graveyard desecrations in Western Europe; if you can't find a live Jew, defile a dead one—of the longevity of anti-Semitism). The possibilities of breakthrough in South Africa contribute to our sense that what seemed frozen, impossible to budge, is not impervious to change.

At home, things are less positive. Especially disturbing is the bland acceptance of people without places to live, and the upsurge in hate crimes of all kinds. Our society continues to fall apart in ways too many to name here, and besides we know all this. I want, though, to underscore a few things. I see feminists who'd gotten a little casual or distracted or involved with everyone else's issues now experiencing intense threat: on the one hand, the assault on choice; on the other, the explicitly anti-feminist murder of the fourteen women in Montreal—never mind that this is a fraction of the number of women killed each year—crystallized something for many of us. We are not even a little safe. And women are mobilizing in response.

I see the militant and creative AIDS activists, ACT UP, QUEER NATION. The Helms assault on lesbian and gay artists and, in response, the revitalization and transformation of the lesbian and gay movement. In both areas, women and men are pulling together.

And I see the students acting up. Having begun with anti-apartheid work, campuses are coming alive. At UC Santa Cruz, they're demanding ethnic studies (and the Jewish students who are part of that coalition are beginning to talk about the need for Jewish studies). At Mills College, in Oakland, their slogan to protect their women's college was no accident: *Keep The Choice.* At CCNY, my alma mater, students sit in to protest tuition increases and the dearth of people of color among the faculty. Derrick Bell, one of the luminaries of Harvard Law School, announced his decision to take an unpaid leave until Harvard hires an African American woman with tenure, admitting with commendable honesty that he, as a Black man, could not pretend any longer to serve as a role model for Black women.[1]

In short, things are in motion. Grace Paley has said, when people stand up, other people discover they've got legs. While there are limits to this kind of analogy (not everyone can stand, or has legs for that matter), the motion is unmistakeable.

So a great deal of change is taking place and the question is how to position ourselves, channel the changes, keep our balance when the ground is shifting. Most left politics in the eighties have been piecemeal, fragmented. What we are beginning to see glimmers of, and what we must see operating in full force if there is to be a human future—not to be melodramatic, but given the level of environmental disaster, this is our last best shot—is more and more unity across our differences.

I want to address a few related areas in which I believe we can and must move forward as progressive Jews. These are areas critical in themselves and through which we can continue to create coalitions with the potential to become powerful alliances. They are not meant to sketch the progressive Jewish movement's total agenda, but to suggest some key directions.

**Pro-Choice**

First, the crucial issue of choice for women. A basic right won by hard struggle is under siege; it's as if the vote (stupid and choiceless as it often is) were being threatened, and progressives everywhere must join this struggle. Yet we don't need to be developing our own rationale, we don't need to do educational work, or open the debate. People have pretty much made up their minds, one way or the other. And as we know, the Jewish community has overwhelmingly come out for choice—meaning, Jewish feminists have done fabulous work.

The task is to demonstrate power on the side of choice. Progressive Jewish groups need to sign on to coalitions, turn out our members in the streets, protect the clinics and their clients against anti-women, pro-fetus fanatics. This should be done visibly, with banners—I like to see the word *Jewish* on banners, especially since the anti-choice forces always manage to dredge up some *hasid,* as if Jews are opposed to choice. We need to make visible Jewish support for choice.

This battle is going to be fought state by state by state, exhausting feminists, depleting resources. On the other hand, the positive side is that when issues get fought locally, they can be won. I don't feel that sanguine when I look at the national government. Aside from who's in power, the question is how to make large-scale change. On the national level, things seem unbudgeable. On a local level we can often exert some influence. This work with pro-choice coalitions will strengthen not only the pro-choice movement, but also the possibility of strong alliance between Jewish progressives and the feminist movement.

## Anti-Semitism and Racism

The second area I want to address is the mine-field of anti-Semitism and racism. Both are on the rise, in the U.S., in Europe, and in the Soviet Union. (Anti-Semitism is increasing in Japan too, according to the *New York Times*—one of those miracle manifestations of Jewhating without Jews). But until recently, I, and I think many progressive Jews, have mostly been content to let other Jews deal with anti-Semitism—except for confronting it among leftists and feminists, a fairly time-consuming endeavor. This means that the response to anti-Semitism, except as it appears on the left, has been choreographed by liberals to conservatives; often the conservative agenda is implicitly or explicitly invoked, positioning Jews defensively alongside privileged whites and in opposition to the agendas of economically oppressed communities of color. Or the liberal non-analysis blurs differences between the situation of Jews and that of other ethnic or racial minorities, seeking dialogue and a friendship not grounded in commitment to social and economic justice.

I have come to believe that anti-Semitism, as it becomes a more and more predictable feature on the national scene, requires a progressive Jewish response.[2] Can you fight anti-Semitism without fighting racism? Can you fight racism *or* anti-Semitism without dismantling the class system? I think a progressive Jewish response to both those questions is *no*.

For one thing, white supremacist ideology is also always anti-Jewish. We may not be a race, but plenty of Jewhaters think we are; they have not evolved very far from the Nazi slogan *No Jews, Negroes, or dogs allowed*. As long as people are predefined and threatened by their genetic line or their people or their culture, every minority group is in danger.

Nor do I believe that we can fight anti-Semitism or racism without attacking the systematic economic injustice that is American capitalism. Racism, because in the U.S., racism is so often expressed in economic terms with economic consequences. Anti-Semitism, because in Christian culture, Jews are identified with evil and treachery in general and with money in particular. Anti-Semitism links Jews with wealth and power in order to protect all those with wealth and power. Only by labeling anti-Semitism clearly and unequivocally as pernicious slime will capitalism be properly revealed as a maker of injustice and as a source of increasing human misery.

As progressive Jews, we need to deepen our understanding of the relationship of anti-Semitism and racism to class. We need to learn about the experiences of the various communities of color, so that we don't lump together these diverse experiences, and so that we can discover our common issues, those where simple decency bids us join in solidarity—and our conflicts.

For example, the clash in my old neighborhood, Flatbush, Brooklyn, between Korean grocers and Black residents, a conflict which exploded into violence against some Vietnamese men (as racism always generalizes, always expands outward to endanger more and more people). The point is, a generation ago that would have been a Black-Jewish conflict because the shopkeepers were Jews. Now they're Koreans, generalized to any Asian. What does color tell us about this conflict? And what do class and available targets for anger tell us about this conflict?

In many cities, there is conflict between African Americans and some other group, often other people of color, and the reason for this is clear. Aside from Native Americans, who have been on this land, obviously, the longest, and who are among the nation's poorest; aside from recent immigrants from Southeast Asia, mostly still very poor; aside from the rural white poor, whose children are leaving their communities and their culture in order to escape absolute poverty; aside from the old and the single mothers who cut across these categories and are obscured by them, most groups come to this country and in a queuing process shove the group formerly at the bottom up the economic and social ladder.

Except everyone cuts in ahead of Blacks. While immigrants open businesses, bring over their families, and seem to thrive; while the Bill Cosby show is the frontrunner on TV and African American language, music, style, etc. are continually appropriated by whites, stolen, adopted, and not even credited, one-half of African American children grow up in grinding, seemingly inescapable poverty.

But even across and through these conflicts and differences, there are some commonalities that can serve as bridges. We need, for example, to create powerful coalitions against hate crimes, including hate crimes against lesbians and gays, and against women. This means rape, battering, and murder. The work of conceptualizing violence against women as a hate crime is critical, and it is interesting to watch the nerve this touches, as some liberals and progressives resist this inclusion. Again, success in creating these coalitions will weaken our common enemies, and strengthen our ability to demand more change.

Finally, I have one last point to make in this section about change, and it is a hard one. I don't like it but I think it's reality. We have all watched the Shamir government block opportunities for peace between Israel and Palestine, so that a time of hope is perhaps lost. Soviet Jewish immigration to Israel supplies a cornerstone for a Greater Israel policy, swelling the demographics, reviving the positive vision of Zionism-as-Jewish homeland, while obscuring the underbelly, Zionism-as-denier-of-Palestinian-national-aspirations.

As progressive Jews in the U.S., we need to address the issue of immigration, and not just Soviet immigration. For us, as Americans, the issue is: *who gets to come here?* Many, perhaps most, Soviet Jews would rather come here than to a turbulent, perpetually-at-war Israel, and so would a lot of other people in the world. Why? Not because of our much-vaunted democracy, but mostly because of money—money they imagine will be available to them. Money created by resources and labor, sometimes money shipped out of their countries into ours.

As progressives, we logically should support open immigration. I don't suggest that this become a major focus; I can't imagine winning, or even having an impact. But just to imagine open immigration to the U.S. demands that we confront the reality of how we live versus how much of the world lives.[3]

We also need to counter the assumption that all Soviet Jews want or need to leave. Many choose to stay, to revive Jewish culture, to recreate the possibility for Jewish life in their homeland.

And we need to address the issue of U.S. aid to Israel. We can do educational work without touching questions of aid, though these questions will surface again and again. What we cannot do is take the next logical step. Coalition work with Palestinian and Arab groups, which provides us with visions of possibility and models for cooperation, is stymied unless we can address the issue of U.S. taxes supporting the Israeli occupation and the continued devastation of the Palestinian people. That's a reality.[4]

### Keeping Balance

When I first made up this title, I thought I meant keeping sane, keeping going. But the more I thought about it, images came to me from tai chi, where the point is to keep in motion and be prepared to respond to what's coming at you. I remembered something a jazz guitarist once told me, *there's no such thing as a wrong note; there's just what you play next.* Keeping balance means being very open to change, especially in a time like now when the ground is shifting. It does not mean digging in your heels.

Leadership, for example, requires different skills and strategies at different stages. There are times when leaders need to step back, loosen controls, welcome more activity and more members into the creative process of political organization. There are times when leaders need to consolidate gains made by the organization, to stabilize it and ensure its survival. And there are times when leaders need to break new ground, to convey inspiration and vision. I think we are entering a time when we need inspiration and vision. We need fresh voices. This means we need people to feel that what they have to say is welcomed, not that they're going to get dumped on the second they open their mouths. We need to create a sense of permission.

We need a new level of sustained activism—not only symbolic action. There have been too many marches where we get a permit and go home afterwards. What is significant about marches is the promise they offer, a promise of trouble, and it is time to live up to those promises. This means more time, more energy, and more risks. It means activated dissent. It means we need to develop broad plans of action with sufficient focus so that we go out demanding something concrete, something we can win, something we can build on. It means recruiting members with energy and time to take some of these risks, meaning young people. The campuses are prime, and groups like AIPAC and CAMERA are busy there.[5]

We need to think about the very structure of our organizations. I suggest that where our structures are working, vital and active, don't touch them. But we should also think about what other kinds of structures might work, and make those structures possible. Geographical division does not always suit every area. Student chapters, women's chapters, lesbian and gay chapters, can make possible a larger unity without infringing on the specific visions and concerns of larger communities.[6] Are we so attached to structures developed years ago as to believe that these are the only structures in which our organizations can function?

## Progressive Jewishness

Progressive Jewishness is about that strand of Jewish tradition which heads toward justice. It must include all the other liberation struggles. Its root is compassion; its assumption, that domination is not only wrong but unnecessary. Progressive Jewishness approaches the world with an ethical imperative and a Marxist slant on constant transformation. Always something needs doing. The world is not a fixed entity but constantly changing, and as progressive Jews our work is to help shape these changes.

What is Jewish about Progressive Jewishness? It roots in Jewish culture. It speaks in a Jewish language, by which I mean not necessarily Hebrew, Yiddish, Ladino, but a language deeply connected to Jewishness. Progressive Jews value Jewish survival—in the flesh and in the spirit. We value Jewish culture. We deliberately recultivate, learn, and use it. Not to show off, not to be more Jewish than someone else. There's a lot of shame among Jews about not being Jewish enough, not knowing, having to learn, blaming ourselves for assimilation, for loss. The point of deepening our knowledge of Jewish culture is to develop continuity between the chasm created by the Holocaust on one hand and the forces of assimilation on the other.

It means we talk to Jews and as Jews. It means we mine the tradition not for our teeny piece of evidence and justification, but for continuous engagement with the tradition and—this is perhaps the hardest stretch for many of us to make, very accustomed to seeing ourselves as powerless outsiders, even in our own tradition—*we engage with the tradition in order to contribute to its evolution* —a very Jewish engagement. We are, after all, members of the adult community.

Sometimes I say this myself, like a mantra: WE ARE THE ONLY ADULTS. This enrages and frightens me. What it means to me is no one will do our work for us. No one can show us the way, or make good on our errors. If the Jewish people need spiritual and political redirection—and we do—if the planet needs saving, and the U.S. needs to spin on its axis, we'd better get busy. No one will do it for us.

A week ago last Friday, I went to synagogue in Montpelier, Vermont, where I live now. Let me say, I was raised a Jewish atheist and I remain one (even though these days it feels about as acceptable as admitting I still believe in germs). But I belong to the synagogue because it's where the Jews are. I go on holidays and once in a while for *shabes* I go to services. This particular Friday I went especially because friends of mine were doing a baby-naming ceremony for their new daughter after *shabat* services. We have no rabbi in Vermont and different members of the congregation take turns leading services. This one was especially musical, lots of singing, lots of joy. When we sang the *shma*,[7] I cried, as I always do; from the first time I remember consciously hearing the prayer, it resonated with a familiarity I hadn't expected and it said to me something unspeakably moving: not what it literally says, a statement of monotheism, which means nothing to me; but a statement of Jewish survival. *Hear o Israel, all over the earth, wherever you are, sing this, say this, we are the Jewish people.*

So I cried over the *shma*. But I also twitched in irritation and alienation when the service leader did not amend the sexist language of our *siddhurim*, "prayer books." I felt depression descend at the language about god standing up for Israel and smiting our enemies, how it justifies the refusal of many Jews in our time to differentiate between defense and aggression, how it encourages a sense among some Jews that we are chosen above others, that our destiny supersedes the destiny of other people. When it was time for the baby-naming, my friends asked me to hold one corner of the *chuppa,* traditionally the marriage canopy, in this case a blanket knit by the baby's grandmother; a sweet task, yet the jokes and assumptions about marriage and motherhood for this girl baby troubled me, and I felt invisible and invalid as a lesbian, whose life choices were not welcomed as possibilities for teeny little Adina.

But I held the *chuppa*—after all, what was I to do?—and caught the eye of a friend in the audience, a heterosexual woman but one who also has chosen not to have children, and I vowed to continue the work of shoving the tradition over a little more to include us. To continue the work of reinterpreting the prayer's *smiting* and *enemies* to incorporate the reality of the IDF and the occupied territories, and to change that reality. And I said silently to Adina, along with the spirit of everyone else in the room, *may you grow up under this community's protection, including mine.* And then I added, *you be whoever and whatever you want, honey.* As the grownups of my childhood somehow must have said to me.

## The Long Haul

When I talk about the long haul I'm talking partly about emulating those wonderful grownups of my childhood: the old Jewish left, some of the most energetic, caring, committed people I've ever met, who through the McCarthy period, which was my childhood, right up through the present never stopped fighting, or stopped and started again, over and over. That is one kind of long haul, how to go on being an activist. And even in a world where almost nothing seemed possible, even then I'd just as soon emulate the women and men I grew up around who refused to stop fighting; because, after all, you never know unless you try.

And, in a sense, this is where I've been for the last few years. But more recently, the changes swirling about raise the question: how do we know what's possible? I have begun again to think about the possibility of profound social, political, and economic transformation. Not that I have a blueprint for strategies or a social design of the world I want. But I know this much. We need to move gropingly towards each other, in both larger and smaller units. We need to balance groups that work, groups small enough to bond fiercely, with the larger units we need to create and strengthen.

And we need the vision that inspires us forward. The couple, the nuclear family as the unit of survival, will not do. The single-issue movement will not do. The single-people struggle will not win. We are up against one of the most powerful, impenetrable machines of human history, our government. I am talking, ultimately, not only about preserving women's choice, or fighting hate, or even about peace between Israel and Palestine, but about massive transformation of society. This is what I had forgotten. This is the vision we need to hang on to. The old activists of my childhood who were my models—now I become them, and so do you. We are the only adults. No one will do it for us.

## NOTES

1. As this book goes to press, Derrick Bell continues his leave of protest, and Harvard Law School still has no tenured Black women professors.

2. In 1990, New Jewish Agenda moved towards making work against anti-Semitism and racism a major organizational priority, which included much debate and discussion about the relationship of these two issues. In 1991, I became Chair of the NJA National Task Force on Anti-Semitism and Racism, and part of a work group that organized a national conference, *Carrying It On: Organizing Against Anti-Semitism and Racism*, in Philadelphia in November, 1991. My talk on the opening night of that conference was a shorter version of "Jews, Class, Color and the Cost of Whiteness," pp.

3. Similarly in Germany, the richest nation in Europe. As I prepare the manuscript, Oct.1, 1991, *The New York Times* reports anti-foreigner skinhead violence in Germany; German prosperity has attracted "guest workers" in droves, and many native Germans resent this influx, some for economic reasons, and many, it appears, for purely racist "reasons."

4. In July, 1990 (a month after I gave this speech), the NJA National Council adopted a resolution to support placing U.S. aid to Israel in escrow, subject to guarantees of a freeze on new West Bank settlements and no human rights violations. A month after that, Iraq invaded Kuwait, and Middle East politics went wild. As I prepare this manuscript, I support the position taken by George Bush on U.S. aid to Israel, namely that it must be tied to a settlement freeze. To agree with George Bush is a disconcerting experience.

5. AIPAC, American-Israel Political Action Committee, the "Israel" lobby, often referred to as the Jewish lobby, though not all Jews support it and not all supporters are Jews; one of the brilliant strokes of the Jewish Peace Lobby has been, in its name, to challenge AIPAC's "ownership" of the Jewish voice. CAMERA is a right-wing group focused on media treatment of Israel; under the guise of supporting fair media practices, they actually challenge any coverage of Palestinian or Jewish peace activities.

6. In June, 1991, the NJA National Council adopted a proposal to consider the creation of all-women chapters.

7. *Shma israel adonai elohenu adonai ehad:* Hear o Israel, the lord our god the lord is one. The most common of prayers.

# *Jews, Class, Color, and the Cost of Whiteness*

(An earlier version of this essay was given as a talk at the New Jewish Agenda National Conference, Carrying It On: Organizing Against Anti-Semitism and Racism, in Philadelphia, 1991.)

> *asleep: dream. i walk down the street wearing shorts and a t-shirt and the new earrings my ex-lover just gave me for my birthday. i pass two young hip-looking women.*

> she's all japped out, *they say. about me. i cringe, self-conscious.*

> *then i look down at my shorts & t-shirt. i'm not even dressed up, except for the earrings. suddenly i understand that no matter what i wear i will be perceived as "all japped out."*

When I wake I realize I've never heard the expression. But I know exactly what it means.

Awake: vision. I walk down 106th street, a big wide street, in the mostly Puerto Rican and Dominican neighborhood where I live, after 25 years away from New York. I spot a man I've seen before on Broadway, asking for money. He's out in the street, shaking his fist at cars, gesturing as if in a silent movie—he looks like he's shouting and no words come out, or at least I can't hear them. He moves in jerky, violent spurts so that when he veers toward the sidewalk, people scatter, afraid. I watch him for a bit, afraid he'll hurt himself, wondering if I should do something. I walk into the copy shop I sometimes use. Everyone's speaking Spanish. I don't, and so I ask, "Do you speak English?" Yes. I discuss the problem with the man behind the counter. We go out into the street and watch. We decide to phone 911, the emergency number.

First question they ask: *is he white black or hispanic?* Like the new baby question: *boy or girl?* Asian doesn't even exist.

*White,* I say, knowing it's only because he's white that I can phone cops on his behalf. If he were Black or Latino, I'd be afraid of how they'd treat him. I keep walking towards Broadway. So does the silently cursing man. He miraculously crosses Broadway to the traffic island without incident and plunks down on a park bench, one of two white men on the Upper West Side asking for money. I watch for a while. No police car arrives.

Awake: more vision. Last night on Broadway I saw the man who had asked me and Helena for money, and I ran across the street against the light and dangerously close to traffic to get away. He scares me. A couple of weeks ago we were walking home, we were almost on my block, 106th between Amsterdam and Columbus, where no one ever asks for money because no one assumes anyone east of Amsterdam has any money. We told him, sorry, not today. I had just given money to two different people, and Helena had three dollars to her name.

By the time we reached the end of the block he'd circled back, stood in front of us, asking again. *You know, I don't want to rob or anything but I just might have to,* he says.

I'm not about to respond, but he keeps talking. *I don't want to be like this, asking for money on the street, but you know I need money, and I don't want to rob or anything....*Finally Helena gives him a dollar.

It seems that he came back to us, rather than the dozen other people on the street, because he (a black man) assumes we have money (we're white) and will be afraid (we're women). The truth is, we are neither moneyed nor afraid, and we give (Helena) or not (me) for our own reasons. The truth also is, he's desperate and we're not.

The next night I'm walking home by myself, late, and there he is, practically in front of my building. He approaches, extends his hand. *I'm sorry about last night,* he says. We shake hands, smile. Then he says, *but I need some money again, could you give me some?*

Late and dark. I don't want to stand there going through my pockets and especially taking out my wallet. Most of all I'm disturbed that he knows me. I am afraid of him becoming mine: *my beggar.* I don't want to be responsible for him. I don't want him to expect anything from me. Half the movies I've ever seen rise up in me, and I know if this were a movie I'd run into him every day for a week and at the end of the week he'd stab me. Everyone watching would recognize the heavy symbolism.

I shove aside the racist movie images. I say, *I can't give you money today*—and now I am stuck with my lie. I could give something. But I want to keep moving, get home.

He demands, *I need money.*

*I can't...*

*I need...*

*I can't...*

*I need...*

until finally I say, *hey man, I dig it but do you hear me?*

He nods. We both know I'm lying, that I'm the one who gets to say yes or no. We say goodnight, smile.

Let me walk you around my neighborhood. On 106th street at Broadway, people of all colors and ages shopping, walking, sitting at street cafes, waiting for buses, heading for the subway, wheeling children in strollers. But notice the people, and there are many, stretched out asleep on the benches and even on the sidewalks—winter is harsh here and still they're in the street, sometimes without shoes—the people shaking cups, asking, *can you spare some change,* saying, *I'm very hungry, can you give me something, even a quarter.* They're almost all African American men, a few women, also African American. Look at the taxi drivers. Step into one of the hundreds of small shops, restaurants, groceries, stationery shops that line Broadway. I see owners and often their families, and hired clerks: Asian, Indian, Arab, Latino, Greek, Jewish, sometimes

Caribbean Black. Rarely are they African American. Practically all of them speak English wrapped in the vowels and consonants of their mother tongue, which is not English; except their kids, teenagers who help out after school and Saturdays, as I used to help out in my parents' store, are fluently bilingual, perfect English, as well as rapid-fire Chinese, Korean, Spanish....They will go to college, their kids will probably lose their language, their culture. This is the American dream.

South of 96th street the balance of color shifts from brown to white, Latino to yuppie. Gentrified, white graduates of elite colleges live in buildings with swimming pools and elaborate doormen, views of the George Washington bridge—men and women in their twenties whose parents, or trust funds, bought them apartments costing maybe a million dollars.

There are lots of old Jews, surviving still in their rent-controlled apartments that will probably turn co-op when they die. Lots of harried thirty-somethings and forty-something Jewish women and men, their Jewishness visible only to those familiar with the intricacies and codes of New York Jews. They had their kids late, they split economically between upper middle and middle, and politically between liberals and radicals. Some are insistent about sending their kids to public schools, and some have given up on the public schools, refusing, in their words, to sacrifice their kids to a principle. They are professionals who live on schedules so tight that any unforeseen disruption is a minor disaster. To cope with the stress of life by the clock, and because they were raised to, or have taught themselves to, expect some joy and fulfillment in life, they see therapists, acupuncturists, chiropractors, and belong to health clubs where they work out and stay in shape. On the Upper West Side (and all over New York City) class shows in well-developed calves and trim forms. Fat is sloppy. Fat is poor. I am sure that the average weight in my immediate neighborhood among the women is 15 pounds higher than 15 blocks south.

One more thing: in my immediate neighborhood, when you see women with children, they tend to be the same color, brown to black. A few blocks west or south, when I see a woman and child of the same color, I'm almost surprised; the norm is women of color caring for white children, what I've come to think of as the underbelly of feminism. Most of the women are immigrants. Some of the children are Jews.

Let me adjust the lens, for accuracy. Not all Jews are professionals (45% are working class or poor); not all African Americans are homeless or poor, generation after generation (though a full third live below the poverty line). Not all whites are yuppies, New York is not the nation, and the Upper West Side is not even all of New York.

For example, I recently visited Seattle; at the Asian community health clinic, the brochures come in ten different languages for clients from Hong Kong and the hills of Laos (imagine in the early part of this century, a "European" clinic had to serve Irish, Poles, Italians, Slavs, Greeks, Jews, and Swedes, from farms and *shtetlekh*, from Sicily, Dublin, Paris and Prague). In Seattle the homeless are white men, and anti-racist coalitions include Jews as a matter of course, because skinheads and other white supremacist groups mustering forces in Idaho target Jews and people of color. Or in New Mexico, where I used to live and where I still return as often as I can, the poor are Native American, and after them, Chicano/a; Anglos buy up the beautiful old adobes; the issues are development and ecology, water table first and foremost. In Maine and Vermont, where I also have lived, and which share with New Mexico and Mississippi the honor of being the poorest states in the union, the poor are mostly white, nationally invisible because small-town and rural and the only news that counts happens in the big cities, where media thrive. For rural and small-town residents, the issues are not street violence; there are few streets and hardly anyone is anonymous, though women and children endure and resist violence in their homes. Rural issues are development and agriculture; the question is whether all food production will rest in the hands of a few multinational corporations.

But whatever is coming apart in the nation is doing so to some extent in New York first. When the public schools are essentially abandoned; when thousands upon thousands of people have no place to live, and everyone who does carries key rings heavy with metal, for the two to five locks required to simply get in one's apartment; when the threat of rape and other street violence against women controls our every decision about where to go, how long to stay, how much it will cost, and how much anxiety we can tolerate; when hate crimes of all kinds are on the rise, this is the future of our nation if something doesn't change. A recent survey found that even in rural areas, nearly half the people encounter on a daily basis people with no place to live. This is the human cost of our nation's priorities.

In the early and mid-eighties, I was working out some thoughts on racism and anti-Semitism, heavily influenced by these places I'd lived, and by my friends, many of whom were women of color, from both poor/working-and middle-class families, and white poor and working-class women. The way the debate was being framed as Black-Jewish or even Black-white obscured, I felt, the issue of class and the complexity of race. I wrote about the ways racism played out very differently against the various peoples of color—Chinese, Japanese, Arab, Native American....I wrote about why I saw anti-Semitism as a form of racism, meaning racist ideology. This last seemed like a truism to me; the camps of Europe were revealed three months before I was born. And in New Mexico, Maine, Vermont, I was certainly an alien. And I said then, the difficulty some people have in grasping anti-Semitism as a serious concern and as a form of racism is that it hasn't kept Jews poor. (In fact, anti-Semitism often claims that all Jews are rich.) I also saw what was getting called Black-Jewish conflict as a mutual scapegoating—Jews were getting blamed for white racism and Blacks for christian anti-Semitism—as well as obscured class conflict.[1]

But I have come to believe that this analysis needs to be pushed further. I am troubled, for example, by analogies between Asians and Jews, between

Arabs and Jews, not because these analogies are not valid—with the difference that Asians almost always look Asian, while Jews and Arabs may often pass. What troubles me is this: while class and general principles of race-hate are illuminated by these analogies, something else gets obscured: the intransigence and virulence of oppression of African Americans...and something else.

The structure of apartheid is useful to contemplate here, not because things in the U.S. are so fixed and clear; they're not. But let me pursue the analogy. South Africa has not two racial categories, but three: white, black and colored. It's the particular buffer zone of colored that I want to examine. Colored are those who will never be white but at least aren't black. Colored are those who have more access to higher status and all that implies—better housing, jobs, education, health, leisure, safety, respect. I want to suggest that in many places in the U.S., Japanese, Korean, and some Chinese, Indians and Pakistanis, Arabs and lighter-skinned or wealthier Latinos get to be colored. Sometimes Caribbean Blacks, by virtue of their accent, their education, the strength of growing up as the majority, also get to be colored. And African Americans, I want to suggest, are not the only "blacks," though they are the most visible. Many Latinos are black—dark in color—and also those most Indian of Chicanos, tracked in the lowest social and economic status. Immigrants from Southeast Asia hold some of the hardest, worst-paying jobs in the nation. And in the Southwest and sometimes Northwest, where there are few African Americans, Native Americans are kept the lowest of the low, and every cruel stereotype of inferiority shows up in local racist culture.

As I've said, these categories are not totally fixed. There is a certain permeability that characterizes the class-race system in the U.S., a certain amount of passing—literally, for those with skin light enough, who shed their accents, language, culture; and approximately, for those who, laboring under the heavy burden of racism, through luck and extraordinary heroism and sometimes through hardness against their own people, still squeak through. Clarence Thomas rises up from poverty to hobnob with the white male club called the Senate precisely by abandoning his people's concerns.

The point of this white/colored/black classification is not to violate the hope of solidarity among people of color by dividing them, but to recognize divisions that exist and must be named in order to bridge them. The Iraqi-Black conflicts in Detroit; Korean-Black in Flatbush and L.A.; Cuban-Black in Miami. Conflicts which a generation ago often were Jewish-Black because they are in part the inevitable result of who owns what in whose community, and who is poor, and who is accessible.

You could say, as my sister did when I was sharing these thoughts with her, aren't you talking about class? Yes and no. I'm talking about *caste as access to class,* as representing the probability either of moving up or standing still. And in the years of Reagan and Bush, standing still means things get worse.

Let me meander for a moment in the swamp of class. Top down, billionaires, millionaires: control and power; wealth so beyond the needs of one person, one family, it staggers the mind; here we find unlimited access to health care, comfort, resources; mostly WASP. 70 % of Congress comes from this class. While most white people aren't in it, most people in it are white, some Jews.

Middle class includes low-level managers, social workers, small shop-keepers, and teachers—K-12, secondary school, junior college, university—as well as business people, doctors, lawyers, and other professionals with incomes of $200,000 a year and more ($200,000, the dividing line under Reagan/Bush, between the rich getting richer and everyone else getting poorer). When a class category includes both those piling up assets and those applying for food stamps, we should recognize an obsolete term and come up with something else. Here is where we find over half the Jews in the U.S., spread throughout the category, and a fair number of people of color, mostly represented at the lower end of the class.

Working class is also problematic as an economic category. The non-unionized women in the chicken factories, Black in the South, white in Maine; Asians and Latinas in the endlessly transforming, infinitely stable New York City sweatshops once worked by Italian and Jewish women: these are working-class, and, as we see, part of the problem with the category is gender. Working class also includes the racially diverse members of the UAW, the men whose sons used to be guaranteed the best paid laboring jobs in the U.S.—but today Michigan, heart of the auto industry, endures 35% unemploy-ment. Working class excludes the endemic poor, the poor without a prayer of breaking out of it, not those who perform backbreaking work of past generations of immigrants but those who can find no work at all, or can only find work that pays so badly that, for example, women with children can't afford to give up welfare to earn money that will all get swallowed by childcare costs. They are African American, Latino, Native American, Asian. As for the rural white poor, because there are no jobs, their children leave for the cities, become essentially immigrants, and in the cities their white skin serves them in finding work— but, like other immigrants, they lose their culture. Working class spans well-paid unionized fields, many of which are now threatened because of automation, and because successful unionization has challenged owners' greed and sent manufacturing jobs abroad to pay workers less and maximize profits. Whole industries abandon communities of workers who have served them for generations; even keypunch work which requires English is shipped to Ireland (lest we miss the dominance of class/poverty as theme, and mistake it entirely for race/color), because Irish women are so poor as to demand so little. The two fields of labor still growing in the U.S., the hardest to organize and the worst paid, are office work and the service industry, including maids and restaurant workers.

Who does this office and service work? Women. People of color, especially immigrants, a replenishing, flexible pool of cheap labor, thankful to work hideously long hours for little money, because it is more than they had, and because they came here, often, not for their own betterment but for their children's. And so they groom their kids to escape the parents' lives, to assimilate, much as I, raised passionately pro-union, was groomed to escape the working class, and even the lower-middle-class shopkeeping existence at which my parents had succeeded.

It is precisely this access to better-paid working-class jobs or lower-middle-class small business opportunities, along with access to education for the next generation, that characterizes the experience of "colored" in the U.S. It is precisely this lack of better working-class jobs and small business opportunities, along with sytematic disadvantaging and exclusion by the educational system, that characterizes the experience of "blacks" in the U.S.. Sherry Gorelick's *City College and the Jewish Poor*[2] describes how City College was created as a path to upward mobility to distract the radical Jewish poor from the revolutionary class struggle predicted by Marx; the path of higher education was taken by thousands and thousands of poor and working-class Jews. But college was free for us, and there was room, if not at the top, then certainly in the middle. Where are the free colleges now? Private colleges cost more than $20,000 a year. And where is room in the middle, when even the middle is suffering?

This shared economic disaster could and should unite most people across lines of color. But the illusory protection of "whiteness" offers a partial escape route toward which anyone who can scrambles. This desire to identify with whiteness, as well as bigotry and fear, blocks solidarity.

In this white-colored-black scheme, where are the Jews?

Of the groups I've named as targeted by a general hate I'll call race-hate, Jews are the closest to white. Many would say we are white, and indeed a common-sense visual response suggests that many of us are.

But listen to the prophet James Baldwin: "No one was white before he/she came to America," Baldwin wrote in the mid-eighties. "It took generations, and a vast amount of coercion, before this became a white country...

It is probable that it is the Jewish community—or more accurately, perhaps, its remnants—that in America has paid the highest and most extraordinary price for becoming white. For the Jews came here from countries where they were not white, and they came here in part because they were not white; and incontestably—in the eyes of the Black American (and not only in those eyes) American Jews have opted to become white....[3]

Now, the point is not for us, Jews, to escape the category "white", to evade confronting our own racism, nor is it to insert ourselves artificially into a category of oppression, as sometimes happens in our movements where oppression in some puny paradoxical way confers privilege. It is to recognize a continuum where we are the closest of the coloreds to white, or the closest of the whites to colored.

This is hardest to see in New York City, where Jews can hardly be called a minority. If there is the diaspora and Eretz Yisroel, I have come to think of New York as a third category, somewhere between the two. "I'm in exile from Brooklyn," I used to joke, but it's no joke. Jews in New York City, except for select neighborhoods, experience the luxury of normality. To assume christianity in New York is to be hopelessly provincial. In New York one finds Jewish culture on a broad spectrum: orthodox, secular, lesbian and gay, Sephardic, Yiddishist, feminist.... The paradoxical result is a majority of Jews who operate without consciousness of their Jewishness. It's not an issue. Anti-Semitism is occasional, focused, and historical, and in recent years, for New Yorkers, has been associated mostly with African Americans. Quite the opposite from what's going on in the farm belt, the Northwest, and the South, where alliances between Jews and people of color are obvious to everyone.

Yet I'm suggesting that progressive Jews recognize our position in between colored and white, a source of tension but also of possibility. I can envision a powerful coalition between Jewish and Asian women, against the JAP stereotype. I can also envision a nightmare coalition between Jewish and Asian men against affirmative action. The challenge is to build progressive coalitions not only among the coloreds but between the coloreds and the blacks, and between these and the economically struggling whites—and then to expand still further. The issue of hate crimes, for example, can unite Jews with people of color, and with lesbians and gays; and we should insist on the legal—and moral—classification of violence against women as a hate crime. That will be a powerful coalition indeed.

What I want to focus on is this: in James Baldwin's phrase, "the extraordinary price of becoming white."

Many of us chose, or had chosen for us, a white path. A path of assimilation, of passing, often accompanied by extreme cultural loss. How many of us speak or read Yiddish or Ladino or Judeo-Arabic? What do we know of our own histories, our literature, our music, our cultural diversity, our rich traditions? What do we know beyond or besides the now-usual sources of American Jewish identity, which are, in a nutshell, religion, Israel, and the Holocaust. Nothing wrong with these sources—but as the sum total of Jewish identity, this is limited. Where does this restricted focus leave secularists or confirmed diasporists? What happens when we disagree, as we do, about solutions to the Israeli-Palestinian conflict? How does this restricted focus help us create and strengthen an authentic Jewish American identity? How does it enable us to see the Holocaust in a context of Jewish history, the tragedy of which was not only the destruction of millions of lives—as though that were not tragedy enough—but also the destruction of a rich and varied culture.

It's called assimilation. We, like others who pass or partly pass, can choose where to direct our allegiance: upward and whitening, restricting our Jewishness to that which assimilation increasingly demands, *a Jew at home, a "man" in the streets,*[4] white people who go to Jewish church, i.e., synagogue; or we can deepen both our identity and our affiliation, with the other "others," the outsiders: the coloreds and the blacks.

Think about shedding whiteness. I don't mean to pretend that Jews who are white endure the same visual vulnerability as people of color; though we should recognize that many Jews, especially outside the U.S., simply *are* people of color, that the definition of Jews as automatically "European" is incorrect. In addition, many Sephardi and also many Ashkenazi Jews are sufficiently dark to be readily perceived, at least in the South and in the heartland, as people of color. Think also about the Hasids; think about wearing a Jewish star, or other item that identifies you as a Jew; think about never taking it off. Think about driving through Mississippi.

So: is fighting anti-Semitism a diversion from fighting racism? Do we think we can fight anti-Semitism without fighting racism? Do we think Jews can be safe within a white supremacist society?

I do not. I believe, along with a great many other Jews, that a color/class barrier means injustice, and our culture teaches us to pursue justice. I also believe that a color/class barrier threatens Jews, in two ways:

1) Because race hate will never exclude us. As long as the world is divided into us and them, minorities are vulnerable. Fascism is on the rise. In our century, can we be naive about the danger?

2) Because the particular nature of anti-Semitism, which defines Jews as money, as powermongers—especially marks us as scapegoats for the abuses of capitalism, and we are living through a time of rampant abuse.

It's also a hard time to be talking about the abuses of capitalism, when it seems that so many people living under communism have rejected it, or tried to. Even allowing for lies and misperceptions, the American left is going through something as massively disruptive to our way of describing and envisioning the world as were the fifties' exposés of Stalinism on one hand, and persecutions by McCarthy on the other. I know that some of us who came to adulthood calling Lyndon Baines Johnson a fascist have a perspective problem, one which Reagan and Bush have helped us address. But we have not yet dealt, even theoretically, with the re-emergence in Europe and the former Soviet Union of toxic nationalism, nor with the dazzling speed with which internationalization of capital is matched by internationalization of labor: "guest workers" in Germany, Kuwait, Saudi Arabia; "illegals" in the U.S. What do national boundaries or national identity mean at this century's end?

Jews with any sense of history are scanning the airwaves for disaster. What I think we must keep poised in response to our knowledge that communism as practiced has failed: *so has capitalism*. We cannot accept what we have as tolerable. It's not okay that, in the richest country in the world, millions are without health care. It's not okay that one out of five children grows up in poverty, or that the figure for Black children is one out of two.

The rich get richer. And who does the dominant culture blame? Jews; Asians, especially Japanese; Arabs; foreigners; let's face it, "the colored" get blamed for various contributions to economic disaster; for controlling the economy, or making money on the backs of the poor; for raising the price of oil; for stealing or eliminating jobs (by importing goods or exporting production). African Americans, Latinos, Native Americans, "the blacks," get blamed for urban violence and chaos, for drugs, for the skyrocketing costs and failures of social programs. That is, coloreds get blamed for capitalism's crimes; blacks for capitalism's fallout. Do I need to point out who escapes all blame?

When we are scapegoated we are most conscious of how we feel humiliated, alienated, and endangered. But the other function of scapegoating is at least as pernicious. Scapegoating protects the source of the problem we are being scapegoated for, the vicious system of profit and exploitation, of plenty and scarcity existing side by side.

And let me address briefly, because it is the glaring omission so far, the pain and difficulty many of us have experienced from hearing about or facing anti-Semitism from African Americans. How are we supposed to be allies? people ask, not unreasonably.

But I want us to understand a few things. First, just as a racist remark by Jackie Mason does not reveal the inherent racism of all Jews, let us not assume that an anti-Semitic remark by Leonard Jeffries, or by ten Leonard Jeffries, reveals the heart of the African American community. We need to recognize the destructive role played by the media in fanning the flames of the "Black-Jewish Conflict." Cornel West, bell hooks, Richard Green, Barbara Christian, Henry Louis Gates, Marian Wright Edelman, Nell Painter, Albert Raby....Why are these names not as well known outside the African American community as the names of Louis Farrakhan or Leonard Jeffries? Are they, in their diversity and dynamism, less representative of the African American community?

Second, no more than racism in the Jewish community should surprise us, should we be surprised by anti-Semitism in the christian and Muslim communities, which includes African Americans. Nor should we be surprised by racism among people of color against each other. We all learn the same lies about one another. Part of our work is untangling these lies.

I want to make one last point about Jews and class, and this is about privilege and power. Hatred, chauvinism, oppression always function to keep people from their power, to mute their strength. Because they're laboring under heavier odds. Because they're taught to feel bad about themselves.

Anti-Semitism has a peculiar edge because the myth is that we're too powerful, too rich, and much too pushy. I began with my dream, where displaying a simple gift of earrings, walking down the street daring to feel okay, means: *she's all japped out.* Any particle of this that we absorb makes us afraid of our strength, loath to use our power, embarrassed by the relative economic and social success of Jews as a people, afraid it will be used against us (and it will).

Jewish progressives often buy into this scheme of contempt for "most Jews," assumed to be uniformly well off, or they experience a nostalgic longing for the time when Jews were authentically the right class, that is, poor and working-class.

I think we need to look critically at this attitude. First, because it erases working-class Jews and poor Jews. Second, because it writes off the political energy and concerns that exist sometimes apart from class, the ripe possibilities for coalition of feminist Jews, of lesbian and gay Jews, of Jewish educators and cultural workers, of Jewish seniors, and on and on, not to mention Jews who see anti-Semitism for what it is, a form of race hate which must be fought along with other forms of race hate, and those who are simply hungry for economic and social justice. Who do not wish to spend our lives deciding whether or not to give quarters or dollars to other human beings who need more than we can possibly give; who do not wish to abandon the cities with their fabulous human variety because of the stresses of economic inequality, alienation, and violence; who still believe a better way is possible.

Third, because this attitude of contempt for Jews who are not poor, which is, after all, a form of internalized anti-Semitism, ignores the fact that education, choice, comfort are all valuable. One cannot walk the streets of any of our cities, see people living in cardboard boxes or wrapped in torn blankets, and not appreciate the material basis for human existence. The problem is not relative Jewish success. The problem is a severe class system that distributes success so unequally.

Used well, education, choice, even comfort, can strengthen people, individually and collectively. As for money—let me say the dirty word—nothing gets done without it. The question is, what do we do with our education, our choice, privilege, skills, experience, passion for justice: our power. Don't racism and anti-Semitism make you sick? Doesn't hatred scare you? Don't you feel at least a little desperate about the way things are going unless something intervenes?

I think Jews need to gather our power, make it visible, and use it right. I'm sick of the more conservative wing of the Jewish community speaking for all of us. Everyone knows that Jews are all over progressive movements, what I've come to think of as the political diaspora. Maybe our task is to ingather the Jews, just a little, into a new civil and human rights coalition, in which we are present and visible as Jews. It means being proud of our collective strength, confident that we can use it right. Someone will always call us pushy. Isn't it time to really push?

NOTES

1. See "To Be a Radical Jew in the Late Twentieth Century," and "Women, Class, and 'the Black-Jewish Question'." Also see "*In gerangl/*In struggle," exercises in *The Tribe of Dina: A Jewish Women's Anthology,* by myself and Irena Klepfisz, with Bernice Mennis (Boston: Beacon Press, 1989).

2. Sherry Gorelick, *City College and the Jewish Poor* (NJ: Rutgers University Press, 1981).

3. James Baldwin, "On Being 'White' and Other Lies" *Essence* (April, 1984).

4. The phrase was used to characterize the "modern" Jew of the European Enlightenment.

# I've Been to Israel
# and to Palestine

*Riverside Church, New York. Eighteen of us, about to travel to Amman, Israel, the West Bank and Gaza, on a Middle East Peace Delegation, an interfaith group co-sponsored by Fellowship of Reconciliation and Pax World Foundation. The room is full of Christians and several, god help me, ministers. Two Muslims. Several Jews, including Selena, a lesbian and writer like me, who jokes about her mother the Zionist. I look for signs of being perceived—by Jews or non-Jews—as paranoid, hypersensitive. I'm wary but engaged.*

*I have been to Israel once before and have deep attachments to friends and family, to the sounds of Hebrew, the smells and tastes of the place. I'm afraid people in this group will lump together all Israelis—Shamir with my friend Dalia who busts ass working in the Israeli peace movement. I'm afraid to hear what they think about Jews.*

*The flight to Amman takes fourteen hours. By the time we arrive we'll practically be married.*

Amman. To come here I needed a new passport that hadn't been stamped by Israel first. Diplomatically Jordan and Israel do not coexist, and even the maps reflect this. Jordanian maps omit Israel; Israeli maps omit the green line—the border between Israel proper and the West Bank and Gaza. I've been afraid of this part, arriving in Jordan, an Arab country, but the reality is calm, controlled, tight. For two days we meet with Palestinians and a few Jordanians, talk talk talk—with scholars, elected mayors expelled from their West Bank towns, the President of Birzeit University, also expelled.

New Year's Day we travel by bus into the West Bank and East Jerusalem. On my first visit I flew directly on El Al, swooped down into Tel Aviv. I have heard that Iraqi, Yemeni, Moroccan Jews, traditional, impoverished, flown here in '48, '49, '50, thought the prophecy about an angel carrying them home to Zion had come true. I've heard Ashkenazi Jews mock this as one more example of *Mizrachi* foolishness.[1] The laughter offends me with its source, sheer prejudice. The truth is it did feel like a miracle to arrive in Israel by air.

By land it's different: Israel has a context and the context is the Middle East. Driving through the rise of bare red rock, still on Jordanian soil (and the whole notion of "soil," "borders," hums with arbitrariness), I'm home—like the first time I saw desert, in New Mexico, and fell in love; I was home, could not bring myself to leave. Even my skin looks better in the desert, centuries of genetic oil glands functioning to purpose at last, and the earth's body exposed, visible, stark....

We arrive at the famous Allenby Bridge spanning the even more famous Jordan River into the West Bank. The river is a thin trickle. The bridge is about a foot long. On the Jordanian side it's called King Hussein Bridge, and it takes thirty seconds to get across. Among ourselves, we've discussed how Hassan and Said, Egyptian and Turkish, will get special scrutiny, and I've offered to carry in Hassan's video equipment, figuring I'll have an easier time than he, with his passport stamped *place of birth: Egypt*. Last night I practiced taking the camera out of the case, switching it on, focusing; I am an excellent liar and believe in being thorough. Now I feel Hassan and Said's tension, my excitement, Selena's, and as we enter the immigration building, I say *shalom* to the Israeli soldiers, partly for the joy of speaking my pitiful few words of Hebrew, partly to walk in easily with the equipment.

Jerusalem. History weighs on everyone's back here, you schlep it around with the fabled tangerines and ripe persimmons. Partly it's ancientness: half the cultures you've heard of and three major religions walked these stones. Partly it's the question you can't help asking: Does anyone learn anything from history? And variants thereof: Is history a sick joke? Do victims only wait their turn? etc. The familiar *hamish*[2] culture of teachers, scholars and shopkeepers re-emerges in the Palestinian diaspora, while Jews institute ID cards, legislate expulsions, ban books, repress their own Left.

Yehezkel Landau, from *Oz ve Shalom*/Strength and Peace, a religious peace group: "In any protracted struggle between two parties over time, there's an exchange of characteristics." Some Palestinians and supporters toss the term *Holocaust* around, as if by invoking it against Israelis they can cancel out the past, even-steven, leaving the Jews stripped of history, devoid of credentials. There is nothing here a clear mind would call a Holocaust, yet expulsions, administrative detentions,[3] book bannings make you wonder: how far will the Israeli government go?

Batya Stein, from *Shalom Akshav*/Peace Now: "The Palestinians are in the position we were in '48. They are young, they have nothing to lose, they've been traumatized."

If anyone should understand that the Palestinians will have a state, it should be the Israelis.

*Intifada*: Palestinian resistance come of age; a concentrated and publicized version of the 21 years of resistance which preceded it. In a remarkable turnabout, the young homegrown *intifada* leadership, shaped by the mud of Gaza and the West Bank, demanded that their PLO elders grow up and deliver something realistic. The result: Algiers and Geneva, the declaration of Palestinian Independence, renunciation of terrorism, punctilious acceptance of all relevant U.N. resolutions, and a definition of Palestinian nationalism compatible with Jewish nationalism: two peoples, two states.

By January, the *intifada's* 14th month, aims have crystallized, hardnosed and practical: maintain energy and momentum, win international sympathy, minimize violence, hurt the Israeli economy while developing the Palestinian one, heighten national identity, strengthen the infrastructure—damaged by Jordanian, Egyptian and Israeli colonialism—to prepare for statehood. Children continue to throw stones, there's no stopping them. Every Friday noon after prayer in the mosques, men demonstrate and are teargassed.

But beyond the street fracases, people are mobilized into a wide range of alternative institutions and activities. Strategies are eclectic, creative and largely nonviolent: boycotts of Israeli goods (estimated at an astonishing 50% successful), carefully orchestrated traffic jams, whistles and pot banging to confuse soldiers, recurring strikes, shutdowns and slowdowns, tax resistance, mass resignations of police and tax workers, illegal secret study groups (schools have been closed by the Israeli authorities on and off for over a year), victory gardens and home production, tree planting to prevent land confiscation, hunger strikes in prison—all these demonstrate and build collective power.

Humor helps keep up morale: pasting a Palestinian flag sticker on the back of the last Israeli soldier in a marching line; creating a dummy with a *kafiyeh*[4] on its head, a lit cigarette in its mouth, to "violate curfew," fool the soldiers and make people in the camp laugh.

Most striking, the military government's chief tactic—of depleting grass-roots leadership by harassing, arresting and/or deporting young, active men—has finally backfired. Israeli prisons, packed with highly disciplined Palestinian youth, intensify political savvy, commitment and prestige, so that the joke goes, *What do you call a graduate of an Israeli prison? A revolutionary.* While close to 30,000 Palestinians, mostly young men and boys, have been in and out of prison since the *intifada* began, Palestinian women, organized as students, workers and housewives, have moved with courage and common sense into the leadership.

The daily shape of resistance is guided by leaflets issued by *intifada* leadership every ten days or so, each apparently from a different press, suggesting endless access to print shops. The leaflets announce activities, instructions, strikes, boycotts, etc. Often they praise heroic acts of individuals and communities or honor the dead, thus building solidarity. On occasion, a leaflet corrects the previous week's instructions; a directive to burn Israeli trees, for example, lasted only between one leaflet and the next. That *intifada* leadership reflects popular will is evidenced by Israeli attempts at counterfeit leaflets, which are instantly spotted as frauds, and by reports like journalist Daoud Kuttab's: "I'd be driving in a taxi and everyone would be talking about decisions in the latest leaflet as though they themselves had made the decisions."

Souad Dajani, a scholar typical of the highly educated multilingual young Palestinian professional, spent last year at Harvard. Her field of research is nonviolence and Palestinian resistance. Beyond the stones and bullets, she explains, the *intifada* is a network of intense, mostly nonviolent organizations. From 1977-84, some 900 incidents of Palestinian resistance were categorized as violent, while more than 10,000 acts of resistance were nonviolent. From 1983 on, *each year,* 3000 acts of nonviolent resistance have been recorded.

Souad clarifies: It's not that the Palestinian resistance is philosophically committed to nonviolence. In fact, the word "pacifism" in Arabic has completely negative connotations, like "passivity." Nor is anyone claiming that stones are nonviolent, not to mention gasoline bombs. But practice has been guided by common sense, and, for Palestinians inside the occupied territories, this does not mean armed struggle against the IDF.[5] In addition, the deportation of Mubarak Awad—a leading proponent of nonviolent resistance—has boosted Awad's credibility, the Center he founded in East Jerusalem and the idea of nonviolence itself.

Nafez Assaily, who replaced Awad as the director of the Center for the Study of Non-Violence, also points to an analysis of *intifada* strategies, the vast majority of which are nonviolent. Nafez has a round face, sparkling brown eyes, a somewhat bald head; he's chubby in his thick, Nordic-looking sweater. Every *intifada*, he asserts earnestly, including India and the American Civil Rights movement, had some exceptions to nonviolence.

On the bookshelves at the Center, works by Gandhi, King. On the wall, a hand-stitched quilt. One square reads:

*This quilt was made by*
*the children of the*
*Concord Area Jewish Group*
*Boston, Massachusetts, 1988.*
*This quilt is presented to the*
*Center for the Study of Non-Violence*
*and Mubarak Awad*
*in friendship and hope.*

On his kibbutz near Tel Aviv, Israeli Amos Gvirtz, whose white hair belies his young face and 40-ish years, describes his development into that rare animal in this part of the world, an ideological pacifist. He and Nafez often work together, and like Nafez he has lots of ideas for civil disobedience tactics, "constructive protest" he calls them. Instead of hundreds of thousands of people demonstrating in Tel Aviv, he prefers a thousand people planting trees or building houses to replace those destroyed. "When you take nonviolent action," he addresses the absent Palestinian people, "you help us Israelis to help you. If we go together it causes a problem for Israeli forces because then they have to fight Israelis." He observes, "Those who fight wars go with guns in their hand like sheep to the slaughter"—playing on the theme of European Jews who (supposedly) went like sheep to the slaughter.

Clever. But I'm angry that he says nothing—does he know nothing?— about the Jews who resisted in a hundred different ways, including with bombs and guns, which may have saved lives. I'm bothered by his emphasis on pacifism as a personal, moral choice; isn't the point to act politically to minimize suffering, maximize survival? I mumble this to Hassan, who's also troubled. "I don't know," he says. "I want to believe in nonviolence."

Rita Giacoman is the first hardcore Palestinian feminist we meet. She cites Virginia Woolf's *A Room of One's Own,* speaks of the deep need to degender education for the young. She's in contact with Israeli feminists, and she comments —quite Woolflike—"Feminists—both Israeli and Palestinian—interpret movement not in nationalist terms, but in terms of cooperation." The alliance, however, is far from simple sisterhood. Rita mentions in passing that she returned from the U.S. to teach public health at Birzeit University in 1969, when Golda Meir announced that there was no such thing as a Palestinian. "So I had to come home," she says, matter of factly, "in defiance of Golda Meir—and today no one dares say it."

Rita describes how the older, bourgeois, more service-oriented women's movement and the newer, PLO-affiliated women's groups (there are four, corresponding to the four main factions) have provided the template for training women to participate in mainstream politics. "I wouldn't have dared to speak up in front of my brother in public." The anonymous, rotating and local nature of the *intifada* leadership has facilitated women's participation, and of course, she says, the women will have to struggle to keep their gains when— never *if*—the men come out of prison.

Meanwhile, the *intifada* is unthinkable without the women. They create production cooperatives. They set up day care and classes in first aid. They plant the victory gardens, organize boycotts, manage all sorts of prisoner relief. With their greater freedom of movement, they carry much of the communication from place to place. Inevitably, they challenge the power dynamics between men and women, though not responsibility for housework or childcare, still considered women's work.

Amal is a seasoned organizer in her late twenties. Active in the Palestinian Federation of Women's Action Committee, she has herself served several months in prison and has since 1978 been banned from travel. She explains: "We do not go behind the backs of the men. We try by diplomacy to convince the men that it's for the benefit of the family, it's not dangerous. We don't talk about women's liberation in a big mouth. This would make them afraid. They say, you are communists, you are against God. But first we have to put confidence in the woman herself, to make her more strong, for when she faces her husband or father."

"Our friend who was in prison for six months had trouble with her husband. When she came out of prison, she was strong enough to tell him, either I will continue with this Federation and my activities or we will get a divorce. So she forced him. And this changes even the mentality of her family. Her father used to be very angry with her, he blamed her for her trouble with her husband, but once she was arrested, he respected her more, he helped her solve problems with her husband."

Amal describes how the women resist the army: when there's a demonstration in the center of the village, the women raise their voices and confuse the soldiers; they bang on pots and pans, blow whistles. "Fear is not in the woman's heart anymore." One woman beat up a soldier to force him to release a boy—he released the boy, but she was shot and killed. "To arrest a woman in the village, this is something the soldiers cannot stand, the women would be all over them." Yet women are arrested, detained, sentenced. The older, often more traditional women channel conventional women's tasks in support of the uprising. They also gather stones for the children to throw, and sometimes they throw stones themselves.

What about rape? Some Israeli women claim that there have been instances of soldiers raping Palestinian women, but no one will talk about it because it's considered so shameful to the woman and her family. Amal flat out denies that it's a problem. The soldiers do things to humiliate the women, like expose themselves "to make the women feel shy," but it no longer works, the women are past caring. "When the soldiers call the women by dirty names, the women say worse names back."

The Federation, of which Amal is a founding member, differs from the earlier women's groups centered in the large cities. The Federation women decided to go into all the villages and camps, to concentrate on housewives and on offering services which also help politicize women, like daycare. The Federation runs kindergartens and nurseries for 1,200 children. They have organized programs to keep alive traditional culture; they train women in Palestinian crafts—embroidery and copper work, for example—and sell these products through marketing cooperatives. Other Federation cooperatives produce jam, biscuits and baby food. The army has not interfered with the cooperatives, but they have on several occasions closed the kindergartens and held at least one teacher in administrative detention. One of the Federation's most important projects has been to train women from the villages and camps as leaders and to familiarize them with the skills and procedures of representative democracy.

Someone asks: What were Amal's struggles to participate in political life as a woman?

"In our society where the man is having all the privileges, the reaction of the woman is to say, why is he having all the privileges? Both are human. So it started with my house and problems with my father and mother and privileged brother (he's in the States, by the way)—so I usually insisted that I have to take my rights as he does. If he gets to ride a bicycle, I have to ride a bicycle. If he wears jeans, I have to wear jeans. If he goes to youth club, I have to go to youth club. We used to have discussion groups, started with the National Question, and also we discussed feminist books."

Ina'm, who accompanies Amal, is a student activist. She speaks in Arabic, with Amal translating. Her story is quite different. In her house they had seven brothers and two sisters. There wasn't any pressure on the girls. She was active in high school committees, her family didn't reject her. They encouraged her to go to Birzeit University. Her family support helped a lot, she could do voluntary work, go on trips, live alone, etc. Amal comments, "She didn't face the problems I faced—she liberated herself. She was lucky." Amal laughs.

Ina'm explains how the student organization works. Founded in 1984, it's aim is to help university and high school students face difficulties concerning curriculum; to help provide money for fees and books; to create the sorts of activities—clubs, arts, etc.—which occupation has inhibited; and to deal with problems of students who return to school from prison, a mission which hints at the numbers of student prisoners: 80% of Birzeit students, for example, have visited Israeli jails, some for two and three years.

Amal and Ina'm are married to brothers. They show us a poster that reads *Expulsion is Transfer*, with pictures of about 30 young Palestinian men marked for expulsion. Amal points to her husband and to Ina'm's.

Where do they get their strength, humor, their lack of bitterness?

Amal laughs again. No time for that. From the work. From the other women.

As in other mass movements of civil disobedience, people have discovered themselves as a unified force. Subject at every moment to arrest, violence, harassment, they have avoided every predictable rift: class (this one will wait till after independence), Christian and Muslim, village and city, "the Bank and the Strip." According to Daoud Kuttab, even George Habash, an insistent rejectionist, was convinced to abide by the Algiers majority decision at the request of Palestinians in the Occupied Territories. Before the *intifada*, Kuttab indicated, Habash's faction would have split.

In Amman, Souad Dajani had observed: "The surprise was not the *intifada* itself, anyone could have told you Gaza was ready to explode. The surprise has been the *intifada's* persistence and self-discovery, the degree of organization, pragmatism, unity and creativity.

"The second surprise has been the fearlessness. People have shed their fear, which resonates in the peculiar sense of invincibility. No one believes the *intifada* can be stopped."

*When I was growing up in Brooklyn, Palestine and Israel were, vaguely, the same place: Jews lived there. Palestinians were Jews from Palestine. But by the time I was an adult, the word Palestine set off a subtle alarm system. People who said Palestine did not say Israel, and vice versa. For many years it has been Palestine or Israel.*

*My third day in East Jerusalem, travelling each morning to the West Bank, I call my friend Chaya Shalom, an Israeli peace activist in West Jerusalem. "You've been here three days and I haven't seen you?" she asks, and I say, with no intention of making a political statement, just to explain, "I haven't been in Israel yet, I've been in Palestine."*

*I hear what I've said. It's true: I've been in Palestine. People speak Arabic (and English). The signs are in Arabic, the food is Arabic, the people are Arab.*

*I walk a few blocks into West Jerusalem. Into Israel. West Jerusalem, Hebrew, Israel. Back a few blocks: East Jerusalem, Arabic, Palestine. Back and forth, Palestine to Israel, Israel to Palestine, they are both here, Israel and Palestine: obvious, palpable.*

*Also palpable: the invisible green line splitting Jerusalem. Jews and Arabs stick to their own part of town.*

Inside the green line, Israeli dissent evokes memories of America in the mid-sixties, but the lack of a common vocabulary between those who oppose and those who favor the occupation suggests the extent of polarization.

For example, at 5 p.m. on a Thursday in Tel Aviv, some 30 people hold a vigil with *Dai L'Kibush* (Stop the Occupation); across the street six teenage boys counter-demonstrate. "You're going to be in the army," I say to one boy. "How do you feel about getting sent to the territories?"

"Well, I don't want to, of course, but if I have to....But, first of all, we don't call them *the territories.*"[6]

Chaim Shur, old leftist Zionist, editor of *New Outlook* magazine; a small man with white hair, familiarly cadenced speech: "People say, If you give them back Ramallah, they'll want Jaffa. So they'll want Jaffa. So what? So I want New York. Do I get New York?" He tells us, between 80 and 90% of ex-army generals say Israel should give up the West Bank for security reasons, and no one has ever imagined that holding onto Gaza did any good. "Can you defend better with the enemy behind your back or facing out? You can see with the *intifada* all around you, it's not so easy to defend."

Defense Minister Rabin gets screamed at in the Knesset. A group of soldiers meet with Prime Minister Shamir to express their anger and shame at the tasks required of them, tasks like breaking children's arms, shooting women and children with plastic or rubber-coated metal bullets, supposedly nonlethal bullets which have killed dozens. Another group of soldiers *(Yesh Gvul*/There's a Limit) has pledged not to serve in the territories; more than 60 have served prison sentences instead, while many others have been quietly reassigned by sympathetic or nervous commanders.

Jeremy Milgrom is a Rabbi, though he doesn't have a congregation—too many compromises, he says. He's also a member of *Yesh Gvul*. He discovered his ability to say *No* in Lebanon, where he began a hunger strike and was sent home. He tells of pinning up a prayer over the barracks gun rack: *Just as I have returned this gun, so may all humanity put their guns away, learn to solve things non violently.* Someone wrote *amen*; someone else copied the words from *Isaiah* about beating swords into plowshares.

Jeremy has decided to refuse his next reserve tour if he's assigned to the territories or the prisons. He's afraid. Every Israeli man, just about, enters the army at age 18 for three years, serves 30 to 50 days a year until age 55. To withdraw from the army is to cut off from the national consensus. Because of this, *Yesh Gvul* is seen as quite radical, as opposed to *Shalom Akshav*/Peace Now, which aims at having a positive influence inside the army. (There's a song satirizing the contradiction, *First you shoot and then you cry*.) But the army unit is like family. Refusal also means being cut off from his unit, with whom he's shared strong social ties over many years.

Why then?

"The evil that we're aware of right now—the evil we're doing right now—is not much worse than what most nations have done. The problem is we're aware of it."

Where does he find the strength?

"The fellowship of *Yesh Gvul*. And I've been blessed with knowing Palestinians in this country—at university, as a dorm counselor. And this—it's simply what I've been taught all along. It's simply Jewish."

He shows us the new *Yesh Gvul* poster. It's a huge black-and-white photo of a crying child—an actual photo of a baby wounded in the territories, in the eye it looks like; and across the eye, the only color in the poster, red crayon more than suggests blood. The caption, in huge Hebrew letters: *What did you do in the territories today, Daddy?*

Israeli women, like their Palestinian counterparts, are newly visible as a political force. Women's Organization for Women Political Prisoners supplies material aid to prisoners, keeps their families informed and educates Israelis about prison conditions. Dressed in black, Jewish and Arab women have stood in vigil against the occupation every Friday for over a year in the three major cities.[7]

Parallelling the soldiers' refusal to serve, a mostly women's group named "Year 21" has drawn up a covenant of refusal to cooperate with the occupation: 2,000 Israelis have signed it. Some 1,200 people travelled to the Negev in late January to camp for several days outside the dread Ansar 3, a major prison where Palestinians are held in subminimal facilities. The demonstrators lived in tents as the prisoners do; each day they presented a program focused on some aspect of the occupation, in general, and prison life, in particular. From the Jewish and Palestinian communities, lawyers and judges, psychologists and doctors, religious leaders, the entire congregation of one synagogue, writers and artists with art classes in tow participated. An exhibit was created of the 2,100 books banned in the occupied territories.

The more the Israeli and Palestinian movements come into communication and coordination, the more possible peace seems. That the Israeli government fears this is evidenced by increased surveillance; the arrest of leftist journalists, like the editors of *Derech Hanitzotz* (newspaper of the Communist Bloc); interrogation and harassment of *Yesh Gvul* leaders. Daphna Golan, from Year 21, says they expect heightened repression.

How do they protect themselves?

"First, we try to build support for our policies and actions. Second, we do everything out in front: *no secrets.*"

We're meeting with Lil Moed,[8] a founder of *Shani*/Change (Israeli Women Against the Occupation), and Dalia Sachs, from Women in Black in Haifa. Dalia also works on the *Dai L'Kibush* coordinating committee that connects peace groups to the left of *Shalom Akshav*. They explain their groups' various activities. *Dai L'Kibush* plans visits to West Bank families, for Israelis to learn about the occupation from those who live under it. *Shani* holds weekly "educationals" for its members, using each session as a base to plan some practical related action. Most recently, a talk by a Palestinian school principal has led to a public workshop for Israeli teachers, to acquaint them with the effects on Palestinian children of being virtually without school for a year.

Dalia explains how Women in Black has helped focus feminist energy. "As we stand there, we can create other activities—political, social." (I've seen these impressive fast-talking gatherings, an organizer's dream.) Gradually, Women in Black has become visible to the Israeli public. "We became an institution where people can come and get information and other people can come and be very angry with us." She laughs. (I've seen this too: people drive by shouting obscenities, curses. Sometimes they drive very close, to frighten the women, or they throw food, garbage. Children scream at them from the bus.)

A recent cartoon in the *Jerusalem Post* showed a *hasid* dressed in the traditional black coat and hat. Someone's asking, "What are you part of?" and he answers, "I'm part of the Men in Black."

"Sometimes you have to learn from a cartoon that you've finally achieved visibility," Dalia observes wryly.

How successful are they at talking with people who don't agree with them?

Lil, in her sixties and a political activist for more than her adult life, in the U.S. and in Israel, takes the question easily. "If you're not interested in communicating, you're not a peace worker. Besides, it helps to be in the Middle East where there's a different view of time. You don't have to win each conversation. There's another opportunity. You need patience. Most important, you have to respect people's process—for me, it helps to remember my own. Then start with what you have in common. Especially with women, this isn't so hard. You both think the killing is terrible. You both want peace."

Dalia's parents grew up in Haifa, emigrated to Egypt to find work—she was born there—and returned to Haifa when she was eight. "I need to remember the Jewish experience, the Holocaust, the pogroms, the deep fears people bring to these issues. My grandmother came to Israel escaping a pogrom in Russia. I need to address these fears or I get nowhere.

"But also I have to remember that most people don't want to oppress other people. And if you can show them a way out, they want that way out."

*Group meeting. Said moves me. From the Turkish left, he has always supported Palestine, but despite this, despite his fear that he and Hassan might not be permitted entry, he felt mixed crossing into Israel: because he rooms with Bill (a Jew) who was so excited about coming to Israel he was singing; because on the bus I kept reassuring him it would be okay; because Selena said to him, "I'm sitting with you because I'm a Jew and when we get to the border, I'm going across with you."*

*Practically everyone moves me: decent people, worth trusting. Selena and I share our anguish over Israeli actions, our suspicion of non-Jews, and they listen. (I don't even remember until later to be moved by the lack of homophobia. Ruth, Nancy, Selena and I have spent several meals spilling secrets, mostly about who we slept with when; Ruth and Nancy are straight and Nancy's a minister.)*

*Rebecca, one of the tour leaders, who has been organizing trips like this for seven years, says, "I wish sometimes I could feel it raw again," and I glimpse her self-protection like a slightly peeling skin.*

*Then we sing* Shalom Chaverim Shalom Chaverot / Shalom Shalom / L'hitraot L'hitraot / Shalom Shalom. *Peace, comrades, see you soon. Peace, see you soon.[9] For a moment everything seems possible.*

Birzeit University is the largest, most prestigious of the West Bank universities; it's also the oldest, founded in 1924, the same as Hebrew University. Birzeit has been closed by the Israelis for over a year. Prior to the *intifada,* Birzeit, considered a hotbed of Palestinian activism, had been shut 17 times for anywhere from two to eight months, but never before without a sign of when it might reopen.

In his Amman office, Dr. Hanna Nassir, President of Birzeit, expelled to Jordan in 1974, had served us sweet strong tea and delicious thick coffee. He was not optimistic that the Israelis would allow Birzeit to open. (By late January, all Palestinian schools had been closed, even kindergartens.) The Israeli government claims that the schools foster demonstrations.

What is he doing with the students to move them towards peace?

"It's too early for the students. The students are fighting. They're in the mood of the *intifada,* like the whole population."

When we talk to people at Birzeit's temporary office on the West Bank— university closed means not only no classes but also no entry to any campus office—the mood is less sanguine. The students have lost a year of their education. Faculty and staff contracts need to be honored, but there's no money from student fees. And the university has just been hit by a retroactive tax claim for five and a half million shekls (over three million dollars). Birzeit has taken a principled stand: While the university is closed, they won't pay taxes. But this new claim has thrown them.

"What would help?" Rebecca asks.

"A miracle."

Dr. Ali Jarbawi is a professor of political science. Somewhat balding, moustached, glasses, utterly familiar, a leftist intellectual—he could easily be a Jew. It fascinates me how none of us can tell the Jews and Arabs apart.

"It's very hard to be and not be a university professor. Our situation contradicts what a university means: free information, free lecturing, people exchanging ideas. If you're prevented from doing that, you're not a university professor anymore. Now we're not even allowed to meet with our students or to go into our own offices, to get books for our research. If you can't find a public library open in the West Bank, cannot get the Journal of Palestine Studies, for instance, you have to make a special trip to Hebrew University [in Jerusalem], where they have everything. Then you have to watch yourself at the checkpoint coming back."

"When school is open, is your teaching censored or restricted? And how do the students react?" Said's question.

Dr. Jarbawi says the curriculum, texts and so on are chosen in the usual way, no overt censorship or even control. But "regarding the military there are restrictions you cannot see. There is a list of banned books, every month it grows, if you have one of those books it can be bad for you. Anything about Palestinian nationalism, anything from the Arab world. During lectures—it's very dangerous when you start thinking that you have to impose restrictions upon yourself. You don't even need somebody from the outside to tell you what you can say. When you start censoring yourself, you are in deep trouble.

"Everyone's in deep trouble. This is the toll of occupation. When you ask yourself each time you say something, *anything* you say may be counted as an incitement; you cannot use the word *intifada* when you listen to it every day, you read it in the *Jerusalem Post* every day."

"And the second part of my question: is there tension between faculty and students?"

"No, no tension. The faculty and students are completely united." (Later, Said expresses disbelief. He says in Turkey, students constantly pressured the teachers to talk politics, to break rules.)

"Given how important Birzeit has been in the Palestinian struggle, doesn't it make sense from the Israeli perspective to try to undermine Birzeit?" My question.

Gabi Baramki, Acting President of Birzeit, disagrees. "We have never said to our students that Palestine is the negation of Israel. The university was established to prepare Palestinian people for responsible leadership in their communities. It's only responsible people who will make peace. Irresponsible people make war. Sometimes I worry because Birzeit University is only in the papers when there is violence or closure. We would like people to see Birzeit operating normally as a university."

Chaifa Baramki, Registrar of Birzeit, an elegant, middle-aged woman with high cheekbones and a dazzling smile. "It is because of this education that the decisions are now coming out of the Palestinians to accept Israel. If you look back thirty years ago, these were not the sentiments, these were not the ideas—now how did this come about? This was not development from God. This was the work of education. This is what happens when people are educated: they are realistic."

After the meeting, we stand around talking. Gabi Baramki shrugs, "Sometimes we feel, we're asking to open the university when thousands of people are being jailed." Chaifa Baramki adds, "Sometimes I wonder if I should be doing more."

We were supposed to go to Deheishe Refugee Camp on the West Bank but it's under curfew. We're going to Jalazon instead, which may be under curfew when we get there, you never know till the last minute. Jalazon had 42 consecutive days of curfew at one point, no one allowed in or out of the camp, everyone had to stay inside their houses. Since the *intifada*, some camps have had 120, 135 days of curfew on and off.

On the bus, our guide tosses off figures: 820,000 Palestinians live on the West Bank, of whom 30-40% are refugees. About 11%—95,000—live in camps in cement block houses. A hundred thousand West Bank Palestinians work in Israel, mostly at the lower paid, lower status jobs.

"Can't people leave the camps and be considered permanently resettled?"

"Yes, but most choose not to. They cling to refugee status. It's a political statement," the guide tells us.

There are also the other commuters, 60,000 Jewish settlers. About half are ideologically committed to the map they see God as having handed Moses along with the Ten Commandments; the other 30,000 are there because it's cheap, decent housing in the tightest of housing markets.

Graffiti on the walls. Each day they're painted over. Each day new ones appear. Today we saw:
*complete strike days*
*yes to Abu Amar's* [Arafat's] *speech*

Jalazon. I was prepared for worse. I was prepared, I discover later, for Gaza. Jalazon is a nasty slum but by no means the worst I've seen in or out of the U.S. It was, however, worse than any Israeli Jewish housing I'd seen inside the green line. Amy, who admits she has never seen a slum, is in deep shock; you'd think the Israelis invented oppression. I feel the familiar, locked center of defense: these are not the worst human abuses on the planet. I'm ranting about context, and Ruth says, "I've been to El Salvador and heard women testify about their breasts being cut off. I see this in context."

In context then. Most grim is not the poverty but the sense of total arbitrariness, rules without purpose, disaster without motive. I identify with the middle-aged minority—70% of the Palestinians are under 30, which partly explains why young people are so evident. Especially I identify with the women, the mothers. How do you keep a life together? You live crowded. The authorities humiliate your husband in front of the family, he lashes out at you or at the kids, and one of the kids throws back in his face his humiliation. You send your kids to school with a ferocity any second-generation American Jew would instantly recognize. The schools are closed repeatedly these days—pre-emptive measures against disorder. It is collective punishment against a people desperate for education. The authorities calculate that in this way, they will force the parents to control their children. But these kids are making history and they know it. They know what we want too, they flash the *intifada* V.[10]

The kids. When we had asked Hanna Nassir why the Jordanians decided to withdraw their claim on the West Bank, he answered, "They gave up. They couldn't control the West Bank. No one can control the West Bank. Almost the PLO can't control the West Bank." If your kid is wild or suspected of being wild, any day, the IDF is at your door giving you fifteen minutes or half an hour to get your things and get out of your house. They blow it up or knock it down with a bulldozer. More than 150 houses have been destroyed. Or they seal the house with concrete. Why one house is blown up and another sealed is a mystery to everyone. Maybe you only live next to someone whose house is blown up, but the soldiers use too much dynamite and so your house goes too. I met a family living in a tent staked in their relatives' courtyard, their house blown up in this way. I met a family living in two (illegal) rooms they'd built on top of their sealed house. On the wall, bright magazine pictures, for color.

"They are not kids. At 4, 5, 6 years old, they know about strike days and resolution 242 and Rabin and Peres and Kahane." This is Ali, a young West Bank Palestinian. He's been going to graduate school in the U.S. and is home visiting. In school, his 12-year-old brother's class had pushed desks against the classroom door and kept out the teachers for a whole day.

"Why did you come?" I ask (meaning, why did you pick now to visit?).

"I am *from* here," he says, and as others ask, "When did you get here?" "What are you doing here?" he repeats "I am *from* here," "I am *from* here," again and again, like he's afraid we won't understand. Then he explains: he came home to help his family. Two of his brothers are in prison, one convicted and sentenced, one administratively detained. Just before he arrived, his parents' house was demolished.

What will his parents do? He doesn't know—live with relatives probably. They can't rebuild the house. You need a permit, and it takes at least ten years to get one.

Al Haq, legal center in Ramallah, is the only public law library on the West Bank, the only place where the 1,250-odd military regulations under which the West Bank is governed are available for people to read. A youngish Dutch man and two very young Palestinian women explain Al Haq's programs. They monitor violations of the law and file reports. They recommend procedures. They prepare to assist the new nation in drawing up its own legal codes.

After the formal discussion, we're looking at publications. Hassan chats in Arabic with the two young women. Then they switch to English. "Who knows what kind of effect it will have on the children," one of the women is saying. Her name is Naima, about 19 years old, a student from Birzeit volunteering fulltime at the center while Birzeit is closed.

Hassan interrupts. "Why do you keep talking about the children? What about you? What kind of effect is it having on you?" His tone is brusque, almost angry, and I'm afraid they'll withdraw, but Naima answers, "I too. I myself saw my best friend killed. The army shot him, he was left bleeding."

"They wouldn't let the ambulance through," the other woman adds, "it's not unusual."

Naima continues, "They were too slow, he bled to death. I keep his picture by my bed and every morning I look at it and remember that he's dead."

Her face is alive and her eyes look into mine. There is not a trace of self-pity. "We studied together," she says.

"What do you study?" I ask.

"Comparative literature. English literature first. Now, since the *intifada*, I want to study Palestinian literature. And South African. And maybe also Irish."

"Do you write?"

"Yes," she smiles, shy. "I used to write stories in English—to reach outside Palestine. Since the *intifada* I find I am writing in Arabic."

"Why?"

"There is a new Palestinian literature being born."

"You're part of it."

Again, the shy smile. "This is my dream."

*East Jerusalem, National Palace Hotel. Sat up late drinking arak with Hassan. Wanting to solve his dilemma for him, yet it's also mine: how do I live my life? By what values? He wants to keep doing Middle East peace work when he gets back, not find a job; but he has to earn a living.*

*On TV, clips from Gaza: kids, faces swathed in white or red kafiyehs, throw stones. Three shot, one killed. Another day in the occupied territories.*

*Tomorrow we go to Gaza.*

*Hassan says he and Said went for a walk in the morning, saw a kid being grabbed and arrested right in front of them. He froze. He asked the kids in Arabic, "What will happen to him?" They sneered at his Egyptian accent, his question. "It's not for fun," they mocked. He felt ashamed. Complicit.*

*I love the mail Nafez Assaily got, several letters delivered through the Israeli postal service, addressed to "Palestinian Center for the Study of Non-Violence, Occupied Jerusalem, Palestine via Israel." And the peace quilt from the Jewish children. I did not love the bumper sticker up on the Center's wall, "Why not a Presbyterian State?"—slamming the need for Israel. Such jokes feed Jewish fear: see, they don't understand, they don't really accept Israel, it's just a ploy.*

*I don't feel fearful, just unaccountably hurt. Why not a Jewish state? The Presbyterians have Scotland, were not decimated by one-third ever and especially not recently. Is forty years so long? Why can they remember their orange trees and not our terror? I have read that Palestinians educated on the West Bank and in Gaza or in Arab countries learn nothing about the Holocaust. Literally, they don't know what it is.*

*In answer, Palestinian feminist Rita Giacoman's face, voice, flash into my mind: "I am very sympathetic to the suffering of the Jews in Europe, though I can never accept what was done to us to solve their problems."*

*For a moment I imagine hearts on both sides beating open, beginning to shed anger and feel grief: their own, each other's. The immense relief.*

*I breathe. Is this the first time I understand they were wronged?*

Gaza. The day after heavy rain, the unpaved streets are flooded. It's like this all winter, we're told, swimming in mud. In Jabalia Refugee Camp, the sewers run open, you can smell them, and everywhere children play there is sewage. The birthrate in Gaza can't go any higher and every one of those children must have some form of dysentery. No one—not the Egyptians, who ruled until '67, nor the Israelis since—has bothered to build drainage or sewers.

"Why," I ask Sara Roy, an American showing us around, "don't they just put in some drains?"
"Because the Israelis don't give a shit about the Palestinians."
"I'm from the U.S., I'm used to co-optation," I explain lamely, and she responds, kind but bitter, "They don't even try to co-opt. They assume no one will come to Gaza. No one will see. No one will care."

Some of these houses are sealed, as punishment. Common: eighteen people in a two-room house. A cemetery. A huge lake of sewage. Donkeys. Camp Jabalia: 55,000 official population; 65,000, realistic estimate. Children wave, make V sign, shout, *In America, help us.*

We drive by a line of people waiting for confiscated IDs, permits, passports —not really passports, since the Gazans are considered stateless (unlike West Bank residents, who at least until now have carried Jordanian passports). Instead Gazans get a *laisser passer* good for single use; you need to reapply each time. And permits: you need a permit to build, travel, plant a tree, dig a well; to print, buy or sell any given book. Even a driver's license can be refused on any pretext. You wait in line for hours for each permit, which may be denied or used as a lever to force you to pay back taxes or fines. This is part of what it means to live here: a profound lack of control. A profound sense of being controlled.

Later, driving through the town of Gaza, we see all kinds of construction but no one working on it; hard to tell if it's halted or a strike day. Sara says that with the economy so uncertain, Palestinians with money put it into real estate and build housing for other Palestinians with money.

"Do they talk about class here?" I ask.

"Not now," she says, "now everyone's united." After independence, she indicates, they will need to talk about class quite a lot.

Graffiti: *that we be ready for any kind of aggression or torture*

At Marna House, a beautiful inn with a broken boiler—no heat, no hot water—we have the building to ourselves, except for the owners. The woman tells Amy that her family has over 100 members and every one of them lives in Gaza. Of all the Palestinian experiences I've heard, this is the least Jewish: I've never met a Jew who knew so many members of her family, or had them all living close by.

Our rooms open onto a huge balcony facing the blue, blue Mediterranean. It's a shock to realize Gaza is beautiful, a former resort town. I keep thinking *Eyeless in Gaza*, Samson, Milton, Huxley. Ruth and I dash out onto the balcony, as do Hassan and Said, Amy and Nancy. We snap pictures of the sea. Then we take pictures of each other, laughing, playing, squished close for the picture, snap, the photographer jumps into the group as a new photographer jumps out to snap another picture. It seems we each take hundreds of pictures in various groupings, but when my photos come back, there are only two: one with me, one without. Everyone laughing.

Sara shares information with us over lunch. A scholar who expanded Meron Benvenisti's West Bank Data Project to Gaza, she is small, thin, dark, intensely serious, with huge dark eyes and a radiant smile. The food is the best we've had on the trip, eggplant soft and spicy, tender chicken.

We ask her to compare Gaza with the West Bank. Gaza is one-fifteenth the size of the West Bank and ten times more densely populated: about 700,000 to the West Bank's 820,000. About 70% of the people who live in Gaza are refugees, many from outside the region, and there's hostility between the original Gazans and the intruders, whose roots are in Haifa, Beersheva and elsewhwere. (On the West Bank, with a refugee population of 30-40%, most come from the general area, have kin and connections.) Gaza is also isolated; cut off from the West Bank and Israeli cities, the people tend to be more conservative. Most of the women wear the traditional Muslim headdress, and class divisions are much starker. The West Bank has a large, well-educated middle class and a solid working class. Gaza has a tiny landed aristocracy, a tiny middle class. Most people are poor.

Sara is scrupulous about distinguishing what she heard, what she knows, what came from several reliable sources, what is sheer rumor. *Hamas* (Muslim fundamentalist party) with its hard-line, don't-give-up-an-inch-of-Palestine position, has lost influence since Arafat's smashing success at Algiers. She says it's well known that *Mossad* or *Shin Bet* (Israeli secret police) funded the Muslim Brotherhood, the precursor of *Hamas,* and it's widely believed that Israeli money backs *Hamas* today, to foster disunity, to make compromise impossible.

A rumor from several sources: Israeli paramilitary hit squads move in during a demonstration very fast, target organizers, kill and get out. Since *intifada* leadership is rotating and quite secret, the ability to target organizers suggests spies. Spies and drug dealers are killed. "There's no grey in Gaza, it's all black and white, you're on one side or the other." She mentions—as had Nafez Assaily—a tactic used by the *Mossad:* they threaten people, "Either you spy for us or we'll say you're a collaborator."

(Amal, from the West Bank, had sketched a more flexible scenario. Hardened traitors, yes, are hung or strung up on an electric pole, in front of everyone. But someone who the Israelis forced to give information—by beating or threatening him—can confess in front of everyone in the mosque and give up his gun; they won't really trust him but they'll "accept him." Amal says it's very easy to tell when someone is a traitor or a spy. I can't tell if the difference between Amal and Sara reflects differences between the West Bank and Gaza or if one of them is wrong.)

Sara says during the PNC (Palestine National Council) meeting in Algiers, 30,000 Israeli troops were sent to Gaza. Firecrackers were banned, with penalties of a $10,000 fine and five years in prison. Electricity was cut off, so people couldn't watch Arafat's speech on TV. Of course people had batteries, so everyone heard the news on the radio, and what didn't work—for three days—were the army search lights. People set off firecrackers and danced in the streets.

We meet with Dr. Haider Abdel Shafi, chairman of the Palestine Red Crescent Society. He begins by stating that of course he accepts the reality of Israel's presence in the Middle East. Every Palestinian we've talked to has said this. Equally of course, he remarks, there must be a geographical link connecting the West Bank and Gaza. This is the first time anyone's mentioned such a thing, and I feel suddenly weary—a new obstacle. But the next morning I wake up thinking, of course the Gazans are pushing for a geographical link. They're afraid of being peripheral, excluded, isolated again.

Graffiti: *our souls, our blood for the martyrs*

In a vocational school run by the Near East Council of Churches, dropout girls learn traditional skills: sewing, cooking, childcare; there is self-help for widows. The NECC people want us to talk to the secretarial students, who speak English. When we pause to smile and say "salaam" to the young women embroidering, the officials rush us through. "No," they say, "talk to these other girls, much better. Ask how *intifada* changed their life."

Practically all the young women wear traditional headdresses. Sara has said that *Hamas* beats up girls in the schools, intimidates them to wear headdresses.

We check out the English class. They're using the East Jerusalem daily *Al Fajr* as a text, even though it's illegal in Gaza.

The teacher asks, "What's the capital of Turkey?"

"Ankara."

"What's the capital of Palestine?"

They all giggle: "Jerusalem."

In one of the rooms older women sew—the self-help widows? Few traditional headdresses. I talk in French to a woman in her sixties, with one eye sealed shut, perhaps infected. She holds up the different dresses they make, and explains what each one is for. We admire. "Life is very difficult," she says, "*tres difficile.*" She says because of the soldiers she was not able to go outside and buy Christmas cards for her family. I wonder how many are Christian.

Finally—to the NECC workers' relief—we talk to the secretarial students. No traditional headdresses here. Several say they're just taking the secretarial course because the universities are all closed; it's something to do.

"How has the *intifada* changed your life?" Someone actually asks it.

"Why do you ask?" says a young woman with short curled hair. "Don't you see it on TV? You want more?"

I find myself explaining, "So we can say, I heard the story myself, this happened to someone I met—"

She turns away in disgust. "TV is better. You want more?"

Back at Marna House, Tawfiq Abu Ghazala, an attorney from the Gaza Center for Rights and Laws explains: "It's impossible to practice law in the occupied territories." He cites the lack of due process, the courts' failure to tell families where prisoners are, or why. Lawyers often can't find or can't see their clients, are not informed of court dates, etc. He explains how law works here. The Military Commander in Gaza writes on a piece of paper, *In my capacity as Commander in Gaza, I hereby cancel Article 14. Why? Security reasons.* Oh.

West Bank lawyers only recently declared a month-long strike, but in Gaza they've been on strike for over a year, an indefinite strike—perhaps a mistake, volunteers Tawfiq: "I believe we have a role to minimize damage, but many

Israeli lawyers from the Civil Rights Movement are always here helping..." His voice trails off.

"How do you spend your time?" someone asks.

"I read history." He grins impishly. "You know, an Israeli general asked me the same question, and I told him: *I'm reading history and I advise you to do the same.*"

In the car with Sara on the way to the hospital, I ask how people would react to my being a Jew. She says you can't say it. "Things are very stark here, there's only two sides, black and white." Her eyes reflect complexity. And pain.

"How do you stand it?"

"I know it seems depressing. But it's not, I love being here. Despite everything. The people make everything worth it." Her face lights up. "They're so beautiful. And determined."

Ahli Arab Hospital is a small private hospital, better than the state-run ones, we're told and will soon see for ourselves: modest but relatively clean, 67 beds plus outpatient services. Sometimes they have 65 wounded in one day. The American doctor says that since the U.S. decision to talk to the PLO, the soldiers have gotten more randomly violent, more provocative. The Border Police, mostly Druse,[11] are the worst. (In the past few months, Border Police have been relied on more; the government explains that they're better trained, but the Gazans say, more brutal.)

In the beds are women and many children, as well as young men, wounded by beatings, burns, steel bullets, plastic bullets, "rubber" bullets....

Do people mind us walking around, going into their homes, staring at them in the hospital?

Most people in Gaza want to share stories, we're told. They're not delighted about the breach of privacy, but they're terrified of being forgotten, again. They are very proud *intifada* started here.

A child—13—a soldier shoved him towards a burning tire and said, "Turn off this fire." He said "no" so they pushed again, he tripped, fell in. His legs are one suppurating burn.

A woman tried to pull her 9-year-old son out of an army jeep, they shot her in the hand, shot her daughter in the head. Her daughter is in critical condition in Jerusalem. Her son was beaten, and they loosed a dog who bit him in the neck. When I ask to take her picture, she raises her unharmed hand in the *intifada* V.

Samira Farah, hospital administrator, explains that they sometimes re-admit the same patient three or four times for different kinds of injuries. She shows us a "rubber bullet," I hold it in the palm of my hand, the size of a large hazelnut, a hard metal center coated with rubber.

We see a 10-year-old boy who has been beaten, arm broken; a 16-year-old was tear gassed outside his house in the camp, soldiers began shooting, shot a plastic bullet in his arm, a rubber bullet in his chest; a 19-year-old, a bullet in his leg bone. A 14-year-old, shot in the thigh a week ago, ran away from soldiers yesterday, so that the bullet wound opened and is bleeding. People pull back the sheets, wounded young men pull down their pajama pants, so we can see the burn, the bullet inflammation. One, around 15 years old, has eight rubber bullet wounds in his leg, each a huge yellow and purple bruise.

*In context.* Case after case of the sort of thing I saw in Harlem during the riots of the early sixties. Cops doing whatever they fucking felt like doing. *The evil that we're doing right now is not much worse than what most nations have done. The problem is we're aware of it.*

Shifa, the public hospital, is quite different. Filth. Grease, grime, dust. An operating room I wouldn't sit in. Cats wandering about. One toilet to the ward (of 30 patients?), stinking. Mostly men and boys in filthy bedding, dressed in street clothes, uncovered bedpans on the floor beside them. One can speculate about conditions in rural Egypt, to which Gaza used to belong, and local people even tell us it used to be worse—two people to each bed, no sheets. Still, the discrepancy between what the Israelis provide for their own people and what they provide for the Gazans is stunning.

One patient, a young man, says, "Bullets easier to us than beatings."

Batya Stein, from *Shalom Akshav*, is small, dark, broad-featured, has a sturdy body—classically Jewish-or-Arab. She tells us people are now saying things they didn't dare say even a few months ago. *Shalom Akshav* is urging Israel to talk directly with the PLO. Labor is accusing Likud of wanting simply to hang onto territory.

"You seem hopeful, why?"

"Finally reality is going to have to dawn on us."

Batya repeatedly mentions "the Arabs" in an angry and mistrustful tone, and mostly avoids the term "Palestinian." I remember how our bus driver and tour guide speak in Arabic not of Israelis but of *yehudis* (Jews). Someone says that *yehudi* has come to mean any soldier or policeman. "Arab work," in Hebrew, means "work sloppily done." At the moment the mutual suspicion feels like a mountain, but there's no detour and no way back.

Chaim Shur, old leftist Zionist: "I think the Palestinian state is a fact already. There'll probably still be spilled a lot of blood. But there's no way back." He tells us a story making the rounds. An Israeli soldier asks an 8-year-old caught throwing a stone—*Who taught you to throw stones?* So the kid shows the soldier his 3-year-old brother. Chaim continues: "My old uncle—he's about 90 years old—says, *When you have participating in the struggle a kid of 8 years old, there's no way back.*"

Every pro-peace Israeli says the same thing: the Palestinians will have a state. The question is not *if*, but *when*. And behind that question, the meaning of the question: how much more suffering? How many wounded, how many dead, how many children will be beaten, lose eyes, live through, grow into how many years of rebellion? How much hatred prolonged, exacerbated, before the inevitable is grasped, and the hard essential work of healing can begin? *Get it over with,* one wants to scream at the recalcitrant Israeli mainstream, but the government has an entire history to defend itself with, and they have a point: who has ever cared about the Jews?

The Palestinians have the same point: who has cared about them? Mohammed Milhem, Mayor of Halhoul on the West Bank, expelled in 1980, says prior to *intifada*, Palestinians relied on, kept hoping for help from outside, especially from the other Arab countries. The *intifada*, created by Palestinians under Israeli rule, is an authentic continuous act of caring about themselves, of bringing the image of Palestine into focus, like a developing photograph.

Milhem remarks, like a simple statement of fact, "The *intifada* won't stop until there is not one Palestinian under Israeli occupation."

*The Palestinians are in the position we were in '48. They are young, they have nothing to lose, they've been traumatized.* Both peoples have common experiences now: diaspora, reliance on education, identity dependent for years not on territory but on culture. In the end—many people say this quietly—the Israelis and the Palestinians will be allies. They will understand each other in this scrap of land, when death is limited to illness, natural disaster and car accidents...

I've been to Palestine. It exists, right next to Israel. The problem is not that Palestine threatens or erases Israel. The problem is that there are Israeli soldiers all over Palestine.

To picture peace is first to imagine absence. Absence of hate. Absence of soldiers. Absence of constant searching, having to show your papers, obsession with radio news. Children do not make the *intifada* V sign. I am not afraid to say, *I'm a Jew.*

Then, peace as presence. Israel, able at last to turn to her own tasks. To explore and define the meaning of a Jewish democratic state, where Jews are safe and a non-Jewish minority is equal; where the secular and the orthodox hash it out, maybe without killing each other; where the economy is self-sustaining; where the best Zionist dream comes true—a culture that enriches Jewish lives all over the globe.

And Palestine? For so many years, the essence of Palestinian identity has been statelessness—like their prefiguring enemies, the Jews. The Palestinians will need to clarify their relationship to the Arab nations, to Islam, to the West, where so many of their best and brightest have been educated and to the institutions of democracy which they have come to value and demand. They will need to repair a brutalized economy. To reconcile rebellion with order and predictability, channel the children's astonishing courage. And to confront their own contradictions: on the West Bank, between the large, educated middle class and the workers; in Gaza, between the few with everything and the many with nothing; between the two territories, the sophisticated, urbane West Bank and bleak, dense Gaza, where it began.

Someone gives Hassan a slingshot, the kind the kids use to hurl rocks at Israeli soldiers. He's proud of it. *I want to believe in non violence.* I think of the shepherd David who brought down the warrior Goliath with a slingshot: Israelite against Filastin. *In any protracted struggle between two parties over time, there's an exchange of characteristics.*

*What did you do in the territories today, Daddy?*

*I'm reading history and I advise you to do the same.*

*Finally reality is going to have to dawn on us.*

*This is my dream.*

April, 1989

*for Lil Moed* (1925-1991)

---

NOTES

Names given in full are of public figures in public situations. First names indicate private individuals; for these, I have used pseudonyms.

1. Ashkenazi Jews are those of German and East European descent; *Mizrachi* Jews (literally, of the East) are those who came from the Arab world. The terms *Mizrachim* and *Sephardim* (Jews from Spain and Portugal, many of whom ended up in Greece, Turkey, and even Holland and Germany) are sometimes used interchangeably.

2. *hamish* (Yiddish), homey

3. To be administratively detained you need not be charged, only suspected of present or future troublemaking. You can be held virtually indefinitely.

4. *kafiyeh* (Arabic), the traditional Arab scarf.

5. IDF: the Israeli Defense Force.

6. Those who favor annexation of the territories call the West Bank by its biblical names, Judaea and Samaria.

7. By 1991, Women in Black were standing in silent vigil at nearly 30 sites across Israel to protest the occupation.

8. Lil Moed died of cancer in early 1991. Her wisdom and strength continue to animate women's peace activity in Israel.

9. *shalom* (Hebrew) means both "peace" and "hello" or "goodbye."

10. The *intifada* V is a V-for-Victory sign, commonly done with both hands, palm out.

11. The Druse, many of whom are Israeli citizens, are neither Arabs nor Jews but a distinct people.

# *While Patriarchy Explodes*

# Culture-Making: Lesbian Classics in the Year 2000?

**First published in *Sinister Wisdom* 13 (1980) and reprinted in *Women Identified Women*, eds. Potter & Darty. Mountainview, CA: Mayfield.**

What is a classic? Is a classic a book that stays in print? Who decides what stays in print, what gets remaindered, what makes it into paperback, onto the supermarket displays, back into hardbound collected works? Alice Walker's first novel, *The Third Life of Grange Copeland,* was out of print for seven years.[1] It didn't change. By what mechanism is it now available in paperback? Pat Parker's *Movement In Black* is out of print, as is Barbara Deming's work.[2] How might their work come back to us? By their deaths? "Discovery" by an influential critic?

In fact, much of the work of Aphra Behn, Emily Dickinson, Christina Rossetti, Angelina Weld Grimké, Willa Cather, Gertrude Stein, H.D., and others, was out of print or hard to come by prior to the second wave of feminism (and who knew that all of these women loved women!) Is this work classic now, but not then? Can we only talk about classics after a suitable passage of time?

One fact is clear. To be a classic, a book must at least get published. A book no one reads has no chance of becoming a classic, no matter how wonderful it is. And while many perhaps worthy books go out of print, many never make it into print in the first place.

But if a book is printed and distributed and well-read and many like it, will it then become a classic? Yes, if—those who read and like it include an editor from Doubleday; a critic from the *New York Times Review of Books;* a few highly reputed writers; and several professors of literature at prestigious universities who will mention the book in their lectures and in their books, include it on their reading lists and class syllabi, encourage their graduate students to write dissertations on the author and on the author's circle of friends and colleagues, develop sessions about the author at Modern Language Association meetings to pursue heated discussions about the author's imagery and fictional persona, and, perhaps most insidiously, school the tastes of future writers on the author's perspective and style.[3]

## A HISTORICAL DIGRESSION, BY WAY OF EXPLANATION

Shakespeare in his own time was extremely popular, the best. His popularity developed in the context of a popular theater, a whole audience accustomed to regular play-going; a "hot" audience with a shared and growing frame of reference, like the audience for rock in the late sixties, or, on a smaller scale, women's poetry in the early seventies, exploding with mass energy and creativity.[4] Shakespeare's popularity meant that many of his contemporaries were familiar with his work, language, and ideation. Thus Elizabethan/Jacobean culture, theater, language, literature, conversation—at least around London—incorporated his work, so that he went on being familiar to succeeding generations of writers and audiences[5] The cultural web around him spun larger and he was part of it. He schooled the ears of those who shaped the language. He gave the storytellers his version of stories that interested him.

Consequently, today his sentences sound "poetic," while those of Ben Jonson— a gifted contemporary—seem peculiar, because Jonson's rhythms and even vocabulary are unfamiliar. The intrigues of *Volpone* (one of Jonson's better plays) are harder to absorb than those of *Romeo and Juliet,* who have, at least on the level of stereotype, passed into mainstream culture.[6] So questions of "greatness" aside (including the question of why Shakespeare *was* more popular than Jonson), no one today approaches the work of Shakespeare and Jonson with an equal headset; Shakespeare is another word for "great writer": Who do you think you are, *Shakespeare?* Nor is anyone likely to experience the pleasurable rush of recognition when confronting Jonson's work: Volpone, Volpone, wherefore art thou Volpone?

It's not that a classic is necessarily great—what's "great"? It's that something large and encompassing grows from it. A classic is a chosen book or writer; and it is also an institution. As an institution, a classic is hard to avoid. It will be crashed into here and there, openly or covertly. We breathe it—a signpost of our culture, or one of its common foods. A classic knits a connection among people of a culture, so that many people can respond with a kind of intimacy and knowledge. The face that launched a thousand ships. Machiavelli. The green-eyed monster. A solid liberal arts education will locate these images at the source. And those who don't respond with intimacy, who remain unfamiliar with the signal or reference, are excluded. Depending on the hierarchy of a situation, this exclusion can be intentional (academic cocktail party) or incidental.

But whatever the intent of this connective tissue and its somewhat mysterious growth, a classic in a given culture always has a supportive relationship to that culture and to those empowered in that culture. A classic may praise or critique, but never ignore, what the people empowered in that culture consider important. Turning once again to Shakespeare: it doesn't matter much what he says about heterosexual love and marriage, or the death of kings. That his plays ask us to obsess about these subjects is enough indication that male Elizabethans took heterosexual coupling and royal death very seriously. Furthermore, though marriage concludes the majority of Elizabethan plays (called comedies), and royal death ends most of the other plays (called tragedies), contemporary Western male criticism has mostly managed to avoid the glaring question: What does it mean when people can envision only two possible ends to any story? Religious parallels of salvation and damnation aside, we can deduce some meaning from the fact that contemporary culture tends to value the "death" plays as higher art than the "marriage" plays. This valuation suggests that the tragedies embody, and are used to tutor us as contemporary evaluators toward, the assumptions of individualism and capitalism (*my* life and what's *mine* matter),[7] and away from the principles of communalism (marriage equals birth equals continuity of life).

In more recent literature, the central plot that emerges as individuals feel far too powerless to matter is the love story, where the individual matters, at least to one other person.[8] But what if the lovers are of the same gender?

## LESBIAN CULTURE

Lesbians have been around a long time. And like all people who constitute a group, lesbians have had a culture, albeit a subculture. Even that relatively tiny group of women whose lives are documented—white Western middle-class—offers evidence of women-loving women: witness the elaborate rituals and traditional intensities of women's relationships in the nineteenth century, as detailed by Carroll Smith-Rosenberg; or Nancy Sahli's account of women's passionate crushes on one another, censured only in the last hundred years.[9] In our own century, how many lesbians grew up, alas, haunted by Radclyffe Hall's 1928 novel, *The Well of Loneliness?* Or consider *The Ladder,* for many years many lesbians' only contact with lesbian culture.[10]

But lesbian culture as a context aware of itself, with its own networks and presses and connective tissue, is a recent creation. Contemporary lesbian culture blooms at the convergence of gay liberation and women's liberation, and in the realization by quite a few feminist cultural workers that, as Alix Dobkin bluntly, if musically, put it: "Any woman can be a lesbian."[11] In the consciousness of many heterosexual women, lesbians suddenly ceased to be a third sex, and became our own self. The impact of this convergence of homophiles and feminists on lesbian culture-making has been powerful and pervasive.

For example, one task in creating a culture is to reclaim what one ought to have learned but that somehow went by and was lost. I think of Emily Dickinson's

> Witchcraft was hung, in History,
> But History and I
> Find all the Witchcraft that we need
> Around us, every Day—

Why does a women's studies classroom break into laughter when I read this poem? A flash of feminist resistance? We were not exterminated, we survived. Possible lesbian implications? We are here, hiding, if you knew to see us; implications perhaps suggested by knowledge, recently acquired, that Dickinson loved and desired a woman.

But there is more to the story of Emily Dickinson and her poem. Where did I read the poem? Not in grade school, along with "I'm nobody, Who Are You?" and "I Never Saw a Moor"; but in an anthology of women's writing gathered by Louise Bernikow because she wanted to uncover the unknown and suppressed work of women writers. Whence this desire? The feminist movement had created or tapped or articulated a need in women readers for women's work. I read Dickinson's poem because of this need, in myself as well as in Bernikow;

and because a publisher was astute enough to recognize the anthology as something women needed.[12]

But the story is still not over. I pass over the recent research, sometimes wistful, inconclusive as yet, but provocative and inspiring, on witches and witchcraft; information and possibilities that have sifted into contemporary feminist and lesbian imagination, that suggest lesbianism as one possible deviation among many for which women were tortured and killed. There remains the question: How do I know that Dickinson loved a woman? Because Lillian Faderman rejected the popular mythology in which Dickinson, a pathetically shy spinster, hopelessly in love with Higginson, sent letters to a world that never wrote to her. Instead, Faderman read over Dickinson's letters to discover that Dickinson wrote to her sister-in-law Sue Gilbert in the following terms:

Susie, will you indeed come home next Saturday,
and be my own again, and kiss me as you used to?
Shall I indeed behold you, not "darkly, but face
to face" or am I *fancying* so, and dreaming blessed
dreams from which the day will wake me? I hope for
you so much, and feel so eager for you. Feel that
I *cannot* wait, feel that *now* I must have you—that
the expectation once more to see your face again,
makes me feel hot and feverish, and my heart beats
so fast....[13]

Faderman explains her work on Dickinson: "Six or seven years ago I stopped consenting to the conspiracy to hide lesbian history." Her resolve was facilitated by a newly blooming lesbian culture, and her work contributes to this culture. Thus Emily Dickinson, the oddest duck in American literature, may perhaps be considered in a new light.

In addition, despite the risks involved whenever a writer or teacher (or almost anyone) identifies her/himself as homosexual—and simply mentioning the word is sometimes equated with self-identification—a climate has been established where many culture-makers find it possible to take this risk.[14] When Jan Clausen concludes the title poem in *after touch* with the words "I am a lesbian," we recognize this more accepting climate. When Lorraine Bethel and Barbara Smith write that one lesbian publishing in the journal *Conditions: Five—The Black Women's Issue* felt the need to use a pseudonym, we know the culture is not accepting enough yet.[15]

Lillian Faderman writes openly of Dickinson's passion for Sue Gilbert; Louise Bernikow supports the possibility that when women say "she" in their love poems, they *mean* "she," and demonstrates that women creators often bond with women in primary intensity; these are facts. Such facts are products of culture; and they are also producers of culture, in a chain extending from Dickinson through Faderman, Bernikow, myself, and all those who may read this combination of materials and talk about what they've read, write books, and think, knowing that Dickinson loved a woman; that love between women was possible and restricted; and that women poets, even those who write in brusque original phrases, are not necessarily loveless and contemptible. The impact that this cluster of information may have on future generations, especially women, especially lesbians, perhaps most especially writers, is incalculable. This is what I mean by culture-making.

And it is happening all around us; by us and to us. While writing this essay, I have been reading *Beginning Book* by Maricla Moyano[16], which I'd picked up in a women's bookstore (which existed because of a burgeoning feminist culture) and bought because I liked how it looked and because on the back Ti-Grace Atkinson was quoted: "I loved it. It's beautiful. I think it the most beautiful writing to come out of the new women's literature." I recognized Ti-Grace's name—her name *is* a name—because there has been a women's movement; and her praise asks me to read Moyano in a context of feminism and rebellion, a context that until recently was invisible[17].

The story, about Moyano's "beginning," weaves a childhood narrative against passages that seem to leap out of the narrator's journal, until a second narrative emerges: Moyano abandons a male lover and commits herself to a woman; a spare and slightly surreal coming-out story. Without the gay and women's movement, Moyano's story would probably not have been told, at least not published and republished and flagged by Ti-Grace to me with recognizable signals: *Read this one.*

I read it and find myself delighted by her mind at work/play, by her distinct voice telling a clear honest story. I have learned to value clarity and accuracy. But I was trained in graduate school to mock the concept of "sincerity" in art, to equate art and artifice, as I was steered away from contemporary writers, those untested and unapproved by my betters. No one told me that classics were also *becoming.*

Nor was I told that as a woman with access to print, I would be able to bring literature into a circle of awareness, as I do now with Moyano, by writing about her work; knowing that if her work is widely read by lesbians and loved and used to inspire other writings, or is critiqued and answered with contrasting stories, then *Beginning Book* some twenty or fifty years from now may be considered a lesbian classic. And, conversely, if no one reads it...

## CLASSICS IN WHICH LESBIAN CULTURE?

But, says the idealist, who believes in the cream theory of greatness (greatness rises to the top, like cream on milk), "Isn't it different with lesbians? None of us runs the *New York Review*; we aren't owned by Shell Oil; some few of us teach college, but not all of us go there. Many of us have other, freer, connections with writing. So won't our great works survive (assuming they get written and published, that is)?[18]"

It's true that lesbian culture, like any culture that matters to people, if not completely suppressed and driven underground, thrives on scanty resources, outside universities and other traditional institutions of cultural production and evaluation. We exchange, are inspired by, and learn from each other's works in a variety of publications, bookstores, classes, grapevines. These alternative institutions exist because of the vitality of lesbian and feminist cultures. Only because of this dynamic, nourishing relationship does the concept of a lesbian classic even arise.

But we should recognize that to the extent that lesbian culture represents the experience, insights, values, and interests of most lesbians, it will have a combative relationship to the dominant culture—as long as in that culture, lesbians are oppressed. *Rubyfruit Jungle* doesn't alter this oppression. Lesbian culture, for it to belong to and represent most lesbians, will be pro-woman, pro-working people, and multiracial.[19] This means that a genuine culture of lesbians will always be in danger of repression, co-optation, and absorption, until such time as lesbians have control of our lives.

It's clear that a racist society that makes a best-seller of, for example, Baldwin's *The Fire Next Time*, must have a bizarre and indirect relationship to the content of creative work[20]. The dominant culture can tolerate a few clear thinkers, even revolutionary artists; anthologize their sappiest work ("How Do I Love Thee?" by Elizabeth Barrett Browning, not "Aurora Leigh"[21]); put them on panels; or isolate them, make them stars, interview them on television, deprive them of the deep popular connection that fed their work in the first place and gave them support, information, and, above all, honest criticism. When all else fails, publish their books and don't promote them;[22] destroy their presses or encourage them to destroy one another's; buy film rights to their books and don't film them; or film and distort them.

But not so separate from the dominant culture are the patriarchal outposts in our heads. The fact: whenever we are not consciously fighting against the hierarchies we were born and raised into, we will imitate these hierarchies and reinforce the oppression of other women.

We can say this more simply. How many lesbian or feminist publications, presses, coffee houses, galleries, how many women's studies programs, conferences, how many of our culture-making institutions are controlled by women of color? By women of working class background or without college training? By women who are poor?[23]

White middle-class lesbians can ignore, co-opt, or patronize poor lesbians and lesbians of color. This happens not mysteriously or through moral flaw, but through the facts of oppression. The less oppressed tend to have more access to money, education, and other resources required for cultural nourishment; and to old-girl networks that influence such decisions as what gets printed, heard about, reviewed in which publications, who gets invited to speak at what college on which panel, who gets money to fly to the opposite coast to appear at which conference, who wins which fellow [*sic*] ships and grants or gets which teaching positions where.

The effect of this is much larger than dictating the particular people who do and don't get to make a living off their creative work—though this is large enough. These unofficial networks bear on the questions: which lesbians will lesbian culture honor and support? Whose experience will come to be represented in the books women will read years from now? Which languages will be preserved and extended and given fruit: The Barbadian-Brooklyn English of Paule Marshall's characters in *Brown Girl, Brownstones?*[24] The witty explosions of Bertha Harris's *Lover?*[25] The working class inflections of Sharon Isabell's *Yesterday's Lessons?*[26]

It's simple. If I teach everyone to talk, future generations will not find a woman's Brooklyn Jewish accent unpoetic or comical. But if British aristocrats— or even William Carlos Williams and Allen Ginsberg—prime our poetic sensibilities, my voice will *never* sound classic.[27]

But the questions extend even further: What kind of consciousness will women have when they pick up which books in which languages representing whose experience? Who will be encouraged to write? Who will be silenced and made invisible? Who will women become, to choose *great/not great?*

## LESBIAN CLASSICS

In talking about classics, then, I mean who and what will become central to who we, as a people, become, and to what our culture becomes. And we can't know these things yet—though we know that we will become partly *through* our culture. Our classics will be chosen partly because they have shaped the choosers.

But if we can't know, we can suspect which values are significant for us now and what directions our culture may turn. Adrienne Rich's *Women and Honor: Some Notes on Lying,* for example, filled a need and has been taken instantly into the culture.[28] How many lesbians have given a new lover a copy, either to start things off right, or after the first big fight? A value: to be honorable with each other. A form: women and (Susan Griffin's *Woman and Nature;*[29] my "Women and Violence"[30]). All of us asking to be read in a context of women as the lens on the world.

Monique Wittig's *Les Guérillères*[31] seems another core work. The tribal voice ("the women say...") made possible, it seems, the collective voice in *Woman and Nature,* as well as the nonlinear form of Griffin's book and much of new women's writing. So that although Wittig's work seemed strange to many women when it first was getting passed around (in the early seventies), it seems less strange now.

Nowhere is this process more evident than in the work of Virginia Woolf. As women readers have articulated not just separate taste, a separate list of best-sellers, favorites, but also a developing network we can call culture, Woolf's role in this culture has become clearer, more obviously key. She wrote about textured lives, the secret currents between women, towards each other, against men, even against each other, but always with a piercing consciousness of sexual conflict. Many of us have imitated/will imitate Woolf to discover what she has to offer in the way of style and vision. And since so many women read and use Woolf, her work becomes familiar, "easier."[32]

Judy Grahn, on the other hand, accessible from the start—language, subject, price—reclaimed the word common, a reclamation that continues to echo through our literature: Rich's *The Dream of a Common Language,*[33] my "Are we ready to name/with a common tongue?"[34] Grahn celebrates the speech of ordinary women: "The common woman is as common/as a rattlesnake." Has a sentence ever crackled so across a page?[35] A value, supported in Tillie Olsen's *Silences,* broken;

Alice Walker's mother's garden.[36] As long as we cherish the creativity of ordinary women and value what women themselves have valued, we center exactly on the passionately egalitarian vision named in "women's liberation."

But if those who control what gets passed on are antagonistic to this vision, and claim that Grahn's language is flat and a bit rhetorical (instead of powerful and incantatory, which is what I think); or that Rich has lost something (elegance of form? compelling imagery?) bringing her work progressively towards clarity and accessibility to the vast majority of women; or that Walker has unfortunately fallen prey to white feminist man-hating in her last two splendid articles in *Ms.*;[37] then Rich, Grahn, and Walker may appear in literary history—if at all—as minor writers. And since "lesser" writers whose work connected with theirs in a common tradition will be excluded altogether, none of them will be read in a context of like-minded peers, and their work will seem eccentric rather than central, and will become marginal to the culture that passes on.[38]

Conversely, if tentative explorations are pursued, the original probings will come to seem/be pivotal in the culture. For example, if Black and white women confront—in life and in art—the substance of what is between us, historically and currently, separating as well as joining us, so that an authentic bi- or multiracial, anti-racist tradition is incorporated into lesbian culture, then the relationship between Meridian and Lynn in Alice Walker's *Meridian*, or between Lillian and Sophronia, in Hellman's *An Unfinished Woman*, will be recognized as (painful) beginnings; thus classic.[39]

We can watch a classic becoming. When Audre Lorde tells a room full of women, many lesbians, many Black women, "Your silence will not protect you,"[40] and Gloria Hull writes "Poem," dedicated to Audre Lorde, which concludes:

Dear Eshu's Audre
please keep on
teaching us
how
to speak
to know
that now
"our labor *is*
more important than
our silence"    ©1979 Gloria Hull

and this poem is chosen to introduce *Conditions: Five—The Black Women's Issue*, we know we're in the presence of something classic. The invocation. The passionate connection. The exhortation to speak.

Similarly, Muriel Rukeyser celebrates Käthe Kollwitz: "What would happen if one woman told the truth about her life?/The world would split open";[41] and Louise Bernikow lifts these lines to title her anthology of women's poetry over four hundred years, one which makes a point of including women's blues, prison, and work poems—as much truth as she could find.[42]

Or take *Conditions: Five—The Black Women's Issue*, which I have already referred to four times, a sign of its impact. *Conditions: Five* represents another facet of women's truth telling and is important for its mode of production—the *Conditions* editors gave control of the journal to guest editors, Black women—and for the high quality of the gathered work. Smith and Bethel, the guest editors, vigorously solicited material from many women, including some who had not considered themselves writers. The result was twofold: many new writers were included, and *Conditions: Five* not only recorded an emerging Black feminist/lesbian culture, but helped to evoke it.

All cultural institutions can open their doors to those who have been excluded. In the past year, *off our backs* and *Heresies* have published issues for and by women of color. If feminist and lesbian institutions—not just journals, but anthologies, women's studies programs, presses, radio programs, and so on—do extend themselves to other communities of women, then *Conditions* and *Heresies* and *off our backs* will be seen as pioneers in Third World feminist and lesbian culture. Otherwise the entire burden of this work of enlarging the circle of women makers will fall to groups like the *Azalea* collective, a group of Third World lesbians, and a multiracial lesbian culture will not flourish. Moreover, if one of our values is inclusion of many different lesbians, and support for personal and cultural uniqueness, then as Asian, Native American, and Latina lesbians, and those in the new immigrant cultures—Vietnamese, Cuban, Haitian—and those yet to come to this country, begin to articulate their cultures, then those of us with access to cultural resources will welcome the opportunity to move on over and expand our circle.[43]

And one of our themes will be how we joined the circle of women. Coming out, glorious, excruciating, sometimes so natural it went unnamed for years, will occupy a central place in our classics. And since lesbian possibility is often curtailed, then whenever women matter to each other, or choose women, or reject or betray women with a consciousness of pain or necessity, we will discern this possibility.[44] Perhaps our tragedies will be stories where women could not or did not stand by each other, bond together against oppression, or reach out to each other with sufficient strength and tenderness to transform, at least partly, each other's lives. Our comedies would unfold tales of women joining to resist all kinds of damage visited on women in a sexist world, to promote the survival of life on the planet and the creation of a just, generous, multicolored world.

## LESBIAN PASSION

But we stray far from any recognizable boundary of lesbian culture. It may be that on the level of platonic forms, lesbianism means a vast and holy bonding with women. Yet if I were attracted to a particular woman and asked, "Is she a lesbian?" this is not what I'd mean. I would be asking: Might she be open to me? Will she put me down for wanting her?[45]

While love and comraderie among women have been mocked, discouraged, and often punished, sex between women has been made almost unspeakable, thus unthinkable. In light of this destructive taboo, it's not surprising how little we find in our art that is explicitly sexual, as if we're embarrassed by the sexualness of lesbian sexuality: oceans, flowers, caves, and revolution, okay—but sex?[46] If we remember that some of our people lived—and live—sexless, in terror; and that, as Michaele Uccella has remarked, "To some people, our very existence is pornographic";[47] then as we work to rid our lives of violent offensive pornography, we will be careful at the same time to expand protection for sexual freedom, and to support sexual honesty in our culture.

And one way to expand protection for sexual freedom is to assert this freedom. If our developing culture does support sexual honesty, then perhaps explicitly sexual art and literature will replace exclusively floral interpretations of our cunts. June Arnold's *Sister Gin*[48] will reverberate for us not only as a celebration of female love and middle-aged sexuality and integrity, but also as a depiction of explicit lesbian sexuality. We will laugh with Joan Larkin's "'Vagina' Sonnet":

Is "vagina" suitable for use
in a sonnet? I don't suppose so.
A famous poet told me, "Vagina's ugly."

Meaning, of course, the *sound* of it. In poems.[49]

Olga Broumas's poems will make us flush with pleasure; for example:

...Marine
eyes, marine
odors. Everything live
(tongue, clitoris, lip and lip)
swells in its moist shell.[50]

And this incredible poem of Stephanie Byrd's will be honored for the courage it gives us to know our sex:

I can feel it in my lips
My ass moves towards warmth
Press warmth upon my buttocks
my breasts
rub my crotch the lips
I am warmed, hot water in a bath
I can feel breath in my throat
I choke up phlegm
Lick my chest, the lips
dart in to make me choke again
I can feel sight in my eyes
Push sight into my eyes, the eyelets
I see writhing eyelets clearer
Eat me
Eat me
Eat me
alive[51]

## LESBIAN VISION

So our culture must allow for both sex and solidarity. From our deepest eroticism to our hardest struggles: if we know ourselves and each other, and that our lives depend on one another, we will cherish "the courage to be there when another woman needs you";[52] we will teach our daughters and our students to believe, and to act on the belief, that "Any woman's death diminishes me."[53] Then lesbians in the year 2000 will read Judy Grahn's "A Woman Is Talking to Death" a bit the way the Greeks, they say, sat around listening to Homer. Grahn's poem will be key in our culture, not just because it is—let's face it— great, but because the values it embodies will be our cultural values—and because Grahn will have helped to make them ours. We will remember that the love we make with each other was called *indecent*. We will have redefined indecent.

Have you ever committed any indecent acts with women?

Yes, many. I am guilty of allowing suicidal women to die before my eyes or in the ears or under my hands because I thought I could do nothing, I am guilty of leaving a prostitute who held a knife to my friend's throat to keep us from leaving, because we would not sleep with her, we thought she was old and fat and ugly; I am guilty of not loving her who needed me; I regret all the women I have not slept with or comforted, who pulled themselves away from me for lack of something I had not the courage to fight for, for us, our life, our planet, our city, our meat and potatoes, our love. These are indecent acts, lacking courage, lacking a certain fire behind the eyes, which is the symbol, the raised fist, the sharing of resources, the resistance that tells death he will starve for lack of the fat of us, our extra. Yes I have committed acts of indecency with women and most of them were acts of omission. I regret them bitterly.[54]

## NOTES

1. First published in 1970 (NY: Harcourt Brace Jovanovich).

2. Pat Parker, *Movement In Black* (Oakland, CA: Diana Press, 1978); Barbara Deming, *Prison Notes* (Boston, MA: Beacon Press, 1966); *Running Away from Myself: A Dream Portrait of America Drawn from the Movies of the Forties* (NY: Grossman, 1969); *Revolution and Equilibrium* (NY: Grossman, 1971); *Wash Us and Comb Us* (NY: Grossman, 1972); and *We Cannot Live Without Our Lives* (NY: Grossman, 1974).

3. Louise Bernikow's introduction to her anthology *The World Split Open, Four Centuries of Women Poets in England and America, 1552-1950* (NY: Vintage Books, 1974), gives a lively and accurate description of how literary history gets written.

4. Judy Grahn notes that she, Susan Griffin, and Alta, later joined by Pat Parker, led a renaissance of women's poetry in the early 1970s on the West Coast; in her introduction to selected writings by Alta, *The Shameless Hussy* (NY: The Crossing Press, 1980).

5. Similarly, any writer situated in New York, Boston, San Francisco, or Los Angeles has more chance of influencing the culture than one living in Oshkosh.

6. Jonson's most brilliant play, *Bartholomew Fair,* is practically unintelligible by nonscholars, partly because it is so original, thus unfamiliar; partly because the texture and language of the play reflect so faithfully Jonson's culture.

7. See, for example, R.H. Tawney, *Religion and the Rise of Capitalism* (NY: Harcourt Brace & Co., 1926); and the work of his predecessor, Max Weber, *The Protestant Ethic and the Spirit of Capitalism* (NY: Scribner's, 1958).

8. I received a shot of cultural relativism in 1975, while visiting the People's Republic of China. Some students asked us what American books and movies were about. We described a romantic plot; they were amazed. "That's all?" they asked. "A whole book just about

two people falling in love and getting married?" Their basic plots at the time revolved around a person or small group struggling to transform the world, and succeeding.

9. Carroll Smith-Rosenberg, "The Female World of Love and Ritual: Relations Between Women in Nineteenth-Century America," *Signs* #1 (Fall 1975): 1-29; Nancy Sahli, "Smashing: Women's Relationships Before the Fall," *Chrysalis* 8 (1979): 17-27.

10. Barbara Grier and Coletta Reid have edited three volumes gleaned from *The Ladder*, all published by Diana Press in 1976: *The Lavender Herring: Lesbian Essays from The Ladder; Lesbian Lives*; and *Lesbians' Home Journal*.

11. On the album *Lavender Jane Loves Women*, 1975, from Ladyslipper Music, Box 3124, Durham, NC 27705.

12. Bernikow.

13. From the unexpurgated edition of Dickinson's letters, eds. Thomas Johnson and Theodora Ward (1958), cited in Lillian Faderman, "Who Hid Lesbian History?" *Frontiers* 4, no. 3 (1979): 74-76. See also Faderman's article, "Emily Dickinson's Letters to Sue Gilbert," *The Massachusetts Review* 18 (Summer 1977): 197-225.

14. See, for example, Judith Schwarz's recent survey of women researching lesbian history, in *Frontiers* 4, no. 3 (1979): 1-13. Most of the women indicated that they are risking their careers simply by doing this research.

15. Jan Clausen, *after touch* (Brooklyn, NY: Out & Out Books, 1975); Bethel and Smith, "Introduction," *Conditions:Five—The Black Women's Issue* (1979): 12.

16. (NY: Magic Circle Printing, 1979; first published in 1973).

17. Novelist Blanche Boyd, shared with me her insight that a blurb on a book jacket helps to place the book in the context in which it was meant to be read; conversation, January 1977, in which she was explaining why she especially wanted Tillie Olsen to write an advance notice for her second novel, *Mourning the Death of Magic* (NY: Macmillan, 1977).

18. By idealist, I don't mean visionary; a visionary should be clear-sighted. I mean someone who still thinks as she was taught, in terms of essences (Kant, not Hegel); who fails to recognize that what we consider "great" is an historical phenomenon; that *we* are an historical phenomenon.

19. Internationalist as well; Gertrude Stein spoke perhaps more insightfully than she intended: "Patriarchal Poetry is the same as Patriotic poetry": (excerpts from *Patriarchal Poetry* reprinted in Bernikow's anthology).

20. By the sixties, American intellectuals and critics had rejected the idea that content in art mattered, perhaps because (1) a new generation needed new theories to publish new books and to see freshly; (2) McCarthyism had taken its toll—they were suspicious of any political implications, especially "pinkish" tints; and (3) they felt profoundly empty. As Susan Sontag argued, if you're sensually, emotionally, spiritually, morally dead, the priority is to *wake up*; from "On Style," in *Against Interpretation* (NY: Farrar, Straus & Giroux, 1966). The movements of the sixties and seventies brought back to American culture a concern for content.

21. See Bernikow, pp. 29-32, for a discussion of how the Barrett mythology was created.

22. Blanche Boyd's inventive and compelling novel, cited above, received little promotion from Macmillan, the publisher. See also Kathi Maio's account of trying for a year to locate a copy of Andrea Dworkin's *Woman Hating*, published by Dutton in 1974, but unavailable from book distributors for some time; Maio's review of *Woman Hating* in *The Second Wave* 4, no. 1(1975).

23. I have heard only of *Azalea*, a publication for lesbians of color; see below, discussion of *Conditions: Five*.

24. First published 1959; republished by the Feminist Press, Old Westbury, NY, 1982.

25. Plainfield, VT: Daughters, Inc., 1976.

26. Oakland, CA: Women's Press Collective, 1974. For a shrewd and sprightly discussion of "nonstandard" English, see Judy Grahn's introduction to volume 1 of *True to Life Adventure Stories* (Oakland, CA: Diana Press, 1978), entitled "Murdering the King's English."

27. The first time I heard Muriel Rukeyser read—she was a large woman with a loud New York Jewish accent—my heart sang. I realized I had needed to hear her voice as I had needed to hear women's voices against a drone of male voices. This has implications for all oppressed cultures.

28. Originally published in *Heresies* 1 (Jan. 1977); then as a chapbook by Motheroot Publications (Pittsburgh, PA: 1977); and reprinted in the volume *On Lies, Secrets, and Silence, Selected Prose, 1966-1978*. Sometimes the instant leap into usage encourages the growth of jargon, almost passwords. When women talk about "spinning" as a political activity, without awareness that they're using a metaphor, I know something's out of control (*spinning*, from Mary Daly's *Gyn/Ecology* [Boston, MA: Beacon Press, 1978]); but there's no mistaking our need for our own namings.

29. NY: Harper & Row, 1978.

30. In *Sinister Wisdom* 9 (Spring 1979): 75-78.

31. Translated into English as *Les Guérillères* (NY: Avon).

32. Woolf's talent and achievement are so taken for granted now that we risk forgetting that initially she had to publish herself.

33. (1978).

34. From "Naming," in Melanie Kaye, *We Speak in Code* (Pittsburgh, PA: Motheroot Publications, 1980).

35. That these lines barely require citation shows how they've taken hold; but early lesbian publishing efforts should be recorded: *The Common Woman* was distributed in 10 cent mimeographed copies; then printed by the Oakland Women's Press Collective in the

early seventies (undated, with *Edward the Dyke and Other Poems*); and now appears in Grahn's collected poems, *The Work of a Common Woman* (Oakland, CA: Diana Press, 1978).

36. Olsen, *Silences* (NY: Delacorte Press, 1978); *Walker*, "In Search of Our Mother's Gardens," *Ms.*, May 1974, 67-70.

37. Walker, "Confronting Pornography at Home—A Fable," *Ms.*, February 1980, 67-70; "Breaking Chains and Encouraging Life," a review of *Conditions: Five* and a tribute to the courage of Black lesbians, *Ms.*, April 1980, 35-41.

38. For example, Tillie Olsen tells of returning to writing after decades of abstention to discover that Josephine Herbst (an older contemporary and another rare woman writer on the left) was out of print and virtually unknown. In her own day, Olsen reports, Jo Herbst was as popular and as major a writer as Hemingway or Odets. Perhaps Elinor Langer's biography of Herbst, in progress, will restore her to an appropriate place in our map of American literature.

39. Walker, *Meridian* (NY: Harcourt Brace Jovanovich, 1976); Hellman, *An Unfinished Woman* (Boston, MA: Little, Brown, 1969). Adrienne Rich treats this subject eloquently, in a talk she gave as part of the Lesbians and Literature panel at the 1977 Modern Language Association meeting (on the topic "The Transformation of Silence into Language and Action," published in *Sinister Wisdom* 6 (Summer 1978): 17-24; and, more fully, in her essay "Disloyal to Civilization: Feminism, Racism, Gynephobia," first published in *Chrysalis* 7 (1979), and reprinted in the volume of her collected prose, *On Lies, Secrets, and Silence.*

40. In her talk for the 1977 Lesbians and Literature panel, cited above, also published in *The Cancer Journals* (San Francisco, CA.: Aunt Lute Press). pp. 18-23.

41. From "Käthe Kollwitz," in Muriel Rukeyser, *The Speed of Darkness* (NY: Random House, 1968).

42. Bernikow.

43. Since I wrote this essay early in 1980, Third World lesbian and feminist activity has born much fruit; for example, the publication of *This Bridge Called My Back: Writings by Radical Women of Color*, edited by Cherríe Moraga and Gloria Anzaldúa (Watertown, MA: Persephone Press, 1981); of *Black Lesbians: An Annotated Bibliography*, compiled by J.R. Roberts (Tallahassee, FL: Naiad Press, 1981); of a double issue of *Sinister Wisdom* by and for Native American women, edited by Beth Brant (1983); and the creation of Kitchen Table Press and of the Third World Women's Archives (1982). The domino theory is true. In addition, in 1982 I find myself part of a movement of lesbian and feminist Jews; the emergence of a strong proud Jewish identity and the struggle against anti-Semitism begin to gather momentum. The publication of *Nice Jewish Girls: A Lesbian Anthology*, edited by Evelyn Torton Beck (Watertown, MA: Persephone Press, 1982), records and accelerates this momentum.

44. Barbara Smith, discussing Black women writers, argues that a lesbian perspective emerges when we look for primary female connections; in "Towards a Black Feminist Criticism," *Conditions: Two* (1977): 25-44. Smith's classic essay is also available from Out & Out Books, Brooklyn, NY (1981).

45. Women who were never permitted to express their love for women erotically, or who faced scathing queer-hatred for years, often feel the need for a clear word that means "women who desire women." I'm reminded of Adrienne Rich's pronouncement at the 1976 Modern Language Association meeting: "It is the lesbian in us who is creative...." Dolores Noll, a long-time gay activist, responded that it was all right with her if the word acquired a figurative meaning, but then she wanted a word that expressed who she was. See Rich's talk and later remarks on this point in her collected prose.

46. I discuss some reasons for lesbian reticence about explicit sex in "Sexual Power," *Sinister Wisdom* 15 (Fall 1980: 45-50, cocreated with Michaele Uccella): defensiveness; lack of a sense of privacy; and reluctance to feed stereotypes in which lesbians are nothing but sexual beings—these facts explain, in part, our silence.

47. Uccella, conversation, Fall 1979.

48. (Plainfield, VT: Daughters, Inc., 1975).

49. From *Housework* (Brooklyn, NY: Out & Out Books, 1975).

50. Broumas, "Amazon Twins," in *Beginning With O* (New Haven, CT: Yale University Press, 1977).

51. "I Can Feel It in My Lips," in *25 Years of Malcontent* (Boston, MA: Good Gay Poets Press, 1976). Byrd's work deserves mention also as strongly Black-identified poetry.

52. Michaele Uccella, defining womanhood, Spring 1979.

53. Adrienne Rich, the last line of "From an Old House in America, in *Poems, Selected and New, 1950-1974.*

54. Grahn, "A Woman Is Talking to Death," in *The Work of a Common Woman*, cited above.

# The Issue Is Power:
# Some Notes On Jewish Women & Therapy

(Before being published in *Jewish Women In Therapy: Seen But Not Heard*, Rochelle Siegel & Ellen Cole, eds. Binghamton & London: Harrington Park Press, 1991, this was first published as an article in a special issue of *Women & Therapy* 10.4 [1990].)

It begins with power, and why not? Jews are supposed to be all-powerful: controlling Wall Street, the world's money, media, colleges: the world itself. Tucked under the myth of the all-powerful Jew is the victim-Jew, the old-world-Jew, the *shlep*, the *nebish*, and—somber but receding into the vague, undifferentiated past—the Holocaust Jew. Riding the myth of the all-powerful Jew is the Israeli, the soldier, the one who breaks the hands of Palestinian children; inherently worse than other soldiers, worse than other men; the one who justifies hatred, is pointed to as proof of the problem: *you see what they're like?*

And the Jewish woman? As a Jew, she's assumed to have so much power already; as a woman, so little that any power she has is excessive. Stereotypes of Jewish women combine with prejudice against powerful women, pressuring us to cloak our strength lest we be seen as pushy; hide our desire, lest we be deemed oversexed (or, fuck on demand, lest we be considered frigid); mute our feelings, lest we be judged overemotional. Jewish lesbians to some extent escape this pressure—we are already displeasing to men, already outside the limits of acceptable female behavior;[1] to some extent, but not entirely. Jewish women are asked to sit on ourselves, lest we seem too...too...too powerful. Too powerful for men, Jews and non-Jews, who consider male dominance their birthright. Too powerful for women, Jews and non-Jews. Often non-Jewish women who are poor, working class or of color, automatically define Jews as privileged, and can only imagine Jewish power being used against them.[2] Often privileged WASP women, raised on politeness and privacy, see Jewish women as *aggressive, bossy, tense, driven, difficult*, not to mention *loud* and *pushy*. Jewish women, too, depending on the extent of our assimilation and our feelings about our own Jewishness, may respond negatively to strength in other Jewish women. We fear the male/gentile response to that strength. And, loving ourselves insufficiently, trafficking too much in other people's conception of us, we fear our own strength. What will we do with this strength? Make trouble? Hoard privilege? Justify anti-Semitism? Remind us we are Jews?

And the therapist, Jewish or non-Jewish: what is her response to a Jewish woman coming into her strength?

The task of self-love is endless. It is also, for many women, the task of therapy. Learning to love, trust and nurture ourselves, as we were insufficiently loved, trusted and nurtured. But what if a woman has been taught that she is especially selfish, especially unlovable, especially not to be trusted; that she already has too much, takes too much, occupies too much space?

A Jewish woman in the U.S. may well look around to see once poor but now comfortably middle-class relatives saying, *We made it, why can't they?* (Poor Jews, especially women and the elderly, are invisible, disguised by assumptions of Jewish wealth and by the general lack of attention to women and the elderly.) She hears prominent Jews—Jackie Mason, Ed Koch—make horrendous racist statements, while the gritty day-to-day anti-racist work of many Jews in and out of the Jewish community gets ignored.[3] She reads media hypes about Black-Jewish conflict, dreary rehashed incidents, in which Jews get scapegoated for white racism and Blacks for christian and Muslim anti-Semitism. She wants to feel proud of her Jewish tradition, but she finds elements she is not proud of, and it seems this is what non-Jews know best. More feminists know the obscure male prayer that thanks god for not being a woman than any other detail about Judaism. On one hand, she may feel profoundly threatened by a legacy of hate that haunted, at least, her grandparents; probably her parents; possibly herself. On the other, she may feel profoundly ashamed of, and oddly responsible for, the oppression visited by Israelis on Palestinians and masquerading as defense of the Jewish people. About the Holocaust legacy: is she paranoid or foolishly off guard? About Israel: the same question.

If she moves in progressive circles, she may discover that she cannot say she's a Jew without being called to account for the Israeli army. If she has bothered to educate herself and points out that armies are armies and that a huge movement of Israelis oppose their government's policies,[4] she may be shocked by the animosity such a common sense observation provokes. If she attends a family gathering and offers similar observations, she may be confronted by enraged and terrified relatives who accuse her of not caring about Jews. *You don't know,* they tell her, *you were born here, you're protected,* and often she knows this is true. They say she believes the lies of, strengthens the hands of her people's enemies.

Either way, she risks anger, dislike, alienation. Either way, it seems as if she is forced to choose. Between being Jewish and being progressive. Between the right and the wrong sides of history. Between her people and the other.

Even a Jew who doesn't identify strongly as Jewish, even if she responds to these scenes, observations, events with bewilderment—*what has this to do with me?*—her question hangs in the air. She may pass as gentile, unconsciously and with no sense of guilt or loss (as in, *my parents were Jewish, but I'm Unitarian*). But assimilated, identified, or, like most Jews in the U.S., somewhere in between, she will grapple with her Jewishness or she will be split from herself.

What is a therapist's task when a Jewish woman becomes her client?

There is a common assumption that Jewishness is an insignificant identity and shouldn't matter—except to those oddball few who practice the religion. A therapist who makes this assumption can damage. Here are some things I want to say to therapists.

Don't assume Jewish identity is unimportant. With Jewish clients, consider the possibility that some blockages relate to alienation from one's Jewish self and think about how to raise this issue. You work with a woman you could swear is "really" a lesbian; another who claims her working-class background is the past....I assume that most of you have developed strategies for clients like these. Understand that what appears to be a client's casual attitude towards her own Jewishness may be just that or may mask a loss of which the client is not yet aware or may protect a tenderness the client feels around her Jewishness because of the common assumption of insignificance.

Don't assume you know how assimilated a given Jewish client is; the woman you know as a radical lesbian carpenter may have spent hours of her childhood in Hebrew school. Ask. Don't assume you know what a given Jewish symbol, holiday, ritual means to your client. A friend tells her therapist she doesn't want to schedule an appointment for Yom Kippur. "What, do you need to pray or something?" cracks the therapist, evoking in my friend feelings of exposure, shame and alienation. Ask a real question. "What does that mean to you?" The first task is not to assume you understand. Assume you need to listen and learn.

Don't assume that Jewishness equals Judaism. Religion is only a part of Jewishness. Jewishness is a peoplehood, a culture, a shared history, an ethnic identity. Conversely, women who struggle to reclaim Judaism are reclaiming not just their religion but their history, their wholeness. That millions died within familial memory for being Jews means that when we go to *shul*, or attend a Jewish event, or wear a star, or long for the sound of Yiddish, Ladino or Hebrew, or the smell of *tsimes* or *knaidlakh*, we are also asserting, *I am a Jew and I am alive.*

Don't assume that reclaiming Jewish identity is simple. Jewishness is an intensely collective endeavor, to be pursued in a community of other Jews. Sometimes the work of re-approaching one's Jewishness involves exploration, the nature of which may well be mysterious even to the explorer. In this work we feel excruciating vulnerability. We feel ashamed for not already knowing tradition, history, culture, language lost to us via assimilation. We feel exposed and foolish for wanting to encompass these things so little seen, much less valued by the non-Jewish world. We feel guilty for criticizing family and culture. Besides, given the pain—as well as joy—with which being Jewish has usually bathed our families, our Jewishness is often buried under oceans of tears.

Here are some issues which I believe are especially intense for Jewish women or have a particularly Jewish slant to them:

*Children and Family.* The decision to have or not have children; the meaning of family: these issues have particular weight in the Jewish community, as in many other minority communities, especially those subjected to attempted genocide. The people's survival has depended on the strong family and on the woman's reproductive performance. To take a simple example, the therapist who sees in a Jewish woman's anguish about whether or not to have a child only a classic feminist dilemma may miss a dynamic of which even the client herself may be unaware.

On the other hand, Jewish families are probably as riddled with abuse and dysfunction as other families. Yet there is a myth about the close, happy Jewish family, that Jewish men don't drink or beat their wives or sexually abuse their daughters. These myths make the reality hard to bear for the individual suffering in a nonideal family. The anguish felt by many women about revealing family secrets is exacerbated by a sense that Jewish families, in particular, need protection. That we need to be better than the goyim. That by telling the truth we're validating anti-Semitism.

*Money.* To many non-Jews, Jews *are* money. A friend tells me that whenever she mentions money in therapy sessions she feels intense anxiety, lest her therapist click into anti-Semitic stereotypes. Jews' relationship to money is further complicated by the dramatic class shifts many of us have experienced in our own or in our parents' lifetimes. Add to this a concept of charity deep in the Jewish tradition that is fundamentally different from christian charity, as the notion of poverty is fundamentally different; neither a blessed state (Catholicism) nor a sign of damnation (Calvinism), but an unfortunate reality to be ameliorated, anonymously and without fanfare, by those who have more.

*Alienation.* The non-Jewish or assimilated Jewish therapist needs to consider that the woman who looks to her like a "normal white woman" has experienced in her own life or through her parents' experience serious alienation and even danger from being Jewish. Thus the question of Jewish paranoia asserts itself. Many of us were taught that the world is dangerous because the world *is* dangerous. A therapist who treats this fear as pathology seriously misses the point. A friend whose father survived the Holocaust tells of her reluctance to mention Hitler to her therapist; her fear is that her deepest loyalty and rage, her commitment to Jewish survival and memory will be defined as pathology, therapized away.

*"The Real Jew."* Any minority culture which has encountered the force of American assimilation has lost much of itself. Some Jews have lost more than others, and often we feel ashamed of this loss. Many of us have one Jewish parent, or received no religious education, or have a partner who is not Jewish. From a relatively homogenous culture not so many generations back we have developed a tremendous range of experience and relationships to Jewishness but without a corresponding sense that this range is valid, acceptable. Jews tend to feel judged by other Jews as not Jewish enough; this projection includes our own self-judgment and makes us either undermine our sense of self or turn from Jewish community, in an effort to avoid this undermining.

To be a Jew is to tangle with history. Even Jews born post-World War II in the U.S.—that is to say, even the most protected Jews the world has known—are formed not only by a personal history that begins at birth but also by the often turbulent experience of our parents and grandparents.

Everyone learns distorted, no-longer-accurate lessons through parents and other family members. What I am characterizing here as Jewish is the nature and the extent of those lessons.

There's the issue of how to define the self. Traditional therapy focuses on an individual's exploration and healing; its very bias runs counter to the bias of Jewish culture, which is towards the collectivity.[5] Not that the individual should be sacrificed to the community, but that the individual is profoundly connected to the community, so profoundly that separation is not truly possible without extreme loss. In some ways, this stance, deep in the Jewish tradition—as in the tradition of many oppressed peoples—corresponds to feminism.

But even feminist therapists who understand perfectly well that the personal is political, that family and community conflict may be worth probing instead of escaping, who know better than to idealize individuation and demean connectedness; still these same feminists sometimes miss the point about Jewishness and see it only as an archaic construct to shed.

In addition, while you could say that Jews—like many other ethnics—have fuzzy boundaries, the issue of boundaries or their lack seems particularly acute for Jews. Boundaries between the self, the family and the community. Between the generations. Between history and the present. Between national identity and identification across national lines with the Jewish people. Perhaps this is why much of Jewish religion, in fact, involves drawing boundaries, between secular and sacred; between acceptable and not acceptable food. The anguish of Israel and Palestine can be seen partly as a question of boundaries, geographical and metaphysical. Even one's body is barely one's own. A friend says, *You return from the toilet, and everyone wants to know: did you go?* The nosiness characteristic of Jewish culture relates both to responsiblity and danger; if you constantly monitor information, you may be able to ward off disaster.

Fuzzy boundaries between the self, family and community can be a sign of Jewish health. And yet for Jewish women, there is danger in this lack of distinction. How do I live my life if it is not my own? There are injunctions directed at me, as a Jewish member of a larger entity, the Jewish people; as a female member of this same entity; and as a woman. They all agree on one point: *everyone else is more important than I am.* As a Jewish woman, I need protection against these injunctions. But the therapist who attempts to point out the danger without grasping also the positive, life-affirming aspect of Jewish culture forfeits my trust.

She also short-circuits my work. The immunity I develop against the "you are not important" message must be my own authentic version of self-love. This will inevitably involve sorting through the tangle of roots that nourished me,[6] separating the healthy from the diseased from the once-useful but no longer. If, as a Jew, I understand the cultural nature of much of this tangle, I come to understand myself as part of an historical process. *History is a nightmare from which I am trying to awaken*, wrote James Joyce, referring most likely to the tumultuous Ireland he was born into. But no one escapes history, however nightmarish; one can only delude oneself that one has escaped, a delusion almost identical with dominant culture consciousness in the U.S.

As an adolescent blessed with some choices, as a rebel, as a seeker of my own path I may shun the charge and privilege of historical continuity, of agency and responsibility; I may need time out. But as an adult blessed with some choices, I must wrestle my own power, as, they say, Jacob wrestled the angel of god—not just to make myself happy, but to enter the historical flow. This is not a very American way to think, though it is quite Jewish.

Personal change, political transformation, the role of therapy: who is the self, who is the other? I know that healthy suspicion of individual solution may blur dangerously into self-hate and self-deprivation, and I have watched movements, especially feminism, exploit this blur. I also know that self-love and a sense of individual worth can slide cruelly into lack of compassion and responsibility.

This issue of therapy and politics is not particular to Jewish women, and yet Jewish women may have a particularly difficult time sorting it out. I believe that one part of healing is the struggle to change the world, to make visible and to eradicate the conditions that produced pain. I know that not every person who enters therapy is interested in changing the world, and it is a constant source of frustration to me as a teacher and writer that certain crumbs of my wisdom, such as it is, are gobbled up (*you are worthy*) while others, to me inseparable, are often ignored (*everyone else is worthy too*). I imagine that therapists experience this disappointment as well.

I also know that not every Jewish woman who seeks therapy wants to address her Jewishness; nor would I presume to dictate the form this work should take (though as a secular Jew I will also confess to disappointment that so much of it has centered on religion). But since Jewishness is a collective endeavor, the work to reclaim it will be pursued with other Jewish women, in study groups, cultural activities, as well as political work as Jews. Therapists need to understand that this work can constitute in itself a healing, and that it takes courage.[7]

If the personal is political, the political is also personal. In January, 1989, I visited Israel and the Occupied Territories on a peace tour and met with a variety of peace activists. One, Chaim Shur, an old-time Socialist Zionist who has worked towards Israeli-Palestinian reconciliation for most of his life, told us: *Israeli Jews are polarized, and now American Jews have to become just as polarized.*

I believe that Jewish feminists must seek and welcome this polarization. Jewish mainstream leaders, mostly male, rarely raise their voices on our behalf. They claim the right to care only about their own when people are homeless and hungry and desperate. They commemorate the Holocaust but ignore the plight of contemporary refugees. They vociferously oppose anti-Semitism but soft-pedal the horrors of racism, including Jewish racism. They exploit the energy of women, through volunteer networks and the nuclear family, without allowing us equal control of resources. Until recently they screamed for support of Israeli governmental policies, and many still actively persecute those who depart from mainstream positions.[8] Progressive American Jews, who are not represented by these leaders, must make ourselves as loud and as visible as our opposition.

This is political strategy. But it feels like splitting the family. And it feels like our fault. As daughters in Jewish homes, many of us learned to shore up the family, to protect it. Much of the work any of us do in therapy includes unlearning this protection, a counter-education that may be, as I've said, especially frightening for minorities, including Jews.

Even on the left, the people with whom we've worked closely may feel like family. Feminists, lesbians, working class people may have experienced what it means to raise charged and potentially divisive issues in a group that seemed, up until the disruption, to be getting on fine. But perhaps especially for Jews working with Jews, the familiarity may invoke childhood memory and with it great longing and dread.

As we define our relationship to Jewishness we confront our relationship to and role in the family. For Jews who felt constrained by the growing-up demands of their family or Jewish community, who may have created some freedom through distance, the thought of engaging with any level of Jewishness will feel like rejoining the family, with all the attendant conflict. The Jewish woman with a non-Jewish partner, friends and community, may contend not only with her own ambivalence; in addition, her non-Jewish support system may evince distaste or mystification at her new endeavor: *Why does it matter? What's so important?* She will feel alone. She will need a new support system.

Inside the Jewish community, when I criticize the Israeli government's occupation of the West Bank and Gaza, I may experience the same feelings of guilt, the same terror as a woman fighting to pray at the Western Wall in Jerusalem or to transform the sexist language in the liturgy; the same accusations are hurled at me as at the B'nai B'rith women who recently defied the male leadership's order to dissolve their autonomous women's organization. Are we dividing the Jewish people and exposing them to danger? Are we abandoning our fathers and brothers whom we were trained to flatter and protect? Will the community of Jews reject us and will we then be alone, hated by both goyim and Jews?

Yet the truth is, Jewish women *have* disrupted the family. We have challenged patriarchal authority. We have supported affirmative action. We have created a Jewish women's peace movement in support of Israeli and Palestinian women working for peace. We have argued unequivocally for reproductive choice. We have been among the leaders of the feminist movement, challenging the traditional nuclear family. In fact, if Jewish women were to assume leadership in the Jewish community, a leadership which we are well trained to exercise, the traditionally progressive direction of a great deal of Jewish power would become even more pronounced, in support of a feminist, life-affirming agenda.

And what stops us? On one hand, not much. The B'nai B'rith women insisting on an autonomous feminist organization have budged not one inch against the patriarchal call for "assimilation." The largely successful struggle of women rabbis for ordination, the continued battle against homophobia in the various synagogue movements, the strong pro-choice position of most mainstream Jewish groups bespeaks powerful feminist impact. Jewish women are moving, inside the Jewish community, the feminist movement and everywhere people are fighting for liberation, dignity, peace. Name it, we're there.

But I'll ask the question again. What stops us? Sexism. Anti-Semitism. Everything I've said so far. We're afraid of division, of anger. We're constrained by our own ignorance of Jewish history and culture, by our lack of pride in who we are, our lack of trust in one another. We're reluctant to rejoin a family we gratefully escaped.

And we are afraid, deeply, irrationally afraid of our own power. How can we gather and use our power if we're afraid what we'll do with it?

So I return to the theme of power, as I must. Isn't the point of therapy to find our power and use it, to trust what we'll do with it? Let me speak for myself. Beneath self-hate, self-distrust, something more solid and luminous reveals itself as deepest longing, for a just, generous, beautifully diverse world. My task in and out of therapy is to learn to welcome my strength, to believe that I, *I*, in all my individual and collective identities, including as a Jew, a Jewish woman, a Jewish lesbian, can help create this world—not in spite of who I am but because of it.

## NOTES

I'm grateful to Judy Chalmer, Michele Clark and Bernice Mennis for critical suggestions and sharing of experience; Michele's expertise as a therapist was particularly helpful. Responsibility for these opinions is mine alone. Because of the original context in which this essay first appeared, I did not address the obvious and critical issue of the cost of therapy. Until therapy, like other health care, is available to anyone who seeks it, individuals and the collective society will continue to suffer for the cruel and shortsighted conception of health as a privilege instead of a right.

1. In addition, women often find power sexy and appealing in other women, so our strength can be an asset. See "Some Notes on Jewish Lesbian Identity."

2. See, for example, Barbara Smith, "Between a Rock and a Hard Place: Relationships Between Black and Jewish Women," in *Yours In Struggle: Three Feminist Perspectives on Anti-Semitism and Racism* (Ithaca: Long Haul/Firebrand, 1984), pp. 76 ff.

3. For example, Cherie Brown or the late Ricky Shereover Marcuse, whose coalition-building work has been a model for the feminist anti-racist movement.

4. Proportionately more Israelis oppose their government in some way than Americans opposed ours at the peak of activity against the Vietnam War.

5. In this it is quite distinct from Christianity, especially from Protestantism, which is the religious version of individualism.

6. The image is Bernice Mennis's, from one of our many fruitful conversations.

7. The critical importance of groups like New Jewish Agenda, Jews for Racial and Economic Justice and Jewish Women's Call for Peace (which holds vigils in support of the Israeli Women's Peace Movement and in opposition to the occupation) is that they allow us to work as Jews and to use organized Jewish power in positive ways.

8. Recent studies by Steven Cohen (1989, sponsored by the Israel-Diaspora Institute at Tel Aviv University and by the American Jewish Committee) indicate that American Jews have become more peace-oriented and that leadership is actually more dovish than its constituent communities. On the other hand, David Biale points to retaliation in the Jewish community against leaders who advocate talking to the PLO, a Palestinian state, etc.; "The Rhetoric of Occupation," *Tikkun* (March/April 1990), pp. 41-43.

# *The Next Step: Coalition Building in the Nineties*[1]

(This is a revised version of a talk given at *Parallels & Intersections: Conference on Racism & Other Forms of Oppression* (April 6-9, 1989, Iowa City), as part of the final plenary session, *Rethinking Alliance Building,* and published in the *NWSA Journal* (Spring 1990). The other speakers were Rachel Sierra, Lakota Hardin, and Angela Davis)

As feminists in the widest possible sense—fighters for the liberation of all women—we look into the nineties with an odd problem. Our analyses are plentiful and often acute. We understand what and how we think and most often we know what positions to take. What is harder is figuring out what to do; how to act effectively. And sometimes, because we are uncertain about where a given political act will lead, we refrain from all but the most familiar and predictable action.

What would we in this country know about civil disobedience had Rosa Parks not refused to give up a seat she had a right to? (And what do we know about it now that anti-abortion people are using our tactics?) We learn through doing. Bernice Johnson Reagon has said we're stumbling because we have to take the next step.[2] There are two parts to this statement, and both are crucial. First, *we are stumbling. We will stumble.* We cannot act without clumsiness and error. Yet the second part insists *we have to take the next step.* We have to move forward without quite knowing where our feet—or wheelchairs—are going. Choose or not, we are perpetually moving across a "perilous chasm that only later gets called history."[3]

But this is abstract and if we know anything about our lives, we know they are filled with concrete details which determine the possibility of change. So let me describe one hard journey of mine, as important as yours: no more, no less.

This journey begins with two separate, parallel stories which ignore each other. There has been no room for these two stories to coexist. I refer of course to the history of the Jews and the history of the Palestinians. As a Jewish child born into a working- and lower-middle-class neighborhood in Brooklyn, I grew up on one of these stories. I think I'm correct in saying that Palestinian children grew up on the other. These divergent and mutually exclusive histories are mirrored in the mutually exclusive claims to the land of Israel/Palestine. They are mirrored in the naming of the piece of land: for years people have said *Israel* or *Palestine*. No one said *both* or *and*. It was one or the other.

I will not here rehearse the histories. What I want to discuss is the process whereby I, a Jew raised on one of these two stories, one of these names, to feel connection to one of these peoples, have changed so that I can honestly say I also feel connection to the other, the people who are not supposed to be mine. I say this with some trepidation, a sense of shame. Who cares about my story, how I came to this place? What's important is that Palestinians are suffering and being killed, and by Israelis. I know that the very slowness of this process, my process, the process of change in which I hope to continue to engage the Jewish people, means the suffering continues.

And yet I have no other story but my own. If I am to use myself as an agent of change, I have to understand both my power and its limits.

Interesting—and it's why I need to speak so personally—through years of change the one thing that has not changed is my political position on the Middle East. From the time I first paid attention—not until the mid-seventies—I thought there should be two states, and I still think so. Something else has changed.

Where does change begin? Born in 1945—Israel came into being in 1948—I grew up knowing Israel existed, that this was good, and that was the end of it. First I left Brooklyn when I was 20 and discovered anti-Semitism. I became increasingly engaged with Jewish issues, increasingly needy of Jewish community (considering I was living in Oregon, New Mexico, and Maine during this time, just finding other Jews was not easy). In the women's movement, the Middle East was often discussed, and the discussion was totally polarized. Depending on the stripe of the speaker's politics, it was again one or the other story. *Israel* or *Palestine*. It made me very nervous. I was aware—and still am—of a double standard on the left, a left that often demonizes Israelis and forgets the most elementary wisdom of any radical: people are not the same as their government.

So I started educating myself and sharing that information. This meant I read and studied, and that I went to the Jewish community, to their events, to learn some of what they knew. I wrote on Jewish themes. Jewish identity. Anti-Semitism and racism. Black-Jewish relations. And the Israeli-Palestinian conflict. I spoke at my local Vermont synagogue about the lesbian and gay civil rights bill. I offered workshops and talks in the women's and in the Jewish community. From all of these, I learned.

This is very important: I did not come to my communities with received wisdom. It has been an honest exchange, and I believe to the extent that I am effective in the Jewish community and in the feminist community, it's because people know I'm really there, that I identify with them, that I'm listening as well as talking. Also important: deepening my Jewish identity did not mean I sat around contemplating my Jewish navel, contrary to what some people seem to think. Developing my identity as a Jew brought me to the Israelis and to the Palestinians.

But I'm getting ahead of myself. In 1982, Israel invaded Lebanon. This marked an important shift for many American Jews: a new sense of urgency. Jews began to speak publicly and critically of Israeli policy, and I did too. But what I felt most keenly was terror: historical Jewish terror, fear of how Israeli actions would be used against Jews. And all this time in the Jewish community the word *Palestinian* was a dangerous word. I assumed that Palestinians hated Israelis, hated Jews, and hated me. If I had knowingly met a Palestinian, I would have been afraid. My state of mind at that point is documented in a poem I wrote called "Kaddish,"[4] about the Holocaust, the death of my father, and the invasion of Lebanon. I'm going to read part of this poem because, as kaddish is the prayer of mourning, this section of the poem is a prayer for openness, an invocation, a refusal to separate either from my people—in this case, the victimizers—or from those victimized.

and...when I heard about children  women
families shot  stabbed at the table in  Shatilla
Sabra  I couldn't breathe
and I was  almost  too afraid to mourn

let me be plain
Jews sent up flares
for christians  to kill by

let me absorb
yes  they are men  soldiers  also, my people  my father loved
all things Jewish  and should I disown?
I  who will be blamed  with the others  again

let me mourn  if anything
is holy  flesh
so readily  torn  from the skeleton

let me rock  my body  like a scared child—
what skin?  what hair?  which language?
*whose child is this?*
*whose child is this?*

the answer says if the child shall
live  die  suffer  kill

let me be strong  as history
let me join those  who refuse
let there be time
let it be  possible

let no faction keep me
from those who suffer

let no faction keep me from those who needed a home
and found one

let no faction keep me from those
who need a home now

In 1982, I, a secular Jew, prayed my own strange prayer to find connection
with both peoples. When I wrote this poem I was grieving, but I asked for
something and It has come. All I knew was the first step: a motion not away from
but deeper into my own community. I found my way to those among my own
people closest to the ground and to the issues—Israelis working towards peace.
I was extremely lucky to get a grant to go to Israel, and interview Israeli women:
feminists, lesbians, peace activists. I learned their commitment to end the
occupation, the devastation that this constant war, the militarism of Israeli
society wreaks especially on the women, the children, the whole social fabric.

Their faces are vivid before me. As a white person who worked in the Civil Rights movement; as an American who worked against the Vietnam war, it was easy for me to identify with the Israeli left. Suddenly I was not frozen with guilt or horror. People were busting ass in some very familiar ways and they needed help.

I not only visited Israel, I visited Ramallah and Hebron on the West Bank. The meaning of "Occupied Territories" was suddenly clear, even visceral. Just about everyone spoke Arabic. The signs were in Arabic. The restaurants served Arabic food. The people were Arab. Only the soldiers were Israeli.

From this trip and the ensuing connections came work primarily directed at the Jewish community in the U.S., especially the women. Writing. Speaking. Workshops. The book *The Tribe of Dina*.[5] And again, I taught and I learned.

One thing I learned was how mystified the issue was. The "Middle East" was like science: only men could understand it. That has changed, and a lot of the breakthrough has been because the women—Palestinian, Israeli, Jewish and Arab—have pushed for change. But did I have any idea where I would end up when I began work on this issue? Not the faintest.

We learn by doing. In January of this year I travelled to Israel and Palestine as part of a peace delegation, to meet with a wide range of Palestinians and Israelis. There is change among the Palestinians and among the Israelis. A solution between the Palestinians and the Israelis seems utterly possible, looming just out of reach. Through the Palestinian *intifada*, the uprising, people—especially women and children—have discovered their own creativity, persistence, and fearlessness. One astonishing example of people discovering their direction— and their power—through doing.

One exercise of this grassroots power has been to demand that their leaders deliver something realistic: the two-state solution. This realism, including Palestinian recognition of Israel, of course makes possible broader international support. It has moved the center of the Israeli peace movement to the left. It has been an enormous relief to Jews, who have, after all, reason to fear extermination. For the first time in years, I can imagine a unified left without feeling much ambivalence, and it's the Palestinians who made this possible. But it's obvious that the self-criticism of American Jews in response to Lebanon, the gritty work of groups like New Jewish Agenda, readied us to receive the message of the *intifada*.

And something else has happened. The two separate narratives have begun to overlap, or, rather, people on both sides have recognized that these two stories have always overlapped and cannot be told except by reference to each other. Largely through Israeli contacts, I've met and spoken with many Palestinian people, and now their faces, too, are vivid before me. I can picture right this minute the ten-year-old boy I met in Ahli Arab Hospital in Gaza, his arm broken from beatings by soldiers; or the woman who had been shot in the hand protecting her kids, smiling and raising her other hand in the *intifada* victory sign.

I picture Naima[6], a young student at Birzeit University except that Birzeit—like all Palestinian universities—has been closed by the Israeli government for nearly two years. Naima writes stories—she used to write in English but now, since the *intifada*, she writes in Arabic, because, in her words, "There's a new Palestinian literature being born." She has a round face, a dazzling smile. She's a feminist. She saw her best friend bleed to death, shot by Israeli soldiers and the ambulance took too long. There are many faces and each face has its own story.

Faces? Human contact? This is exactly the sort of thing I used to think was soppy when I was seventeen and joined the Civil Rights movement out of a sense of outrage. I was very angry, along with most of my generation, and I believed the men when they quoted Mao, "Power comes from the barrel of a gun." I heard the words of Che Guevara, and thought I understood them. But I believe I am only coming to understand these words now: "At the risk of seeming ridiculous, I have to say that the true revolutionary is guided by feelings of great love."

I know we can't all go around meeting and loving each other. It's not possible or practical. Even when we live in the same city, sometimes we are too angry, hurt, or just plain busy. Besides, for those of us who are U.S. citizens, our power extends dangerously around the globe, far beyond the reach of neighborly conversation.

At the same time, I'm reminded of the slogan from the French movement S.O.S., against anti-Semitism and anti-Arab racism (of course in France many are both, Jews and Arabs). They chant, *Ne touche pas à mon pote.* "Keep your hands off my buddy." Far from the complicated, bloodless language with which we have often envisioned coalitions. I know that if we all responded in this way to an injustice done to any of us, we would be unstoppable.

But something stops us. In the poem "Kaddish," I asked—of myself as much as anyone—"let no faction keep me from this group, from that group." Who are these factions? They are three characters and when I introduce them you will recognize them.

One faction says, *Keep away from those who suffer.* This is the all-American faction. Watch it, homelessness is catching. Don't even look. The plague of AIDS striking now so relentlessly at the gay male, Black, and Latino/a communities is used to justify fear and discrimination. The American dream says, *don't fight oppression, escape it;* escape your people, melt into the great white American marshmallow: I'm ok you're ok everything's ok. If you can't escape...tough. Try harder. This is the lure of assimilation and of individual solution.

These people who want to deny suffering, including their own, are also our people. Our job is to remind people where they suffer, and to demand of them their best, most ethical selves. My friend Dalia Sachs, an Israeli leftist, says, "We have to remember most people don't want to oppress others. And if we can show them a way out, they want a way out." Our job is to show people a way out.

Another faction is represented by the self-hater among one's own people who says, *Disown.* She too wants to escape, not from oppressed people but into someone else's experience. Step away from your people. She can see nothing in her own identity but guilt and shame—or, at best, emptiness. She claims to feel like an Indian. She was African in another life. She wants to join the oppressed, the groovy, the hip. You can hear it in the accent she didn't grow up on, you sense it in the way she avoids or mocks her past. You can see it in her clothes. When I was 17 she wore the Southern Black farmworker's overall; at 20 it was Che Guevara's beret, or Mao's jacket or....When I see a Jew wearing a *kafiyeh*, I want to ask, *did you earn this? What are you saying to your own people? Is this what the Palestinians need from you, that you should wear their clothes?*

These folks have internalized society's hatred, and they are hard cookies. They can be extremely destructive. Yet their impulse is to be decent, to work towards change. They need to be met with compassion and they need to be taught compassion. They need some healthy pride in their identity.

But I want to say something about identity politics. The point of identity politics is not to feel good about ourselves, though this is a necessary and inevitable result. The point is to identify with our own people, however we define this; to struggle with them and bring them along with us, so that we build coalitions which represent a true joining.

A third faction cares only about its own people. This can be a defense of privilege or a mark of fear and distrust. Often it is both. When this woman is a Jew she speaks from a deep, terrible history, but she might also be Black or Native American or Chicana or Latina or Asian or lesbian or a mother or poor or simply female, and she will also speak from a deep, terrible history. She says, *No one gives a shit about you but your own.* Your own people.

Sometimes, in its smallest nugget—as we are trained to feel in this fragmented capitalist society—no one but your own family counts. This is the smallest, the pettiest of existences, that we should care for, that we should love so little, so few. Does it matter if people are homeless as long as your few connected folk are provided for?

We carry this over to our movements. If your issue is homelessness, do you care if a football stadium full of college students chants "JAP JAP JAP" when a woman someone thinks is Jewish walks by? If you're fighting for lesbian and gay rights, do you care if a fraternity at the University of Wisconsin (and I am deeply mortified to say it was a mostly Jewish fraternity) runs an auction where pledges dress up in blackface and Afro wigs to be sold as slaves?

In confronting people who focus only on their own, our job is to struggle honestly with their fear, which is often, given the various horrible experiences all our people have been through, quite reasonable. Fear of the hatred or indifference of others. Fear that one's own issues will get lost. In the Jewish community, this has been a large part of my work.

What I've learned is just how big a heart can stretch, and like any muscle, it hurts. But in that amazing paradox of struggle, in conditions you wish no one had to confront, conditions which destroy many, too many—one is too many—people demonstrate the most astonishing capacity for invention, compassion and courage. I hear an Armenian man who says his mother asks him why he's involved with the Palestinian cause, and he explains, "Because if the Palestinians do not stand fast, they will end up like the Armenians in perpetual exile, and therefore

I stand with them." I meet a daughter of Holocaust survivors working in the Gaza Strip to collect stories of Israeli abuse; she says, "It's my own history that brings me here." I listen to a Palestinian schoolteacher describe the first time she entered the refugee camps in 1978; she was so appalled by the conditions that she began working to organize housewives and workers. Ten years later, 25,000 women are organized and, it is said, are the backbone of the *intifada*.

Israeli women too are newly organized and visible: groups like Women in Black who stand in silent vigil every single Friday at 23 locations across Israel, and who are often subjected to abusive language and even to violence by their political opponents; *Shani* (Israeli Women Against the Occupation); Women's Organization for Political Prisoners; *Shutafut* (Partnership); as well as the women's strength evident in mixed peace groups, from the centrist *Shalom Akshav* (Peace Now) to the radical Year 21.[7] Similarly, everywhere I look in Jewish peace activity in the U.S. I see feminists—and lesbians—out in front, pressing the Jewish community to remember our history of oppression and tradition of justice.

The Israeli-Palestinian conflict is one issue in a tiny part of a world that is in big trouble. I was trained in the sixties and seventies in mass movements—civil rights, anti-war, women's liberation. In the eighties we have responded with a proliferation of single-issue movements. This sometimes means that many of us get to pipe up just a little to a desperately cynical Washington and to media far more interested in splash than substance, who contribute to what is often a hit parade of oppression—lesbians and gays up two slots, Salvador down two, Eastern Airline workers up one, coal miners and Guatemala off the charts, South Africa leading, women at the bottom as always....This is not total silencing but it's not reaching for power either.

What does it mean to reach for power?[8] The Rainbow Coalition? A new, untainted communist party? I have my own grounded suspicion of hierarchy, of political leaders, of manipulation and constraint. How we treat each other, how we work with one another is crucial, yet we need to learn again to work in units larger than three or five or twenty.

I think, like everything in this late 20th century, reaching for power will require some fine-tuned balance. It will mean reaching in to our communities and particular issues and reaching out to others—at the same time. We need to be fighting our closest, most passionate battles, whatever and wherever they are. And if the vivid faces before me, demanding my attention, are not Black students in Soweto; are not North American women incarcerated for defending themselves or for refusing to reveal the whereabouts of their sexually abused daughters; are not the indigenous people of Guatemala, then let me be close to people who know these faces well. Who can help weave the connections among all our battles clearly and closely so that our work joins us and we are more and more able to move as one force.

We have to learn by doing. We're stumbling because we have to take the next step. And it's risky, yes. But as one of the Jewish sages, Rabbi Nachman, said almost 200 years ago, "The whole world is a very narrow bridge, but the main thing is not to be afraid." Isn't it, this beautiful, fragile planet, a very narrow bridge, and there is no place to stand but on this bridge, all together; nothing to do but discover how to save, protect, and cherish ourselves and each other? Here we are on the bridge, moving across the perilous chasm that only later gets called history, stumbling because we have to take the next step. The whole world is a very narrow bridge, but the main thing is not to be afraid. Here it is in Hebrew:

*kol ha-olam kulo*
*gesher tzar me'od*
*v'ha-ikar lo l'fached k'lal.*

## NOTES

1. I want to thank the organizers of this conference for many things but in particular, I want to thank them as a Jew for offering kosher food at this conference, a clear option on the registration form. Whether I keep kosher or not, that notice says Jews are welcome, and this touches me deeply because, while Jews have been prominent in radical politics, the left has often forgotten or discarded us. I want to thank them also for making this conference free, donations accepted—an early principle of women's liberation, too often forgotten.

2. Bernice Johnson Reagon, "Coalition Politics: Turning the Century," *Home Girls*, ed. Barbara Smith (Latham, NY: Kitchen Table, Women of Color Press, 1983), p.368.

3. From Melanie Kaye/Kantrowitz, "Some Pieces of Jewish Left," *My Jewish Face & Other Stories* (San Francisco: Aunt Lute, 1990).

4. "Kaddish," in *Sinister Wisdom* 25 (1984). Reprinted in the expanded edition, *Nice Jewish Girls: A Lesbian Anthology*, ed. Evelyn Torton Beck (1990).

5. *The Tribe of Dina: A Jewish Women's Anthology*, eds. Melanie Kaye/Kantrowitz and Irena Klepfisz (Boston: Beacon Press, 1989).

6. A pseudonym.

7. For example, in what may have been the first Israeli civil disobedience action against the occupation, 27 members of *Year 21*, including 19 women, were arrested in May, 1989 and held for several days without bail, until public outcry forced their release.

8. This question has even less answers in 1992, as this goes to press, than in 1989. We will have to create the forms in which we reach for power.

# *Swords Into Plowshares: Jews For Middle East Peace*

(This talk was given to introduce a *Swords Into Plowshares* event on April 7, 1991, at the Stephen Wise Free Synagogue in New York City. The event included music, poetry, saying kaddish for all who died in the Gulf War, and presenting petitions signed by Jews who support the creation of a Palestinian State alongside a secure Israel.)

Welcome. I'm Melanie Kaye/Kantrowitz, greeting you on behalf of SWORDS INTO PLOWSHARES: JEWS FOR MIDDLE EAST PEACE, a project created by individuals and groups including the International Jewish Peace Union, the Jewish Peace Fellowship, the Jewish Women's Committee to End the Occupation of the West Bank and Gaza, and New Jewish Agenda/Manhattan Chapter.

As Jews, friends, and allies, we've just finished celebrating *pesakh*, our holiday of liberation, and we gather to recommit our already committed selves to the work of liberation, which in our tradition—and I love this about our tradition—is also the work of making peace. Because the word *shalom* does not mean passivity; peace is not an absence, it is a full, harmonious presence. It means freedom. It means justice.

We need this as Jews. We are sick of the sickness of the Israeli occupation of the West Bank and Gaza. And we're here especially today on our holiday of liberation to refuse oppression in all its forms. I don't have to tell you what's right, you're here today instead of somewhere else because you needed to be among your people, friends, community—who are sick with grief about the 100,000, 200,000 Iraqis dead, the civil war still raging, the Kurds seeking refuge at closed or open borders, as Jews so often sought refuge at borders sometimes closed, sometimes open, always for reasons that served those in power.

As Jews, we're taught to learn from history. That's why at *pesakh* we tell the story of the exodus, our escape from slavery. We must always remember the lessons of slavery and freedom, exile and return, strangeness and home.

And it is because we're faithful to history that we oppose one of history's sickest jokes: the Palestinian diaspora, the Palestinians without passports, the Palestinians showing their identity papers over and over. We're sick about children killed for throwing stones, schools closed, incessant curfews, women stabbed in the marketplace, and the daily humiliations and abuses which are inevitable companions of occupation. We're sick about the endless cycle of violence in Israel and in Palestine, that we are determined to end as it only can be ended: with justice.

In a time like this we need all the wisdom and nourishment we can get, and we have gathered today to share these things. I invoke one of the wisest, bravest voices of our century: the late Muriel Rukeyser, poet, activist, Jew, lesbian, relentless fighter for freedom. In 1968, Rukeyser published a poem titled simply "poem," which goes like this:

POEM

I lived in the first century of world wars.
Most mornings I would be more or less insane,
The newspapers would arrive with their careless stories,
The news would pour out of various devices
Interrupted by attempts to sell products to the unseen.
I would call my friends on other devices;
They would be more or less mad for similar reasons.
Slowly I would get to pen and paper,
Make my poems for others unseen and unborn.
In the day I would be reminded of those men and women
Brave, setting up signals across vast distances,
Considering a nameless way of living, of almost unimagined values.
As the lights darkened, as the lights of night brightened,
We would try to imagine them, try to find each other.
To construct peace, to make love, to reconcile
Waking with sleeping, ourselves with each other,
Ourselves with ourselves. We would try by any means
To reach the limits of ourselves, to reach beyond ourselves,
To let go the means, to wake.

I lived in the first century of these wars.*

Here we are, at the end of this same century, imagining acts of courage, trying to reach beyond ourselves. I was thinking this morning about people I knew who'd be coming today and their reasons for doing so. We created this event out of a need that was both personal and political. Politically, the need to be visible as Jews in support of Palestinian rights and aspirations, of the spirit of land for peace, of negotiations. Our political opponents in the Jewish community are vocal as Jews; our task here is to make plain that they do not speak for us or for thousands of others. We are also here in solidarity with the African American community's designation of today as Justice and Peace on Earth Sunday.

On a personal level, I think many of us need—I know I need—to look around the room and for a moment shed our differences, in political stripe, in gender and sexual orientation, in class, age, degrees of religious observance and secular identity, and among our friends and allies, in religion, race, ethnicity. To look around the room and feel our unity in our commitment to justice, and the sense of possibility, the strength we derive from that unity.

I think in the end we are here out of loyalty—to individuals, to principles, to what is best in ourselves. And what is best in ourselves must answer to what is worst in our nation, in the Jewish community, and in Israel; the anti-wisdom of the Gulf War and of the Israeli occupation. The war, the occupation's lesson is the same: it is the lesson of scarcity, of *us and them*, of someone gets protected at the expense of someone else. It is the anti-wisdom that leaves thousands in this city without homes, without food; that leaves unchallenged the violence of racism, the violence of sexism.

And what will this continued anti-wisdom of Israelis or Palestinians bring? We're here to say we refuse this anti-choice: not either/or, but both. We know that we do not abandon the Jewish people because we embrace the Palestinian people as well.

I want to ask you to think for a minute about yourselves as political beings. Many of you are activists, that's why you're here. I know some of you are teachers, who pour your political energy into your students. Many of you, I know, work so hard, usually at jobs for pay and do political work over and above that. I want to ask you—not to do more quantitatively—for many of you here, that's not possible—nor do I want to ask you for money.

I want to ask you to think about risk. I think we are here because we recognize that events in Israel and the Occupied Territories will move one way or the other: towards the two states and the opportunity for peace and justice, which we long for, or towards mass expulsion, repression, and destruction of the Palestinian people.

Given this, we need to think about escalation—not from bombs to ground war, but from writing letters and petition drives, like this one, and lobbying, and educational forums and fundraising and vigils—all the things we are doing—to some next steps. What will we do next? Mass protest? Sit-ins? Tax resistance? Fill in the blank, it is ours to fill. What are we willing to do for peace and justice? What are we willing to do to heal this sickness perpetrated in the name of the Jewish people?

I ask this not to inspire fake dramatics and I certainly don't mean to guilt trip. I ask because I think we are all a bit confused, shocked, dazed by this war, its swiftness, its devastation. We need to think about how to move next. We will need to do things we have not yet thought of or planned for. We will need to be bold and experimental. The years have tamed us, neutralized our strategies, domesticated our demonstrations, and demonstrations are only as powerful as the evident determination behind them, and that is the determination to do more.

What will we do? Take an obvious example. What if everyone in this room showed up at the Israeli independence day parade to say we have a different vision for Israel, a vision of peace, justice, and equality? What if everyone here performed civil disobedience in the name of self-determination for the Palestinian people? Imagine how these actions would embolden our community—and how they would embolden us.

Muriel Rukeyser, again, wrote in 1944, "To be a Jew in the 20th century is to be offered a gift." Let us seize this gift. We gather today for mourning, for sustenance, for rededication to action, and for emboldening. Welcome.

NOTES

*"Poem," as well as a selection of Muriel Rukeyser's other poems, is now back in print; *Muriel Rukeyser Out of Silence: Selected Poems,* ed. Kate Daniels (Evanston, IL: TriQuarterly Books, Northwestern Univ., 1992).

# *Anti-Arab Racism*

(This talk was presented at a panel on Anti-Arab Racism organized by Brooklyn Residents Against Bias-Related Violence, March 13, 1991.)

I want to talk about common issues of racism against Arabs and against Jews; about how anti-Arab racism made possible the slaughter of perhaps 200,000 Iraqis—you could not fight such wars were it not for racism—and how it is used in the U.S. at large and in the Jewish community, in particular, to block peace efforts between Israelis and Palestinians. Finally I want to talk about Jewish efforts to fight racism against Arabs and how these efforts are an integral part of our Middle East peace work and our work to fight Jewhating, Arabhating and racism of all kinds.

Notice I'm avoiding the term anti-Semitism. In my community this term means, and has meant for over 100 years, *Jewhating*. That Arabs and Jews are both of Semitic origins has led some to use the term to mean hatred of Jews and Arabs. What is important I believe is not what we call it but what we are saying about it. If, for example, Jews use anti-Semitism to mean Jewhating, because of its traditional meaning in the community, but always talk also about, and always act also against, anti-Arab racism, this seems fine to me. Similarly, though it's not my community's usage or tradition, if people say anti-Semitism against Arabs and Jews and *mean* the "and Jews" part, always act also against Jewhating, I feel fine about this too. But there are no rules of usage by which you can tell where people's politics line up, or what is our commitment to stick up for each other. What counts is the commitment.

*Stereotypes of Jews and Arabs.* Jews are money and Arabs are oil. Jews are communists and Arabs are terrorists. Jews are pushy, rude, while Arabs are over-polite, unctuous. Neither is trustworthy: Jews will do anything for money and Arabs will readily lie. Jews are faggots and Arabs are sodomites. One of the ugliest slogans of this war, which I encountered in an upstate New York diner: *Saddamize Hussein*, showing a man being raped in the ass, exploiting anti-gay as well as anti-Arab stereotypes of perverse, untrustworthy sexuality.

*Women.* Notice I'm talking about men. Jewish women are mothers, domineering guilt-tripping martyrs, or Jewish American Princesses, rich from their fathers' money, parasites, either frigid or nymphomaniacs. This stereotype is a serious problem on college campuses. The relationship of this stereotype to racism should be plain even without its acronym *JAP* and the revival on some campuses of the World War II slogan *Slap a JAP* (racist propaganda is always a weapon of war), or the fact that dormitories with a lot of Jewish women on at least two campuses I know about get called *Tokyo Towers*.

The level of discourse in the mainstream American community is different for Jews and for Arabs. Stereotypes of Jewish women circulated in the mainstream U.S. community are drawn largely from the misogyny of certain Jewish men, who seem not to recognize its relationship to Jewhating.

Arabs, on the other hand, are not often heard in the mainstream U.S. community speaking for themselves. There has not been an Arab *Portnoy's Complaint* to familiarize mainstream U.S. with Arab cultures generally, or with Arab men's attitudes towards Arab women, in particular. In the U.S. there is a basic, vague, outsider attitude—"they're so backward they don't let their women get educated or drive or vote." There's vast ignorance about the diversity of Arab cultures, and about what life is like for Arab Americans. Americans simply "know" that Arab women are the most oppressed on earth, they live in harems (where they satisfy unnatural desires) or they wear the veil and are prevented from any independent interaction with the world.

*Religious Bigotry.* Of course, many Arabs are christian, but the majority are Muslims, and they're perceived as Muslims, non-christian. And Jews, of course, are Jews, the people who had the honor to produce Christ but not the virtue to recognize him as the messiah.

In a country which is ostensibly secular but insistently christian, both Jews and Arabs are perceived as evil, morally lacking, beyond the pale. Anyone who is not christian is suspected of immorality. Christianity is not a very generous religion, though it considers itself so, since anyone can join. But those who choose not to become christian are, by its theology, damned to eternal torment: not exactly an appreciation of diversity. "Act like a christian" means "act decently," act humanly (or as we would say in the Flatbush I grew up in: act like a *mentsh*). But history suggests that "act like a christian" might well mean "slaughter all non-christians in the name of Christ"—from the Crusades to the bombing of Baghdad.

*The Jewish Community.* Speaking as a Jew, all the attitudes I've just named affect us too. Plus. As Jews, Israeli racism affects us. There's a permeable border between Israel and the American Jewish community (as with Arabs and their homelands, including Palestine), so we often are privy to those Israeli attitudes shaped by fear, hatred and just plain bigotry, as well as the cynical manipulation of all these in the interest of hanging onto the West Bank and Gaza. Continued possession of these areas entails continued occupation and oppression of another people, and, ultimately—as the *intifada* has made clear, there is no status quo—a choice between two options: transfer or murder, on one hand, or self-determination for the Palestinian people, on the other.

One tactic used by those who support the concept of a "Greater Israel"— code for annexation of at least the West Bank—is to continually paint a picture of nonpeople. This is done most commonly about *The Arabs*—the name *Palestinian* is seldom even used by those who would depict all Arabs as essentially barbaric, primitive, violent and untrustworthy. The truth, as observed by American Jews like myself who have visited with West Bank Palestinians, is in many ways a very familiar culture, a culture of diaspora, landlessness and attachment to education as a way to provide some security (the Yiddish proverb *toyre is di beste skroyre*, "learning is the best merchandise," felt very appropriate). Lots of Ph.D.s, scholars, students. A nation of small shopkeepers.

*Why Anti-Arab Racism Must Be Fought Among Jews,* as well as in society at large. I could say, and it's true, strategically, that anti-Arab racism alienates us from Arabs and we are possible allies. I could say, and it's true, that I'm not free until everybody else is. This is all true. I could even say more specifically that in the dominant culture, those who hate Arabs probably also hate Jews, and vice versa. They are christian fundamentalists (very scary people, as are all fundamentalists, including Jewish and Muslim fundamentalists). They are xenophobes, hating all foreigners, all difference, all other. They are repressive, constraining forces of death, and any one who loves freedom has to fight them at all times.

But I want to say something else too. Let me backtrack for a moment. Something I noticed in most of the discussions about this war: even those who were anti-war used for the most part a certain discourse. They talked about foreign policy, oil, U.N. resolutions, geopolitical this and that....

I don't mean to trivialize these issues, but there has been another discourse on war, primarily heard among the women. The language of outrage: *it's disgusting,* we say, *it's wrong, unacceptable, we will not allow this to continue.* I think we need to trust more to the discourse of outrage and morality, to encourage in our people what is best and most generous, not only what is in our own narrowly defined self-interest.

So I want to say, we fight anti-Arab racism because it's disgusting. And something else, which can best be said through two poems, both by women, one Israeli, one Palestinian-American.

GAZA

I

After the final heave, house collapsing
in and all the prayers that had held
the ceiling up for years rushing
through dust with a low moan
but leaving, you have seen her
sifting through the rubble,
sandaled foot striking an iron
bedframe, splintered picture
of a prophet's resting place.
With no tears you have seen her,
dry like stone, like tile, and alone.

Then understand the law as I did not;
we tore the house down and she may not rebuild
there or elsewhere. *Her kitchen smelled of zatar
and of bread.* She will have no home here, no home.

II
Consider the prayers' desertion and our faith
crushed where it had been tucked neatly
between headscarves in the top drawer
even as our walls still stand;
*there is no believing now.*
*There are only children in the alleys,*
*their blood darkening the dirt.*

After the rains, this mound will settle,
sink into itself and forget what it was.
But she, who salvaged
herself, will not forget.
This you cannot see, but listen;
how the storm rises, and the hills
move closer to the river.[1]

FOR THE 500th DEAD PALESTINIAN, IBTISAM BOZIEH

Little sister Ibtisam,
our sleep flounders, our sleep tugs
on the cord of your name.
Dead at thirteen, for staring through
the window into a gun barrel
which did not know you wanted to be
a doctor.

I would smooth your life in my hands,
pull you back. Had I stayed in your land
I might have been dead too,
for something simple like staring
or shouting what was true
and getting kicked out of school.
I wandered the stony afternoons
owning all their vastness.

Now I would give them to you,
guiltily, *you, not me.*
Throwing this ragged grief into the street,
scissoring news stories free from the page,
but they live on my desk like letters, not cries.

How do we carry the endless surprise
of all our deaths? Becoming doctors
for one another, Arab, Jew,
instead of guarding tumors of pain
as if they hold us upright?

Little sister, once our supple fingers
curled around any twig.
Now even the orchards weep.
People in other countries speak easily
of being early, being late.
Some will live to be eighty.
Some who never saw it
will not forget your face.[2]

As Jews we need to say, along with Naomi Shihab Nye, *we will not forget this face.* We need to identify, as Rachel Tsvia Beck does, with the woman whose home has been destroyed. For to remember the face, to feel our beliefs challenged by the blood of children is to become the storm, the river challenging the hills.

## NOTES

1. Rachel Tsvia Beck, "Gaza," *Tikkun*, Vol. 4, No. 5.

2. Naomi Shihab Nye, "For the 500th Dead Palestinian, Ibtisam Bozieh," *Fine Madness* (1991).

# *Some Notes On The Gulf War*

## 1. WAR

The problem with war is that it's simple. You kill or you don't kill. But conflict is not simple. Conflict involves edges. Edges cause friction. Friction makes heat; sometimes fire. Only once it becomes fire, it's simple. It burns or it doesn't burn.

Non-violence assumes a way of resolving conflict that pays attention to the edges.

## 2. SOME EDGES IN THE MIDDLE EAST

The legacy of colonialism, false national boundaries, bitterness against Europe/the U.S./the West; distribution of wealth in the Arab world in general and the Gulf States in particular; rivalry between Iraq and Syria, between Saddam and Assad, over who gets to be the new Nassar; Israel's continued refusal to acknowledge Palestinian rights; manipulation of Palestinian grievances by various Arab leaders, most recently Saddam; the matched trauma of the Jews and the Palestinians claiming the same small piece of earth...

## 3. IRAQ

Until the hostage crisis in 1979, how many people in the U.S. could tell Iraq from Iran? People are learning for the first time the name of Iraq's capital, as in 1979 we learned Tehran.

But that's the iceberg tip. We, as the dominant culture, never have learned where the other places are. Never have learned to see through the eyes of another. We don't speak the languages. We don't bother learning anything about them. We know our way is the best damned way there is. WE'RE RIGHT. Consequently we rarely know what's happening, until a crisis erupts. TV specials, newspaper maps abound. Where is it? Who are they? In what ways are they odd, eccentric, inferior to us?

## 4. KUWAIT

Then there is the particular complexity called Kuwait. Tiny, rich, with borders as artificial as any in the once-colonized Third World, Kuwait was hardly free to start with—like Athens, cradle of Western democracy, where women, slaves and non-citizens had no rights. That's our hero. Sixty percent of the pre-war residents were non-citizens, and thus had no rights, plus 50% of the remaining 40%, who had no rights because they were women. That leaves 20% up for liberation. Kuwaitis (non-citizens excluded but wives and daughters of citizens included, as citizen property) had an average per capita income of $13,000+ a year. Not the workers, of course; the workers were Palestinians, Filipinos, Egyptians...holding the worst jobs, lacking all rights and benefits of citizens.

Given this, one can't help asking, *How did George Bush talk about the liberation of Kuwait with a straight face?*

Or answering, *years of practice in the CIA.*

## 5. GEOPOLITICAL REALITY, OR THE BIG DICK

War does not allow you to care about the other people's lives.

I am not a pacifist. Pacifism depends upon faith that you can contact a spark of goodness in each human being, or you'll die trying. Whereas I, as a woman and a Jew, am unwilling to trust in this spark. I used to have screaming fights with a friend, Salvation Army by origin/Buddhist by conviction. She didn't lock her door and insisted she'd rather be raped and murdered than carry around the distrust of that locking gesture. I'd argue vehemently for killing someone who attacked me, thus protecting myself and every other woman he'd go on to attack, if not stopped. And I would still argue this point vehemently.

But the stupidity of this war is so stark I can't believe everyone didn't laugh Bush and Congress off the stage. Except the consequences are also so stark they smother humor. Except it's about people's lives. War does not allow you to care about the other people's lives.

War is simple. You kill or you don't kill. If you muck up this simplicity with weapons you long to use, an economy you need to stimulate, medals you ache to win and award, a country desperate for distraction, an empire in its last gasps, something simple remains. You start a war because you want to start a war. The Gulf War began because the U.S. wanted a war, and because Saddam Hussein didn't not want a war enough to stop it. This is called Saving Face.

What was settled by this war? Whose face got saved? To live in a century of computers, jets and open-heart surgery, a century of mustard gas, xyklon B, napalm and 2,600 bombs a day dumped on Iraqi cities. The century of war-caused famine, plague and pollution. Whose face got saved?

I know people who care about lives more than saving face. Personally. I've watched them in action. Women. Women take life more seriously than men. Not always, but often.

Patriarchy needs war. Because patriarchy too is simple. It likes good guys and bad guys, adventures with clear goals and no ethics to ponder. Especially in the U.S. We have never lost a war. We have never fought a war on our own soil, except for a civil war and massacres against people who for thousands of years had managed with more or less grace to share the land with each other and all other living creatures. We wanted to preserve the union. We wanted the land. What do we know of complexities?

Who do I mean by *we?*

Why was this war fought? They say oil. Oil is money. But beyond a certain point, money is an abstraction. For control. Wealth. Power. Who gets to decide. Who will live and who will die. And how.

Beyond a certain point, power, control are abstractions. Yet power must feel very concrete to men who seek it at the expense of human life. Other human lives. Never their own.

## 6. CONQUERORS, RAGE AND SCAPEGOATS

Frantz Fanon, an Algerian psychiatrist, wrote about the psychology of oppression, rage and violence. Why do oppressed people strike out at their own, or at other oppressed people? What keeps the violence turned inward, backward or downward, instead of focused as revolution against those in power? Fanon was exploring the relationship of Algerians to French, Africa to Europe, colonized to colonizer.

What were the British doing in Palestine, Transjordan, Egypt? What were the French doing in Lebanon, Syria?

Put another way, why do Jews hate Arabs? Why do Arabs hate Jews?

The early Zionists came from Europe and wanted to build a new world free from hatred of Jews, free from marginalized existence as a despised minority. They wanted to normalize Jewish existence, to have a government, an army, a language, most significantly, a geographical location—a homeland—the same as every other nationality.

Think, though. Europe had already mistreated the Jews beyond belief. The U.S., generally kinder to Jews, shut its doors when Jews were desperate. Before the Nazis, there were various terrifying pogroms. Under the Nazis it was only more, a lot more, of the same. To stay meant death. And there was no place to go.

But what we see is not Jewish rage at Europe or the U.S.—on the contrary, relations are fine, especially cordial between Israel and Germany, while the U.S. and Israel are more than dating again, they are in, it would seem, a committed relationship.[1] Israel has even let the U.S. move in.

And where do we find the rage, the fear, the insistent "Never Again" directed?

At the Arabs.

And the Arabs? Their hatred is of course partly about the displacement of their people by—from their perspective—one more set of colonials. The Jews intruded, did things differently, upset the culture (lest anyone romanticize that culture, the apparent freedom and equality of Jewish women was considered deeply offensive).

Since 1948 Israel has meant for the Palestinians *ghurba*/exile, hordes of young men in prison or expelled from Israel and the Occupied Territories, and always the increasing facts on the ground, the continuing expansion of settlements, the priority given to Hebrew as language, to Israeli as culture, to Jews as people. There have been wars and deaths. There is still an occupying army and occupying armies do pretty much the same thing all over the world. Repress, suppress, oppress. Keep the people back, down, under.

Then too there are real obstacles to settling the conflict. Concrete losses. Land. Water. Margin of border safety.[2]

Set all this aside for a moment. The hatred is also about Europe. Europe colonized the Middle East. But in Fanon's terms the West is too frightening to hate directly, too powerful to fight directly.

Whereas Israel—now that's a hatred you can act on. Zionists were Europeans weak enough to attack safely. The reachable Europeans. Israel is the reachable West.

Israel has played into this identification with the West, especially with the U.S., developing an economy and a military that depend on U.S. money, evading the need to make peace with its neighbors, most pressingly the Palestinians. As if Israel were not a small Middle Eastern country in the middle of other Middle Eastern countries.

There are actual injuries perpetrated by Arabs and Israelis against each other. There are continued injuries perpetrated by the Israeli government against Palestinians.[3]

Yet something is obvious, dangerous and even tragic. Arabs and Jews play out *colonialism* and *Holocaust* on one another, displacing their rage, compressing and eliding their sense of injury so that what was done to them is partly acted out against people who didn't do it; a mutual scapegoating in which Europe and the U.S. emerge innocent. What happens to Europe? Nothing. What happens to the U.S.? Nothing. Except the opportunity to use up weapons which are not even counted as costing, since they've already been paid for.

## 7. AMERICA

As we have seen with the fall of Eastern Europe's regimes, the world's love affair with America, best symbolized by jeans, is quite complex. If the public face is hateful, disapproving, the hidden face is probably a passionate slightly smutty attraction. That's how repression works.

The Arabs hate and love us. Islam is blurred in everyone's mind with this hate, its sacred task to ward off not just christianity but the West itself. Yet everyone knows the West means freedom, personal happiness, an unconstrained future. Israelis love and hate us. Need our money. Think we're stupid, naive, spoiled, bossy, rich cousins at best. Are grateful that for once someone is sticking up for the Jews. Besides, they too want to come here: for jeans, for the good life, the easy, protected life.

Let's face it. Everyone has been seduced by America. Everyone wants jeans. Everyone wants to come here. Even the name of two continents is claimed by us, and you have to utter awkward locutions to be politically sound. North Americans? But Canada. United Statesians? Only in Spanish is there a word: *Estadounidenses*.[4] "We are the world" spoken by *Estadounidenses* resonates dangerously; we may not know that we are not in fact the world but a rather small and ignorant corner of it.

## 8. GLADIATORS

It's Europe and Japan who need the oil. It's the U.S. flailing about for control, dying gasp of the old patriarch struggling against a nightmare new order possibly as nasty as the old. Will we take the planet with us? Radioactive debris scattered by our side; oilfields burning from their side.

Who do I mean by *we?*

Soldiers are always gladiators, fighting a war that rarely pertains to their direct interest. But in this war civilians, too, were gladiators, bearing the risk for others. They are joined by the American poor. Those who cannot possibly win. The war that was protested before it began. The war no public figure would openly oppose.

## 9. A JEWISH RESPONSE TO THE BOMBING OF ISRAEL

War is simple. The problem is complex. Yet what are we supposed to say, as Jews, when Israel is attacked?

The validity of our response to the missiles lobbed at Tel Aviv hangs on our response to the bombing of Baghdad. A civilian city. Our army spokesmen say, "military targets," but the non-information of this war was staggering, and estimates range from one to two hundred thousand casualties. People who did not care about Iraqi life—are they entitled to care about Jewish life?

And vice versa? At an anti-war rally on a California campus, someone announces that Tel Aviv was bombed. Some people clap.

Simona Sharoni, an Israeli. *Of course I'm afraid for my family. After every attack I call home to see if everyone's okay. But who's calling home for the Iraqis, to see if they're okay? Do we even know if there are any phones left in Baghdad?*

## 10. JEWISH *ESTADOUNIDENSES* AND JEWISH SURVIVAL

Contemporary Jewish experience is characterized by desperate situations in which the real subject is not us; worse suffering is always elsewhere. Sabra and Shatilla. Baghdad. West Bank and Gaza. Bed-Stuy.

So why am I talking about Jewish survival?

Jewish survival is not only the banner waved over Tel Aviv, over Israel. As if it were at stake. It is not only the banner always waved over Jewish life. Always at stake.

It is also one end of a polarized choice. We are told by many Jewish institutions, we get to be Jews, Jewish bodies with Jewish blood and Jewish genes by giving up our progressive ideas. We are told Jewish survival is contradicted by progressive ideas, progressive movements. Solidarity vs. *take care of your own, no one else will.*

On the other hand, we are told by many progressives, we get to be progressives only by abandoning our Jewish selves and Jewish community. Jews devoted to their Jewishness are inherently reactionary, though quite a few transcend. Transcend both their reactionism and their Jewishness. Since these are identical.

Until we articulate a pro-Jewish, anti-war position, we are trapped, silenced, turned against some part of ourselves.

Jewish tradition isn't clear on this question: I wish it were. It says both. The ugly *chosen chosen chosen* voices. The dangerous *protect us, smite our enemies* voices. As well as the *welcome the stranger* voices, *beat swords into plowshares* voices, passages in which god is more mother than father, protector, giver of life and holiness.

We have to choose. That too is Jewish.

## 11. JEWISH SECULAR PRAYER IN A TIME OF WAR

I am a secular Jew, an atheist, but in the last few years sometimes I go to synagogue. In Vermont, where I lived for five years, because it's where the Jews were. In New York City, where I live now, returned from the diaspora, because there are Jewish communal events which move me, holidays; a talk by Yael Dayan about the possibilities for peace between Israel and Palestine (she didn't quite call it Palestine, but she spoke of trading land for peace). And on the evening of January 18, 1991, on the 3rd day of this war—where the days should be counted *erev,*[5] since each day's fighting began after sundown, whether for the safety of darkness or more cynically for network prime time—I went to B'nai Jeshurun for a program in honor of Martin Luther King's birthday. A choir from an African American church sang, and Julian Bond spoke, and it was good for a moment to interrupt the war and remember the tasks the war had interrupted.

But when the rabbi told us to turn East towards Jerusalem to pray to god the protector for peace for the peoples of the Middle East, all I could think was *shame shame shame, god, if you exist, shame, with all this wisdom, how could anyone with power to stop it not stop it?*

Because war is simple. You kill or you don't kill.

NOTES

1. As this goes to press in 1992, relations between Israel and the U.S. are again somewhat unstable.

2. The West Bank did not protect Israelis from SCUD missiles, and there are security arguments in favor of Israel giving up the West Bank and Gaza. See Jerome Segal, *Creating the Palestinian State, A Strategy for Peace* (1989).

3. This is not to pretend that no Palestinians have harmed Israelis, but in 1991 there is no symmetry between Israeli state power and the responses, however hostile and even violent, of Palestinians.

4. Not surprisingly, since most Spanish-speakers are also Americans, in Central and South America.

5. The Jewish day begins at sundown; *erev* is the period between dusk and dawn.

# Nine Suggestions For Radicals
# or Lessons From the Gulf War

## 1. ACKNOWLEDGE CHAOS.

Anyone who claims s/he understands fully the events of the whirlwind Gulf War is lying, crazy or god. We have been lied to so that we don't know which way is up. Even as information about the war's damage comes to us, we have lost faith in our ability to find out what really is happening at any given time, and we have learned that the popular media will not tell us.

As radicals, we have been outsmarted; they learned more from Vietnam than we did. We saw a war coming and responded as if this were 25 years ago. But something was missing. A certain determination to do more. The threat of potential force that must lurk behind the marches and demonstrations of any mass movement. The sense of strength restrained—*for now.*

In addition, we assumed a public and an enemy (the government) that would function in familiar ways. We remembered people's disgust with the Vietnam War that manifested in its late stages, when many Americans had died, when the economy squeezed the poor, working and lower-middle classes, when information about napalm, My Lai, brothels in Saigon, were all over the news.... We thought we could mobilize this disgust immediately. We did not count on the strength of anti-Arab racism.[1] We remembered U.S. military strategy as not only criminal but also stupid, and were not prepared for criminal skill, their chilling, efficient strategy of entirely discounting the lives of Iraqi civilians. The military learned to win fast, to avoid the body bags we kept invoking as "our" cost in this war. We didn't expect their stranglehold on the media, their preparations for our mass demonstrations, their muffling of our impact.

Perhaps most significantly, we soft-pedalled talk about morality, counting instead on U.S. casualties to mobilize our people against the war.

So what happened when the body bags failed to come home? Essentially the U.S. had a free war, practically costless to the American people. Money, yes; but since we were not able to mobilize mass opposition to the military budget prior to the war, how much less did people object when a demonic enemy was dangled before them; when it was such smashing evening entertainment; when it ended so quickly...or seemed to.

We failed to talk much about morality and principle, but the government did not. They were fighting for freedom. They were stopping the new Hitler. We were not able to expose their rhetoric. We didn't have time. We didn't have access to mass media. We didn't have people's confidence.

Moreover, the discourse of anti-war morality risks sounding unmasculine, soppy. To say war is wrong or a desperate last resort makes patriarchy wince. Anti-communism has been the U.S.'s powerful pro-war tool since 1945. Speaking out against a war when the enemy was communism was like rooting for Satan.

In January, 1991, when the red menace had practically devoured itself (the finishing touches would soon appear), the government had two brilliant strategies.

First, lie. Deny that people were being killed, present this as George Bush's kinder, gentler war. The press's collaboration with these lies was shameful, but moral indignation will get us about as far as it got those of us who were shocked in the sixties when cops beat us. Doesn't our analysis tell us whose interests are served by mass media; by police?

Second, lacking the red menace to wave about, invoke the lavender one. Anyone who objects to war as a means to settle disputes is a faggot or a woman. Because what needed to be said clearly was this: the Gulf War was wrong because people got killed and life is precious. Because Iraqis love their lives just as Americans do.

Yet the movement itself was rarely ready to say anything so fruity. At rallies, panels and teach-ins I heard two wildly different sorts of discourse, mostly though not entirely corresponding to male and female speakers. The men mostly spoke about foreign policy, oil, statistics, U.N. resolutions, the serious issues; the women mostly spoke about disgust and horror and wrong, *girl talk,* a discourse little respected even in our movement.

We need to talk among ourselves about mistakes, assumptions and new possibilities. We need to be thinking more long range, not to get caught so off guard, so responsive/reactive. We need above all to acknowledge that neither this war nor the state of the world itself is as we knew it. We are confused. Only by admitting our confusion can we begin to build something new.

## 2. EXPERIMENT.

New movements are created by and create new forms: unions/walkabouts, which became strikes; civil rights/sit-ins; women's liberation/consciousness-raising groups. The most interesting new political forms, using the term loosely, of the past couple of years have been the lively disobedience of ACT UP and QUEER NATION, the campus rebellions opposing tuition increases and in support of multicultural agendas and—from the war—the Military Families Support Network and the GI Resistance. We need to learn from the most politically bold and creative among us. (We also need to offer concrete solidarity and support to those we learn from, lest *learning from* mean *ripping off.*)

The need to experiment becomes especially apparent when we think how, yippies onward, we have oriented movement activities towards the media and have in fact become dependent on the media which, in this war, neither provided us with information, nor reported our anti-war activities.[2] Important work is being done to pressure the media to shape up and to force the government to release information in a timely fashion.[3] But we also need to find ways around this dependence. We are stuck with a pernicious assumption which we have in part created: that a huge march on Washington is the way to go. Yet Washington has seen a thousand marches and is, by now, perpetually unimpressed by whatever we muster in symbolic strength. And anyway, how huge is *huge* in the face of 1/2 million, 3/4 million from past marches: this is the century of numbers.

We need to try new strategies and tactics, some of which we have not yet thought of. This means encouraging creativity, seeing what works. (The *let 1000 flowers bloom* approach to politics.[4])

Some of these "new" strategies might actually be old. Many political organizations, operating from the nation's media centers, have attempted shortcut alternatives to the slower process of involving large numbers of people in grassroots organization. Seduced by the promise of mass media, we imagine a mass movement can be created by the eleven o'clock news. Faxing a press release to the major newspapers and TV stations is seen as taking action. In this war, as in our political work of the last decade or so, we did a lot of our fighting with paper. Now we discover the limits of paper. Even if our press releases achieve publicity—and often they did not—whom do they engage? Who gets mobilized? How do press releases build a movement's strength? How do they deepen the militancy of participants?

### 3. TO POLARIZE OR NOT TO POLARIZE

Anti-war activity during Vietnam was probably retarded by the initial hostility toward G.I.s and "ordinary" Americans espoused by often privileged white kids (and stressed by media). Snobbery hurt the anti-war movement. Right-wing forces were able to portray radicals and peaceniks as aberrations, barely human, as opposed to ordinary, decent folk. We ourselves contributed to this polarization. Hip and square. Summer of love vs. suit and tie or lunch bucket.

In this war we saw polarized thinking in the mainstream and on the sectarian left: we were ordered to choose between Kuwait or Iraq, Israelis or Palestinians. To choose one side meant death or abandonment to the other. Sometimes we, on the left, even chose by default: everything they loved, we hated. Thus in some segments of the movement, Saddam Hussein, Hitler to the mainstream, became Ho Chi Minh.

Where we best transcended this kind of split was in our insistence that support for the troops did *not* mean support for the war; or, in the Jewish peace movement, that support for Israeli security—even under SCUD attack—did not mean abandoning the aspirations for justice and self-determination of the Palestinians.[5]

Polarization, either/or, has been called patriarchal thinking and (as in "all-or-nothing") alcoholic thinking. Too much or premature polarization or polarization along incorrect lines, can destroy communication and, along with it, the possibility for an unfolding process of change.

Yet polarization also helps us to move: *this way, not that.* It fuels rebellion.[6] In building a movement to oppose the war in Vietnam, for example, we learned to stress an evil cluster of government-business-military ripping off practically everyone else and killing poor Americans and half of Vietnam. It was the radicalizing civil rights/Black liberation movement that pressed this point, and

Malcolm X and Dr. King were probably both murdered because each in his own political development was isolating the racist, moneyed, ruling elite. This sort of polarization retains its sharp edge, but positions most people firmly on our side.

In other words, radical politics is not about being hipper than our parents or neighbors. It is about enlarging the circle. It is about being inclusive of practically everyone except those few on top.

How do we enlarge our circle? We begin close to home. The danger for any of us who do not root deeply in our communities is that we skim the surface and contribute only ourselves. We can be witnesses and single individuals, but we cannot be effective unless we go back "home," whether that be workplace, neighborhood, growing-up community, present-day community, friends, profession...and bridge the gap between our people and ourselves.

## 4. DON'T UNDERESTIMATE THE IMPORTANCE OF HUMOR

Humor, particularly ridicule directed against the powerful, bonds the rest of us against them, in laughter and in common understanding. One of the most effective pro-choice images was a pregnant man, with a text that read: *If men got pregnant, abortion would be a sacrament.* About the war, *It's a dick thing* was practically irrefutable. We need to create a public consciousness to support our political positions. Anger, denunciation, outrage are often ineffective openers; they demand willingness to experience unpleasant and threatening emotions. Humor softens people up. Humor empowers the disempowered. It's hard to feel afraid when you're laughing. It's hard to deny what you've laughed at.

## 5. LOOK FOR OPPORTUNITIES TO BRIDGE CHASMS

A chasm can be seen exactly as an unbridgeable space. This is easiest to see physically. But chasms are also made possible by racism, sexism, classism, all kinds of chauvinism. Chauvinism blocks empathy. Empathy builds bridges. Bridges cross chasms.

As ever, the empowered side of the chasm owes the labor to create trust. Reaching out to build trust includes actions as varied as attending demonstrations organized in other communities than your own, seeking advice and leadership, attempting coalition. Simply being present, on local, community issues as well as national ones. Weaving a fabric in which the fragmented groups from the late seventies and eighties can get acquainted and begin to work together. The Rainbow Coalition, the anti-Gulf War movement recreated this vision. Our job is to transform this vision into the reality of a multiracial, multicultural, feminist, pro-gay, anti-empire movement.

One major opportunity for U.S. city dwellers who are monolingual is to learn a language spoken in our city. For most of us this will mean Spanish, though it could mean Creole, Hmong, Thai, Korean, Chinese....As U.S. citizens or residents, our perspective is entirely skewed by a U.S.-centrism that lacks even a name. We expect everyone to speak our language. Otherwise, we assume they're stupid: *they can't even speak English.* Marie Antoinette's *let them eat cake* is this sort of self-centered response. Learning a language stretches a long way to help create trust, to strengthen our ability to communicate and to understand another people. It also signals willingness to give up centrality.

## 6. DON'T BE AFRAID OF THE STRENGTH OF SUBGROUPS

A movement, even a radical movement, is also an institution with its own set of leaders, power dynamics and hierarchy. New clusters inside the movement (as when feminism emerged in the sixties) or developing their power outside the movement are often seen as a threat. They will shake things up.

And this is true. They *will* shake things up. But shaking up is often exactly what's needed. The strength of emerging groups, instead of posing a threat, instead of needing to be kept in line, can be a positive force for change.

Different groups and communities responded differently to the Gulf War. The African American community opposed the war strenuously. The Jewish community was strongly split, with the pro-war voice heard much more forcefully than the anti-war voice. The labor movement divided lopsidedly, obnoxiously pro-war except for some bold dissent. In many places, the anti-war movement was practically a women's movement, judging by who was doing the actual work, though most of the major spokespeople continued to be men.

The mostly white male leadership of the movement reacted in a variety of ways. The strength of African American opposition to the war was greeted warmly by white radicals, though they often tried to absorb, co-opt or seek tokens to work in a movement over which whites continued to exercise control. Students, too, were welcomed, but often treated with some suspicion and condescension. Jews were often seen as automatically pro-war (even, in some analyses, as the war's cause). And the strength of women was seen by some as a detriment, evoking fear that men would be alienated and that a women-strong movement is inherently frail.

If we seek to strengthen progressive activity, we will seek full participation by new constituencies. But this does not mean finding tokens, the ones who stick out most, who often are those who most identify with the dominant culture and are thus most accessible to dominant culture folk. It does not mean selecting a community's representatives or leaders for it. Instead it means actively encouraging people to participate in large numbers, by seeking out their authentic representatives and leaders. It means also seeking their political positions, ideas and vision. It means accepting leadership, where appropriate. A movement created by equal partners will take a different shape, even develop different politics than a movement created by any of the groups working separately. The point of creating a multiracial, multicultural movement is not only numbers, but *wisdom:* to encompass the widest possible experience and vision.

## 7. WELCOME THE ENERGY AND COURAGE OF THE YOUNG

Especially the young. The age conflicts in the movement have been among the most interesting. I am so thankful for this next generation; for many years they were absent from political work, and the work suffered, in numbers and in boldness.

But the conflicts often play out in child/parent terms: the younger generation fights their parents and the older generation acts like their parents....*What do you know:*

*you're old/things are different now*
*you're kids/did you ever get teargassed, arrested, etc...*

So each of us tries to keep the other in line, when we need to pool ideas and strength. As Bernice Johnson Reagon sings,

*The older I get, the better I know*
*that the secret to carrying on*
*is when the reins are in the hands of the young who dare*
*to ride against the storm...*[7]

This means, *the young dare, the rest back them up.*

Some of the bravest political work in this country and around the world has happened because people often too young to grasp their own mortality stick their necks out. The job of the rest of us is to rise to the occasion of their bravery. The young inspire the middle-aged and old with courage, and they project our vision where it belongs, into the future.

This doesn't mean that youth is always right or even always brave. It does mean the rest of us need to check our impulse to control, to say we know best (we don't always), to scan our own motivation for fear, both simple (as in, danger) and complex (as in, losing control of strategy, events, etc.).

One failure of the sixties, with major consequences, was a poor working relationship between the old and new left. Many of us who were then young, repeated, *Don't trust anyone over 30.* We were not willing or able to harvest and absorb our elders' experience. They were not able or willing to leap forward with our courage and boldness. The success or failure of our end-of-the-century anti-empire movement will depend on the ability of the three generations of activists, from the thirties, sixties and nineties, to learn from each other and to work together with mutual respect.

## 8. PAY ATTENTION TO PSYCHOLOGY

One of the most detrimental and false polarizations to permeate the American scene is that between politics and psychology. From the right through the middle through liberalism, we have the individual, shaped by the nuclear family and seeking individual happiness. From the left, we have the masses, shaped by and shaping history, seeking collective transformation. Only a few sensible souls try to put these together. Anyone who has lived, as I have, through the sixties into the nineties, recognizes a nauseating, increasing insistence on psychological explanation for everything, including, most recently, turning the war into Bush's anti-wimp strike or Saddam's paranoia.

But history is shaped by people operating as people do, making choices with their consciousness limited by material reality and by their perceptions of material reality. This means by their perceptions of possibility too. Simply put, if people don't think change is possible, they won't try. Thus we can't pretend away the significance of psychology, of learned helplessness, of the seeming unavailability for most people of historical options. How many of us feel that what we do matters in the world? We are for the most part utterly untrained to think and move collectively. The discrediting of communism has only enhanced American individualism. Yet communism created a people able to overturn even itself, because they took seriously the rhetoric of collectivity.

What blocks people's sense of possibility?

*Failure. Exhaustion. Stress. Competition for limited resources.*

What exhilarates people's sense of possibility?

*Success. Victory. Community, since you are together making something possible.*

Therefore:

## 9. LOOK TO EXPAND PEOPLE'S SENSE OF POSSIBILITY

Few have written about the joy of political life, the sense of comradeship and achievement. As activists we need to believe in vision and imagination; communicate a sense of possibility. Bleakness is not the whole story, and escape is not the only alternative. Change *is* possible.

For example, the original feminist Take Back the Night marches not only demanded safe streets for women, but also offered women the opportunity to make the streets safe for ourselves for that night, so we could feel our freedom and thus be inspired to work for it. Also important, these marches were fun. They made us feel great.

In the war's wake, the MADRE/organized Mother Courage Peace Tour brought together women from the Middle East—including Egypt, Turkey, Israel, Palestine, Jordan and Iraq—and from the U.S., especially from the Family Military Support Network. Together these women forcefully expressed the possibility of dialogue, communication, working things out in other than militaristic ways, by presenting the reality of dialogue and communication.

Sometimes, in order to communicate a sense of possibility, we have to expand reality. The events of Eastern Europe, Germany and the Soviet Union best demonstrate how people are inspired to action by successful action. This means not policing ourselves, not keeping ourselves in check, not limiting our own sense of what's possible. We need to break rules, experiment. We need to pay attention to those who, from desperation and inventiveness, are already breaking rules, already experimenting. Squatting, for example, challenges the notion of private property in a very concrete way; it assumes housing as a right and seizes this right. Even an individual squatter, providing her/his own housing out of need and without particular attention to political theory, is a potential source of political motion.

## IN SUM:

We should be nosing around our neighborhoods, communities and cities, our workplaces, schools and children's schools for issues which are compelling in themselves and which provide opportunities for developing leadership, skills, militancy and growth. There is no dearth of issues. How much hunger, how many homeless and jobless, how much depleted ozone, how much fouled water, how many oil spills, how much rape, battering and other hate crimes, how many schools closed or lacking books, how much cancer, AIDS, tuberculosis and other devastating disease....and I am only talking about the richest, most privileged nation in the world. How we fight, how we enlarge our circle of fighters, will determine our ability to build collective power sufficient to turn things around.

Or we are lost.

*—Winter 1991*

*With respect for Saul Alinsky, who wrote* Rules for Radicals, *though as Alinsky himself said over and over, there are no rules; radicalism demands extraordinary flexibility and agility. Radicals have to improvise, not kneejerk. Thus, these are suggestions....*

## NOTES

1. Not that we understood or truly managed to counteract anti-Asian racism in the sixties and seventies.

2. The Yippies were among the most innovative of sixties politicos. Mostly white (and, at least in leadership, mostly Jewish), they emphasized outrageousness and flashy media events; for example, giving away money on Wall Street. Their leaders were Jerry Rubin and Abbie Hoffman. Their legacy has been selective—more media focus, less value placed on innovation and outrageousness— though, of course, they were not alone of the New Left in emphasizing the importance of mass media.

3. E.g., Fairness and Accuracy in Reporting (FAIR), the *Mother Jones, et al.* suit against the government.

4. When I named this approach at a 1991 New Jewish Agenda Steering Committee meeting, Roger Hurwitz, Chair of the National Middle East Task Force, quipped, "Or, in our case, let 1000 Blooms flower."

5. This wisdom needs to be communicated to the rest of the anti-war/anti-empire movement, which often kneejerks a "Zionism = racism" response, as though Jewish nationalism were inherently different, inherently more pernicious, than other nationalisms. Nationalism empowered is *always* problematic at best, potentially racist at worst.

6. At the same time, fuzzing the difference between us and our opposition works in favor of the *status quo*. On the issue of abortion, for example, emphasizing *Roe v. Wade* and its "right to privacy" basis as a *status quo*, pro-choice strategists have sometimes tried to direct people's attention away from the hard fact: the choice *is* between a woman and a fetus. Pro-choice means unequivocally placing that choice with the woman. The difference between a militant and a liberal stance can be seen in the recent slogan of pro-choice militants: *Abortion on demand and without apology.* When an issue has been kicking around as long as abortion, we can assume communication is not the issue. Everyone who's going to form an opinion already has. Now the question is which opinions are expressed most forcefully by how many people.

7. "Ella's Song."

# *While Patriarchy Explodes: Writing In A Time Of Crisis*

(This talk was presented at the Out/Write Conference in San Francisco, March, 1991. An earlier version was presented at Concordia College, Montréal, through the Simone de Beauvoir Institute.)

For some time, even before the Gulf War began, I have had a sense of things falling apart, of impending crisis. Ecological disasters. The devastations of AIDS and of cancer, particularly breast cancer striking younger and younger women in staggering numbers. The increasing numbers of people without homes, wandering the streets begging. Cuts in social services so extreme that basic assumptions have vanished about what we can expect in the way of schools, medical care, welfare, firehouses, bridge maintenance, financial assistance for students. The colleges are all in financial crisis. Jobs are being slashed, in the public and private sector, at the rate of many thousands at a time. Support of the arts has slipped from minimal to pitiful.

Some of this is about money. A lot. But there's also simple increase, simple astronomical increase of societal plagues like violence—random violence, violence against women: rape and battering. Increase in racial violence, anti-Semitic violence, gay and lesbian bashing. Skinheads, neo-Nazis, Aryan Nation, Ku Klux Klan—these groups are growing and are being scanned by right-wing political leadership for likely candidates, who are being groomed for political office. Radical racism, once again, is no longer marginal in U.S. electoral politics.

Gains won by the civil rights movement, women's liberation, gay and lesbian liberation, won in hard struggle—affirmative action, the right to abortion, no forced sterilization, gay and lesbian rights—are being lost on the national level or state by state—or enormous resources are being required of us to fight for these things all over again. Censorship is clamping down, made most visible by news coverage of the war or lack thereof, but really preceding that, as funding of lesbian and gay artists has come under attack and in some cases been blocked. Surrogate mothers—or the paid use of women's bodies for producing babies—even the relatively benign procedure of those in the more affluent nations adopting babies from poorer nations—bespeaks some radical change in the concept of the right/ability to parent. I haven't even mentioned the changing shape of Eastern Europe, the Soviet Union, Germany, and what all this means for the left and the right, for the futures of socialism and capitalism.

And then the crisis erupts. A crisis which exacerbates all the money issues, strengthens at least for now mindless patriotism and diverts the energies of many of us working on a variety of needs—personal, social and even political—into a single, desperate flow.

And now, suddenly, it's over. We who opposed this war have been out-smarted: they learned more from Vietnam than we did, and one to two hundred thousand people are dead at the hands of our government. I'm not a pacifist but it doesn't take much to see that this war did not need to be fought.

In November, because I was obsessed with certainty that, crazy as it seemed, this government wanted, longed to go to war against Iraq, I reread Tolstoy's *War and Peace*. I wanted the comfort of a long novel and one which tries to make sense of willfully caused massive deprivation of all anyone has: our paltry little lives.

In fact, I found Tolstoy far from comforting. It seemed exactly like what I could see today, except for a few technological shifts. Life seemed as precious and as vulnerable, male heroism as stupid and wasteful of life, especially young life. The discrepancy between the ostensible causes of war and the result, the war itself—because, in Tolstoy's novel, Napoleon was offended and Alexander proud—or for that matter because Saddam Hussein wanted to be the new Nassar and George Bush wanted to be the new god knows what—why then in Tolstoy's words should thousands of people commit unspeakable crimes against each other which are not even seen as crimes?

And what is the relationship between all this and the writer? I know that Virginia Woolf's entire literary project was to find the space, the frozen moment in time, where the individual might matter, because whenever time, that is to say, history intervened, the individual was lost....And Virginia Woolf went mad the last time and killed herself at least partly because it was another war, and who could bear such a thing? I know that second-wave feminism produced a bevy of writers determined not to abandon the public world to men, or to devalue the private world usually inhabited by women.

As a writer produced by second wave feminism, what does this mean?

Most of the writing I've been doing lately takes two forms:

1) the personal journal, raw, in which personal/political boundaries blur. Unfinished. Art is the last thing on my mind, and audience next to last.

2) press releases, speeches, statements, project descriptions, leaflets, chants. Finished writing, for me, in this crisis, has focused outward, to what's immediately useful.

I've been thinking about Brecht's comment on creating apolitical art: it's like painting a still life on a sinking ship, he said. You could argue that painting *anything* on a sinking ship except maybe a sign to the lifeboats is beside the point. But we're writers and we know the uses and the limits of metaphor. In some ways we're on a ship and in others not. It is not sinking but eroding and rotting and maybe about to explode. Besides, some people are on the ship lounging around getting fed huge portions and others are in the bone-cold water, treading to stay afloat.

But the question *What am I supposed to write about?* is a very personal one. For me, and I think for many of us, there are two issues. One, the sense of pressure, the inescapable measuring stick of what is important enough. Especially for those of us already fighting cultural messages that our experience is trivial, marginal—lesbians and gays, women, working class and poor people, people of color, Jews, among others—this prejudging stifles creativity. Before you even say it, it's not good enough. How petty, how useless seem the small spaces of our lives. It's hard to take them seriously. Did I suffer as a child? Am I falling in love, even bravely and wonderfully, with another woman? Did I come out as a lesbian in the neighborhood synagogue? Am I engaged in painful struggle with a friend? Does any of this matter?

These things matter as much as, as little as, life itself. In the one piece of "creative" writing I've done since this war began, a hodgepodge of news commentary and response called "Some Notes on the Gulf War," I wrote: *War is simple. You kill or you don't kill.*

War reduces things to a very simple level. Maybe this is why patriarchy likes war: the simplicity of it. The longing for good guys and bad guys, the goal-directed win-or-lose male adventure—and of course for this country it's almost always been *win.*

This particular sort of crisis, this simplicity of it, *kill or don't kill,* is antagonistic to the mode of the imaginative writer, who should have some interest in complexity. What the writer must value—the small life, the daily life, the significance of the individual consciousness and experience—are exactly what war violates.

At the same time—Brecht again—it's hard to value writing which doesn't include some sort of context.

The other issue is about process. Imaginative writing is in some sense a work of play, a meandering adventure, seeing what happens, what emerges: it is wildly inefficient. I often need to pretend to myself that I have infinite time, in order not to short circuit the painstaking process of bringing something new into the world. I can knock out a press release, position papers, etc., but fiction, or poetry? For me, and I think for many writers, the very nature of fiction, poetry and other forms that get called, loosely, 'creative,' demands freedom of subject, the possibility of anything happening. We cannot be dutiful and creative at the same moment. This doesn't mean the alternatives are either a slavish political correctness or total inattention to political issues and consequences.

The poet Audre Lorde has said, *Poetry is not a luxury.* I think it is no accident that these words were spoken by a Black lesbian radical poet, and that they have been echoed throughout the feminist writers community. We have experienced, in the open readings of early women's liberation, in the heady thrill of those first publications—Judy Grahn's *Common Women* poems were mimeographed and sold for ten cents on the streets of Berkeley—the necessity of poetry. I think too of the early sixties and the Black poetry movement inspired in part by the anti- colonialist Négritude movement from formerly French Africa, Haiti and Martinique.[1] These were immensely creative times. I suspect we are entering such a time.

But what characterizes writing created at the hub of such activity? It tends to be fairly short, because at least for the activist/artist—who has the time for solitude and withdrawal necessary to the long work? Because short pieces are more suitable for public presentation (as opposed to the long novel, a solitary adventure if there ever was one), for quasi-ritual, where part of the meaning is that the work is heard in a community—a common experience, a shared frame of reference. I suspect we'll see more interest in poetry, because of its affinity with ritual, and in theater and performance pieces and mixed media. Collaborative work. Perhaps the ego end of things will shrink a bit, as satisfaction is derived more from a sense of shared purpose and less from personal aggrandizement.

At the same time, I notice a shift, a subtle shift in the role of the writer. Muriel Rukeyser, one of the great poets of our century—a lesbian and a Jew—wrote, "In our period, they say there is free speech. They say...there is no penalty for writing poems. They say this. This is the penalty."[2]

Now, first outside the U.S., in the attacks on Salman Rushdie; in a very different way, in the election to the presidency of Czechoslovakia of the playwright Vaclav Havel, we have a sense that at least somewhere writers are taken seriously. In the U.S., censorship has become a serious issue, as I've said.

Coinciding with this censorship is, paradoxically, a sense of empowerment for artists, including writers. The opposite of no penalty: the prize is we begin to feel a bit more taken seriously.

I suggest that this seriousness is one we need to welcome but also to earn.

You can say, *It's useless* or *I don't care about the impact of my art* or *I just want to get known and maybe even make a living.* Writers are workers too, and it's too bad we get paid so little that we start eying the box office, so to speak. Or eying each other. The competitiveness around writing, the careerism I see even at this conference, depresses me. And I understand it, that's what's so sad. But we don't have to accept these conditions. The task is to increase opportunities for cooperation instead of competition. I think this has particular implications for us as writers and is connected to the growth of a healthy counter-empire movement in this country as well. How much can we hang together? A writers' union would help a lot, I think, in limiting the arbitrariness of our contracts and speakers' fees and in lobbying for increased funding for artists. The money not spent on arts in this country is a scandal. And don't tell me AIDS is more important. I agree. But don't set us against each other, when there is so much money being spent on weapons that one day's warfare would have paid for just about everything anybody needs.

The other thing about a writers' union: our condition as writers is hideously individualized. How then can we communicate a sense of possibility of anything else? Working to create a union would help us develop collectivity, a sense of possibility, which some of us experience elsewhere, in other movements. We could also have this as writers.

I want to say one more thing related to competitiveness, careerism: the desperation to publish. I understand it, and for many of us, who have been so silenced, publication is critical. But sometimes we rush, and sometimes we're obsessed with the next publication credit. Sometimes we get ahead of our purpose, not only the larger purpose I'm suggesting but we even forget what we owe ourselves: to become the best writer we can, the most ourselves. I put out a book in May and immediately people ask, *What's your next book?* I want to say, *Leave me alone, I just wrote a book, I'm living my life, I'm gathering experience. What else would I have to write about?* We're all different this way, but consider that your ultimate goal may not be quantitative.

But that's kind of a digression. I want to suggest we continue to act as if the war were not over, for indeed it is not. You know about the war against people with AIDS, fought by willful withholding of compassion and resources. But there are many wars, too many to name here, against which various peoples—many of whom are represented here—struggle to survive. And god only knows what George Bush is going to do next in the name of the new world order. How bad does it have to get before we take it seriously? So I've been thinking. It seems to me to be fully alive is to seek justice. Otherwise, what's the point? I think I'm speaking as a writer, but maybe I'm just speaking as a Jew. In my culture we take very seriously both books and the injunction to pursue justice. Why should anyone read a book by someone who doesn't care about justice? Brecht's still life on the sinking ship again....

This war has reminded me to take my time seriously. I have become extremely ambitious and by this I don't mean I want an NEA fellowship or even a bestseller, although of course I'd welcome either. I mean I believe in the power of writing to do something very important. No, we cannot be dutiful and creative at the same time, but we can think about what is our purpose and commit ourselves to this purpose.

This doesn't mean lies and boredom. As writers we should be hungry for and extremely respectful of truth, even if often the truth is told—as Emily Dickinson would say—slant: *tell the truth but tell it slant.* That is all the room in the world for imagination and creativity. But at least let's think about what it would mean to write with a moral purpose.

This sounds prim, puritanical. That's because our time has so cheapened and reduced the concept of morality that it seems to equal repression. I'm talking about seeking the connection between the excruciating facts we live in—among which the war against the people of Iraq looms particularly large at this moment—and our own work. I'm not talking about moral cops, thought police. Tell it slant. But tell it.

This may be something we can do with our writing and it may not always be. Yes, we should demonstrate. Give money, give time, use our speaking/teaching skills by getting out into the community and talking to people, writing leaflets— people joke about leaflet prose, but I've been writing and reading leaflets and I challenge my sister and brother writers to try to write a leaflet that moves people to action. I've seen it done. The Women's Pentagon Action statement, written in 1980 by Grace Paley in collaboration with dozens of women, actually inspired a lot of us to take action. Organize community poetry readings, bridge the gap between art and political life. These are things people are doing, I'm not making this up. Let's do it more.

As radicals and as writers, we should know by now there are no rules, we need to think for ourselves. Let me summarize some things to think about. Bridging the chasms between:

—our career as a writer and the purpose of our writing

—political responsibility and creative freedom

—valuing subjectivity and placing ourselves in the larger context

—individual talent and skill and collaboration and collectivity

and each of us has to decide what that means for her or himself.

Let this war be a terrible sacrifice to the end of the American Empire as we know it. And let us think how we can honor that sacrifice by preventing its repetition. Let us choose to create a time of penalty for writing poems, in Muriel Rukeyser's words. Let's be dangerous, as dangerous as, more dangerous than they fear. Why should we settle for less?

NOTES

1. A cultural/political movement associated with Black pride and national liberation, especially with the poet Aimé Césaire.

2. Muriel Rukeyser. From *Muriel Rukeyser Out of Silence: Selected Poems*, ed. Kate Daniels (Evanston, IL: TriQuarterly Books, Northwestern Univ., 1992).

# Reviews

# CROSSOVER DREAMS
## Review of Borderlands/La Frontera by Gloria Anzaldúa (San Francisco: Aunt Lute, 1987)

**Published in the *Village Voice* (June 28, 1988)**

Shame is a knife that carves out a culture's heart. To name, describe and defy shame is thus a profoundly rebellious, strengthening act, and nobody writes about shame like Gloria Anzaldúa—the shame of the other, the minority, the one whose face, hair, eyes, skin, speech, sexuality is different, not right. The child who doesn't have money clothes lunch, whose mother cannot protect her/him, who has to work while other children get to spend their time as the dominant culture says children should.

Those familiar with Anzaldúa's writing from *This Bridge Called My Back*, the groundbreaking collection she co-edited with Cherríe Moraga, know her as one of the most important and original voices of Third World feminism. No coincidence that *Bridge*, the first anthology by radical women of color, was edited by two Chicana lesbians, those excluded both from white feminism and from the initial discussions of race and racism in the women's movement, polarized between black and white. The tension between separatism and coalition is a principal theme of *Bridge*.

Anzaldúa's new book, *Borderlands/La Frontera*, takes up where *Bridge* left off. The border, "this thin edge of barbwire," (13) is as much a spiritual state as a geographical one. From the borderlands you can see both, all countries; all languages are spoken, and survival depends on understanding all modes of thought. In the borderlands new creatures come into being, including the "new mestiza" Anzaldúa celebrates in some of the boldest experimental writing to come out of the women's movement. Monique Wittig comes to mind, experimenting with language as well as form, or June Arnold, or the innovative English/Yiddish poetry of Irena Klepfisz, cited several times by Anzaldúa.

The book's first half is composed of a long essay, "*Atravesando Fronteras*/Crossing Borders," the second of poems. The sense is of the same body of truth passed on in two radically different ways. The essay interweaves theory and visceral tale, prose and poetry, history, anthropology, psychology, literature, personal and collective experience. The experiment is sometimes a smashing success, as in the section on language—"How to Tame a Wild Tongue"—a linguistic and intellectual tour de force. Sometimes, though, personal narrative follows historical analysis too abruptly, the juxtaposition of parts fragmenting the text. And sometimes the stretch toward absolute theory falls short; to those not already convinced that dualistic thinking prepares for and shores up patriarchal violence, the assertion seems curiously flat.

The book demands attention to Spanish, and for readers who don't know the language, lines and whole poems will be lost. Anzaldúa translates some passages, but her choices seem haphazard. She cites her commitment to those Chicanos/as robbed of Spanish by assimilation. Why not help people back to their language? A systematic glossary would have been ideal.

Yet Anzaldúa moves with grace and erudition through a sprawling and diverse landscape, nothing less than a history of the people of the Southwest, a survey of both sides of the border, a critique of Western patriarchal civilization and a manifesto of true counterculture: the nondominants, the Third World, women, artists, queers, outsiders. Given the scope of the material and the boldness of Anzaldúa's reach, it seems churlish to ask for a smooth product. Even the seams of the experiment are lessons, both for the North American English speaker trying to disengage from linguistic entitlement and for the bilingual Spanish-English speaker who will, I imagine, delight in Anzaldúa's bold linguistic mix.

The emotional and intellectual impact of the book is disorienting and powerful. Logic and image are confounded, as well as English and Spanish, the literal and the figurative. Anzaldúa's writing is especially strong in two contrasting traditions: naturalism and surrealism, sometimes combined, as in the poem "*Mar de Repollos*/A Sea of Cabbages."

Some of the strongest writing focuses on the sexual victimization and exploitation of *mojadas/os*, wetbacks and farm workers (which Anzaldúa knows both as a worker and an organizer). "*El sonavabitche*," the tense story of a poet/teacher who forces a cheating boss to pay "his illegals" their wages, ends:

...His eyes were pin pricks.
Sweat money, Mister, blood money,
not my sweat, but same blood.
Yeah, but who's to say you won't abscond with it?
If I ever hear that you got illegals on your land,
even a single one, I'm going to come here
in broad daylight and have you
hung by your balls.
He walks slowly to his desk.
Knees shaking, I count every bill
taking my time. (128)

The staunch solidarity, the juxtaposition of fear and courage are pure Anzaldúa, as in the excruciating but exquisite prose poem "Cervicide," in which the poet—a child—must bludgeon a pet fawn to death to protect her father from arrest by the gringo game warden.

Deeply political, these poems mostly manage to steer clear of rhetoric. Anzaldúa is more afraid of lies than of how the truth may be misinterpreted or used against her people. One poem, "that dark shining thing," depicting self-hate in women of color, begins:

You've shut the door again
to escape the darkness
only it's pitch black in that closet. (171)

Elsewhere she criticizes the sexism and machismo of Chicano culture, but from the perspective of someone solidly of her culture: "I am a turtle, wherever I go I carry 'home' on my back." (21) She chides Chicanos/as for "trying to out-Chicano each other, vying to be the 'real' Chicanas..."(58) And her challenge to white racism is unflinching.

Yet the dominant note in the book is neither scolding nor grim. Anzaldúa loves her culture, language, people. Many of the poems are wildly humorous or optimistic simply by dint of their inventiveness ("Interface" or "Holy Relics," for example). She invokes new human possibility in the name of the new mestiza charged with pulling the human race into a future free from destruction, exploitation or oppression. The new mestiza does extra work:

I am the only round face,
Indian-beaked, off-colored
in the faculty lineup, the workshop, the panel
and reckless enough to take you on. (171)

But she gets extra vision:

I see *oposición e insurrección*. I see the crack growing on the rock. I see the fine frenzy building. I see the heat of anger or rebellion or hope split open that rock...And suddenly I feel everything rushing to a center, a nucleus. All the lost pieces of myself come flying from the deserts and the mountains and the valleys, magnetized toward that center. *Completa*.

Something pulsates in my body, a luminous thin thing that grows thicker every day. Its presence never leaves me. I am never alone. That which abides: my vigilance, my thousand sleepless serpent eyes blinking in the night forever open. And I am not afraid. (51)

# RUTH RUBIN: YIDDISH SONGS OF THE HOLOCAUST: THE STRUGGLE TO SURVIVE.
## Lecture-recital recorded live, narrated and performed by Ruth Rubin

**Published in *Jewish Currents* (April, 1988)**

Anyone even mildly interested in Yiddish culture knows the name Ruth Rubin. By the late forties, Rubin was already collecting Yiddish folksongs and translating them into English, virtually the first to do so. Particularly focused on the lives of ordinary working people, of women, on the struggles of the Jewish people to stay afloat, her *Treasury of Jewish Folksong* (1950) as well as her collection-cum-analysis *Voices of a People: The Story of Yiddish Folksong* (1979) established her as an authority in the field and themselves as instant classics. More recently, a commercial videotape by Cindy Marshall (*A Life of Song: A Portrait of Ruth Rubin*) has been shown widely in the Jewish community.

Now from Ruth Rubin, we have another collection which promises to be at least as significant as those already received: an audio cassette of a lecture-recital, *Yiddish Songs of the Holocaust: The Struggle to Survive.* Recorded live on Yom Hashoah, the tape continues Rubin's work in an extremely potent vein. Rubin has subtitled the tape *Shoa V'Hagvura/*Destruction and Courage, and in insisting on the *gvura* (courage) as well as the *shoa*, her respect for people and love for Jewish culture animate the lecture, as she lets the songs tell us in the words of those who lived the events "what their *gvura* consisted of..."

The tape fills a great need. For many Jews, it's a struggle to know what to do with the Holocaust. The Holocaust is a list of statistics any one of which can freeze the blood, and there are a thousand of these statistics. The Holocaust is a scream of intense betrayal and loneliness; why didn't anyone help? The Holocaust is a source of shame; why didn't they resist? (The Holocaust is a well of ignorance, because of course "they" did resist, where they could.) The Holocaust is a vast cataclysm, not a series of historical events that happened to actual people who had actual human responses.

What Rubin offers here, quite purposefully, is a way of approaching the Holocaust, for the lecture-performance serves to demystify; to present the victims in human terms, not flattened or deprived of dignity but as full, suffering, thinking, grieving, scheming, fighting, creating individuals. As the lecture makes plain, these songs and poems, written between 1938 and 1945, reveal a portion of the historical events not yet called Holocaust, and how Jews responded to these events as they occurred. The Jews of Eastern Europe come again to life—because the songs are about their lives, and the melodies are from their lives. The lullaby that croons unforgettably, "They will shoot us if they hear us, so darling don't you cry"—because bearing children in the ghetto was forbidden—communicates more graphically than a hundred statistics the impact of the Nazi war against the Jews (*"Her mayn kind, vi vintn brumen/*Listen child, the wind is howling"). Or listen to the *"Yugnt Hymn/*Youth Hymn," sung by the young Jews of Vilna, marching through the ghetto streets, inspiring their elders:

> *Undzer lid iz ful mit troyer,*
> *Dreyst is undzer muntergang.*
> *Khotsh der soyne vakht baym toyer,*
> *Shturemt yugnt mit gezang:*

*Yung iz yeder, yeder, yeder, ver es vil nor.*
*Yorn hobn keyn batayt.*
*Alte kenen, kenen, kenen oykh zayn kinder*
*Fun a nayer, frayer, tsayt.*

Our song is filled with grieving,
Bold our step, we march along,
Though the foe the gateway's watching,
Youth comes storming with their song:
Young are they, are they, are they whose age won't bind them,
Years don't really mean a thing,
Elders also, also, also can be children
In a newer, freer spring.[1]

This song speaks more vividly about courage, about art as literal encouragement and about the responsibility of ghetto youth, than a mountain of facts.

But the songs do more than document the experience. They testify to the determination of people in the ghettos under conditions of terrible privation and fear to write, to sing, to create musical events and performances, to express their feelings, to build solidarity. In Rubin's words: "Through the songs there flows the will to live, to preserve one's self-respect, one's dignity, along with the traditions and customs they cherished for centuries, and the love of learning, teaching and creating....Creativity became the channel for the yearning to survive, in spite of everything."

It is especially good for artists, writers, composers and performers to know that many of these songs were specifically created for cultural events in the ghettos; that performances were planned and carried out under the most trying circumstances; that poems were published in journals in Bergen-Belsen and smuggled out. In a culture like ours, so predicated on packaging, hustling and individual success, it is at least bracing to come up against the real thing: culture for people because it is necessary.

Rubin, a dynamic speaker, is both precise and emotional. She presents the songs as recitative, talky, dramatic monologues—not performance, but utterance. Created as powerful expression of experiences that never should have happened, these songs are far from entertainment. People sang them because they needed to. At the same time the melodies, some composed specially, some traditional folk tunes, are haunting, enchanting.

The lecture and the songs are organized chronologically: here is what happened and here are the songs they wrote and sang in response to the events we now call Holocaust. First come songs which reflect disbelief, bewilderment, shock, isolation, shame, anger: songs of prophetic awareness, as Mordkhe Gebirtig's 1938 description of the ghetto's conflagration in *"Es brent, briderlekh, es brent*/It's burning, brothers, it's burning." With each song, Rubin presents the contexts: the forced labor (*"Rivkele di Shabesdike"*); the children selling cigarettes, smuggling messages, old with responsibilities, tough with bravado (*"Yisrolik"*). She remarks and then lets the songs and poems themselves reveal the shame of the (temporary) survivors: *"Ir geyt farbay*/You pass us by, leaving us to serve your murderers with our work and sweat, straining to win their sympathy"; the isolation of *"Aroys iz in Vilne a hayer bafel*/In Vilne, a new decree has been issued"; the intense estrangement from people not subjected to the occupation, people who still lived normal lives, worked, ate, were happy (the poem, *"Tsvey bazundere veltn*/Two different worlds"). Rubin offers a constant corrective to the painful distortions about Jews going like sheep to the slaughter; she tells of Jewish belief in preserving life, and honors the dignity of the religious Jews of Poland, who—when it was obvious no escape was possible—sang, as they were being led to the gas chambers, "*Ani ma-amin*/I believe the Messiah will come." Her voice in this song is what Kafka said a book should be: an axe for the frozen sea within us.

From these songs of stunned disbelief, she moves to songs of, one can't say hope, but songs that absorb and respond to the conditions, with encouragement or despair. The sardonic "*Hot zikh mir di shikh tserisn*/My shoes were torn," which speaks of the frosty wind blowing from Siberia—i.e., rescue will come from the Russian front. She tells of the concert singer Luba Lubitski, famous in Vilna, who could have escaped but chose to return to the ghetto with her mother. She tells how Lubitski would sing folk songs at the ghetto cultural events, how she got caught smuggling lentils into the ghetto (and who survived without smuggling something?); and then she sings the song Lubitski is reported to have sung as she was being led to her death: "*Tsvey Taybelekh*/Two Little Doves," which says, "Be brave, don't kill yourself: survive. Survive." Especially painful in this section are the lullabies, and the songs about children, including "*Yeder ruft mikh Ziamele*/Everybody calls me Ziamele," rich in pathos:

| | |
|---|---|
| *Kh'hob gehat a tatele,* | I once had a father dear, |
| *Hot er mikh gehit;* | His love for me was true, |
| *Itst bin ikh a shmatele,* | Now I'm just a little rag |
| *Vayl ikh bin a yid.* | Because I am a Jew. |

In the final section of the tape are songs reflecting people's realization that the Nazis intended total destruction, that the evil which had seemed nightmarish was in fact absolute. Here the mood of the songs changes, the sense of tragedy and sadness dissipates, and the songs stir people to become fighters. This is the period conventionally called the resistance, though Rubin deliberately expands the definition of resistance. Here is the well-known partisan song by Hirsh Glik, "*Shtil, di nakht iz oysgeshternt*/Still is the starry night," written for Vitke Kempner of the Vilna ghetto; and the incredibly charged account, from Shmerke Kacerginski's diary (himself a poet and the author of the *Yugnt Hymn*), of Glik's creation of the song inspired by the Warsaw Ghetto Uprising—"*Zog nisht keynmol az du geyst dem letstn veg*/Never say that you have trod the final road"—which immediately became the Partisan Hymn. As Rubin sings we hear, for the first time, the audience at this Yom Hashoah lecture; several of them are singing along every word. For this moment alone, the tape is a treasure.

Rubin's voice is strong, tough, infinitely expressive, essentially dramatic rather than lyrical. Hearing each song provides the listener with the space and texture of that song's experience. As I listen I am for the duration wrapped/rapt in the experience of Yisrolik the cigarette boy, of the mother hushing her child, of the Jews of Vilna hearing the latest Nazi decree, of the partisans sharing and shoring up their courage. There is nothing detached about the experience of listening. The tape creates an atmosphere of total identification with those who wrote and sang and heard these songs, so one is caught, as the tape's subtitle suggests—*shoa v'hagvura*/destruction and courage—between the gaping horror of what was done to the Jews of Europe and the incredible beauty of these songs they created and sang and wept with and were strengthened by.

I have only one small criticism. Though the lecture gives frequent translation and enough of a hook to hang the songs' meaning on, I wish Rubin would include in future editions an accompanying "libretto": each song in Yiddish, transliterated and translated. One of the Nazi near-victories has been over Yiddish language and Yiddish culture. The lecture, the collection and retransmission of the songs strikes back; but specifically bridging the language chasm, so that non-Yiddish speakers can follow the text and learn the words would be an extra *mitzvah*. (Most of the songs can be found in *We Are Here: Songs of the Holocaust.*)

Need it be said: *Yiddish Songs of the Holocaust: The Struggle to Survive* is a gift from one who has already regaled the Jewish community with her collector's and analyst's talent. Hear it, share it, talk about it with people you love. Play this tape for classes and political groups, get your local libraries to order it. Learn the songs. And on Yom Hashoah, gather friends or family to hear the tape, to mourn together, to honor the suffering, ingenuity, courage and creativity of the Jews of Eastern Europe. Hear the music they made from the deepest pain, and imagine the music we are deprived of.

## NOTES

1. All transliteration and translation taken from *We Are Here: Songs of the Holocaust,* compiled by Eleanor Mlotek and Malke Gottlieb, translation by Roslyn Bresnick-Perry (NY: Workmen's Circle, 1983).

# AN IMMIGRANT LIFE:
### Review of Anzia Yezierska: A Writer's Life
### by Louise Levitas Henriksen with assistance from
### Jo Ann Boydston (New Brunswick: Rutgers U. Press, 1988)
### and
## Love In The Promised Land: The Story Of Anzia
## Yezierska And John Dewey, by Mary V. Dearborn
## (NY: The Free Press, 1988)

**Published in** *Women's Review of Books* **(July, 1988)**

Anzia Yezierska was a Jewish immigrant who lived in a New York ghetto, worked in a sweatshop and in the twenties became a best-selling author of unpolished gems written straight from the heart. She was brought out to Hollywood, inundated by money, alienated and confused by her success. Within ten years she was a has-been.

That, at any rate, was the Yezierska myth, created by a newly budding public relations industry and especially by Yezierska herself—an appealing myth, but less interesting than reality. Yezierska, it turns out, was educated at Columbia Teachers' College, and left the sweatshop to teach for nearly twenty years before her literary discovery. At the time of her first success, far from being an innocent young greenhorn, she had married and separated twice, given birth to a daughter and was hanging out with the hottest radicals and boldest feminists in New York City in the twenties. Her writing was hardly raw; she revised and polished constantly, striving to achieve the "natural" sound of Yiddish-inflected English. A diligent, determined artist throughout her long life, she wrote some of her finest work as an old woman.

Yezierska's best-kept secret was her short, intense, probably unconsummated but obsessive love affair with John Dewey, the high priest of American progressive thought, WASP to the core. Years later Dewey remained for her an animating presence; his approval, eternally sought, still symbolized achievement and acceptance by the American literary establishment.

Two new books tell Yezierska's story from different angles. Louise Levitas Henriksen has written a compelling and astonishing biography, so even-handed that one continually forgets that the author is the subject's daughter. *A Writer's Life* commands attention first of all because it offers comprehensive information about this remarkable woman. Utterly dedicated to the craft of writing, compulsively mythmaking about herself, Yezierska, in her broad outlines, recalls another woman writer of the period, the fabulously inventive Zora Neale Hurston, who also wrote about her (non-WASP) people in their own language and also died in obscurity. Henriksen discusses the literary world that exoticized Yezierska, accepted her "roughness" but was not in the end willing to hear her voice on a plane and volume equal to its more familiar cadences. To the literary establishment Yezierska would forever be anomalous: a sweatshop escapee, a hyphenated writer.

*A Writer's Life* joins Kim Chernin's *In My Mother's House* and Vivian Gornick's *Fierce Attachments* as a splendid, if odd, Jewish mother-daughter book; but in this one the mother is in no way defined by her maternal role. In real life, too, Yezierska rejected this role—for hauntingly modern reasons, Yezierska gave over Louise to be raised by her boring but economically reliable ex.

"I have decided to tear my heart out of my body," Anzia wrote to Rose Pastor Stokes..."I have decided to send Tynkabel [her pet name for Louise] back to her father for a few years until I get back on my feet..." (73)

The few years stretched to include Louise's entire childhood. Yezierska chose her writing over her daughter, and the daughter's response, it seems, was to mother the mother, soothe, humor and above all *listen* to her.

Such a daughter might tell her story with anger; Henriksen does not. The dominant emotion in her account is a piercing informed respect for the struggles of an extremely hard-working writer.

No matter who helped her in the selfless task of reading, editing and bouncing back to her own ideas in different words, the manuscript would evolve unmistakably hers, because she vigorously attacked it afresh the next day, by herself or with another helper, and slashed away pitilessly whatever now seemed stiff or foreign to her. Her instinct as she hacked away at the words she didn't like, to get closer to her own truth, was usually infallible. (203)

As a child, Louise pitied her mother's loneliness, adored her uniqueness and cherished the freedom her oddball mother allowed her: on her Saturday visits, she could stay awake till all hours reading any book on her mother's decidedly hip shelves. She took for granted Yezierska's devouring egotism and obsessional devotion to craft. Henriksen's description of her mother's creative process continues:

But "dirt and disorder" returned with each new story, and her devouring need for hand holders, as she groped her way out of her chaos, consumed friendships and family relationships. For she confronted almost everyone she knew sooner or later with her manuscripts, including her young daughter. (203)

The scenes of Louise's visits, during which she would be inevitably trapped into critiquing the manuscripts, delight but also horrify in the blatant inappropriate use of child by parent.

The daughter grew up "impatient with her mother's sentimentality and Jewish colloquialisms..." (241) Henriksen's is perhaps the archetypal response of Jewish daughter to mother and of hyphenated-American to immigrant ethos and taste: embarrassment.

When she was dissatisfied, her mother created scenes....Anzia always wanted things done differently than anyone else; she always called attention to herself...It was embarrassing to a child who wanted only to be a normal sheep like everyone else. (241)

The gravest Jewish sin in a WASP world: *she always called attention to herself.* As a college student, Louise found Yezierska's writing excessive, crude; she scorned yet exploited her mother's need for approval, especially from "real" Americans, including her native-born daughter. Some of Henriksen's descriptions of Yezierska make me, second-generation American, cringe; Helen Yglesias records a similar response in her *New York Times* review of the book. The portrait reminds me how Jewish women appear to a polished WASP world; reminds me too of what we shed trying to adapt. Yezierska, bless her, didn't try very hard: striving desperately for acceptance, she nevertheless refused to give up very much of herself.

Finally and most significantly, the book is indeed a writer's life. The most impressive discussion is not about the mother-daughter relationship or even about Yezierska's rags-to-riches-to-near-rags trajectory, documented less accurately but more dramatically by the writer herself in *Red Ribbon on a White Horse*.[1] It is Yezierska's dedication to writing, her determination to *speak*, just like the characters she wrote about, first sentimentally, later with great subtlety: characters who had in them something to express. She insisted. She struggled with language to shape what she understood of freedom, cages, love and her "own people," the immigrant Jewish poor whose hands were building urban America. Oppression's literal meaning is rarely felt so forcefully as in Yezierska's descriptions of young women longing for freedom but weighed down by machine work and slum dwelling. The measure of burden is their corresponding desire for beauty, their capacity for joy:

> She sipped the grape juice leisurely, thrilled into ecstacy [sic] with each lingering drop. "How it laughs yet in me, the life, the minute I turn my head from my worries!" [2]

The most moving section in the biography describes Yezierska's response to the publication of *Red Ribbon...*, the quasi-autobiography that took her eighteen years to write, years of disregard, aging, poverty and loneliness. Henriksen portrays a demanding, self-centered woman who watched the book earn praise but not money. Most touching is Yezierska's glee at finding herself again as a writer. She barely cared about the money. She wrote:

> "Why had I no premonition in the wandering years when I was hungering and thirsting for recognition, that this quiet joy, this sanctuary, was waiting for me after I had sunk back to anonymity? I did not have to...sweat for glory, strain for the smile from important people. All that I could ever be...was in myself." (275)

Those years of success and then "failure" had in some sense freed her. Her last published story earned the same fee as the first story she had ever published fifty years before—$25. Even ignoring the insult of inflation, her determination to write for the sake of what she had to say is inspiring.

Yezierska remained a productive woman into her eighties. "Growing old is like entering a new profession," she said (284), challenging with characteristic buoyancy her fears about increased physical frailty and possible dependence. "Trying to accept age in herself by examining it in others," (284) she volunteered several hours a week at a home and became something of a spokesperson for the elderly, pressing for "rehabilitation... to restore the elderly to jobs and social acceptance." (285) Indeed, Ellen Gruber Garvey has argued persuasively that old age represented for Yezierska another, final "immigrant stance" from which she could write.[3] In her last years it appears she was even more herself: passionate, somewhat self and other-deceiving, a monster of self-absorption, "the same vigorous egotist fiercely centered on herself and her own sufferings." (284)

Though Henriksen's account is utterly credible, I can't help wondering: was Louise really such an unresentful daughter? What are her resulting issues with intimacy, boundaries? Is the amazing balance of this book an accurate portrayal of the relationship? In an afterword, Henriksen hints at her struggle to achieve this balance:

> Out of loneliness and despair she made art. When I was a small child, I chose her against my father and never changed my allegiance. But whenever I was with her, close up, and fighting, she was always infuriating, demanding too much.
> Only now, in her absence, can I come this close to her again. (301)

Despite Yezierska's temporary obscurity, and the bittersweet taste of posthumous fame, one is left with a sense not of regrets but of completion, of a life lived fully. *Anzia Yezierska: A Writer's Life* is a triumphant biography, not less for being a good read, absorbing and shapely despite the unshapeliness of real life.

Yezierska's unabashed passion and vitality first attracted and ultimately repelled John Dewey. Their relationship—which lasted perhaps a year—was not revealed until the excavation of Yezierska's out-of-print, out-of-favor books by feminist scholars, notably historian Alice Kessler-Harris, and the discovery and publication in the seventies of Dewey's poems. Consigned by their author to oblivion, these poems speak about finding love; about East meeting West and immigrant meeting America; about sexual longings he projected onto the exotic, erotic Jew, who—he briefly imagined—could heal his overintellectual alienation from body and emotion.

These metaphors were real and paramount for both of them. Dewey wrote a number of not-for-publication poems about their relationship; Yezierska wrote about it obsessively for years in books, some of which became best sellers. (Some quoted without credit his poems and speeches, making possible the recent detective scholarship.) She wrote versions of their encounter which seem fairly accurate (most notably in *Red Ribbon...*), fantasy versions with happy endings, maudlin versions with heroine suicides... In some way the relationship served her better in its failure.

Henriksen deals mildly with Dewey. In her version he appears simply outclassed: if his poems are evidence, Yezierska brought him emotional and erotic life, but she was quickly too much for him. For her, he was never enough, though he encouraged her to become a writer, to value her own perceptions. Most important, he was her muse. It's hard to say if the recurring pattern in her fiction—Jewish immigrant woman meets, falls for, and is embraced or rejected by American WASP man—is modelled on her encounter with Dewey, or if the encounter took on such mythic proportions because the pattern predated it in her mind. The young-to-youngish women in Yezierska's fiction always recognize in an instant *this is he* when they meet the Dewey-ish hero. Interestingly, Henriksen's book, which honors Yezierska so movingly, is far less sympathetic to her in the Dewey encounter. Clearly the daughter identifies somewhat with Dewey, overwhelmed by her mother, the emotion factory.

Dearborn's *Love in the Promised Land*, as the title indicates, focuses on the unlikely/inevitable relationship between the 58-year-old king of the liberals and the 35-year-old immigrant and aspiring writer: Supergoy meets Superjew. Chapter by chapter, Dearborn traces the life of each, gracefully evoking the social and intellectual context, until their lives intersect. Two concluding chapters sketch their post-encounter lives. If Henriksen's triumph is the recreation of a struggling, feisty, literary matriarch, Dearborn's is the situating of Yezierska—and the immigrant experience—in the tumultuous context of the progressive era, including the settlement houses, the trade union movement, a vibrant socialism, first wave feminism and the sexually liberated, economically autonomous new women. While Henriksen occasionally names Yezierska's friends and acquaintances, the overall impression in the daughter's version is of a woman so driven by her own impulses that she barely notices what these people—lions of the period—are doing.

Dearborn pays less attention to Yezierska's personality, and more to her acquaintances and activities. Yezierska read Olive Schreiner, Charlotte Perkins Gilman and Swedish feminist Ellen Key. She was close friends with socialist-feminist Rose Pastor Stokes (an immigrant Jew and a journalist, Pastor married a millionaire and joined the Communist Party), and "radical schoolteacher and dress reformer" Henrietta Rodman, who lived cheerfully with her husband and his mistress, and "challenged the Board of Education's rules regarding married women holding teaching jobs." (72-73) Even Emma Goldman, anarchist and champion of free love, ran in these circles. Thus Yezierksa's self-presentation as greenhorn acquires an edge of sophisticated intent, while her extreme reticence about sex—typical of her home culture but not of the milieu in which she was living—emerges as an intriguing question.

Dearborn's book lacks Henriksen's narrative flow, and the first chapter, on Dewey's early life, is deadly (perhaps not to a Dewey enthusiast, which I confess to not being). But after this deceptively tedious start, the brief book builds engagingly towards the encounter of these two fabulous symbols; a smaller portion concludes. In between they meet, interact and it's quickly over, a missed opportunity for drama.

But Dearborn draws much meaning from the encounter. She sees the two as doomed, having each idealized the other, expecting from one another some profound and impossible reconciliation of the sort contemporary therapists tell us can only come from the self. Dearborn, however, points out what Henriksen overlooks: that when Dewey retreated, he simply refused to talk to Yezierska about his change of heart. "You misunderstood," he claimed, pretending nothing had happened, a classic gambit from the gaslighting repertoire of WASPs and men. In short, Dewey treated Yezierska shabbily. He acted irresponsibly to a woman who turned out to be different and more troublesome than he'd imagined.

Though Dearborn's respect for the man is evident, she does not spare him an unflattering exposure in his lack of candor with Yezierska, as in his refusal to repudiate his close friend Albert Barnes, an explicit anti-Semite. Noting that "Time and again [Yezierska's] Deweyan heroes accuse their immigrant lovers of excessive emotion," Dearborn observes:

> It is a stock in the trade of sexism to accuse women of hysteria, over-emotionalism. To accuse a Jewish woman of these traits is to traffic in anti-Semitism. Yezierska well knew the pattern: Her novels were first welcomed by native-born America, but as she continued to play the same tune the reviewers began to find her overemotional, hysterical, even—some reviewers were explicit—"too Jewish." (132)

Dearborn properly attends to the symbolic nature of the relationship for each and for the changing U.S. Dewey's initial attraction to and ultimate rejection of Yezierska might, she proposes, represent the rejection of Yezierska's writing as too emotional, "too Jewish." The analysis includes the exotic/erotic projection of sexuality by WASP men onto dark women and extends convincingly to the rise of nativism, chauvinism and anti-Semitism, mirrored in the conviction and execution of Sacco and Vanzetti, "the specter of Jew as Bolshevik," (134) Henry Ford's creation of *The Dearborn Independent* and publication of *The Protocols of the Elders of Zion*, as well as the abrupt closing of immigration in the period around the Great War.

The two books go well together. What is most compelling about Yezierska emerges in the amalgam of both, and should send an appreciative reader back to her fiction. At a time when American Jews, among other cultural or racial minorities, are examining the nature of assimilation in America, when feminists are needing to deepen our understanding of class, when stereotypes of Jewish American Princess and Jewish Mother are considered humorous, Yezierska offers much wisdom. Henriksen's—or my—embarrassment is the internalized anti-Semitism of the American Jewish woman that keeps us from our own strength and power. It needs examination and healing, and in this work Yezierska's writing can play a central role.

I hope that these books, appearing at the same time, herald the republication of Yezierska's work still out of print, and the according of an appropriate place to her in the canon of American letters. Then Anzia Yezierska will be recognized not as a patronized primitive but as an artist and a woman who persisted through praise and rejection, fame and obscurity, to write what she had to say, "to make herself for a person"; and as a Jew who recorded her people's passage into the American urban landscape of the twentieth century:

> "Ach! At last it writes itself in me!" she whispered triumphantly. "It's not me—it's their cries—my own people—crying in me! Hanneh Breineh, Shmendrik, they will not be stilled in me, till all America stops to listen."[4]

## NOTES

1. *Red Ribbon on a White Horse* (NY: Persea Books, 1981; 1st pub., 1950).

2. "My Own People," *Hungry Hearts and Other Stories* (NY: Persea Books, 1985; 1st pub., 1920), p. 241.

3. In a paper entitled "Anzia Yezierska and Dorothy Canfield Fisher: Correspondences and Incongruities," presented at the Multi-Ethnic Literature of the U.S. Conference, 4/17/88.

4. "My Own People," p. 249.

# OTHER VOICES FROM THE OTHER SIDE
## Review of The Other Side by Mary Gordon
## (NY: Viking, 1989) and
## Jasmine by Bharati Mukherjee
## (NY: Grove Weidenfeld, 1989)

Published in the *Women's Review of Books* (April, 1990)

It's been a while since women writers began to tell our side of the story; not quite so long since women of color first pointed out that the category "women," if unexamined, masks a dominant experience, that of white middle-class women. Meanwhile, the significance of the category "American" remains a vast given, unacknowledged and unexplored. U.S. citizens often learn our "national character" only by travelling, but immigrants, among others outside the dominant culture, are poised to describe to us our society and ourselves.

In *The Other Side*, Mary Gordon explores the Irish immigrant's America, named the "other side" in Ireland; the dream place to which the young might escape in order to survive, move up, have breathing room. Ireland is depicted from conflicting perspectives, reflecting the different experience of the male and the female, the village and the bleak countryside, but the Other Side is the place one's ancestors aimed at, where the present generation is now. What, Gordon asks, is this present her ancestors labored to create?

Chronicling several generations of a large working class Irish family, Gordon shapes a mass of unwieldy material through focus on the events of a single day, like her great Irish predecessor James Joyce. But Joyce's event was rooted in the life of a city and justified by symbolic alliance with classical mythology. Gordon's is personal, rarely documented, one day in the dying of an Irish family's matriarch, Ellen McNamara. Joyce's modern Ulysses returned home not from the Trojan War but from a day on the town in Dublin, while Vincent McNamara returns home neither from war nor from the male arena of public life. He leaves a nursing home, because sixty years ago, he promised Ellen she would die at home and he would be with her.

The novel opens with Vincent's reluctance to keep this promise, moves with extraordinary grace through the consciousness and history of a huge cast of family members, who have also gathered or refused to gather for Ellen's death and Vincent's return, and it ends with his return. Throughout the novel, Gordon depicts beautifully the link between past and present—the connection, for example, between Ellen's shame about her mother, abandoned by her husband after she is driven crazy and physically ruined by constant pregnancy and miscarriage and the joyful mid-life extramarital sexuality of Ellen's granddaughter Cam, a lawyer and advocate for women. We can see how one generation becomes the other, even in the dizzying twentieth century. Dan, another grandchild, returns to Ireland for a visit and recognizes:

> ...they could never be happy, any of them, coming from people like the Irish. Unhappiness was bred into the bone, a message in the blood, a code of weakness. The sickle-cell anemia of the Irish; they had to thwart joy in their lives. You saw it everywhere in Irish history; they wouldn't allow themselves to prosper. They didn't believe in prosperity. Perhaps, he thought, they were right not to....He understood the Irish. They were a colonized nation and had taken from their colonizers all their symbols of prosperity and of success...(160-61)

A harsh vision, manifest in Dan's glumness, implicitly critiqued by his energetic buoyant cousin Cam, but still casting the past's shadow.

Gordon is the sort of writer you'd like to hand your life to, because you know she'd feed it back so that you'd understand it better. An old-fashioned novelist in the best sense, she grounds her characters in material reality and creates them so substantial that I left the book knowing them. She offers a constant stream of wisdom about relationships and families, children and generations, the legacies we carry into adulthood like genes, a powerful steady feminist consciousness about the experience and options of women.

Even rarer, she understands and can write about the power of both class and history. Ellen, dying, strapped to her bed, remembers the shame and rage of being a servant over 70 years ago. She remembers, too, her urge towards resistance; when her "mistress" claimed her day off, Ellen had refused.

"Surely it can't mean that much," Claire Fitzpatrick had said. It means my
life. *It means I draw my breath outside your presence and your will...* (118)

The class shift upward of the generations of McNamaras reflects the pattern of European immigrants typical of the period, from extreme poverty and wretched living conditions, through solid working class (one of Vincent and Ellen's daughters celebrates her move as a young bride from living with her parents to her own apartment above the butcher's) to small shopkeepers, to social workers and lawyers, whose children almost automatically will go to college. The family also includes members who are economically and socially marginalized: one crazed Viet Nam veteran; one hippie, financially struggling, single mother.

Aside from offering a wealth of historical information, the novel yields a quantity of illuminating images: pride is "the secret jewel she hoarded in her mind: the stranger's envious stare" (89); back in Ireland, the family member who made good in America becomes "the imaginative center of the family, the knot of color around which it spread, like a peacock's tail." (96) Vincent observes how a random act of Ellen's becomes, for her daughters,

one more thing for which they never will forgive her. He can see this as it
happens...He knows they store up her offenses. Even now, women in their
sixties, they take them out, examine them like jewels, precious for having
endured. Shining, intact. Their grievances against their mother. (300)

Ellen's presence dominates the book. A splendid woman, smart, both brave and timid, an avid reader of newspapers, anti-social except for kin, she is the animating force of this family, the one whose love or not-love sustains or haunts the various offspring. The novel carries the staggering impact of a dying, disintegrating parent on the family.

And in the silence, shaped around the cleft, the guttural, inhuman noise of
Ellen's cry boils up. Speech without communication, words unmoored form
meaning, thrown out, an offense. *I will remind you how frail your grasp is
upon what you determine to be human. At any moment you can be the animal
I am.* (342)

She is and is not herself. She has not had all she wanted. Her shame, her disappointments, her cruel humor and its source in pain, all this is evident, and yet her vitality sticks. In her mockery of the Irish, we see the bitter self-hatred of the betrayed plus a realistic assessment of a woman's options in the Ireland of her time, of her mother's Catholic bride's fate. (Simply by telling the truth about Irish women's lives, Gordon has written a superb propaganda piece for women's control of our reproduction.)

Vincent understands how Ellen was thwarted by the sexist demands of family, by the constraints of history:

> She'd given up too much of that part of herself for the family, and it was wrong for her, he knows it now, but at the time, what could you do? What could you do when the times were against you, against who you really were? (234)

Is Vincent too good to be true? Better than most, many of us will respond, and some will wonder how typical was the McNamaras' powerful sexual relationship among marriages of the period, much less Irish Catholic marriages. But Gordon keeps Ellen and Vincent from seeming idealized; first, by detailing the many conflicts of their marriage; and, second, by strongly suggesting that the successful heterosexual marriage is a thing of the past, part of what will die with Ellen and, soon, Vincent. Marital failure, boredom, alienation and disaster plague every single child and grandchild. Only Cam, the feminist, has a joyous heterosexual relationship, from which she deliberately withholds the dailiness of marriage. (A subsidiary character, a gay male family friend, has a committed nourishing partnership.) Yet Vincent's determination to keep a promise that Ellen is probably in no condition to witness or appreciate smacks of existential commitment, making this a novel of extraordinary faith, by which I mean not religion but loyalty beyond reason, an odd but earned happy ending.

Bharati Mukherjee's *Jasmine* traces the contemporary immigrant experience of a young Indian widow from the Punjab—feisty, lucid and venturesome, one of the most appealing women to appear in recent fiction. *Jasmine* is not a sprawling family tree, but a story of individual transformation, meandering through flashbacks but firmly controlled by the flawless voice of Jasmine. It is a witty, dazzling fairy tale disguised by naturalism and made possible by the whirling world of late twentieth century America, where people— at least the bright, beautiful and lucky—get to pick who they'll be. Its subject is, first, identity; second, hovering mortality, what haunts the immigrant; third, the contrast between the escapee/immigrant vision of America and the vision of the protected American.

In one sense *Jasmine* is an equivocal hymn of praise to the personal freedom of America, the whoosh by which the present becomes the future. America is the place where change is so rapid that it cannot be contained or predicted. Farms become golf courses become malls. Du, the Vietnamese boat child adopted by Jasmine and her banker lover, is an electronics buff whose first telephone conversation to them begins, "You have television? You get?" (18) Contrast between traditional and modern strikes from the first sentence, where "Lifetimes ago, under a banyan tree in the village of Hasnapur, an astrologer cupped his ears—his satellite dish to the stars...." (1)

Mukherjee's particular gift is montage, a jump-cut movement which creates a bond with the first-person narrator and distance from everyone else, thus underscoring with great economy the immigrant's isolation, by-product of American opportunity. Take the scene in which Jasmine has arrived in America, been raped, kills her rapist, burns her dead husband's wedding suit (and her symbolic self) and walks empty into her first American morning. Next scene, she's eating lunch in an Iowa faculty club with a middle-aged professor who describes her out-of-body experience as an Aborigine speaking the tribal language. Of course, she's been unable to have a conversation with an Aborigine anywhere in Iowa, though not for lack of searching. One Australian in the music department has listened to a few sentences from her and said it *sounded* Abo to him.

> "Theoretically, I believe in reincarnation," I say. I am astounded by all this, the American need to make intuition so tangible, to *possess* a vision so privately.... (124-25)

The scene continues:

"This can't be new or bizarre to you. Don't you Hindus keep revisiting the world?"
The waiter has 'HI, I'M DUANE' pinned on his white shirt. (126)

Against the flat racism of the Australian, the American appropriation of another culture's heart, Mukherjee lightly places the—equally American—chain-restaurant attempt at personalizing an increasingly impersonal exchange. HI, I'M DUANE.

Jasmine's version of reincarnation is somewhat different, pointing to a definition of personal identity that is far from constant, but shifts into the space provided by the culture.

> Jyoti of Hasnapur was not Jasmine, Duff's day mummy and Taylor and Wylie's *au pair* in Manhattan; *that* Jasmine isn't *this* Jane Ripplemeyer having lunch with Mary Webb at the University Club today. And which of us is the undetected murderer of a half-faced monster, which of us has held a dying husband, which of us was raped and raped and raped in boats and cars and motel rooms? (127)

By the passage's end, she is no longer an individual self, but joins with all immigrant women, all women sexually victimized in places and vehicles of transience.

Between the scene of arrival in America—Jasmine's first sight is of two nuclear cones and some plastic garbage—and getting raped, the novel flashes forward and she wonders if Bud, her banker lover,

> even sees the America I do. We pass half-built, half-deserted cinder-block structures at the edge of town, with mud-spattered deserted cars parked in an uncleared lot, and I wonder, Who's inside? What are they doing? Who's hiding? Empty swimming pools and plywood panels in the window frames grip my guts. And Bud frowns because unproductive projects give him pain. He says, "Wonder who handled their financing." (109)

The book is also an ambivalent hymn to assimilation. As a woman, Jasmine finds freedom by escaping first India and then the immigrant Indian community. The task of healing the rift (and this rift is not Mukherjee's subject) will belong to the next generation; Jasmine's task is escape, from old world constraints, and from mortality, the stench of "the soft waterlogged carcass of a small dog" with which the first chapter concludes: "...every time I lift a glass of water to my lips, fleetingly I smell it. I know what I don't want to become." (5)

Mukherjee does not focus on American poverty, violent racism, woman-hate. What interests her is contrast between the protected, taken for granted, "ordinary lives" of the Americans she sees, and the immigrant's longing for that protected, ordinary life. On intellectuals: "For them, experience leads to knowledge, or else it is wasted. For me, experience must be forgotten, or else it will kill." (33) At Du's school,

> they say Du's doing so well, isn't he, considering. Considering what? I want to say. Considering that he has lived through five or six languages, five or six countries, two or three centuries of history; has seen his country, city and family butchered, bargained with pirates and bureaucrats, eaten filth in order to stay alive; that he has survived every degradation known to this century, *considering all those liabilities*, isn't it amazing that he can read a Condensed and Simplified for Modern Students edition of *A Tale of Two Cities*? (214)

Yet even in safe America, the man who killed Jasmine's young husband appears, somewhat improbably, as a New York hotdog vendor. Even in the heartland, farmers crazed from their farms going under shoot bankers or hang themselves. Americans enjoy more safety than most, but not for long.

In the end, Jasmine is released from obligation and from her existence in middle America, where any mention of Hasnapur is like naming an old lover, disloyal and threatening. Rescued by the man she loves, she escapes into a fairy-tale American happiness, an ending which rings false but not fatally so. There are plenty of unhappy endings in this book to contradict any suggestion of facile optimism, so that the book manages to keep its cake and feed us too. Never mind that Jasmine's leaving the man who left his wife for her, who has become paralyzed in a wheelchair and whose child she's carrying; she doesn't hesitate and neither, in my sympathies, do I. Partly this is due to contingencies, a sense that his ex-wife will probably take him back; but mostly it's because Jasmine is the novel's moral anchor. Besides, I want her to live happily ever after as Mukherjee makes it appear she just might.

Each of these novels represents an interesting development in its interesting author. Gordon probes historical roots, the native soil which shaped them, and the force they continue to exert. Mukherjee, whose earlier collection of stories included a variety of immigrant characters, chooses here to explore female experience. Taken together, the two novels contradict and confirm each other's sense of collective and individual possibility.

Among Gordon's characters are a smattering of unionists, socialists, feminists and others involved in social change, an activism that mirrors the historical swell of mass movements. Gordon's activists are intermittent, not leaders but ordinary people whose commitment runs deep; at various times they stand at the sidelines and are then drawn into the heart of struggle. Gordon is most concerned, however, with the personal meaning of such activity; its relationship to actual social change appears only in soft-focus. That Ellen sacrifices her desire to work for political justice is her personal tragedy, not a movement's loss.

In *Jasmine*, the world itself and the forces that control it are dangerous as misery and as remote as the stars. Political activists are bombthrowers in India, neo-Nazis in Iowa; the danger, not the solution. Solution for the immigrant is survival. What comes to fascinate Jasmine is the American quest for something beyond survival: personal happiness. She ponders a woman's choice to leave her marriage for a new man:

> She wasn't happy? She looked happy, sounded happy, acted happy. Then
> what did happy mean? Her only chance? Happiness was so narrow a door,
> so selective? The microwave pinged its readiness... (182)

Very much the present, the microwave reminds us, so that at the end, when Jasmine too walks out on a life that is pleasant, solid, even sweet, I taste irony in the vision of just how American she's become.

# WHAT DEENA DIDN'T NOTICE:
## A Review Of What Dinah Thought by Deena Metzger.
## (NY: Viking, 1989)

Published in *Women's Review of Books* (July, 1990)

*My name is Dinah. It is a desert name. My father was Jacob and I was his only
daughter, the only soft flesh, the only breasts to bud from his leathery hands.
Who would have thought that he could have a daughter, but it was in his old
age when his limbs were also beginning to soften as if they had been chewed,
as hide is, by the teeth of time. Because I am a woman, I was not taught to kill.
To everything that happened, until now, I have only been a witness.* (5)

Thus begins the novel, with a deliberate confusion of fictional and actual, past and
present, Jewish women: Dinah/Dina/Deena. Through the central character of Dina Z., a
feminist and creative artist like herself, Deena Metzger explores an American Jewish
woman's encounter with her biblical past, with the storied homeland of Eretz Israel, and
with the contemporary reality of the Israeli nation-state, including its occupation of the
West Bank and Gaza. The novel is psychologically layered and boldly experimental, an
ambitious weaving of myth, psychology, history, philosophy, and politics, with a heavy dose
of eroticism, symbolism, and dreams. At its center Metzger juxtaposes a reinterpretation
of the biblical Dinah's experience against that of the contemporary Dina Z. To know
herself and her tradition—which contributes little information about women—Dina Z.
needs to know what Dinah thought.

What did Dinah think about what? you ask. Ah, that is the novel's obsession and
its problem. In the age-old Jewish tradition of *midrash*, the story about the story, Metzger
explicates from *Genesis 34* the tale of Dinah, daughter of Jacob and Leah, who went out
to see (or *seek* or *serve*, depending on the translation) the women. Shechem, a Hivite,
"took her and lay with her and defiled her" (6), Metzger quotes from *Genesis*. ("And
humbled her," reads one translation, not quoted, and another, "And lay with her by
force.") Sounds like rape to me, but the point is, who knows what really happened?
Dinah's brothers then trap Shechem's people; the men are slaughtered, the women
enslaved. Jolly. The question Metzger and her narrator Dina Z. pose: What did Dinah
think of this?[1]

An intriguing question, and I wish Metzger had begun with and circled around the
vast silence, the not-knowing. Instead, we are told, "*I am Dinah. I loved a heathen. My
brothers killed him. It was thousands of years ago.*" (6) Dina Z. knows that she herself is
the modern counterpart of Dinah. She emphasizes repeatedly that Dinah was not raped
but was beloved of Shechem and loved him in return (is your feminist skin crawling
yet?) and she knows that she too has a Shechem to find. Her trip to Israel, ostensibly to
make a documentary about people who live on ancient holy ground and to visit her
close friend Sibyl, becomes a mythologized quest for a sacred union with her Shechem.
This search is concretized in her ultimately successful attempt to reach the West Bank
Palestinian city Nablus (ancient name, Shechem). En route she sleeps with the most
eligible Israeli man around and, finally, she connects with a (much sexier) Palestinian
male lover, her Shechem.

A fair portion of the book consists of Dina Z.'s letters to the not-yet-met Shechem,
detailing her search. At last, she finds him and has sex with him on top of a mountain,

where he pulls out her diaphragm so she'll get pregnant. Dina Z.'s work evolves into making a movie about her two men, and giving birth to the Palestinian's daughter for the Israeli to marry. I know surrogate sex when I see it, and I wish that Metzger, a therapist, had imagined the men expressing their sexuality directly with each other, thus freeing the narrator for less stereotypically female adventures.

In plot summary, the novel sounds foolish, and it is far from foolish, though peak moments sometimes flop into wordiness and failed intensity:

> We are not two people coming together in the flesh, but history, the entire past coming together and altering, you must be willing to do this, to alter the past, even at the risk of erasing it, them, you, me, because the moment we come together, we inevitably erase everything that has come before, everything that has prevented our joining for centuries. There will be peace. Are you brave enough? (344-45)

Especially the book's early reliance on Dina Z.'s letters to a yet non-existent Shechem doesn't exactly move the plot along. But Metzger mostly avoids the danger of self-satire through sheer intelligence, irony, psychological probing, and shifts in voice and tone—from mystical identification with the biblical Dinah, "I knew, felt, everything that Dinah knew, that Dinah felt, that Dinah thought. I was Dinah, it was as simple as that," insists Dina Z. from the top of Mt. Sinai, (233), to self-mockery:

> Bye-bye, Shechem. What a big deal I made. You'd think a girl had never lost her boyfriend before. You know she didn't have a bad deal. She took all his flocks, all his money, a few servants, and everyone wanted to marry her, and then she married Joseph even though she was knocked up and after a few hard years—who doesn't have a few hard years?—she became a priestess or what do you call the wife of the Viceroy, a Lady at the very least, and she was living on the fat of the land in Egypt when her father and brothers were starving here. She was one of the great complainers of all time. (256)

There is much in this novel to like. I like that it's about a Jewish American woman's encounter with Israel, a powerful experience for many diaspora Jews, and that her Jewishness is stirred and examined. I like that she extends in her emotions and actions to the Palestinians. I like that politics is part of her subject, and I like her politics: her anti-militarism; her assumption that women have been excluded from history and must be included; that the Palestinians, like the Jews, need a state. I like that the central character is 40 years old, not a young woman; that she's come to Israel to visit her dearest friend, a woman; that she's a creative and successful artist.

Finally, I admire Metzger's lyrical gifts, her ability to probe the psyche, her bold experimentation. She moves in and out of the consciousness of her characters, not seamlessly but with deliberate emphasis on the novelist's task of imagining other people. Dinah's voice speaks, often hauntingly, against the voiceless authoritative prose of *Genesis*. Dina Z. imagines the thoughts of the ancient Dinah; of her Israeli lover; of her friend Sibyl; she "writes" in Sibyl's voice the posthumous autobiography of Sibyl's dead fantasy-lover. These experiments often work and are unfailingly intriguing, both psychologically and aesthetically.

This is a risky book. Metzger is aiming at mythology, symbolic significance, but the novel's veneer of realism, her talent for exploring nuances of intimate relationships, force questions from this reader like: they've slept together once on top of a mountain and now they're getting married? She's a feminist arranging her daughter's marriage—and to a man 40 years her senior? I have trouble with Metzger's flat rejection of the possibility that Shechem raped Dinah, her facile assumption that Dinah and Shechem were lovers, though this offers an interesting challenge to the prevailing counter-assumption that explains the story as a parable of Arab male wickedness and a justification for Jewish male militarism. But when Dina Z. confounds her Palestinian lover-to-be with various rape memories, the novel's eroticism makes me queasy, with its borderline racism and sexism: are Palestinian men exotic? Do Jewish women find rapists sexy? And I found the quasi-sacred mountain-top impregnation flatly ridiculous. (I admit to being literal-minded and suspect that those more Jungian than Marxist will like this scene better than I did.)

In addition, Metzger writes as an American, but with only intermittent conscious-ness of her Americanness. On one hand, she creates the following incisive portrait of American privilege. Here is Dina Z. describing herself through the imagined perspective of her Israeli lover:

> She treated the country, the people, and its government as if they were her reluctant employees and she complained bitterly that she could not get them to do her will. She seemed to have no respect for the laws or customs of the country when they did not conform to her sense of law and justice, to the procedures which she would have found accommodating or convenient, or, to be straightforward about it, when they prevented her from doing what she wanted to do....Patronizing is the best word to describe her attitude. Yes, patronizing, exactly. She patronized us while we found her adolescent. (280-81)

On the other hand, while Dina Z. understands that the West Bank is another world, neither Dina Z. nor Metzger seems to recognize that Israel too is another world. I share Metzger's political sympathy and vision, but her idea of how to further peace is frankly embarrassing. If the male American solution to conflict is to send in troops, Metzger's is to send in a sexy American woman. Fuck for peace? Maybe I should have expected this from the author of *The Woman Who Slept With Men to Take War Out of Them*. But couldn't she have let Israeli and Palestinian women heal their own male comrades? Could no one but a glamorous, wealthy (money is never an issue for one minute) American do the trick? Significantly, there are no local women. No Israeli women. No Palestinian women.

Truly moving are Metzger's attempts to breathe life into the ancient Dinah, to explore the patriarchal nature of war, and the mixed blessing of female distance from it: *Because I am a woman, I was not taught to kill*, the biblical Dinah tells us in the novel's first paragraph. And I think women, especially Jewish women, should read this novel, for its rich wisdom as well as its dangers.

Still, in the last days of 1989, 6,000 Israeli and Palestinian women dressed in black marched towards each other from opposite sides of Jersualem; they sang and danced in the streets. Against this backdrop of reality, where women on both sides work desperately hard for peace, Metzger's constant apostrophes to Shechem when she might have addressed, just once, Shechem's sister Bonah; her refusal to imagine the women the biblical Dinah went to seek or see or serve, depending on the translation; to imagine how the sisters Leah and Rachel might have transcended the rivalry foisted on them by patriarchal possession of women and children; finally, to imagine what Israeli and Palestinian women might do to achieve peace, makes the book, in my admittedly biased judgment, an interesting, infuriating failure of feminist imagination.

## NOTES

1. This same question is posed by myself and Irena Klepfisz in our anthology *The Tribe of Dina: A Jewish Women's Anthology* (Boston: Beacon Press, 1989.)

# LEAPS OF FAITH
## Review of JUMP and Other Stories by Nadine Gordimer
## (NY: Farrar, Straus, Giroux, 1991)

**Published in the *Women's Review of Books* (December, 1991)**

If ever a writer had a grasp of the umbilical connection between individual experience and historical possibility, it's Nadine Gordimer. The miracle of the Nobel prize is not only that someone got it who deserved it, but that the writer of our century who portrays most insistently how people wrestle with, resist and create political change was rewarded for her vision. An existentialist with an emphasis on both political commitment and efficacy, Gordimer is one of the few writers to depict the activist life. No surprise then to find her quoting Camus: "It is from the moment when I shall no longer be more than a writer that I shall cease to write."[1]

So far it's not a problem. A leftist publicly critical of communism since the early eighties, she named the challenge

> to love truth enough, to pick up the blood-dirtied, shamed cause of the left,
> and attempt to recreate it in accordance with what it was meant to be, not
> what sixty-five years of human power-perversion have made of it.[2]

Comparisons with Doris Lessing, that other vast-minded leftist white woman writer from Southern Africa (Zimbabwe, formerly Rhodesia), seem inevitable; but Lessing left Africa and political vision. Gordimer stayed.

In her novels, apartheid is always the context, "for apartheid is above all a habit."[3] Since *The Late Bourgeois World* (1966), Gordimer has explored the edge of change, toying futuristically with movement towards revolution, examining the leap or slide by which uncommitted people commit themselves. South Africa is rendered with a textured realism and with the symbolic weight of a regime where the guiding principle—racism— is, simply, evil; no one is untouched.

What is a writer with such a large scope doing with short stories? Gordimer has turned to short fiction throughout her career. Least constrained by plot, she is wildly exploratory, and with several of these stories, you can almost see the triggering newspaper article, event, observation. Less visionary than the novels, most of these stories root firmly in the present. Nor does she invent memorable characters; they are always social types, though vividly rendered with great psychological subtlety. Instead she creates unforgettable moments, situations. Gordimer has a reputation for being hard to read, yet in a class I taught of mostly rural Vermont working class women, many found her easy because she's so visual, so precise. As one student put it, "Nadine Gordimer can make you see anything." An almost random example:

> Siza drives with slow-motion rocking and heaving of the human load,
> steadily nearer. Four shapes come forward along the beams; and stop. He
> stops. Motes of dust, scraps of leaf and bark knocked off the vegetation float
> blurring the beams surrounding four lionesses who stand, not ten yards
> away. Their eyes are wide, now, gem-yellow, expanded by the glare they face,
> and never blink. Their jaws hang open and their heads shake with panting,
> their bodies are bellows expanding and contracting between stiff-hipped
> haunches and heavy narrow shoulders that support the heads. Their ton-
> gues lie exposed, the edges rucked up on either side, like red cloth, by long
> white incisors. ("Spoils," 171)

Many writers today are tugging at the story form; from the short shorts for readers in the fast lane, to the character-linked quasi-novel. In *JUMP and Other Stories*, Gordimer creates a powerful context on which the stories mostly depend; the overall effect is like casting an out-of-focus awareness on a huge painting filled with tiny intricate scenes and zooming in—first here, then there; you can't see the whole but its existence informs every detail.

Or almost every detail. A couple of the stories—"A Find," about a man who uses a lost ring to meet women; "A Journey," about a marriage disrupted by the man's infidelity and reunited, perhaps ironically, by a new baby—have the feel of parables manqué, remnants. (Though let me add that Gordimer's manqué is a lesser writer's best shot; these stories are hardly weak, they just lack a resonance characteristic of her work.)

Most of the stories are about jumps and failures to jump—from what into what? The title story offers the too-late jump of a white mercenary into cooperation with victorious black revolutionary forces; he is physically protected but utterly isolated; not quite ready for the jump of suicide which promises his only release. More generally, it's the jump from the present, from something safe, known, but wrapped in illusion, into a possible future. In 1984 Gordimer wrote:

In South Africa the ivory tower is bulldozed anew with every black man's
[sic] home destroyed to make way for a white man's. Yet there are positions
between the bulldozed ivory tower and the maximum security prison.[4]

Repeatedly humble about her personal risks—though a member of the African National Congress, she is, of course, protected, as an internationally renowned white writer—she explores the rarely charted territory between tower and prison, and thus enlarges it.

These stories are also about home, often what is jumped out of, most longed for or most devastated; the home as fortress become prison of the white minority ("Once Upon a Time"); the destroyed home of the fleeing black Africans ("The Ultimate Safari"); the elegant home of a white activist serving lunch to four young blacks, all of whom have been imprisoned ("Comrades"); the myth-like "Teraloyna," the island home where color blurs through breeding and inbreeding, allegory for the bitter kinship of all people, while on the mainland the color line completely defines reality:

When a certain black carpenter draws a splinter from under his nail, the
bubble of blood that comes after it is Teraloyna. And when a certain young
white man, drafted into military service straight from school, throws a
canister of tear-gas into a schoolyard full of black children and is hit on the
cheek by a cast stone, the broken capillaries ooze Teraloyna lifeblood. (51)

One story is called "Home," and another, "My Father Leaves Home," and another, "Safe Houses." The final story in the collection, "Amnesty," from the point of view of a black African woman whose common-law husband—("I know he wants to get married but there's no time for that at present. There was barely time for him to make the child" [247])—makes the jump from worker to union activist. The amnesty in the story includes his release from prison, which she imagines will allow them to create an ordinary life, but ordinary life in South Africa is a mark of privilege. He has become an important political leader, engaged even more deeply in struggle, and the story, and the collection, end with the narrator "...waiting to come back home." (248)

Neither his revolutionary aspirations nor her bereavement is given short shrift. The woman in "Amnesty" is herself and also illuminates the almost stereotypical unsung contribution of thousands of black South African wives of male political leaders.

Gordimer has never been particularly attuned to feminism, though when she trains her eye on women's condition or on heterosexual power dynamics, her savage accuracy reveals more than most analyses. And brave women, fierce activists, sources of hidden strength are nothing new to her work. *Burger's Daughter* (1979) is practically a bildungsroman of a white revolutionary cutting loose from her hero father's legacy, only to claim it as her own. Most recently, the heroic transformation of stereotypical "coloured" women is the surprise fabulous feature of *My Son's Story* (1991). As ever, I eagerly await Gordimer's next, at least partly to see where she's gotten with feminism.

Even less does Gordimer focus on her Jewish background, though her novel before last (*A Sport of Nature*, 1987) had a range of Jewish characters, including a heroine who names herself Hillela, presumably after the great Jewish moralist Hillel. In this collection, the narrator of "My Father Leaves Home" visits an Eastern European village the father might have emigrated from; retraces in her mind his journey; places the anti-Semitism he escaped from next to the racism he entered, assimilated to and participated in. Reacting to his gentile wife's anti-Semitic contempt,

> ...whipped into anger he knew the lowest category of all in her country, this country.
> *You speak to me as if I was a kaffir.* (66)

And the narrator remarks,

> I didn't ask him about his village. He never told me; or I didn't listen....I did not know that I would find, here in the wood, the beaters advancing, advancing across the world. (68)

The large numbers of Jews among white anti-apartheid activists in South Africa, perhaps even higher than the proportion of Jews among white progressives in the U.S., makes this more than a curious point.

But Gordimer's major theme is the impersonal, inevitable chasm between white and black and colored. In "Home," the political arrest of a colored woman's mother and siblings threatens her marriage to a loving yet fearful white husband. In "Keeping Fit," a white jogger escapes an outburst of violence by running into the black area of squatters' shacks, where a woman with "a churchgoer's face, her eyes distant and narrowed behind butterfly-shaped spectacle frames with gilt scrolls" (199) protects him, resentfully but effectively. She explains to him how the police break in, beat people, how they might take her son. The man asks why, and the two sides of the chasm come into focus. She answers, "—My son's in the Youth—the street committee...." And he thinks:

> The kind who burned government appointees' houses, stoned buses, boy-cotted schools. And lived here—slowly he was making out of the dimness and his own shock what this habitation was. Its intimacy pressed around him, a mould in which his own dimensions were redefined. He took up space where the space allowed each resident must be scrupulously confined and observed. The space itself was divided in two by curtains which stretched across it, not quite drawn closed...He saw now there were three children as well as the grown daughter and son; seven people lived here. (201)

In "Comrades," Mrs. Hattie Telford, with her maid's help, prepares lunch for the young revolutionaries she has met at a conference on education,

> but...she suddenly did not want them to see that the maid waited on her. She herself carried the heavy tray into the dining room. (26)

Yet two pages later

> She looks at them all and cannot believe what she knows: that they, suddenly here in her house, will carry the AK 47s they only sing about, now, miming death as they sing. They will have a career of wiring explosives to the undersides of vehicles, they will go away and come back through the bush to dig holes not to plant trees to shade home, but to plant land mines. She can see they have been terribly harmed but cannot believe they could harm. They are wiping their fruit-sticky hands furtively palm against palm. (28)

Many of these stories reveal like a landscape what Gordimer wrote in 1985 during a State of Emergency, as

> ...that extraordinary sense of whiteness, of having always been different, always favoured, always shielded from the vulnerabilities of poverty and powerlessness...We whites in South Africa present an updated version of the Emperor's clothes; we are not aware of our nakedness—ethical, moral, and fatal—clothed as we are in our own skin.[5]

If whites must jump out of their skin's protection, Gordimer projects a caustic, uncertain but compelling vision of what they jump towards: solidarity, not intimacy, is Gordimer's grail. Even the white activist in hiding, who dallies for a while in a suburban romance in the ironically titled "Safe Houses," back in prison, experiences "the exhilaration, after all, of being once again with his comrades, the fellow accused..." (236)

Gordimer is never sentimental. You would not catch her making mealy-mouthed statements like, "Slavery hurts the slave owner as much as the slave," which concrete experience contradicts at every turn. Yet she rejects none of her characters, tracing the limits apartheid, in particular, and oppression/repression, in general, place also upon most of those privileged by the system. That is, she can look at Mrs. Hattie Telford in her moment of revelation; like all white South Africans, she has her maid, her help, her food and fruit and art; but she doesn't have comrades.

Gordimer writes of herself:

> There are two absolutes in my life. One is that racism is evil—human damnation in the Old Testament sense, and no compromises, as well as sacrifices, should be too great in the fight against it. The other is that a writer is a being in whose sensibility is fused what Lukács calls "the duality of inwardness and outside world," and he [sic] must never be asked to sunder this union.[6]

In feminist terms, the personal is political. But she toes no line. Her eye is merciless when it comes to political corruption, ineptitude, cruelty, egotism, pretensions, and she explicitly refuses to place any consideration higher than truth.

> I have a superstitious notion that if I lie, my characters will be damaged... [this] has become a minor obsession with me because in a society like that of South Africa...there are people whom one trusts absolutely who turn out to be police agents...I often say that the best way to write would be as if you were already dead.[7]

This is evident in the complex truths she delineates. Teresa, whose mother becomes a political prisoner, hates her and suffers from intense guilt. ("Home") Terrorism is conducted with despicable cynicism. ("Some Are Born to Sweet Delight") "Spoils" begins,

> In the warmth of the bed your own fart brings to your nostrils the smell of rotting flesh: the lamb chops you devoured last night. Seasoned with rosemary and with an undertaker's paper frill on the severed rib-bones. Another corpse digested. (152)

This, in a story that will climax with a house party of whites led by a black servant into the night to observe lions hunting zebra, the title invoking "to the victor belong...": the conquest of Africa. In "What Were You Dreaming?" a white woman explains to a younger male tourist about the missing front teeth of a "Cape Coloured" man:

> "It's—how shall I say—a sexual preference. Most usually you see it in their young girls, though. They have their front teeth pulled when they're about seventeen."
>
> She feels his uncertainty, his not wanting to let comprehension lead him to a conclusion embarrassing to an older woman. For her part, she is wondering whether he won't find it distasteful if—at her de-sexed age—she should come out with it: for cock-sucking. (180)

Typical Gordimer to come out with the word, and with the truth of the character's fleeting but not trivial dilemma; typical to mix farts with colonialism. Nothing is off limits, but she's no cynic. A fierce moralist who insists on change, Gordimer summons us to our best selves:

> There is no forgetting how we could live if only we could find the way. We must continue to be tormented by the ideal.[8]

## NOTES

1. "The Essential Gesture," in *The Essential Gesture*, Stephen Clingman, ed. (NY: Knopf, 1988), 288.

2. "Living in the Interregnum," in *Gesture*, 283.

3. "Interregnum," 266.

4. "Gesture," 294-95.

5. "Letter from Johannesburg, 1985," in *Gesture*, 303.

6. "Interregnum," 277; Lukács quote from "The Theory of the Novel."

7. "A Conversation with Nadine Gordimer" (interview by Robert Boyers et al.), *Salmagundi 62, Nadine Gordimer: Politics & The Order of Art* (Winter 1984), 5, 9.

8. "Interregnum," 284.

Photo: Sarah Bolden

# Melanie Kaye/Kantrowitz was born in 1945 in Brooklyn,

and has worked in social change movements since the sixties. A graduate of CCNY, she went on to earn her Ph.D. in Comparative Literature from the University of California at Berkeley. A writer, activist, and teacher, she lives in New York City where she is director of *Jews for Racial and Economic Justice*. She is author of *My Jewish Face & Other Stories*, co-editor of *The Tribe of Dina: A Jewish Woman's Anthology*, and former editor and publisher of *Sinister Wisdom*, a lesbian/feminist journal. Her writings about violence and resistance, Jewish identity and anti-Semitism, race, class, and culture have been widely published.

*aunt lute books* is a multicultural women's press that has been committed to publishing high quality, culturally diverse literature since 1982. In 1990, the Aunt Lute Foundation was formed as a non-profit corporation to publish and distribute books that reflect the complex truths of women's lives and the possibilities for personal and social change. We seek work that explores the specificities of the very different histories from which we come, and that examines the intersections between the borders we all inhabit.

Please write or phone for a free catalogue of our other books or if you wish to be on our mailing list for future titles. You may buy books directly from us by phoning in a credit card order or mailing a check with the catalogue order form.

Aunt Lute Books
P.O. Box 410687
San Francisco, CA 94141
(415) 558-8116